Using
WinFax PRO®

David Haskin

Using WinFax PRO

Copyright© 1994 by Que® Corporation.

Library of Congress Catalog No: 94-65521

ISBN: 1-56529-617-6

97 96 95 94   4 3 2 1

Interpretation of the printing code: the rightmost double-digit number is the year of the book's printing; the rightmost single-digit number, the number of the book's printing. For example, a printing code of 94-1 shows that the first printing of the book occurred in 1994.

This book is based on WinFax PRO version 4.

Publisher: David P. Ewing

Associate Publisher: Corinne Walls

Publishing Director: Lisa A. Bucki

Managing Editor: Anne Owen

Marketing Manager: Greg Wiegand

Dedication

For my parents, Jack and Mickey Haskin

Publishing Manager
Thomas H. Bennett

Acquisitions Editor
Nancy Stevenson

Product Director
Stephanie Gould

Production Editor
Elsa Bell

Copy Editors
Rhonda L. Rieseberg
Pamela Wampler
Sally A. Yuska

Technical Editors
Bob Shimer
Janice A. Snyder
Michael Watson

Book Designers
Amy Peppler-Adams
Paula Carroll

Cover Designer
Dan Armstrong

Production Team
Teresa Forrester
Joelynn Gifford
Bob LaRoche
Joy Dean Lee
Tim Montogomery
Aren Munk
G. Alan Palmore
Dennis Sheehan
Ann Sipple
Amy Steed
Tina Trettin
Sue VandeWalle
Mary Beth Wakefield

Indexer
Johnna VanHoose

Editorial Assistant
Michelle Williams

Composed in *Stone Serif* and *MCPdigital*
by Que Corporation

About the Author

David Haskin is a software marketing consultant and freelance writer based in Madison, Wisconsin. A former daily newspaper reporter, David became involved in the desktop PC revolution early. He served in a variety of marketing roles in the software industry, ranging from public relations and product manager to vice president of sales and marketing. David has authored or coauthored several computer-related books, including *Using PC Tools for Windows (Que)* and *Word for Windows HyperGuide (Alpha)*. He also is a regular software and hardware reviewer for several national computer trade publications. You can reach David via CompuServe (71162,776).

Acknowledgments

Writing a book like this is a daunting task that would be impossible without help from many talented professionals and profoundly patient family members. I'm grateful to the crew at Que for their professionalism and unflagging support and good spirits during the inevitable down periods. Nancy Stevenson, the acquisitions editor at the beginning and end of this project, kept things moving forward on an even keel, not a small task when deadlines loom and authors start getting cranky. Tom Godfrey, the acquisitions editor in the middle of the project, struggled successfully, often against the odds, to keep the project moving forward and on time.

Special thanks are due to Stephanie Gould, Elsa Bell, and the other editors, whose editing proves that you can turn a sow's ear into a silk purse. Lisa Dickinson worked hard to make sure that communications with Delrina were clear and open, always an important task when time is of the essence. And big thanks also are due to technical editors Jan Snyder and Bob Shimer for jumping in under difficult circumstances and doggedly ensuring the accuracy of the book.

At Delrina, special thanks go to Allan Lahosky. Getting a new software product out the door is just as intense and crazy-making as creating books, but Allan responded to my endless stream of questions promptly, thoroughly, and with remarkably good humor given the pressure he was under. Also, special thanks at Delrina to Josef Zankowicz, Shelly Sofer, and Tim Callan.

Writing a book can be a consuming task, so a special thank you is due to my wife, Mary, and the still-at-home kids, Sam and Liz. Without their support and encouragement, this book simply would not have happened.

Trademarks

All terms mentioned in this book that are known to be trademarks or service marks have been appropriately capitalized. Que cannot attest to the accuracy of this information. Use of a term in this book should not be regarded as affecting the validity of any trademark or service mark.

Windows is a trademark of Microsoft Corporation.
WinFax PRO is a registered trademark of Delrina Corporation.

Contents at a Glance

Contents

II WinFax PRO in Everyday Operation   107

6 Using Phonebooks   109

7 Creating and Managing Cover Pages   139

8 Sending Faxes   183

15 Converting Faxes to Text   345

16 Different Ways to Send and Receive   367

Introduction

WinFax PRO has been the leading fax program for Windows for many years. With each release, it introduces exciting new technology to make faxing from your computer both more powerful and less difficult.

WinFax PRO 4 makes it easy to send, receive, and manage faxes, incorporates new technology to speed up the faxing process, and even connect to network electronic mail packages.

Why You Should Use this Book

Using WinFax PRO is a valuable addition to WinFax PRO. It is much more than just a repeat of WinFax PRO's documentation. Rather, it provides an in-depth look at WinFax PRO so that beginning and intermediate users not only learn how to use it, but learn how to use it *effectively*.

Que's *Using* book series shows ways to use software effectively. Que has refined the series to help users get the most out of products such as WinFax PRO.

Like all *Using* books, *Using WinFax PRO* doesn't just describe *how* to use WinFax PRO—it tells you *why* you should use specific features and *when* specific features are useful and when they are not. This book helps you get the most out of WinFax PRO in the real world.

Throughout this book, tips and notes tell you how to get the most out of WinFax PRO. Cautions warn you to beware of certain conditions that can slow you down and reduce your productivity.

Also, *Using WinFax PRO* includes chapters about special uses of the product. For example, the book devotes an entire chapter to using WinFax PRO when you are away from the office. Another chapter is about using WinFax PRO when your computer is attached to a network.

Another benefit of this book—and all *Using* books, for that matter—is that its structure helps you pick and choose precisely the information you need. If you read this book from cover to cover, you'll learn about WinFax PRO in great detail. But you also can easily pinpoint precisely the information you need at a specific moment and go right to that section of *Using WinFax PRO*.

This combination of thoroughness, real-world applications, and the ability to quickly find the information you need, makes *Using WinFax PRO* an invaluable companion to WinFax PRO and the documentation that comes with it.

Why You Should Use WinFax PRO 4

WinFax was one of the first fax software products. It helped introduce the world to the concept of sending and receiving faxes from your computer, without the need to get out of your seat and go down the hall to a fax machine. It also helped introduce the concept of creating documents in your normal Windows applications and faxing them directly from that application.

The original WinFax also made it simple to perform basic tasks like scheduling faxes for transmission after the phone rates go down and forwarding received faxes to other recipients.

WinFax PRO 4 continues to simplify these basic fax procedures, and adds extraordinary power. The next few sections briefly describe the advantages of WinFax PRO 4.

Managing Faxes Is Simple and Flexible

From the beginning, fax software has had logs that list all sent and received faxes. However, WinFax PRO manages the unique feat of adding power to this basic capability and making that power simple to use.

WinFax PRO accomplishes this feat in several ways:

- The Send and Receive Logs use the concept of folders for storing faxes. You create your own system of folders to reflect the way you work. If you are a salesperson, for example, you can have folders containing faxes for each major account. Or a bookkeeper can have folders for accounts receivable and accounts payable.

- The Send Log and Receive Log have three easy-to-understand windows. One window is for folders, another window lists the messages in each folder, and the third window lists information about the fax you select. Although you can refine and customize this system quite a bit, the basic information has virtually no learning curve.

- You can add keywords and billing information to each message, enabling you to easily search for messages based on the keyword or billing information. You also can search on other factors, like the date of transmission.

- WinFax PRO automatically compresses messages so that they take less space on your disk.

The result of these refinements is a product that is simple to understand. The three-window approach described applies to more than just the Send and Receive Logs. It is repeated through many aspects of the program. For example, this interface is virtually the same interface as that used for managing phonebooks of fax recipients and files that you attach to faxes.

WinFax PRO Is a Windows Program

If you use other Windows applications, you probably will quickly become comfortable with WinFax PRO. Its interface is similar to those of most other Windows applications.

WinFax PRO also includes some features that make it particularly easy to use. For example, its toolbar has buttons that execute commonly used commands with a single mouse click. Its status bar keeps you informed about what WinFax PRO is doing at the present moment.

WinFax PRO 4 Adds Powerful New Technology

Fax technology has evolved for many years but, until recently, it evolved slowly. However, WinFax PRO incorporates some exciting new technology that adds speed and power to faxing. Specifically, WinFax PRO adds three related types of technology:

■ Binary File Transfer (BFT) enables you to send computer files at the same time you send faxes. These files can either be data files you create, such as word processing documents, or the files needed to run programs.

■ WinFax PRO has a proprietary transmission capability that uses BFT. When you send a message to another WinFax PRO user, the product transmits with a special version of BFT that is much faster.

■ A variation of BFT, Microsoft At Work adds various security measures. It enables you to communicate with other software programs that support this emerging standard as well as, ultimately, office machines such as standard fax machines.

This new technology saves you time by transmitting information you couldn't previously transmit by using the fax process. And it transmits this information very quickly.

WinFax PRO Works with Your Network

If your computer is attached to a network, WinFax PRO provides some powerful capabilities. Perhaps WinFax PRO's most noteworthy network capability is that you can use it to send, receive, and store network electronic mail messages. Also, WinFax PRO enables you to receive a fax in the normal way and forward the fax via electronic mail to others on your computer network.

These capabilities presage the day when computers handle all your messages seamlessly, and you needn't worry about the type of message or the method used to transmit or receive it. Rather, you simply create your message and let the software do the rest of the work.

WinFax PRO's networking capabilities also focus on the everyday realities of using networks. Specifically, WinFax PRO enables you to share its resources with other WinFax PRO users on your network, which, in many cases, is a great convenience.

WinFax PRO Is Highly Customizable

You can customize virtually every aspect of WinFax PRO. For example, you can easily alter the contents of the Send and Receive Logs. Similarly, you can customize the contents of the WinFax PRO toolbar so that it includes buttons for the functions you most commonly use.

You also can change the contents of many of WinFax PRO's other basic tools. For example, you can customize the cover pages that accompany faxes or even create your own. You can even draw on or add graphic images to faxes.

Working with WinFax PRO

You don't have to be a heavy faxer to make optimal use of WinFax PRO. This program is so flexible and powerful that it naturally lends itself to virtually any use. For example:

- Sales personnel can prepare a single fax to key customers announcing a new product. They can schedule WinFax PRO to send the fax after the phone rates go down, or can even hold the fax pending confirmation about details such as pricing.

- Support personnel can quickly and easily fax product instructions and other support documents to customers. They can share phonebooks over the network so all personnel in the department can fax to the same customers.

- Project managers can keep folders containing information about specific aspects of a project under development. The folders can contain sent and received e-mail messages and files transferred using the BFT file transfer process described previously.

- Attorneys can receive faxes of contract drafts. Using WinFax PRO's optical character recognition (OCR) capabilities, they can turn the received fax into editable text, edit the contract in their word processing program, and fax the contract back for further comment.

- Engineers can receive faxes of drawings and, using WinFax PRO's annotation capabilities, can make simple annotations to the drawing, add comments, and forward the drawing on to other engineers involved in the project.

The specific applications for WinFax PRO are practically endless. After you start using it, it won't be long before you start thinking of additional ways you can benefit from WinFax PRO.

How this Book Is Organized

The contents of *Using WinFax PRO* provide a logical progression for learning and using WinFax PRO. It has three sections, each of which builds on the preceding section:

- Part 1: *Understanding WinFax PRO Basics* is for people who either haven't used WinFax PRO before or who need a refresher course. It tells you about the following:

    Understanding the way that faxing works, which is useful background that can help you with troubleshooting.

    Installing WinFax PRO.

    Configuring WinFax PRO.

    Customizing WinFax PRO.

- Part 2: *WinFax PRO in Everyday Operation*, details the basic procedures you must know to operate WinFax PRO. These procedures include the following:

    Sending faxes.

    Receiving faxes.

    Using WinFax PRO to send and receive electronic mail messages.

    Storing and finding fax and electronic mail messages.

    Creating and managing phonebooks of message recipients.

    Creating and managing libraries of cover pages.

    Adding and managing files that you attach to faxes and e-mail messages.

- Part 3: *Power Faxing with WinFax PRO* tells you about WinFax PRO's advanced features and provides some specialized ideas about using WinFax PRO. Specifically, this section includes chapters on the following:

    Using a scanner to scan faxes.

    Understanding WinFax PRO's advanced new methods of transmitting faxes and computer files.

    Understanding how to use WinFax PRO when you are away from the office.

    Understanding how to use WinFax PRO on your organization's network.

    Connecting WinFax PRO with other programs.

Remember, though, that you need not read the entire book to get the maximum benefit from it. Feel free to scan the table of contents and index to find topics on which you need specific help.

Conventions Used in this Book

The conventions in this book help you learn how to use WinFax PRO quickly.

The book prints the letters that you press to activate menus, commands in menus, and options in dialog boxes in **boldface type**. The letters or numbers in boldface type in this book are referred to as *hot keys* because they initiate an action.

For example, to access the User Setup dialog box, this book tells you to choose Setu**p** **U**ser. You access this option in two ways:

- Use your mouse to click Setu**p** in the menu bar. This opens the Setup menu. In the Setup menu, you click **U**ser to display the User Setup dialog box.

- Press Alt plus the menu bar hot key for the Setu**p** menu, which in this case is the boldfaced **p**. When the menu opens, press the hot key for the **U**ser Setup dialog box, which in this case is **U**.

Also, look for three specially formatted items sprinkled throughout the book:

- *Tips* provide shortcuts or other special tricks for using WinFax PRO more efficiently.

- *Notes* provide information, background, and reminders for efficiently using WinFax PRO to perform specific tasks.

- *Cautions* warn you about potential problems that can result if you don't follow instructions precisely, or if certain conditions exist.

Part I

Understanding WinFax PRO Basics

Chapter 1

Installing WinFax PRO

In this chapter, you learn about the following:

- Hardware requirements for WinFax PRO.

- Software requirements for WinFax PRO.

- Various installation options.

- Configuring WinFax PRO during installation.Before you unleash the power of WinFax PRO, you must install it on your system. WinFax PRO's installation procedures make this process simple and offer lots of flexibility.

This chapter describes how to install WinFax PRO. Chapter 3, "Starting and Navigating WinFax PRO," gets you started using WinFax PRO.

Minimum (and Recommended) Requirements

Like most software programs, WinFax PRO has minimum system requirements. If your computer system doesn't meet these minimum requirements, WinFax PRO cannot function.

Also, like most software programs, WinFax PRO has recommended requirements. These requirements typically require more resources than the minimum requirements, and ensure that WinFax PRO runs more efficiently. The next two sections describe these requirements.

Hardware Requirements

WinFax PRO requires the following hardware in order to operate (these are minimum requirements):

- An 80386 or greater PC.

- 4M of random-access memory (RAM).

- A hard disk with at least 5.5M of free space. This doesn't include disk space for storing fax messages.

- At least one floppy drive (required for installation).

- A fax modem. Chapter 2, "How WinFax PRO Works," describes the different types of fax modems, most of which work with WinFax PRO.

If your system just meets the minimum requirements, performance will be sluggish at times. For optimal WinFax PRO performance, the following hardware is suggested:

- An 80386 or greater PC.

- 8M RAM or more.

- A mouse or another pointing device such as a trackball. You can use WinFax PRO without a mouse or other pointing device; however, a mouse or pointing device makes WinFax PRO much easier to use.

- A printer for printing faxes.

Software Requirements

Compared to hardware requirements, WinFax PRO's software requirements are simple. You need only Windows 3.1 or a later version.

In addition to these requirements, WinFax PRO supports virtually all networks. Read Chapter 18, "Using WinFax PRO in Other Programs," for a description of how to use WinFax PRO on networks.

The Installation Process

Whenever you install any new software, it is always a good idea to back up files that are particularly important to the operation of your system, because the installation process often changes those files. Specifically, just to be on the safe side, you might want to back up your AUTOEXEC.BAT and CONFIG.SYS files in the root directory of your C drive. These are the files that your computer looks to for instructions when you start up.

You might want to back up two files in your \WINDOWS directory for safety's sake. Those files are called WIN.INI and SYSTEM.INI. These are the files that Windows looks to for instructions when you first type **WIN** at the DOS prompt. To back up these files, use your normal backup program or simply copy them to a disk.

WinFax PRO's installation process gives you maximum flexibility. To start the installation process, follow these steps:

1. Place WinFax PRO Disk 1 in your floppy drive.

2. In Windows Program Manager, choose **F**ile **R**un. Windows displays the Run dialog box.

3. In the Command Line text box, type **A:SETUP** and press the Enter key. This, of course, assumes that you inserted the disk in your A: drive. If you placed the disk in another drive, substitute that drive letter.

The preceding steps start the WinFax PRO Setup program. Installing WinFax PRO largely requires only that you follow the on-screen directions of the Setup program. However, the Setup program provides a series of options from which you must choose. The next several sections walk you through the installation process and explain various installation options.

Choosing Installation Options

After starting the Setup program, dialog boxes may appear asking some preliminary questions, depending on whether you had a previous installation. For example, if the Setup program detects a previously installed version of WinFax or WinFax PRO, it displays a dialog box asking if you want to continue with the installation.

The Setup program displays a dialog box where you fill in basic information about yourself.

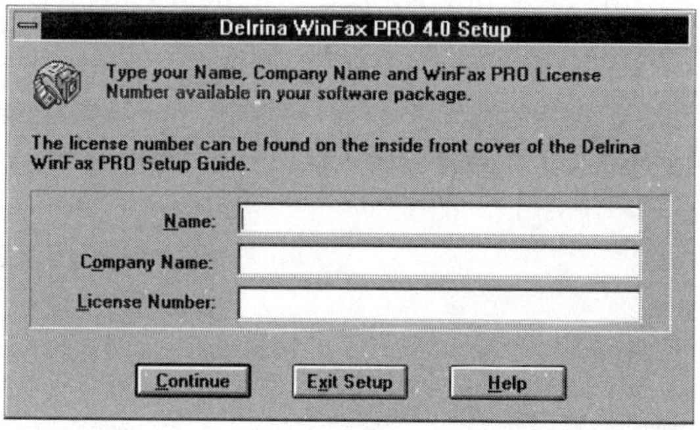

Fig. 1.1
Enter information about yourself in this initial setup dialog box.

Type your name in the **N**ame dialog box and your company name in the **C**ompany dialog box. Type the license number for your copy of WinFax PRO in the **L**icense Number dialog box. You can find the license number on the inside front cover of the WinFax PRO Setup Guide, which Delrina includes with the product.

When you finish this initial dialog box, click **C**ontinue. WinFax PRO then displays a dialog box asking you to confirm the information you typed. If it is correct, click **C**ontinue again. WinFax PRO next displays a dialog box where you decide among three installation choices (see fig. 1.2).

Fig. 1.2
Decide which type of installation you want with the setup dialog box.

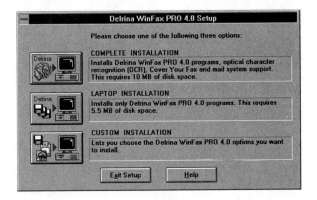

Tip
If you aren't sure which type of installation you want, select Laptop Installation. This option takes the least amount of disk space. You can run Custom Installation later to install additional options.

The three installation options are as follows:

■ *Complete Installation.* This option installs all WinFax PRO's capabilities and requires about 10M of free disk space.

■ *Laptop Installation.* This option installs the minimum number of files possible for using WinFax PRO's faxing capabilities. It does *not* install the following:

WinFax PRO's optical character recognition (OCR) capabilities for converting faxes into editable text. Read Chapter 15, "Converting Faxes to Text," for a description of OCR.

A series of special-use fax cover pages. Read Chapter 7, "Creating and Managing Cover Pages," for more information about creating and using cover pages.

The files necessary to use WinFax PRO with electronic mail. Read Chapter 10, "Using WinFax PRO with Electronic Mail," for more information about electronic mail and how WinFax PRO works with it.

■ *Custom Installation.* This option enables you to choose the specific parts of WinFax PRO that you want to install.

The Complete and Laptop Installation Processes

If you select either Complete Installation or Laptop Installation, WinFax PRO's Setup program displays a dialog box asking for the drive and directory on which to install the program and related files (see fig. 1.3). The dialog box also provides a suggested drive and directory.

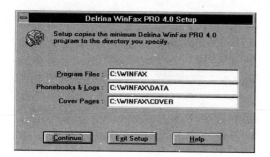

Fig. 1.3
Decide where to install WinFax PRO in this dialog box.

In this dialog box, you need to do the following:

1. In the **P**rogram Files text box, type the drive and directory in which you want the WinFax PRO program files.

2. In the Phonebooks & **L**ogs text box, type the drive and directory in which to store program information. This selection determines where you store the files containing your phonebooks of fax recipients and also the logs of sent and received faxes.

3. In the Cover Pa**g**es text box, type the drive and directory in which to store files containing the cover pages you use to accompany fax messages.

4. Click **C**ontinue to go to the next step in the installation process, which is described a bit later in this chapter.

Tip
Unless there is an overriding need to change them, it is easiest to ac-cept WinFax PRO's sugges-tions for plac-ing programs and files.

The Custom Installation Process

If you choose the Custom Installation option, WinFax PRO displays the Custom Installation dialog box (see fig. 1.4).

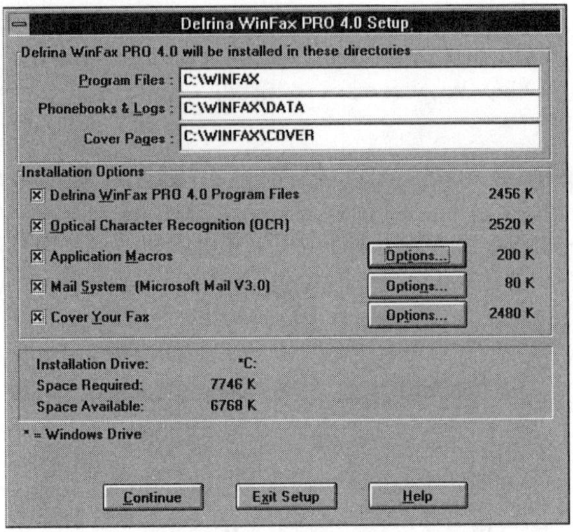

Fig. 1.4
Use the Custom Installation dialog box to select precisely the WinFax PRO elements you want to install.

Tip
If you have multiple drives that are almost full, place different WinFax PRO components on different drives.

Tip
You can add elements to your WinFax PRO installation. Start the Setup program and use this dialog box to determine which elements to add.

The top section of the Custom Installation dialog box is identical to the dialog box for determining the drives and directories on which you install the various WinFax PRO components (described in the previous section). Either accept WinFax PRO's suggestions for installation drives and paths, or type your own in each of the three text boxes.

The bottom of the Custom Installation dialog box lists each drive you designate in the top section of the dialog box. It also lists the space required for the parts of WinFax PRO you choose to install and the available space on each drive.

Use the Installation Options area of the Custom Installation dialog box to determine precisely which elements of WinFax PRO you want to install.

If this is your first installation of WinFax PRO, or if you are upgrading from a previous version, you must select the first option, Delrina **W**inFax PRO 4 Program Files. This option installs the files necessary for running WinFax PRO. If you already installed WinFax PRO 4 and are using the Custom Installation dialog box to install additional options, deactivate the **W**inFax PRO 4 Program Files check box.

The following four sections describe the remaining installation options.

Optical Character Recognition

The **O**ptical Character Recognition (OCR) check box installs the files needed to convert faxes into editable text. As explained in Chapter 2, "How WinFax PRO Works," faxes actually are graphic images.

As such, you can't edit faxes as you can a word processing file. OCR is the process of converting fax images into text that you can edit with your word processor or other application.

OCR is useful if you sometimes must edit faxes you receive. For example, a lawyer who receives a fax of a draft contract can edit the contents of the contract after applying OCR to it.

Also, text files created by OCR take up less disk storage space than fax image files; however, OCR is a time-consuming process and is not always completely accurate. Read Chapter 15, "Converting Faxes to Text," for more information on OCR.

Application Macros

WinFax PRO comes with several macros for popular Windows applications such as Microsoft Word for Windows and WordPerfect for Windows. Installing the macros into these applications creates tight links between WinFax PRO and the application. Read Chapter 18, "Using WinFax PRO in Other Programs," for more information on how these macros operate.

To load the application macros from WinFax PRO's installation disks, select the Application **M**acros check box. To select the specific application macros to install, click Options. WinFax PRO displays the dialog box for selecting the application macros (see fig. 1.5).

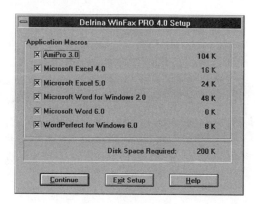

Fig. 1.5
Select the application macros to install in this dialog box.

In the Application Macros area of the dialog box, there is a check box next to each application. Select the check box next to each of the applications you use.

After finishing, click Continue to return to the main Custom Installation dialog box. Read Chapter 18, "Using WinFax PRO in Other Programs," for more information on application macros.

Electronic Mail

During the installation process, WinFax PRO checks to see if you have connected your computer to a network electronic mail system, also known as *e-mail*. Electronic mail systems enable you to exchange messages and files with other persons whose computers are part of your organization's computer network.

WinFax PRO can serve as the collecting point for e-mail that you both send and receive. To set up WinFax PRO for this option, select the Mail System check box.

To further set up WinFax PRO to work with your e-mail system, click the Options button. WinFax PRO displays a dialog box for setting up WinFax PRO to work with your e-mail system (see fig. 1.6).

Fig. 1.6
Set up WinFax
PRO to work with
your e-mail system
in this dialog box.

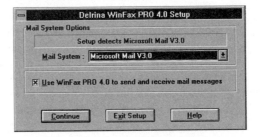

The top section of the e-mail setup dialog box displays which mail system WinFax PRO has determined that you are using. You can select another e-mail system from the Mail System drop-down list.

> **Note**
>
> WinFax PRO does not work with every type of e-mail system. For more information on e-mail and how to use WinFax PRO with it, read Chapter 10, "Using WinFax PRO for Electronic Mail."

To use WinFax PRO as the focal point for your e-mail, select the **U**se WinFax PRO 4 to send and receive mail messages check box. When you finish with the e-mail setup dialog box, click **C**ontinue to return to the main custom setup dialog box.

After you select the options you want to install, click **C**ontinue. WinFax PRO continues with the installation process.

Cover Page Collections

WinFax PRO comes with special collections of cover pages. Many people use cover pages as the first page of the fax. Cover pages explain what the rest of the fax message is about and can even contain the entire message if the message is short.

WinFax PRO calls its collection of cover pages Cover Your Fax. Many of the cover pages are for specific situations, such as setting up meetings or collecting overdue invoices. Others are somewhat humorous. To install the Cover Your Fax cover page library, select the Cover **Y**our Fax check box.

Choose specifically which Cover Your Fax cover page libraries you install by clicking the Op**t**ions button. WinFax PRO displays a dialog box listing all the Cover Your Fax collections (see fig. 1.7).

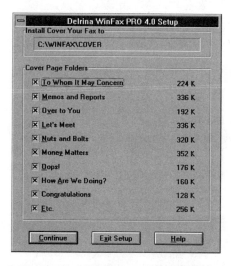

Fig. 1.7
Select the cover page libraries to install in this dialog box.

In the Cover Page Folders area, WinFax PRO automatically has selected the checkboxes next to each collection. To select a collection, keep the check box activated. If you don't want to install a particular collection, deactivate the check box next to it. When you select a check box, the amount of disk space that the cover page library requires appears to the right.

Note

WinFax PRO installs a cover page library called the Basic library even if you don't choose any Cover Your Fax cover pages. The Basic library includes several general purpose cover pages.

When you finish selecting your cover page libraries, click **C**ontinue.

You now finished selecting the items you want to include in your custom WinFax PRO installation. Click **C**ontinue to move on to the next stage of the installation process.

Configuring WinFax PRO during Installation

From this point forward, the installation procedure is the same, no matter which installation option you chose.

Tip
WinFax PRO provides default settings for most of the configuration options. Usually, you won't need to change these settings.

The next series of installation options configures WinFax PRO for operation. Remember, however, that the configuration options you complete in this phase of installation also are available from within the program itself.

This means that you need not complete these options during installation. If you do complete them during installation, you can change them later.

The following sections describe the configuration options. For more details on these options, read Chapter 4, "Configuring WinFax PRO."

Setting Up Your Modem

Whether you selected Full, Laptop, or Custom installation, the next dialog box asks whether you want Setup to test your communication ports. Select **Y**es. WinFax PRO tests your communications ports and displays the following dialog box (see fig. 1.8).

Fig. 1.8
WinFax PRO displays the results of its communications port tests in this dialog box.

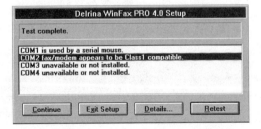

Testing your communications port is a good idea for several reasons. First, the test tells you whether you properly connected your fax modem. Also, WinFax PRO uses test information for later configuration options.

For technical details of what the testing program found, click **D**etails. These details sometimes are of interest to communications experts, but most people do not need to use the information.

To retest your communications ports, click **R**etest. To continue to the next step of installation, click **C**ontinue.

WinFax PRO then examines your fax modem more closely and provides a dialog box for fine-tuning your modem setup (see fig. 1.9).

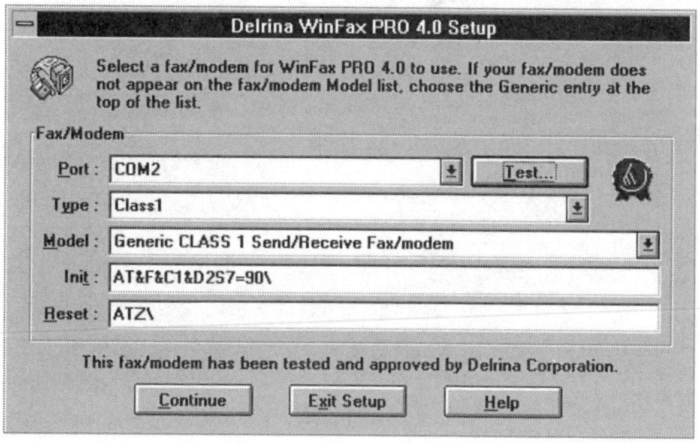

Fig. 1.9
Fine-tune your modem setup during installation in this dialog box.

In the modem setup dialog box, follow these steps:

1. Select the modem port in the **P**ort drop-down list.

2. Select a type of modem in the **T**ype drop-down list.

3. Select a model in the **M**odel drop-down list.

4. Type an initialization string in the Ini**t** text box. An initialization string is the set of instructions WinFax PRO sends to your modem to get it ready to operate.

5. Type a reset string in the **R**eset type box. A reset string is the set of instructions WinFax PRO sends to reset your modem.

Because WinFax PRO automatically places settings in this dialog box that match what it found while testing your communications ports and modem, in most cases there is no need to change these settings.

The settings can be changed at any time in the Fax/Modem setup dialog box in WinFax PRO, which can be accessed by selecting Setup Fax/Modem after you load WinFax PRO. Read Chapter 4, "Configuring WinFax PRO," for more information on these settings.

To move to the next stage of installing WinFax PRO, click Continue.

Changing SYSTEM.INI

Next, WinFax PRO displays a dialog box telling you about changes that should be made to your SYSTEM.INI file (see fig. 1.10).

Fig. 1.10

This dialog tells you about changes you make to your SYSTEM.INI file.

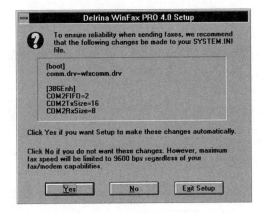

This file is located in your WINDOWS directory. It is one of the files that Windows examines when it loads. SYSTEM.INI contains a long list of technical parameters necessary for running Windows.

Unless you know of a technical reason to not accept WinFax PROs recommendations, click Yes. WinFax PRO automatically makes the technical changes to your SYSTEM.INI file.

Setting Up Your Phonebooks

If you are upgrading from a previous version of WinFax PRO, you may already have a well-established phonebook of fax recipients. If you already use a previous version of WinFax or WinFax PRO, Setup displays a dialog box asking how to handle your existing phonebooks (see fig. 1.11).

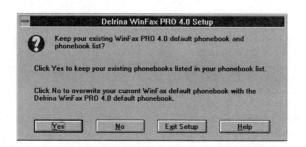

Fig. 1.11
Tell Setup how
to handle
your existing
phonebooks in
this dialog box.

Your options are the following:

- Click **Y**es to keep your current phonebooks. WinFax PRO automatically makes them compatible with WinFax PRO 4.

- Click **N**o if you don't want to convert your previous phonebooks. This means you will start out with empty phonebooks.

Read Chapter 6, "Using Phonebooks," for more information on collecting phonebooks of fax recipients.

Note

You do not see this dialog box if you are installing WinFax PRO for the first time.

WinFax PRO displays a brief screen describing an extra-cost faxing service that you can acquire from Delrina. Fax Broadcast is a service for disseminating large numbers of faxes without tying up your fax modem.

This is a message box only, telling you how to get more information about these services. To clear the message box, click **C**ontinue.

Finishing Installation

Next, WinFax PRO installs program files. Follow the on-screen instructions for inserting new disks.

Depending on which installation options you choose, you may not need to use all the installation disks that came with your package. An on-screen gauge shows the progress of the installation process.

After Setup installs the WinFax PRO files, it asks if you want to install WinFax PRO as your default printer driver. As described in Chapter 2, "How WinFax PRO Works," WinFax PRO prints faxes to fax machines in much the same way that your word processor or spreadsheet prints files to a printer.

Tip
Only select the **Y**es option if you rarely print from your regular printer, but plan on doing a lot of faxing.

If you select **Y**es to install WinFax PRO as your default printer driver, WinFax PRO starts the faxing process by default every time you print something from an application. If you select **N**o, your regular printer remains the default printer. Read Chapter 8, "Sending Faxes," for more information on the printing and faxing process.

Next, WinFax PRO creates your Program Manager program group that includes icons for all elements of WinFax PRO. Those elements include the program itself, the viewer for viewing faxes, the Cover Page Designer for creating your own fax cover pages, the Delrina TEST program for testing your communications port, the Install Log, which is a log of the installation process, and any application macros you added.

Next, WinFax PRO displays the User Setup dialog box, which asks you to set general options about you, your phone numbers, and other basic information. (see fig. 1.12).

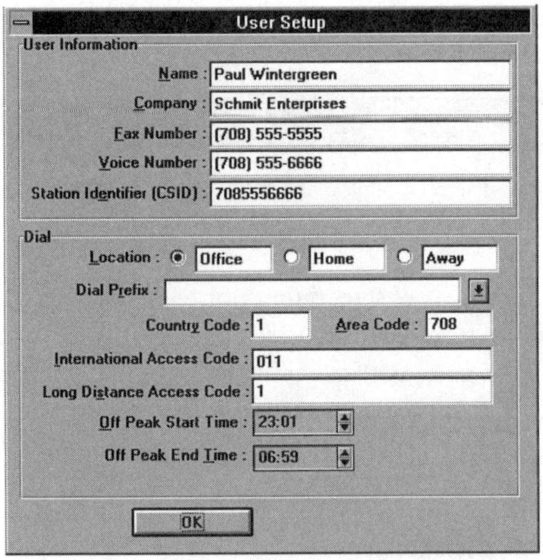

Fig. 1.12
Set up your basic user information in the User Setup dialog box.

The Program Setup dialog box options enable you to select:

■ Your name, company, and fax and voice numbers.

■ Your station identifier (also known as a CSID), which is a unique identifier for your fax device.

■ Dialing information for any of three locations—Office, Home, or Away.

Read Chapter 4, "Configuring WinFax PRO," for information about filling in the User Setup dialog box.

After you click OK in the User Setup dialog box, your installation is complete. WinFax PRO displays a small dialog box informing you of that fact (see fig. 1.13).

Fig. 1.13
When you finish installing WinFax PRO, it displays this dialog box.

Click OK to return to Windows. You can start WinFax PRO by clicking its icon in the Delrina WinFax PRO 4.0 program group in Program Manager.

Troubleshooting

I installed an application macro for my word processor, but there seems to be no change in that program.

Typically, you must run the application macro from within the application. This creates special links to WinFax PRO. Most often, these links create a special option for using WinFax PRO in the File menu of that application. Read Chapter 18, "Using WinFax PRO in Other Programs," for more details on application macros.

I told WinFax PRO installation that I wanted to use it for electronic mail. However, I'm still not able to send or receive electronic mail messages with WinFax PRO.

Setting up WinFax PRO for electronic mail has more steps than simply designating it as such during the installation process. For more information on setting up WinFax PRO for use for electronic mail, read Chapter 10, "Using WinFax PRO for Electronic Mail."

From Here...

This chapter covered how to install WinFax PRO on your computer. To learn more about WinFax PRO, you might want to read the following:

- Chapter 2, "How WinFax PRO Works," describes how the faxing process works.

- Chapter 3, "Starting and Navigating WinFax PRO," covers how to start up WinFax PRO and how to navigate through its interface.

- Chapter 4, "Configuring WinFax PRO," details how to set up WinFax PRO to work optimally. That includes fine-tuning some of the options you set during the installation process.

- Chapter 6, "Using Phonebooks," describes how to create phonebooks of fax recipients.

- Chapter 7, "Creating and Managing Cover Pages," covers how to create and use fax cover pages.

- Chapter 8, "Sending Faxes," tells you about using WinFax PRO to send fax messages.

Chapter 2

How WinFax PRO Works

In this chapter, you learn about the following:

- The way faxing works.

- Types of fax modems.

- Types of fax machines.

- Electronic mail and the way WinFax PRO works with it.

- The way to transfer files as well as faxes.

Whether you transmit between two standard fax machines or between PCs that use fax modems and fax software such as WinFax PRO, faxing is a complicated process. Faxing involves a carefully contrived and complex series of actions involving your PC, WinFax PRO, the telephone lines, and the receiving fax machine or fax modem.

This chapter provides background about the faxing process and the way that WinFax PRO operates, and describes how WinFax PRO transmits and receives computer files and exchanges electronic mail.

This chapter gives you information to help you better understand the faxing process. This information can help you troubleshoot problems more easily and make intelligent modem purchases.

An Overview of How Faxing Works

In the simplest terms, sending a fax requires the following broad steps. The steps described here are meant only to provide an overview of the process and show what WinFax PRO does at each step along the way. Those steps are as follows:

1. *Converting the source document into an electronic image.* This image replicates the document with an organized series of dots, also known as *pixels*. The process of converting a document to a series of pixels is called *rasterizing*.

2. *Dialing and connecting with the receiving fax.* You set up these capabilities in WinFax PRO's phonebook and in the Fax/Modem Setup dialog box. See Chapter 4, "Configuring WinFax PRO," for more details about setting up your modem and Chapter 6, "Using Phonebooks," for details about setting up phonebooks.

3. *Transmitting those pixels over the telephone line to the receiving fax machine.* Your fax modem does most of the work in this stage. However, WinFax PRO monitors progress and determines how to transmit the fax image.

4. *Reconstructing the received fax so that it resembles the original document.* With a traditional fax machine, the result usually is a paper document. With WinFax PRO, you can print the document or save the document on your computer as an image.

In fact, WinFax PRO gives you several additional options. You can resend the fax or forward it to another machine. You also can use *optical character recognition* (OCR) to convert the reconstructed image into editable text that your other programs can use. See Chapter 4, "Configuring WinFax PRO," to learn how to set up WinFax PRO for receiving faxes; Chapter 11, "Using the Send and Receive Logs," to learn how to set up your Receive Log; and Chapter 9, "Receiving Faxes," to learn how to receive faxes.

Understanding the Transmission Process

WinFax PRO plays a larger role in getting the fax ready to send and reconstructing it after receipt (steps one and four) than in the other two steps. That isn't to say that WinFax PRO has no involvement in the other steps—connecting to the receiving fax machine and transmitting the fax. WinFax PRO guides those steps and reacts if problems occur during the middle two steps. For example, if the transmission unexpectedly breaks off, WinFax PRO resends the fax.

Because connecting to the recipient's fax (also called the *remote fax)* and transmitting the fax depend more on the fax device, this book doesn't discuss those steps in depth. This book does, however, provide an overview of those steps. Often, problems transmitting or receiving faxes are the result of a problem with the middle two steps of the process.

> ### Note
>
> Read Chapter 4, "Configuring WinFax PRO," to learn how to set up WinFax PRO so that it displays the progress of a fax connection and transmission.

The middle two steps, connecting to the remote fax machine and transmitting the fax, have a generally accepted series of substeps. That is to say, standards have evolved for these rather complicated processes.

After you dial and connect with the receiving fax, the following steps occur:

1. *Call Setup.* You hear this stage if you inadvertently dial a fax number instead of a voice number. The tones you hear are the signals fax machines use to communicate with each other. In this initial stage, the fax devices use these tones to begin to "talk" to each other and agree on how to communicate.

2. *Pre-message procedure for identifying and selecting facilities.* In this stage, the fax machines exchange technical information. The receiving machine tells the sending machine about its capabilities, such as how many pixels per inch it can handle when it receives a fax, the size of the pages it can print, and the speed at which it operates. Then the calling machine tells the sending machine how it intends to send the document. The two machines must agree on these issues and also on the maximum transmission speed before the sending machine transmits the fax.

   The two fax devices also check for "line noise," which often sounds like static. If the line is not clear, the two machines slow down the transmission speed. Slower transmission speeds are less susceptible to problems due to faulty lines. If the line is too noisy, the fax machines stop the process and hang up.

Tip
A wide variety of problems can cause line noise, including faulty or old wires. However, it is ordinarily an erratic problem. If line noise is a persistent problem, call your telephone repair service.

WinFax PRO Basics

3. *Message Transmission.* In this part of the process, the sending device actually transmits the fax. The length of this phase is the time it takes to send a single page. After transmitting a single page, the process moves on to determine whether there are more pages to transmit. If there are more pages, the process returns to this step.

4. *Post-Message Procedure.* This procedure occurs after each page is transmitted, and includes a tone from the sending machine indicating that it has completed the transmission of the page. The sending machine then tells the receiving machine what comes next—for example, it can send another page or end the call. Then the machines proceed to the stage they agreed upon.

5. *Call Release.* This stage is the last one, when the fax machines or modems hang up.

Learning About Standards and Classes

If every manufacturer of fax machines, fax modems, and fax software did things their way, faxes would rarely get through. Each fax machine or modem wouldn't know how to communicate with fax devices made by other manufacturers.

Over time, standards evolved to make it easy for a fax modem developed by one manufacturer to "talk" with a fax machine or modem developed by another. In fact, international organizations are devoted to helping manufacturers develop standards for all kinds of items, not just electronic transmissions.

The reasoning behind standards is to develop generally accepted protocols—in this case, for the faxing process. Then, in theory, if all manufacturers adhere to the protocols, there should be no difficulty when different machines talk to each other.

The good news is that there are plenty of standards for faxing. The bad news is that some of the standards leave room for interpretation. As a result, sometimes two fax machines that ostensibly agree on a standard still can't communicate, because their manufacturers implemented the standard slightly differently.

More potential bad news is that as telephones, fax machines, and modems develop increased capabilities, new standards must evolve to handle these capabilities. That's good news if you buy a new fax modem or fax machine, but it means that your old fax machine or modem will become out of date.

The two broad types of standards that concern us here are those regarding fax machines and fax modems. Confusingly, the standard for traditional stand-alone fax machines refers to those machines as members of a specific *group.* The standards for fax modems refer to those devices as members of a *class,* which can be confusing.

The next two sections outline those two broad standards. They are important because they affect how successfully you send or receive faxes and also whether your present equipment continues to be useful and generally accepted.

Classes of Fax Modems

The most common type of fax modem is Class 1. In general, Class 1 modems concentrate on sending and receiving the signals—the middle two steps discussed in the last section. Fax software, such as WinFax PRO, does most of the other work, such as rasterizing the document and reconstructing it after reception.

Because Class 1 modems require software to conduct much of the background work, one advantage is that your modem isn't likely to get out of date as quickly. Also, it is easier to build new technology into the software, which is easier and less expensive to upgrade than hardware.

Though reliable, Class 1 modems are more sensitive to the activities of other software. This is particularly true when a system such as Windows tries to operate more than one software application at a time (known as *multitasking).*

By contrast, Class 2 lets the modem do more of the work than Class 1 modems, such as exchanging information with the other modem prior to receipt of the fax. However, even with Class 2 fax modems, the software still must do chores such as reconstructing the fax image after reception.

Because Class 2 modems do more of the work transmitting and receiving faxes than Class 1 modems, it is harder for other software to disrupt the transmissions. However, because the Class 2 standard took so long to develop, not all modem manufacturers adhere to it completely. Rather than

Tip
Unless you have special needs related to high performance and network usage, Class 1 modems are more reliable than Class 2 modems for everyday use and, at this writing, tend to be less expensive.

Tip
Make sure that
WinFax PRO
works with
a new fax
modem, par-
ticularly if it
is a Class 2
modem. To see
if WinFax PRO
supports your
modem,
choose Setu**p**,
Fax/Modem.
Then look in
the **M**odel
drop-down
list for your
modem's brand
and model.

waiting for final approval of the Class 2 standard, many modem manufacturers used interim standards. This means that one Class 2 modem does not
necessarily act like another Class 2 modem. The good news is that WinFax
PRO handles a wide variety of Class 2 modems.

Complicating matters further is the emergence of the Class 2.0 standard (notice the decimal). This is the "final" specification to which Class 2 modems
supposedly must adhere. However, because so many Class 2 fax modems were
developed and released during the waiting period for the final specification,
there actually is more support for Class 2 than for Class 2.0.

> **Note**
>
> At this writing, Class 2.0 modems are both relatively rare and very different from
> Class 2 or Class 1 modems. In fact, while WinFax PRO 4.0 supports Class 1 and Class
> 2 modems, it does not support Class 2.0 modems.

> **Caution**
>
> Buying a "higher" class modem, such as a Class 2 modem, doesn't necessarily mean
> that you also are buying support for Class 1. Some fax modems support both specifi-
> cations, but many modems—particularly lower priced modems—support only one
> standard or the other.

One final type of fax modem that you should know about supports the CAS
standard. Two companies developed the CAS standard, and the market has
not widely embraced it. Still, CAS modems have advantages, including special
processors that make them faster, particularly in heavy use environments
such as networks.

Classes of Fax Machines

Because fax machines have been in existence longer than fax modems, the
standards for the fax machines are more cut and dried. Even though you use
a fax modem with WinFax PRO, you should know at least a little about specifications for fax machines, because your fax modem must be compatible with
the fax capabilities of the machine to which it connects. If the machines are
not compatible, you may find yourself trying—and failing—to exchange
faxes with older fax machines.

In reality, though, compatibility isn't much of a problem in this area, as the
following descriptions of fax specifications show.

For fax machines, the first standard was Group I. This class of fax machines has been obsolete for so long that few remain. The machines transmitted at the now unreasonably slow speed of about six minutes per page. Virtually no fax modems support this standard.

Group II fax machines are still around in somewhat greater numbers than are Group I machines, but they are becoming rarer. Transmission took about three minutes a page. Relatively few fax modems support this standard.

Group III fax machines are currently ubiquitous. These machines transmit about one page per minute. Fax machines purchased in the last several years undoubtedly are Group III machines.

The good news is that virtually all fax modems are compatible with Group III standards. More good news: While a Group IV standard is under development, the Group III standard is likely to remain the dominant standard for quite a while.

Using the WinFax PRO Printer Driver

In computer language, a *driver* is a special piece of software that enables software and hardware to interact. A common type of software driver, the printer driver, enables you to take formatted text from your word processor or other application and send that data to the printer, where it comes out as *hard*, or printed, copy. Because each printer is different, Windows and most DOS programs come with a wide variety of printer drivers to facilitate printing.

WinFax PRO uses a printer driver that works virtually the same as any other printer driver. When you use WinFax PRO to send a fax, think of the remote fax machine to which you send the fax as a printer. WinFax PRO, in effect, prints your fax on the remote fax machine.

There is one fundamental difference between a normal printer driver and the WinFax PRO printer driver. Although a normal printer driver facilitates moving data from your PC to your printer, the WinFax PRO driver facilitates moving data from your PC to your fax modem. After the data arrives at your fax modem, other elements of WinFax PRO take over in conjunction with your modem and the receiving fax device.

You set the resolution of the fax in the WinFax PRO driver. As stated previously in this chapter, the first step of sending a fax creates an image of the document comprised of tiny dots called pixels. The higher the resolution, the more pixels there are on the page. More pixels create cleaner and crisper pages. WinFax PRO's driver supports standard resolution, which is 100 *dots per inch (dpi)* by 200 dots per inch, and fine resolution, which is 200 dpi by 200 dpi. Read Chapter 4, "Configuring WinFax PRO," for more details about setting up the WinFax PRO driver.

An important difference between the WinFax PRO driver and other printer drivers is resolution. Fax standards don't support transmissions of fax images with resolutions greater than 200 dpi by 200 dpi. However, many printers—and the drivers that support them—support resolutions several times higher.

As with other printer drivers, the WinFax PRO driver enables you to send your fax either in *portrait mode* or in *landscape mode.* Portrait mode prints on paper the standard way, with the short edges of the paper at the top and bottom. Landscape mode prints a normal page turned on its side, so the long edges make up the top and bottom. You also can set the size of the printed fax page in the WinFax PRO driver.

Managing WinFax PRO Files

WinFax PRO faxes really are images of the pages you send or receive. Computerized images are different from the text you edit in an application like a word processor. Practically speaking, you can't edit individual words or letters in an image any more than you can edit the words or characters in a photograph of a printed page of words.

It is important to understand that faxes are images, which affects how you store them on your computer and how you use them. Because each page of an image contains a huge number of pixels, images take more disk storage space than a comparable page of text.

So if you send many faxes, periodically clear old faxes from your hard disk; otherwise, you eventually will run out of disk storage space. WinFax PRO helps you with this task by automatically deleting faxes after a user-set amount of time after you receive them.

To save disk space, you can also create a series of folders and subfolders for storing the faxes you sent and received. When you place a fax in an archive folder, WinFax PRO automatically *compresses* the fax image, or makes it fit in less space on your hard drive. Read Chapter 11, "Using the Send and Receive Logs," for more information about using the Send and Receive Logs to archive faxes.

At times, you will want to actually edit the words in a fax. Say that a co-worker faxes you a draft of an important report. Because the fax is an image, you can't extensively edit the words in it. You could retype the fax, but that would be time-consuming.

A better solution is to apply WinFax PRO's optical character recognition (OCR) capabilities to the fax. OCR is the process that converts the words in an image into text your other applications can use. There are two benefits to OCR: You can edit the text with your word processor; also, storing text takes less hard disk storage space than does storing the fax image. Read Chapter 15, "Converting Faxes to Text," to learn more about WinFax PRO's OCR capabilities.

Using WinFax PRO with Electronic Mail

WinFax PRO can send and receive more than just faxes. In the last several years, the use of electronic mail to exchange messages and other computerized information has grown enormously. There are several different types of electronic mail, and several variations of each type.

The most commonly used type of electronic mail is network-based electronic mail, which enables computer users with computers connected to their organization's computer network to exchange messages and files. This method of communicating is increasingly popular in organizations because it is fast and does not require the electronic mail recipient to be present in order to communicate. In other words: no busy signals, and no "telephone tag," that you might get when you exchange messages with voice mail.

WinFax PRO can act as a front end to several popular types of network electronic mail packages. The term *front end* refers to WinFax PRO's ability to create, send, receive, and store electronic mail messages.

Of the electronic mail packages that WinFax PRO supports, the best known are cc:Mail and Microsoft Mail. You can use WinFax with those electronic mail packages or any packages compatible with them. Read Chapter 10, "Using WinFax PRO for Electronic Mail," to learn more about using WinFax PRO with network electronic mail.

Note

If you use a different network electronic mail package, consult your network administrator to determine whether it is compatible with cc:Mail and Microsoft Mail.

Using WinFax PRO to Share Files

In addition to faxing, people commonly use modems to send computerized files to other computers. In fact, long before people started using modems to exchange faxes, the most common use of modems was to exchange computer files.

You can fax an important spreadsheet to somebody, but the recipient of that fax couldn't edit the file to make permanent changes. To do that, the recipient needs the actual file created by a spreadsheet program.

Computerized files sometimes are called *binary files*. The process of exchanging computerized files via the modem is called *binary file transfer.* Over the years, there have been many specialized communications programs that use modems to transfer files. To transfer files, these programs use *file transfer protocols*. These protocols are methods for transferring files between two modems and ensuring that the entire file arrives precisely the same as it was sent.

A new file transfer protocol is called *Binary File Transfer (BFT)*. BFT is a special protocol because it works in conjunction with faxing. In simple terms, BFT enables you to send computer files at the same time you are sending a fax, which means that you can send a two-page fax explaining a spreadsheet file and, at the same time, send the spreadsheet file itself.

WinFax PRO supports three kinds of transfers with BFT:

- BFT transfers to any other fax modem and fax software that supports BFT.

- Direct transfers to somebody else using WinFax PRO.

- Transfers through a new set of computer protocols called Microsoft At Work. To do this, the recipient of your files or fax must be using WinFax PRO 4.0, or have Microsoft At Work capabilities.

Note

If you transfer lots of files to many individuals, you still may need a separate communications package, because WinFax PRO is set up to transfer files primarily with other WinFax PRO 4.0 users and other devices using Microsoft at Work. If you transfer files with others who do not use WinFax PRO or Microsoft At Work, you need a separate program that specializes in transferring files.

From Here...

You might want to review the following chapters, which tell you more about the topics discussed in this chapter.

- Chapter 6, "Using Phonebooks," tells you how to set up individual recipients to receive faxes, electronic mail, or binary files from you.

- Chapter 10, "Using WinFax PRO for Electronic Mail," tells you how to use WinFax PRO with network electronic mail.

- Chapter 16, "Different Ways to Send and Receive," discusses sending and receiving binary files.

Chapter 3

Starting and Navigating WinFax PRO

In this chapter, you learn how to do the following tasks:

- Start WinFax PRO.

- Become familiar with views.

- Navigate between views.

- Navigate within views and dialog boxes.

The previous chapters told you how to install WinFax PRO, and provided a brief overview about how it works. Now let's start WinFax PRO and get to know it. This chapter describes what you see when you start using WinFax PRO, and discusses how to navigate through its various views and windows.

Starting WinFax PRO

You start WinFax PRO just as you start any Windows program. If you are an experienced Windows user, you may want to skim this section, as you undoubtedly are familiar with many of the procedures.

To load Windows and start WinFax PRO, follow these steps:

1. Start Windows by typing **WIN** at the DOS prompt and pressing Enter.

2. In Windows, open the WinFax PRO group window—if it isn't already open—by double-clicking its icon.

Figure 3.1 shows the open WinFax PRO group window.

Fig. 3.1
The open WinFax
PRO group
window.

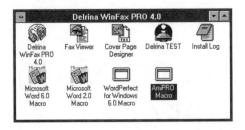

3. To start WinFax Pro, double-click the WinFax PRO icon in the group
   window.

Initializing the Modem

Before WinFax PRO can send or receive faxes, the program must send instructions to the fax modem. This is the *initialization process*.

If you previously set WinFax PRO to automatically receive faxes, the initialization process automatically works when you first start WinFax PRO. If
WinFax PRO isn't set to automatically receive faxes, however, the initialization process only works when you choose to manually receive faxes. Read
Chapter 4, "Configuring WinFax PRO," for more information about how to
set up WinFax PRO to automatically receive faxes. Read Chapter 9, "Receiving
Faxes," about receiving faxes both automatically and manually.

The *status bar*, located at the bottom of the WinFax PRO window, displays
the status of the initialization process. The status bar has several sections that
contain information. The left section tells you how WinFax PRO is interacting with the modem at the present moment. The next section to the right
tells you whether WinFax PRO is set to automatically receive faxes.

If WinFax PRO is set to automatically receive faxes, the words AUTO RCV
appear in the second section from the left. When WinFax PRO finishes the
initialization process, the word Ready appears in the far left section of the
status bar. This means that WinFax PRO is ready to send faxes and to
automatically receive faxes.

Troubleshooting

When I double-click the WinFax PRO icon, the program doesn't start.

Make sure that your WinFax PRO directory is in the path statement in your
AUTOEXEC.BAT file. A path statement tells your computer where to look for files.
When you start a program like WinFax PRO, DOS looks through all the directories in

the path statement for the programs you are trying to start. Read your DOS users manual for more information about path statements. After you change your path statement, you must restart your computer before it goes into effect.

If that doesn't work, click the WinFax PRO icon once. Then, from the Program Manager menu bar, choose **F**ile, **P**roperties. In the Properties dialog box, make sure the drive, path, and file name information about WinFax PRO in both the Command Line and **W**orking Directory text boxes are accurate.

When I start WinFax PRO, I get a message that says WinFax PRO can't communicate with my modem. What's the problem?

Make sure you switched your modem on and properly connected all the cables and phone lines. If you still get the error message, choose **F**ax/Modem from the Setu**p** menu in the WinFax PRO applications screen and select your modem from the **M**odel drop-down list. If that still doesn't work, click on the **T**est button. This runs a diagnostic test on your communications port and modem to see whether they are operational. It is possible the test will find that you did not select the correct port in the Fax/Modem Setup dialog box. If the test tells you so, select a different port from the **P**ort drop-down list.

If your modem still doesn't work, recheck the modem initialization and reset strings in the Fax/Modem Setup dialog box. See Chapter 4, "Configuring WinFax PRO," for more information about selecting a modem type, and initialization and reset strings.

I don't see a status bar at the bottom of the WinFax PRO window. What's the problem?

You probably inadvertently switched off the display of the status bar. Choose **W**indow, Status **B**ar to toggle the status bar display on and off. When the status bar display is visible, a check appears next to the Status **B**ar option.

Understanding Windows

If you are new to computing and to Windows, a few explanatory words may be in order before you turn your attention back to WinFax PRO.

The word "windows" is used in several ways, which can become confusing, even for experienced users. This section tries to clarify some of the potential confusion. The purpose isn't to provide a primer on Windows—use the Microsoft Windows user's guide or books such as Que's *Using Windows 3.1* for that. Rather, this section provides the information you need to get up and running in Windows so that you can start using WinFax PRO.

Working in Microsoft Windows

When capitalized, Windows is a trade name for the Microsoft Windows operating environment within which WinFax PRO works. Windows undoubtedly received its name because it organizes your computing environment by placing programs and other information into *windows* (notice the lowercase *w*), which you can easily access, move, resize, open, and close.

Each program you run in Windows, such as WinFax PRO, operates in its own *application window*. The application window is the entire application as it appears on-screen (see fig. 3.2). You can keep multiple application windows open at the same time.

Fig. 3.2
The WinFax PRO application window (with a small w) is open within Windows (with a capital W).

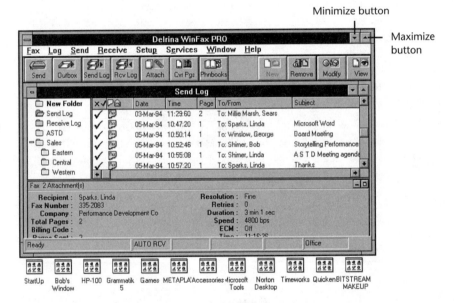

You change the size and screen location of application windows with your mouse (as described in the Microsoft Windows user's guide). You also can minimize the application window by clicking the minimize icon in the upper right corner of the window. When you minimize the application window, it appears as an icon at the bottom of your Windows screen.

Working in WinFax PRO Windows

There are still more types of windows. In most applications, there are typically *document windows*. In a word processor, a document window really is a document—it is the word processing file on which you are working.

In WinFax PRO, a document window doesn't contain a document per se. Rather, it usually contains a *view*, such as the Send Log or Receive Log. WinFax PRO enables you to keep multiple document windows—or views— open at the same time and enables you to switch among them quickly. As with application windows, you can minimize document windows to become icons and change their size and position.

The term "windows" often describes even more things. Within document windows like the Send Log, there are three windows: the folder list window, the fax list window, and the fax display area window.

If you are new to Windows (with a capital *W*), all these different types of windows (with a small *w*) can be confusing at first. But most people find that it doesn't take long before it becomes natural.

Figure 3.3 is similar to the previous figure. However, it highlights the various elements of the WinFax PRO application window.

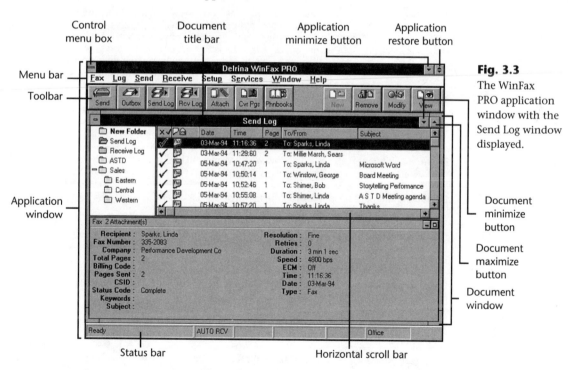

Fig. 3.3
The WinFax PRO application window with the Send Log window displayed.

Table 3.1 lists each part of the opening WinFax PRO application window and what it does.

Table 3.1   Parts of the Opening WinFax PRO Screen.

Part	What It Does
Application title bar	Tells you the name of the application.
Application window control menu box	Activates the close button when clicked once. This enables you to manipulate or close the application window or switch to other windows.
Application window restore button	Increases the application window to its largest possible size. In the case of WinFax PRO, the maximized application window occupies the entire screen.
Application window minimize button	Minimizes the application window to an icon at the bottom of the main Windows screen.
Menu bar	Lists all the main menu options. Click one of the options in the menu bar to drop down a menu that lists program options. The second menu bar option from the left changes to reflect the active document window. For example, when the Send Log document window is active, the second menu item from the left becomes **L**og.
Toolbar	Contains buttons that automate various procedures. In most cases, you can accomplish the same tasks by accessing the menus. Read Chapter 4, "Configuring WinFax PRO," to learn how to customize the toolbar.
Document window	The window where WinFax PRO displays its various views (in this case, the Send Log).
Document title bar	Tells you the name of the document window (also called a "view" in WinFax PRO).
Document window control menu box	Click this button once to produce the document window's System menu, which enables you to manipulate or close the window.
Document window maximize button	Increases the document window to its largest possible size.
Document window minimize button	Minimizes the document window to an icon at the bottom of the WinFax PRO document window.
Document window scroll bar	Scrolls through the list of items in the window—in this case, the Send Log item list.
Status bar	Provides information about how WinFax PRO is interacting with your fax modem.

Here are a few initial navigation hints for application and document windows. Later sections of this chapter discuss in greater detail navigation within and between document and application windows.

■ Because you can keep multiple application windows and document windows open at the same time, it is important to know which one is "active." You can give Windows many color schemes, but typically, the active window is the one in which you currently can work, it has a solid, or darker, title bar.

■ As stated previously, changing the active application window in WinFax PRO changes the contents of the menu bar. Specifically, the second menu option from the left changes to reflect the active document window. If there is no open document window, the second menu option from the left is **S**end.

■ You make an application window or document window active by clicking it or by clicking its title on the **W**indow menu.

■ In WinFax PRO, you open additional document windows either by clicking the appropriate button in the toolbar or by accessing the window from a menu in the menu bar.

Introducing the WinFax PRO Views

WinFax PRO is notable because it provides a consistent interface for many tasks. That is to say, the look and feel of many WinFax PRO document windows—also known as views—is similar. This saves learning time because you needn't learn a new interface for every function.

This section introduces you to several WinFax PRO views that look and act similarly to each other. You learn how to access each view and what the view does. Other chapters of this book describe in detail how each of these views work.

These views, which are focal to WinFax PRO's operations, are as follows:

Send and Receive Logs

Cover Pages

Attachments

Phonebooks

Outbox

Viewer

Send and Receive Logs

You keep track of all faxes you sent and received with WinFax PRO in the Send Log and Receive Log. You access the Send Log by clicking the Send Log button in the toolbar, or by selecting **L**og from the **S**end menu. You also can double-click the Send Log folder while viewing the Receive Log. You access the Receive Log by clicking the Rcv Log button in the toolbar, choosing **L**og from **R**eceive menu, or by double-clicking the Receive Log folder. Figure 3.4 shows the Receive Log.

> **Note**
>
> Because these two logs look and act like the other views, much of this section also applies to the sections that follow.

Fig. 3.4

The Receive Log.

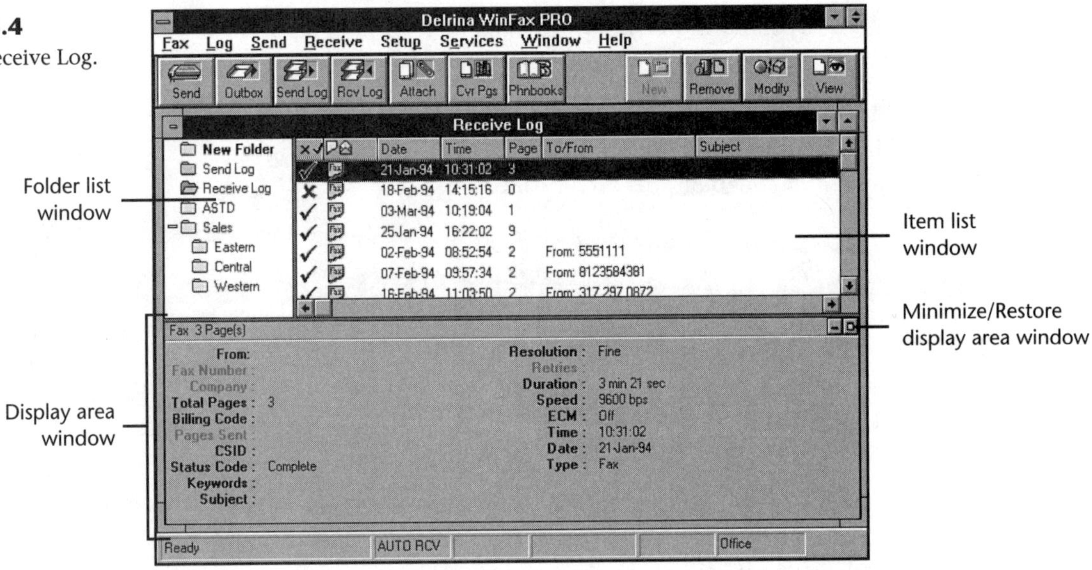

Both logs have the same three windows:

- *The folder list window.* This window contains folders for storing faxes. Read Chapter 5, "Customizing WinFax PRO," for more information about creating and deleting folders.

- *The item list window.* This window lists the items handled in a particular view—in this case, sent or received messages. It also provides basic information about each fax, such as whether the transmission was completed; the date, time, and recipient of the fax; and the number of pages in the fax. This window is highly customizable. Read Chapter 5, "Customizing WinFax PRO," for information about customizing the Send Log or Receive Log item list window.

■ *The display area window.* By default, this window provides detailed text information about the fax highlighted in the item list window. This information includes the fax recipient's name and fax number, the number of pages of the fax, keywords, and billing information. Read Chapter 5, "Customizing WinFax PRO," for more information about customizing the display area window.

In addition to the default information, you can switch to two different views for the display area window: a thumbnail view of the fax or the full image of the fax itself. Read Chapter 5, "Customizing WinFax PRO" for information about customizing WinFax PRO, including information about how to customize the display area window.

You can eliminate the display area window entirely, which increases the size of the fax item list window. Below and to the right of the fax item list window are two buttons. The left button eliminates the display area window, which makes the item list window larger. The right button displays the display area window.

> ### Note
>
> The Send and Receive Logs are tightly linked. In a sense, those logs are two sides of the same coin, meaning that they are actually the same window displaying different information. You can't display both logs at the same time. Selecting one of these logs when the other is on-screen simply switches information in the item list window. These logs, however, share the same system of folders.

The Cover Page Window

You access the cover page window by clicking the Cvr Pgs button in the toolbar or by choosing Cover Pages from the Fax menu. The cover page window is for managing the cover pages that come with WinFax PRO and any that you create using WinFax PRO's cover page creation capabilities. Cover pages provide basic information about the accompanying fax, such as your name and the subject of the fax.

Often, cover pages also contain a note explaining the contents of the fax. For simple fax transmissions, you can send just a cover page with a note.

The basic shape of the cover page window is the same as the Send and Receive Logs (see fig. 3.5).

Fig. 3.5
The cover page window.

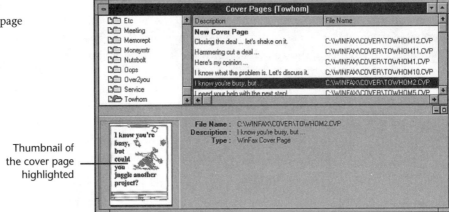

Thumbnail of the cover page highlighted

- The folder list window contains a series of folders and subfolders for storing your cover pages. This is a different series of folders than the one you create for sent and received faxes.

- The item list window lists the cover pages in the highlighted folder and provides basic information about each cover page, such as a description.

- The display area window provides more information about each cover page. This window displays both descriptive information about the cover page and a thumbnail of the cover page.

As with the Send and Receive logs, a button just beneath and to the right of the item list windows enables you to eliminate the display area window so that you can view more information in the item list window. A second button restores the display area window.

Read Chapter 5, "Customizing WinFax PRO," to learn how to customize the cover page window. Read Chapter 7, "Creating and Managing Cover Pages," about creating and managing cover pages.

The Attachments Window

In WinFax PRO, *attachments* are computer files that you add to faxes. Often, these files contain other faxes, although they also can be files created with other applications. Depending on how you transmit your message, WinFax PRO transmits attachments as either a fax or as a computerized file. Read Chapter 12, "Assembling Faxes from Many Sources," for more information about attachments.

You designate specific files as attachments and store those attachments in the Attachments window (see fig. 3.6). To open the attachments window, click the Attach button in the toolbar or choose A**t**tachments from the **F**ax menu. *Attachments* are other faxes or images that you collect. You can assemble new faxes from attachments or add attachments to faxes you create using the usual methods.

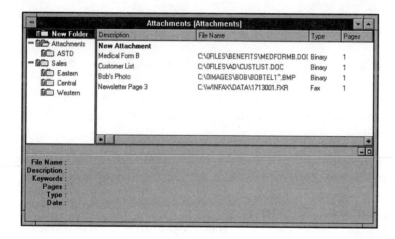

Fig. 3.6
The Attachments window.

Like the previously discussed views, the attachments window consists of a folder list window, an item list window, and a display area window. The system of folders you create for storing attachments is different from those you create for sent and received faxes and cover pages.

The Phonebooks Window

In WinFax PRO, a *phonebook* is where you store information about fax recipients. When you choose to send a fax, WinFax PRO displays the Send dialog box, described a bit later in this chapter. One of your first tasks in the Send dialog box is to access the phonebook and select the name of a person or persons to receive your fax. You can also access the phonebook window separately by clicking the Phnbooks button in the toolbar, or by choosing P**h**onebooks from the **F**ax menu (see fig. 3.7).

Fig. 3.7
The Phonebooks
window.

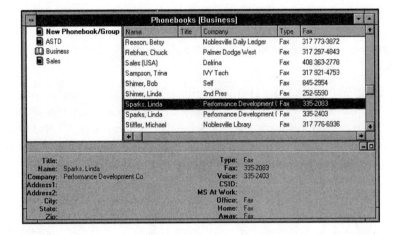

Like the views we already discussed, the Phonebooks window has three sections: a folder list window, an item list window, and a display area window. Each folder in this view represents a different phonebook. For example, one phonebook can store personal fax numbers and another can store business fax numbers.

Read Chapter 6, "Using Phonebooks," for more information about creating new phonebooks and creating and modifying phonebook entries.

The Outbox Window

The Outbox window lists faxes that you scheduled for later transmission. To access the Outbox window, click the Outbox button in the toolbar or choose **O**utbox from the **F**ax menu. This window is different from other windows discussed in this section because it doesn't have a folder list window—the items stored in the scheduled events window are transient: those items move to the Send Log after WinFax PRO transmits them. As a result, you don't need to classify and subclassify them in folders.

Tip
WinFax PRO's ability to send faxes at a later time enables you to schedule non-urgent faxes after the phone rates go down.

The two parts of the Outbox window are the item list and display area windows. Like the other windows discussed in this section, both of these windows are customizable. Read Chapter 5, "Customizing WinFax PRO," for more information about customizing the scheduled event window. Read Chapter 8, "Sending Faxes," to learn about scheduling faxes for later transmission.

The Viewer Window

The Viewer window is the place where you view actual sent, received, or scheduled faxes (see fig. 3.8). Also, in Viewer window, you convert faxes into text that other applications can use through a process called *optical character recognition* (OCR). You also can *annotate* faxes in the Viewer window. When you annotate faxes, you draw on existing faxes or add graphics.

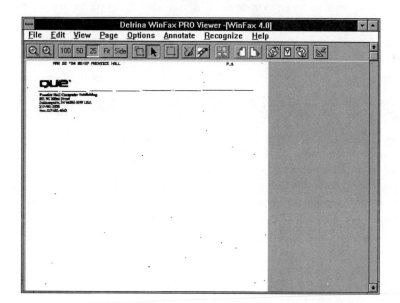

Fig. 3.8
The Viewer window.

Access the Viewer window by first highlighting a fax in the item list windows of one of the other views. Then either click the View button in the toolbar, or, from the **F**ax menu, choose **V**iew. Read Chapter 14, "Viewing and Annotating Faxes," for more information about using the View window to view faxes and to annotate them. Read Chapter 15, "Converting Faxes to Text," to learn about using WinFax PRO's OCR capabilities.

Navigating Among Views

The previous section introduced you to the basic WinFax PRO views and told you, in simple terms, what they do. This section describes the basics of navigating through the WinFax PRO environment. WinFax PRO's capacity to keep multiple windows open at the same time greatly speeds the process of switching from one view to the other.

You would switch between views, for example, when you view the Send Log and want to use the Cover Page window to modify a cover page. The following sections outline basic techniques for switching among WinFax PRO views.

Using the Mouse

The mouse offers the simplest and fastest way to switch between views. The mouse enables you to control an on-screen cursor, called the *mouse pointer*. Depending on activity in Windows or in your specific application, the mouse pointer can look like an I-beam or, more typically, appear on-screen as a single-headed arrow. Position the mouse pointer where you want by rolling the mouse on your desktop; then click the left mouse button to initiate the action.

Note

Most mice are set up for right-handed individuals. So for the most part, you initiate actions with the mouse by clicking or double-clicking the left mouse button, which, for right-handed people, means using the right index finger. This may not be comfortable for left-handed people, however. If you are left-handed, you can switch the functions of the mouse buttons by using the Windows Control Panel. Read your Microsoft Windows user's guide for information about switching the functions of the mouse buttons to accommodate left-handed users.

In WinFax PRO, it is easy to switch among views using the mouse. With more than one view open and on-screen, simply position the mouse pointer over the view you want to switch to and click the left mouse button. The view you clicked becomes the active view.

Say the Outbox and Send Log views are both open and on-screen, but the Outbox window is the active view. To switch to the Send Log, simply click any portion of that window and it becomes active.

Note

You can customize your Windows color schemes. But in most cases, you can tell which view is the active view because both its title bar and outer borders are darker or more solid than those of inactive views.

You also can use the mouse with the **W**indow menu or the toolbar to switch views. The **W**indow menu lists all open windows at the bottom of the menu. To switch to another window, choose **W**indow, and then click the name of the window you want to activate. To switch views using the toolbar, simply

WinFax PRO Basics

point and click the appropriate button. If, for example, you are viewing the Receive Log, switch to the Attachments window by clicking the Attach button in the toolbar.

Similarly, you can find the view you want to activate in the menu system and click it there to switch views. Table 3.2 lists the views discussed in this chapter and describes where in the WinFax PRO menu system you can find them.

Table 3.2 Various Views and Where to Find Them in the Menus.	
View	**Menu location**
Send Log	**S**end, **L**og
Receive Log	**R**eceive, **L**og
Cover Page window	**F**ax, Cover P**a**ges
Attachment window	**F**ax, A**t**tachments
Phonebook window	**F**ax, P**h**onebooks
Outbox	**F**ax, **O**utbox
Send window	**S**end, **F**ax
Viewer window	**F**ax, **V**iew (must have a fax highlighted in a log)

Using the Right Mouse Button

In many WinFax PRO contexts, when you point the mouse pointer at an item and press the right mouse button, a special menu opens with commands specific to the item you pointed to.

The following figure shows an example of these special menus. In this case, figure 3.9 shows the menu that displays when you highlight a fax in the Send Log and click the right mouse button.

Experiment with the right mouse button's capability by pointing at a window with the mouse pointer and pressing the right mouse button. After you get in the habit of using the right mouse button, you will find that it speeds access to many WinFax PRO functions.

Fig. 3.9
Pointing at an
item and clicking
the right mouse
button displays a
special menu with
options for that
specific item.

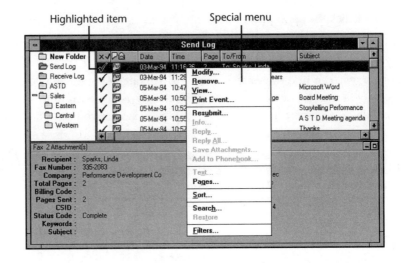

Using the Keyboard

If you prefer, use the keyboard to switch between WinFax PRO views or access menu commands. The easiest way to switch between views is to press Ctrl+tab. This cycles through all open windows.

You also can use the keyboard to access menu commands, including those commands listed in Table 3.2. Each menu and all commands within menus have *hot keys*. Hot keys are letters within the menu or command that you press to select that menu or command. Hot key letters are underlined in both the menu bar and in the menus themselves. (In this book, hot keys are in boldface.)

When you use the keyboard to access menus, you first must select the menu bar. To do that, press F10 and then the hot key for the menu you want to open, or press the Alt key plus the hot key for the menu you want to choose. With the menu open, press the hot key for the menu command you want to choose. For example, to switch to the Receive Log, either press F10 and then R (for **R**eceive), or press Alt+R. With the menu open, press L.

The Multiple Document Interface

As stated previously, WinFax PRO enables you to keep multiple document windows open at the same time. In that way, the WinFax PRO interface operates like the basic Windows desktop, which enables you to keep multiple application windows open at the same time.

To simplify matters, WinFax PRO enables you to minimize each document window so that it appears as an icon at the bottom of the WinFax PRO window, just as you can minimize application windows at the bottom of the Windows screen. Windows refers to the ability of applications to minimize document windows as a *multiple document interface,* or *MDI* for short.

The MDI interface makes navigation simpler by enabling you to keep many windows open at the same time, and avoid a cluttered and confusing screen. You avoid the clutter by minimizing the windows you don't immediately need. Figure 3.10 shows one open window with several minimized windows, which appear as icons in the lower part of the screen.

Minimize button

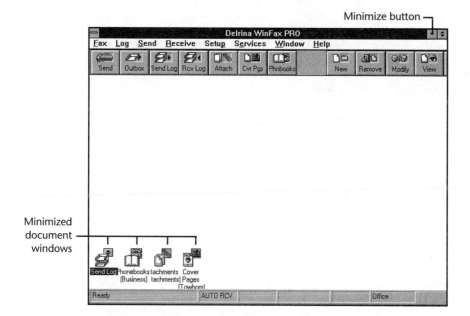

Minimized
document
windows

Fig. 3.10
The MDI interface makes it easy to keep many views accessible.

To minimize an open window, first make it the active window.

Then click the minimize button. (The minimize button is the down arrow in the upper right corner of the window.) There are four ways to maximize the window after it appears as an icon:

- Double-click it.

- Select the window you want to maximize from the list of open windows in the **W**indow menu.

- Select it from elsewhere in the menu system, as summarized in Table 3.2.

- Single-click the icon. In the control menu that appears, choose Ma**x**imize.

Controlling Window Size and Location

You can organize WinFax PRO so that multiple open document windows on the screen are not confusing. WinFax PRO can do this for you, or you can use your mouse to size and position windows manually.

To move a document window to another part of the WinFax PRO application window, click the document window's title bar and hold down the left mouse button. Then move the mouse over your desktop to move the window to the on-screen location you want. (This process is called *dragging*.) When the window is where you want it, release the left mouse button.

To manually change the size of a document window, move the mouse pointer to the border of the window. Once in the proper position at the border of the window, the pointer changes into a two-headed arrow.

On the top or bottom horizontal borders of the document window, the two-headed arrow points up and down. To change the height of the window, place the pointer on the horizontal border you want to change. When it becomes a two-headed arrow, hold the left mouse button down and drag the mouse either up or down until the window is the right height. Then release the left mouse button.

On the left or right vertical borders, the pointer points left and right. Move the cursor to the vertical border you want to change, and when it becomes a two-headed arrow, hold down the mouse button and drag it to make the window narrower or wider. Then release the left mouse button.

You can change both the height and width of a document window at the same time by positioning the mouse pointer over the corners of the window. The pointer turns into a diagonally facing two-headed arrow. When it does this, hold down the left mouse button and drag the mouse to change both the height and width of the document window.

A faster way to create order among open document windows is to use several options in the **W**indow menu. You can place the open windows in a non-overlapping *tile* pattern, or you can *cascade* them so that each open window overlaps the window behind it.

To tile open windows horizontally, choose **W**indow, Tile **H**orizontally (see fig. 3.11).

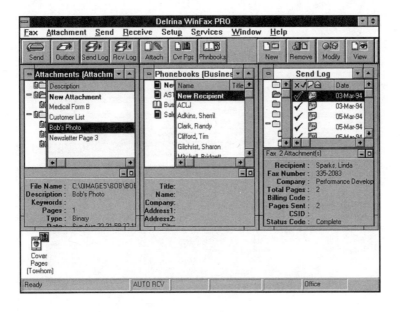

Fig. 3.11
Three horizontally
tiled windows.

To tile open windows vertically, choose **W**indow, Tile **V**ertically
(see fig. 3.12).

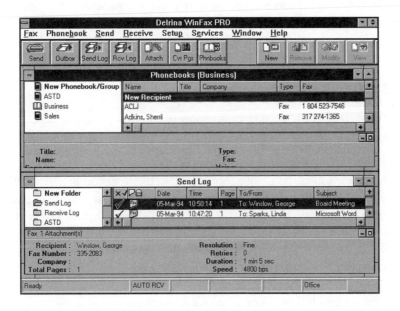

Fig. 3.12
Two vertically
tiled windows.

To cascade open windows, choose **W**indow, **C**ascade (see fig. 3.13).

Fig. 3.13
Three open
windows in
a cascaded
arrangement.

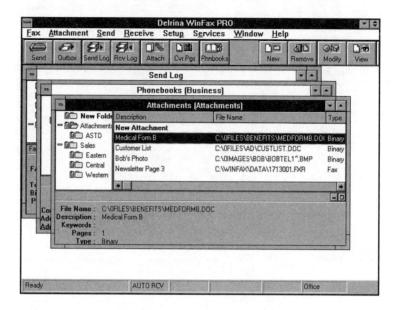

The **W**indow menu also has two other housekeeping options. Arrange Icon**s** arranges all minimized icons neatly at the bottom of the screen. Close **A**ll closes all open windows, including minimized windows.

Using Dialog Boxes

You tell WinFax PRO what to do in *dialog boxes*. They are called dialog boxes because, in a sense, you use them to communicate—or carry on a dialog— with the program.

As stated previously, you move forward to another location in a dialog box either by clicking the part of the dialog box to which you want to move, or by using the tab key. You move backward by clicking the place you want to move to or by using the Shift+tab combination.

Common Elements in Dialog Boxes

This book uses commonly accepted terms to describe the various elements of Windows dialog boxes. Figure 3.14 shows the common areas of dialog boxes.

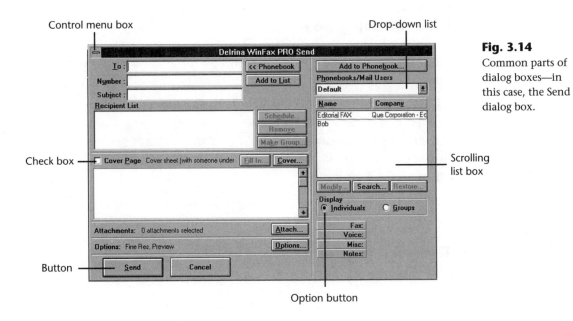

Fig. 3.14
Common parts of
dialog boxes—in
this case, the Send
dialog box.

WinFax PRO Basics

Table 3.3 lists the dialog box elements and gives a brief description of what
they do.

Table 3.3 Common Elements in Dialog Boxes.	
Dialog box item	**Function**
Control menu box	Click once to access a system menu containing basic functions. Double-click to close the dialog box without putting into effect changes you've made.
Button	Initiates an action or leads to another dialog box.
Option button	Selects the item beside it. Typically, when multiple buttons appear, only one can be active.
Check box	Selects the item next to it. Unlike option buttons, you typically can check more than one check box in a group.
Text box	A place for text entry by the user.
Drop-down list	Click the arrow to cause a box to drop down. Highlight the item you want to select.
Scrolling List box	Provides a list of items from which you can choose. Typically, to select an item from the list window, you can double-click it, or highlight it by clicking it once and then clicking a button—usually beneath the list window—that acts on the item.

The Send Dialog Box

The Send dialog box is the control center for sending faxes. It is from this window that you select your recipients, schedule the fax, attach a cover page, and perform other important functions.

Access the Send dialog box from within other applications by selecting the WinFax PRO printer driver, and then printing your file (such as a word processing file) as you usually would. From within WinFax PRO itself, open the Send dialog box by clicking the Send button in the toolbar, or by choosing **F**ax from the **S**end menu.

See Chapter 8, "Sending Faxes," to learn how to send faxes.

Navigating within Views and Dialog Boxes

You can use the mouse or keyboard to navigate within document windows and dialog boxes. With the mouse, position the pointer over the part of the window or the part of the dialog box you want to work with, and then click or double-click the left mouse button.

> **Note**
>
> As a rule of thumb, click once to position the mouse pointer somewhere in the dialog box or window, and twice to initiate an action. For example, to type something in a dialog box, click once where you want to type, and then start typing. To open a minimized document window, double-click the document window's icon at the bottom of the WinFax PRO application window.

If you prefer the keyboard, use the tab key to move around within dialog boxes or application windows. The tab key moves your cursor forward to the next on-screen element in either the dialog box or window. To move backward, press the Shift key and then the tab key.

There is one more basic navigational tool of which you should be aware: *scroll bars*. Scroll bars help you navigate within a document window or within a list when there is more information than can fit on the screen. For example, you may have more messages listed in the Send or Receive Log than can fit in the item list window. You would use scroll bars to scroll through the list.

Vertical scroll bars typically are at the right of the window or list. Clicking the arrow at the top of the scroll bar moves you up one line and clicking on the arrow at the bottom of the scroll bar moves you down one line.

Horizontal scroll bars typically are at the bottom of the list or window. Clicking the arrow at the left of the scroll bar moves you to the left and clicking the arrow at the right of the scroll bar moves you to the right.

Between the two arrows in the scroll bar is the *scroll box*. You can move more quickly through the window or list by positioning the mouse pointer over the scroll box, holding down the left mouse button and dragging your mouse in the appropriate direction.

From Here...

For information about customizing the contents of and using the WinFax PRO document windows, see the following chapters.

■ Chapter 5, "Customizing WinFax PRO," tells you how to customize all aspects of WinFax PRO, including the appearance and contents of document windows.

■ Chapter 6, "Using Phonebooks," tells you how to use phonebooks to keep track of potential fax recipients.

■ Chapter 7, "Creating and Managing Cover Pages," discusses how to use the elements of the Cover Page window.

■ Chapter 11, "Using the Send and Receive Logs," describes the fine points of using these two logs to track and retrieve sent and received faxes.

Chapter 4

Configuring WinFax PRO

In this chapter, you learn to perform the following tasks:

- Set up your fax modem.

- Set up WinFax PRO to send and receive faxes.

- Create and modify fax headers.

- Set up WinFax PRO to use telephone credit cards.

- View and print faxes.

After WinFax PRO is up and running, you can configure the program to operate precisely as you want. You then can spend your time sending and receiving faxes instead of wasting time on fax mechanics.

Although the installation process enables you to set up many WinFax PRO features, you still must understand WinFax PRO's post-installation setup options; the setup procedures discussed in this chapter enable you to use WinFax PRO's more advanced capabilities and to change your previous setup if conditions change. (You may buy a different modem, for example, or decide to change the information in your fax header.)

The Setup menu governs many of WinFax PRO's setup and configuration options (see fig. 4.1). From this menu, you set up the WinFax PRO features that you use most frequently.

Fig. 4.1
The Setup menu
is where you
configure
WinFax PRO.

Setting Up Preferences

The Program Setup dialog box, as shown in figure 4.2, enables you to set a
wide variety of preferences that affect how WinFax PRO operates and how
faxes appear. To access the Program Setup dialog box, choose Setup Program.

Fig. 4.2
You can set up
many appearance
and general-
operation options
for WinFax PRO
in the Program
Setup dialog box.

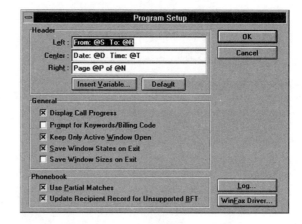

The following sections describe the preferences you can set in this dialog box.

Setting Up Fax Headers

Fax headers appear across the top of faxes and provide recipients with information about you and your fax. WinFax PRO can automatically place your
name and your company's name in the fax header, for example, or list page
numbers for the fax.

During installation, you either accept WinFax PRO's default header or modify
it to suit your needs. You also can modify the header at any time by using the
Header area of the Program Setup dialog box. The Header area contains text
boxes in which you can type information for the left, center, and right fields
of the header.

You can type anything you want in headers, but typically, you use *variables,* which automatically place specific information in the header for you. These variables gather information about your fax, as well as information entered elsewhere in WinFax PRO, and place that information in the header. Variables are useful because they enable WinFax PRO to use information that varies from fax to fax, such as the name of the fax recipient or the current page number.

Variable names begin with the @ sign. After you open the Program Setup dialog box, WinFax PRO displays the current header information in the appropriate text boxes of the Header area.

The default header appears as follows:

```
From: Sender To: Recipient   Date: Time:    Page X of Y
```

To modify header information, eliminate default variables by placing the cursor in the Left, Center, or Right text boxes, and then, using the Backspace or Delete keys, as appropriate. Type the new variable information directly into the text boxes. Header information in each of these positions can contain as many as 39 characters.

To enter a variable in the Header area, select the Insert Variable button. WinFax PRO displays the Insert Variable dialog box, as shown in figure 4.3, which lists the variables you place in your header.

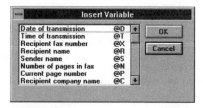

Fig. 4.3
The Insert Variable dialog box lists the variables you can place in fax headers.

To use the Insert Variable dialog box, place your cursor in the text box of the Program Setup dialog box in which you want to insert the variable *before* you access the Insert Variable dialog box. Then choose Insert Variable, and highlight in the list box the variable you want to insert. Click OK, and WinFax PRO inserts the variable at your cursor position.

Table 4.1 describes the variables you use in headers and also where this information originates.

	Table 4.1	Header Variable Codes and Where They Originate.	
	Code	**What Appears in Header**	**Where Information Originates**
	@D	Date of transmission	Your computer's system settings.
	@T	Time of transmission	Your computer's system settings.
	@X	Fax number of recipient	The Send dialog box. (See Chapter 8, "Sending Faxes," for more information about using the Send dialog box.)
	@R	Fax recipient's name	The Send dialog box.
	@S	Sender's name	The User Setup dialog box (discussed later in this chapter).
	@N	Total number of pages in the fax	The fax itself.
	@P	Current page's page number	The fax itself.
	@C	Recipient's company name	Recipient's phonebook record.
	@F	Recipient's first name	Recipient's phonebook record.
	@L	Recipients last name	Recipient's phonebook record.
	@B	Billing code	Recipient's phonebook record.
	@U	Subject	Send dialog box.
	@Y	Your company name	User Setup dialog box.
	@A	Your fax number	User Setup dialog box.
	@H	Your voice number	User Setup dialog box.

Tip

You also can type freeform text into the header text boxes. You can, for example, reserve the center position of the header to say "Seasons greetings to @R!". (Translated: "Seasons greetings to *Your Recipient's Name*!".)

To return to WinFax PROs default header after you've changed it, select the Default button. After you finish, click OK.

General Setup Options

The General area of the Program Setup dialog box includes several additional program operation settings. You activate each option by selecting the check box so that an X appears in the box, and you deactivate the options by deselecting the box to eliminate the X. These options are as described in the following list:

- *Display Call Progress*. If you select this option, WinFax PRO displays the Status message box showing the progress of incoming and outgoing faxes. The information WinFax PRO shows in the Status message box depends on whether you are sending or receiving the fax. In either case, however, the message box provides such basic information as the status of the transmission, the station identifier of the other fax machine, and the current page number sent. For more information, read Chapter 8, "Sending Faxes," or Chapter 9, "Receiving Faxes."

- *Prompt for Billing Code/Keyword* instructs WinFax PRO to automatically display a dialog box that prompts you for keywords and billing information about a fax before you send the fax.

> **Note**
>
> The billing code and keyword information you provide are useful for several reasons. Keywords are particularly useful if you send and receive many faxes. They enable you to search for archived faxes. Chapter 11, "Using the Send and Receive Logs," provides more information about searching for faxes. Billing information is particularly useful in multiuser situations in which long distance and other charges are billed to various departments.

- *Keep Only Active **W**indow Open* automatically closes windows you are not currently using.

- *Save Window States on Exit* instructs WinFax PRO to start with the same windows open as when you last exited.

- *Save Window Sizes on Exit* saves the size of WinFax windows when exiting the program. If this check box is not selected, the windows return to their default setup size.

Setting Phonebook Options

The phonebook area of the Program Setup dialog box contains two options for how your phonebooks operate. Those options are as follows:

- Use **P**artial Matches enables you, when you search for names in your phonebook, to locate names on the basis of part of the name, rather than the entire name. Read Chapter 6, "Using Phonebooks," for more information about searching through your phonebooks.

■ Update Recipient Record for Unsupported **B**FT refers to an advanced
method of transmitting information called *Binary File Transfer (BFT)*.
As described in Chapter 16, "Different Ways to Send and Receive,"
BFT enables you to send computer files at the same time you send a fax.
However, the recipient's fax software must support BFT file transfers. If
you select this option and you try to send a BFT transmission to somebody whose software does not support BFT, WinFax PRO automatically
changes that recipient's phone record so you can't repeat the mistake.

Setting Up Logs

Logs—specifically the Send and Receive Logs—are where you store messages
you send and receive. You *archive* messages by moving them to archive folders you create for the Send and Receive Logs. Chapter 11, "Using the Send
and Receive Logs," describes how to use folders to archive your messages.

You customize the way the logs and folders operate by clicking the **L**og button in the Program Setup dialog box. When you do, WinFax PRO displays the
Log Setup dialog box (see fig. 4.4).

Fig. 4.4
Customize logs in
the Log Setup
dialog box.

The Log Setup dialog box tells WinFax PRO how to handle items that you
archive in folders and whether to automatically delete messages as those
messages age and, if so, how do so. To automatically delete messages, select
the Enable A**u**tomatic Event Deletion check box at the top of the dialog box.

The Archive area of the dialog box has several options that pertain to
archiving messages in folders. Those options are as follows:

■ Select the **D**isplay Archive Options for Move/Copy check box if you want WinFax PRO to display a dialog box whenever you move a message from the Send Log or Receive Log to a folder for archiving. The dialog box, as described in Chapter 11, "Using the Send and Receive Logs," provides options about how to archive the messages. If you don't select this option, WinFax PRO will base its archive decisions on the next options you set.

■ **S**ave Pages with Event tells WinFax PRO to save both the file of the fax and also the notation of the event when you move or copy it to an archive folder.

■ Attachments are computer files that you attach to messages. When you send fax attachments, WinFax PRO converts them to fax images. However, when you send or receive electronic mail (also called e-mail) attachments and send or receive BFT messages, those attachments remain as computer files. Sav**e** Attachments tells WinFax PRO to save electronic mail or binary file attachments when you move a message with such attachments to an archive folder. Read Chapter 10, "Using WinFax PRO for Electronic Mail," for information about files attached to e-mail messages sent and received by WinFax PRO. Reach Chapter 16, "Different Ways to Send and Receive," for information about sending and receiving computer files with WinFax PRO.

You also use the Log Setup dialog box to determine whether, and how, WinFax PRO automatically deletes messages from your logs. If you select automatic event deletion, you next determine which messages to delete and when to delete them.

In the Automatic Event Deletion area of the dialog box, the deletion options are as follows:

Tip
Automatic deletion is a great way to make sure your hard disk doesn't fill up with old, obsolete messages.

■ E**n**able is where you determine whether WinFax PRO automatically deletes messages. Select this check box to enable automatic deletion. If you select this option, you must then set the rules by which WinFax PRO automatically deletes messages. Those options follow:

　All E**v**ents deletes all messages after they are the specified number of days old.

　Failed Events deletes only messages that WinFax PRO did not successfully transmit.

　Comple**t**ed Events deletes messages that WinFax PRO successfully transmitted.

After you select one of the previous three options, type the age of messages you want automatically deleted in the Age **b**y text box. WinFax PRO automatically deletes the messages after that number of days.

You determine which part of the message WinFax PRO deletes in the Delete area. The two options are as follows:

- Events and P**a**ges deletes both the computer file containing the message and the listing of the message in the Send or Receive Log.

- Pages Onl**y** deletes only the file, leaving the listing of the message in the Send or Receive Log.

When you finish the Log Setup dialog box, click OK to return to the Program Setup dialog box.

The final option in the Log Setup dialog box is in the Options area. Select the **C**onfirm All Deletions check box if you want WinFax PRO to display a dialog box confirming all deletions from your Send and Receive Logs.

Read Chapter 11, "Using the Send and Receive Logs," for more information about storing your messages in WinFax PRO.

Setting Up the WinFax Driver

As discussed in Chapter 2, "How WinFax PRO Works," WinFax PRO uses a driver that is functionally similar to a printer driver. Instead of printing your fax on an actual printer, however, WinFax PRO dials the remote fax number and "prints" the fax on that fax machine.

As most printer drivers are designed to work in Windows, you can fine-tune how the WinFax PRO driver operates. To do so, select the Win**F**ax Driver button in the Program Setup dialog box. The WinFax Driver dialog box appears (see fig. 4.5).

Fig. 4.5
You can fine-tune the WinFax PRO "printer" driver in the WinFax Driver Setup dialog box.

> **Note**
>
> You also can access the WinFax Driver dialog box in several other ways. You can, for example, choose **F**ax Printer **S**etup. This displays a list of active Windows printer drivers, including the WinFax driver. Select the WinFax driver from the **P**rinter list box, and then choose **S**etup to access the WinFax Driver dialog box. You also can access this dialog box by double-clicking the Printers dialog box in the Windows Control Panel or by using the printer setup capabilities of other applications. Typically, you access these capabilities from the **F**ile menu of those applications.

The WinFax Driver dialog box contains the following areas:

- *Page **S**ize*, which tells WinFax PRO the paper size of the fax message. In the United States and Canada, the most common paper size is the default setting, which is letter-sized paper (8 1/2 by 11 inches). The other options are legal-sized paper (8 1/2 by 14 inches); A4, which is the paper size most often used in Europe; and Custom. If you choose Custom, WinFax PRO displays two additional text boxes that enable you to select the unit of measure for your custom paper size from the drop-down list on the right and then type the length of the sheet in the Page Len**g**th text box on the left.

  Tip
  If you regularly send only brief faxes, save long distance charges by shortening the length of the page. This helps the fax transmit faster.

- *Orientation* enables you to choose between sending your fax in **P**ortrait or **L**andscape modes. In **P**ortrait mode, the page width—or the lines on which information is printed—is narrower than the page height. This is the most common printing orientation, particularly for letters, memos, and other common business correspondence. **L**andscape mode turns portrait mode on its side so that the page's width is wider than its height.

- *Standard **R**esolution* enables you to choose between Fine Resolution, which transmits and prints the fax at a resolution of 200 by 200 dots per inch (dpi), or Regular Resolution, which prints the fax at 200 by 100 dpi. Fine resolution creates crisper, easier-to-read faxes, but takes longer to transmit.

> **Note**
>
> Standard resolution is the most commonly used resolution mode and, in most cases, is quite readable. Because standard resolution transmits faster, you save on long distance charges. If you really need to make a good impression, however, or you are transmitting many pages and want to spare your recipient eyestrain, send your faxes in fine resolution.

After you finish setting up the WinFax PRO driver, click OK. Click OK again to close the Program Setup dialog box.

Troubleshooting

Headers in the faxes I send don't have precisely the information I specified. What did I do wrong?

This problem probably results from a typing error made as you typed information in the header window of the Program Setup dialog box. If you mistype a variable code, that information does not appear in the headers. Re-examine your header information in the Program Setup dialog box to make sure that you typed it correctly.

I don't know what is happening when WinFax PRO sends or receives faxes. All I know is that while I am in other applications, periodically my PC doesn't work and my hard drive light is on.

During the send and receive process, WinFax PRO sometimes takes complete control of your PC and does not permit any other activity to occur. Displaying the Call Progress dialog box enables you to know when WinFax PRO is in operation. To view the progress of the fax operation, select the Display Call Progress option in the Program Setup dialog box. Some users also like to hear their modem operate during fax sending and receiving. To hear your fax, you must set the modem speaker options in the Modem Setup dialog box, as described in the following section.

Sometimes, if I want to print a document from my word processor or other application, WinFax PRO activates. What causes this problem?

The problem is that you previously sent a fax using the WinFax PRO driver, but forgot to switch back to your normal printer driver. Use the Printer Setup option on your application's **F**ile menu to choose your printer driver.

Recipients complain that the faxes I send are difficult to read. How do I correct this problem?

In the Program Setup dialog box, select the **W**infax Driver button. Then select the **F**ine Resolution button. This sends faxes at a finer resolution that is easier to read. Be aware, however, that sending faxes at this resolution also takes more time.

Setting Up Your Modem

Even though you set up your modem during installation, you may at some point change modems or simply need to change how WinFax PRO interacts with your modem to ensure smooth operation. To make such changes, choose Setu**p** **F**ax/Modem. WinFax PRO displays the Fax/Modem Setup dialog box (see fig. 4.6).

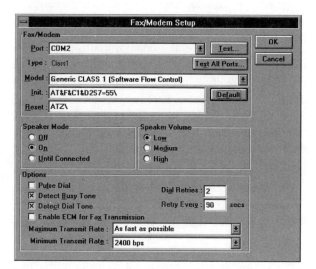

Fig. 4.6
You can make sure that WinFax PRO works correctly with your modem by setting options in the Fax/Modem Setup dialog box.

The Modem Setup dialog box is where you set WinFax PRO to work with your specific modem. The options in the Fax/Modem area of the dialog box are as described in the following list:

■ **P**ort. This is where you change the communications port at the back of the computer to which you connect your fax/modem. Communications ports are numbered COM1 through COM4. The most commonly used communications ports are COM1 and COM2. Select a port location from the **P**ort drop-down list. If you are not sure how your PC numbers its communications ports, check the documentation for the computer, or use the T**e**st All Ports option (described a bit later).

■ **T**est. This button confirms that the fax/modem is properly connected to the port you selected. If you are unsure of your fax/modem port location, select the T**e**st All Ports button instead. WinFax PRO then identifies the port to which your fax/modem is connected. Choose OK to close the Test COM Ports window.

■ **M**odel. This drop-down list is where you select your specific modem brand and model. If you do not find your modem in the drop-down list, the best solution usually is to select the generic setting that best matches your modem's capabilities. The generic settings for Class 1 and Class 2 modems are located at the top of the list. Typically, using the **T**est or Te**st** All Ports options will tell you what class your fax modem is. If the generic settings don't work, try selecting a Hayes modem with a speed that most closely matches the speed of your modem.

■ **I**nit is where you type a special modem initialization string. An initialization string is a series of characters that WinFax PRO sends to your modem to make it ready to operate. Usually, you need not type anything in this text box; WinFax PRO supplies an initialization string that matches the modem you select in the **M**odel drop-down list.

■ **R**eset is the string of characters that WinFax PRO sends to the modem so that you can use the modem again. As it does for the initialization string, WinFax PRO provides the reset string after you select your modem model.

■ De**f**ault makes your modem the default modem type; choose the button.

■ Te**s**t All Ports examines each communications port attached to your computer, determines whether a modem is attached and, if so, tries to determine what kind of modem it is. By contrast, **T**est only tests the port you selected in the **P**ort drop-down list.

Setting Your Modem's Speaker

You can control your modem's speaker by setting options in the Speaker Mode and Speaker Volume areas. Speaker Mode enables you to select whether your modem's speaker is on while you send or receive faxes. The options are **O**ff, O**n**, and **U**ntil Connected.

Speaker Volume sets the speaker's volume as WinFax PRO operates. The options are Lo**w**, Me**d**ium, and **H**igh.

> ### Note
>
> Setting your modem's speaker in this dialog box affects only how the speaker works as you use WinFax PRO. The settings do not affect how your modem speaker works with other communications and fax programs.

Other Modem Options

In the Options area, you can set additional options that determine how WinFax PRO and your modem interact.

- *Pulse Dial* is for use with pulse phones. These days, however, pulse phones, also known as rotary phones, are rare.

- *Detect **B**usy Tone* instructs WinFax PRO to inform you, via the Call Progress dialog box that appears after you send or receive faxes, that the receiving fax line is busy.

- *Detect Dial Tone* instructs WinFax PRO to inform you in the Call Progress dialog box if it detects a dial tone.

- *Dial Retries* instructs WinFax PRO how many times to redial the number if the line is busy or it cannot make a connection for any reason.

- *Retry Every* is the amount of time, in seconds, between retries.

- *Disable Error Correcting Mode* disables a special capability of WinFax PRO when it communicates with standard fax machines. Error Correcting Mode (also known as ECM) breaks a fax page into smaller pieces and examines each piece for accuracy. The result is often faxes with fewer distortions, such as tiny dots around the edges. However, sometimes older fax machines without ECM don't react well to ECM; you may want to disable it with this option.

- *Maximum Transmit Rate* sets the fastest rate at which your modem transmits faxes. The default setting is As Fast As Possible—that is, WinFax PRO sends the fax at the fastest rate that both your modem and the receiving modem support.

- *Minimum Transmit Rate* sets the slowest rate at which your modem transmits faxes. The default is to send faxes at any rate, although you also can set a specific transmission speed.

Caution

Simply having a high speed fax modem doesn't mean that you should set either the minimum or maximum transmission rates to match your modem's capabilities. Enabling WinFax PRO to send and receive at any rate or at the fastest speed possible enables the program to adapt to varying conditions, such as a slow or malfunctioning fax machine at the other end. Setting a specific speed is for special, highly controlled circumstances.

WinFax PRO Basics

After you set all the options for your modem, click OK.

Troubleshooting

*My modem isn't listed in the **M**odel drop-down list, and I get erratic results while sending or receiving faxes. What do I do now?*

First, try using the generic modem settings listed in the Model drop-down list or the settings for Hayes modems. If problems persist and you continue to get erratic results while faxing, the problem often is in the initialization string. Your modem's docu-mentation should provide the correct initialization string. If it doesn't, call technical support for the modem manufacturer to get the correct string, and type it in the **I**nit text box.

My modem worked well the first time I used it after setup, but wouldn't work after that. What is the problem?

If you use your fax modem successfully once, but it does not work correctly again, an incorrect reset string is a leading suspect. As is true of the initialization string, if you don't use one of the settings WinFax PRO provides for the modem you select in the **M**odel drop-down list. You may need to get the correct reset string either from your modem's documentation or from the modem vendor.

Setting Up User Information

The User Setup dialog box, as shown in figure 4.7, provides WinFax PRO with information about you and your telephone system. WinFax PRO uses that information for a variety of other operations. WinFax PRO uses some of the information in the User Information area of the User Setup dialog box, for example, in variables you use in headers and cover page.

You access the User Setup dialog box by choosing Setu**p** **U**ser.

Most of the information you type in the User Information area is obvious, such as your name, your company name, and your voice and fax numbers. Some of the information you must provide is not as obvious, however. The following sections describe that information.

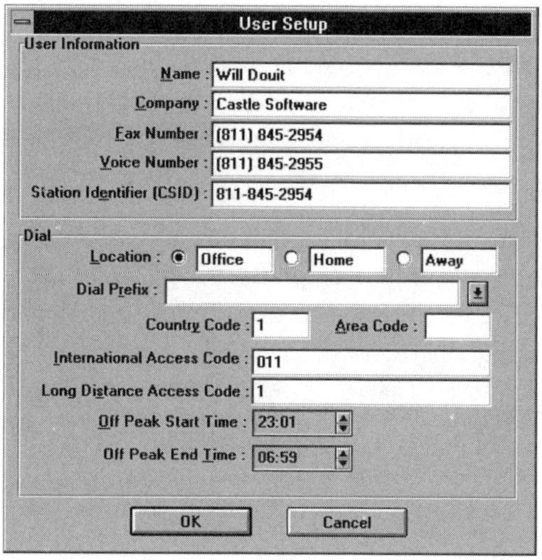

Fig. 4.7
In the User Setup dialog box, you enter information about yourself that WinFax PRO uses elsewhere in the program.

WinFax PRO Basics

Setting the Station Identifier

The last item in the User Information area asks you to establish a *station identifier* (also known as the *CSID*, for Called Station Identifier). This unique series of letters and numbers identifies your fax machine. This number appears on the console of the receiving fax machine as it receives your fax. Using a station identifier is not mandatory, but it can be useful for many fax operations, such as secure sending, as discussed in Chapter 8, "Sending Faxes."

Typically, the station identifier is your fax area code and phone number as a string of characters without spaces. The station identifier can be as long as twenty characters. Creating a station identifier requires only that you type it in the Station Identifier (CSID) text box in the Program Setup dialog box.

Note

Although your station identifier can be any combination of twenty letters and characters, remember that it should be both easily identifiable and easy to remember. The latter is particularly true in multiuser situations. That is why the fax phone number is the most commonly used station identifier.

Setting Location and Dialing Preferences

The Dial area of the User Setup dialog box enables you to set up how WinFax PRO dials out of your phone system, and it also enables you to set up different dialing sequences for three separate locations, which WinFax PRO refers to as home, away, and office.

Tip

The ability to have different dialing sequences for different locations is invaluable for travelers. Read Chapter 17, "WinFax PRO Away from the Office," for more information and tips about faxing while traveling.

This flexibility means, for example, that you can use WinFax PRO at the office, and it automatically will dial a prefix, such as 9, to get an outside line. However, when you use WinFax PRO from home, it automatically dials *70 to disable call waiting when you send a fax.

You set your dialing preferences for each of the three locations in the Dial area of the User Setup dialog box. To do that:

1. Click either the Home, Away, or Office buttons to select the location you are setting up.

2. In the Dial Prefix box, type the dialing prefix you must dial to get an outside line. WinFax PRO will automatically dial this prefix for you.

> **Note**
>
> Dial Prefix is a combination text box and drop-down list box, which means that it can store multiple dial prefixes. This gives you fast access to different dialing prefixes that you use in different situations. For example, you may need different prefixes for working in the home office and in branch offices. To add more dialing prefixes, type them in the Dial Prefix text box and click OK. The next time you access the User Setup dialog box, you can access the prefixes you added by clicking the down arrow next to the Dial Prefix text box to see the drop-down list of prefixes.

3. In the Country Code text box, type the country code of your current location. This is the special code used for dialing your country. Each country has a numeric code you must use if dialing a number in that country. The country code for the United States is 1.

4. In the Area Code, type your current area code. Changing the area code when you travel with WinFax PRO is important, because before it dials out, WinFax PRO compares the current area code and the area code of the number you dial. If the area codes are the same, WinFax PRO doesn't dial the area code.

5. In the **I**nternational Access Code text box, type the number you must dial to get an international number. In the United States, that number most commonly is 011.

6. In the Long **Di**stance Access Code text box, type the number you dial to dial domestic long distance. In the United States, that number is 1.

7. Next, select your off-peak time period for your location. The off-peak time can be anything you chose. This can be a time of lower rates, or a time, in an office situation, in which a shared fax modem is not as heavily used. Select the beginning of the off-peak period in the **O**ff Peak Start Time combo box. Select the end of the off-peak time in the Off Peak End **T**ime box.

> **Note**
>
> You make use of the off-peak time you designate here when scheduling faxes for later transmission. Read Chapter 8, "Sending Faxes," for more information about scheduling faxes.

When you finish setting up your user information for a specific location, click OK to close the User Setup dialog box. WinFax PRO saves the parameter you set for that specific location. You must use the User Setup dialog box again to set parameters for another location.

Using WinFax PRO with Telephone Credit Cards

WinFax PRO automates the process of using telephone credit cards to send faxes. You may need to send faxes from a hotel room while traveling, for example, or if you work at home, you may want to charge the long distance call to your business. To set up this capability, choose Setu**p** **C**redit Card to access the Dial Credit Card Setup dialog box (see fig. 4.8).

Fig. 4.8

The options in the Dial Credit Card Setup dialog box simplify your use of telephone credit cards for sending faxes.

Besides being the place where you type your telephone credit card numbers, this dialog box enables you to automate your credit card use in complex phone systems. After you first display the dialog box, only the following drop-down list box and text box appear on-screen:

- *Long Distance Service* asks you to select the long-distance service that you or your organization uses. Select your service from the drop-down list. If your service isn't listed, select either Custom 1 or Custom 2.

- *Credit Card Number* is where you type your credit card number. WinFax PRO replaces your card number with asterisks as you type it to prevent others who use the program from learning it.

- *Service Access Number* is where you type the number you must dial to access your long distance provider. Selecting some of the selections in the Long Distance Service drop-down list results in the automatic placement of a telephone number in the Service Access Number text box. Type in the number if that does not occur, or if you want to modify the number that WinFax PRO automatically added.

Manually dialing your calls through different phone systems while using a telephone credit card often is difficult enough; the task becomes even more difficult if you must instruct software to do it for you. To simplify the process, select the Dial Credit Card dialog box's Modify button; the dialog box expands to help you set up dialing procedures, as shown in figure 4.9.

Fig. 4.9
Automate the procedure for using your telephone credit cards in the expanded Dial Credit Card Setup dialog box.

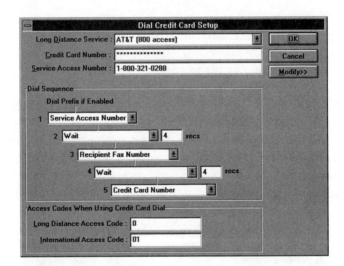

The expanded dialog box adds two areas: One contains a series of five drop-down lists in which you establish the sequence for dialing out and using your credit card. The other enables you to enter special long-distance access and international access codes while using a credit card.

Use the five drop-down lists to give WinFax PRO a series of step-by-step in-structions for using your credit card and connecting to the external fax. Each drop-down list offers the same options. Create the sequence of events needed to dial out using your credit card with these drop-down lists.

The selections available in these drop-down lists are as described in the following list:

Unused. This isn't an appropriate choice for the first drop-down list. Select this option for the fourth and fifth drop-down lists, for example, if dialing out with your credit card requires only three steps.

Service Access Number. This is a special number you must dial to gain access to your long distance carrier. If you choose this option, a special Service Access Number text box where you must type the number appears.

Recipient Fax Number. WinFax PRO uses the number you select from the phonebook.

Credit Card Number. WinFax PRO uses the number you typed in the Credit Card Number text box.

Wait for Dialtone. This option pauses the dialing operation until WinFax PRO detects a dial tone.

Wait. If you choose this option, a text box appears to the right of the drop-down list. You can type in this text box the number of seconds you want WinFax PRO to wait before it goes on to the next step. You often must wait while either your internal phone system or your long distance carrier processes the information you send it.

> **Note**
>
> Although setting a wait time often is necessary, you frequently must use trial and error to discover the optimal wait time. By default, WinFax PRO sets the wait time to four seconds.

The area at the bottom of the Dial Credit Card Setup dialog box contains text boxes for special long-distance or international access numbers you must use if using your credit card.

After you finish entering your information in this dialog box, click OK.

Tip

Type long-distance or international access codes in the Dial Credit Card Setup dialog box even if they are the same numbers entered else-where in the setup options. This tells WinFax PRO specifically to use those op-tions with your credit card.

WinFax PRO Basics

Troubleshooting

WinFax PRO does not dial out from my organization's phone system. What is wrong?

You probably used the wrong Long Distance Access Code or Dial Prefix settings. Check with the person who manages your phone system to obtain the correct settings, and enter these setting in the User Setup dialog box or the Dial Credit Card dialog box. Another possible cause is that you are either waiting too long or not long enough between steps.

I can transmit faxes to domestic numbers by using my telephone credit card, but not to international numbers.

Make sure that your International Access Code setting is correct. In the United States, this setting typically is 011. Yours, however, may be different. Your telephone credit card also may require access codes different from those you normally need. Make sure that you enter the numbers appropriate for your credit card in the expanded Dial Credit Card Setup dialog box. Check with your phone system administrator to obtain the correct information.

Setting Up WinFax PRO To Receive Faxes

WinFax PRO applies many of its most advanced features to received faxes. The Receive Setup dialog box—and the dialog boxes it accesses—are therefore important. These dialog boxes enable you to set WinFax PRO to receive faxes automatically and to display, print, or apply OCR to faxes automatically. This section provides enough information to get you started. Look to other chapters about these specific subjects for more details.

To open the Receive Setup dialog box, as shown in figure 4.10, choose Setup **R**eceive.

The Receive Setup dialog box enables you to determine whether you automatically receive faxes, the way WinFax PRO behaves while it receives faxes, and the way it behaves after it receives faxes, including whether it automatically forwards faxes to a fax number that you specify. You also can set up WinFax PRO so that you can poll it from remote computers to determine whether it received faxes in which you are interested, and then have those faxes forwarded to you.

Fig. 4.10
The Receive
Setup dialog box
contains many
options for
determining how
faxes are received
and what happens
after they arrive.

WinFax PRO Basics

Chapter 17, "WinFax PRO Away from the Office," discusses how to set up
WinFax PRO for automatic forwarding of faxes. This section details other
options related to receiving faxes.

Automatic Receipt of Faxes

To automatically receive faxes, make sure that the **A**utomatic Reception
check box is selected. If you select this check box, you need to fill in the
Number of Rings Till Answer text box. Typically, the phone needs to ring
only once before WinFax PRO answers it and starts receiving the fax.
One ring is the default.

If you don't select this check box, you can receive faxes only manually.
For more information on receiving faxes, see Chapter 9, "Receiving Faxes."

Displaying Faxes During Reception

WinFax PRO can display faxes as it receives them. This process is similar to
that of watching the paper come out of a traditional fax machine as the machine receives the fax. To view the fax as WinFax PRO receives it, select the
View During Receive check box in the Receive Setup dialog box.

To choose the size of the window in which to view the incoming fax, select
the Window **S**ize button. This displays a separate window in which you can
set the size of the window that displays the incoming fax. Adjust the size of
this window by dragging the border with the mouse pointer, and then close
the window by double-clicking the Control menu box in the upper-left
corner of the window.

Next, you need to determine how you want WinFax PRO to display the incoming fax. Selecting the Scroll button in the Display Mode area adds new lines to the bottom of the fax, one after the other, to emulate how a paper fax comes out of a traditional fax machine. Selecting the Sweep button paints the incoming fax image from top to bottom.

> **Note**
>
> Displaying incoming faxes on-screen requires many system resources, which slows down other operations. Unless you have a compelling reason to watch incoming faxes, do not select the View During Receive check box. Your system performs better if you leave this option deselected. If you do select this option, select the Sweep button as well. Sweep requires fewer system resources than Scroll does, because scrolling makes WinFax PRO redraw the entire fax on-screen every time a new line is added; sweeping merely adds new lines to the existing on-screen fax.

Setting Post-Reception Activities

Among WinFax PRO's most powerful capabilities are those that come into play after it receives a fax. You set those capabilities in the After Reception area of the Receive Setup dialog box.

You set most of the options in the After Reception area in two stages. First, you select the check box for the post-reception option you want to activate. Then, if one is available, select the button to the right of the selected check box to actually set the option.

Selecting the Notify check box instructs WinFax PRO to notify you if it receives a fax. If you select this option, WinFax PRO displays a message about the received fax on-screen, even if you are using another application.

If you select this option, you can select a sound to accompany the notification. To select a sound, select the Sound button; the Sound dialog box appears, as shown in figure 4.11, enabling you to select a sound for the message.

Fig. 4.11
The Sound dialog box enables you to pick the sound to notify you that WinFax PRO has received a fax.

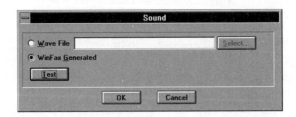

You can use either a sound supplied by WinFax PRO, or a digital waveform file (WAV). Windows includes several WAV files; you also can download them from most bulletin boards and on-line services.

To use a waveform file, select the **W**ave File button and type the path and name of the file in the accompanying text box. If you don't know the path and name of the file, select the **S**elect button to display the Select Wave File dialog box (see fig. 4.12). Use the Dri**v**es drop-down list and the **D**irectories list to select the locations in which you store waveform files. Select the waveform file you want from the File **N**ame window, and click OK. WinFax PRO displays in the Sound dialog box the name of the file you selected.

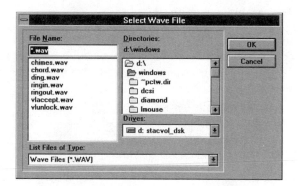

Fig. 4.12
Select a sound file in the Select Wave File dialog box.

To use the sound file included with WinFax PRO, select the Sound dialog box's WinFax **G**enerated button. You can hear the sound you selected play by selecting the **T**est button.

Viewing the Fax

To view the fax in its entirety after you receive it, select the V**i**ew Fax check box. This displays your fax on-screen even if you are using another application.

This option is different from the options used for displaying a fax during reception, as discussed in the section "Displaying Faxes During Reception" earlier in this chapter. Those options display the fax as WinFax PRO receives it, one line at a time. After WinFax PRO completely receives the fax, any other activity is terminated and you see the fax in WinFax PRO's Viewer. (For more information about Viewer mode, see Chapter 14, "Viewing and Annotating Faxes.")

WinFax PRO Basics

Tip
The **N**otify option in the Receive Setup dialog box is useful if you turn off your modem speaker or if your modem is not close enough to your computer for you to hear it, which may be the case if your modem is connected to a network.

Tip
Leave this
option
switched off
most of the
time. The OCR
process takes
time and uses
many system
resources,
which slows
down other
operations.

Applying OCR Automatically

Selecting the **R**ecognize check box in the Receive Setup dialog box instructs WinFax PRO to automatically apply *optical character recognition* (*OCR*) to the fax after reception is complete. Received faxes are actually images, not text like your word processing files. The OCR process converts the images into text usable by your other applications, such as word processors or databases.

You can apply OCR to faxes at any time. This setting automatically applies OCR after WinFax PRO receives the fax.

If you enable this option, select the Se**t**up button to the right of the check box to set up automatic OCR on receipt. WinFax PRO displays the Recognize Setup dialog box, as shown in figure 4.13.

In the Options area of the dialog box, select the **S**tore Text in Receive Log button to keep the recognized text under the control of WinFax PRO. You then can access the text file from the WinFax PRO's Receive Log.

Fig. 4.13
Set up OCR
options in the
Recognize Setup
dialog box.

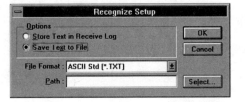

Tip
If you don't
find the pro-
gram you want
to use in the
File Format
drop-down list,
save the recog-
nized text in
ASCII, dBASE,
or Lotus 1-2-3
format, which
virtually all
programs can
import.

Select the Save Text to File button to instruct WinFax PRO to save the text to a specific file, which you can then use with other applications. If you select this option, first select from the File Format drop-down list the file format in which you want to save the recognized text. Type in the **P**ath text box the drive and path in which you want the file saved. If you are not sure which drive and path to specify, choose the Se**l**ect button. WinFax PRO displays the Directories dialog box, from which you can choose a drive and path. When you finish, click OK to return to the Recognize Setup dialog box.

Printing on Receipt

To automatically print faxes as you receive them, select the Print **F**ax check box of the Receive Setup dialog box. WinFax PRO and your fax modem then treat incoming faxes the same as traditional fax machines—except that you don't need to deal with fax paper.

If you select this option, WinFax PRO assumes that you want to print to the default printer you set up in the Windows Control Panel. To designate another printer for your faxes, select the **P**rinter button. WinFax PRO displays the Printer Setup dialog box in which you can select the printer you want WinFax PRO to use. To set up the printer, select the **S**etup button in the Printer Setup dialog box. WinFax PRO displays a standard setup dialog box for each printer you select. You also can access this dialog box from the Windows Control Panel.

Automatically Forwarding Faxes

Among WinFax PRO's most powerful features is its capability to automatically forward faxes. This is a particularly useful capability if you travel. WinFax PRO's forwarding capabilities enable it to automatically forward faxes directly to you. You also can set WinFax PRO to forward specific faxes to others.

Chapter 17, "WinFax PRO Away from the Office," discusses in detail this advanced feature and how to set it up.

Enabling the Toolbar and Status Bar

The toolbar and the status bar are on-screen tools that help you work in WinFax PRO and keep you informed about the program's operation. The toolbar, located just below the menu bar near the top of the WinFax PRO window, consists of a series of buttons that enable you to accomplish common tasks with a simple mouse click (see fig. 4.14). The status bar is located at the bottom of the WinFax PRO window; it describes how the program is currently interacting with your modem (see fig. 4.15).

Fig. 4.14
The toolbar provides fast access to common WinFax PRO functions.

By default, the toolbar and status bar both are visible on-screen. To turn the toolbar on and off, choose **W**indow Tool**b**ar. If a check appears next to the Toolbar menu item, the toolbar is visible. If no check appears, WinFax PRO does not display the toolbar.

Fig. 4.15
The status bar keeps you informed about how WinFax PRO is interacting with your fax modem.

Similarly, to turn the status bar on and off, choose **W**indow Status **B**ar. As is true of the toolbar, a check mark next to the Status Bar menu command indicates that the status bar is visible.

You cannot alter the information displayed in the status bar. You can, however, customize contents of the toolbar. Chapter 5, "Customizing WinFax PRO," describes how to customize the toolbar.

From Here...

This chapter described how to set up WinFax PRO for day-to-day operations. To learn how to set up more advanced options, you may want to review the following chapters of this book:

- Chapter 5, "Customizing WinFax PRO." This chapter tells you how to customize virtually all aspects of WinFax PRO, including how to customize the toolbar.

- Chapter 6, "Using Phonebooks." This chapter tells you how to set up and use phonebooks of your fax recipients.

- Chapter 7, "Creating and Managing Cover Pages." As do the fax headers described in this chapter, cover pages use variables. This chapter describes how to set up cover pages by using this capability.

- Chapter 15, "Converting Faxes to Text." This chapter tells you how WinFax PRO can automatically convert faxes to text you can edit. This chapter describes the process and how you can fine-tune it.

- Chapter 17, "WinFax PRO Away from the Office." Among WinFax PRO's powerful advanced features are those that enable you either to automatically forward faxes to another location or to poll WinFax PRO from a remote location to check for faxes.

- Chapter 18, "Using WinFax PRO in Other Programs." This chapter describes how to use WinFax PRO on a network, as well as how to set up and use WinFax PRO's powerful At Work capabilities.

Chapter 5

Customizing WinFax PRO

This chapter teaches you how to do the following:

■ Add, modify, and delete folders for storing faxes, cover sheets, and phonebooks

■ Customize the appearance and content of document windows

■ Customize the toolbar

One of WinFax PRO's strengths is that it provides a similar interface for performing many different functions. Specifically, its document windows (also called *views*) for listing and storing items—such as faxes and cover pages—are similar. This feature simplifies learning and using WinFax PRO.

As discussed in Chapter 3, "Starting and Navigating WinFax PRO," WinFax PRO divides most of its document windows, such as the Send Log, into three sections. Note that each section also is referred to as a window:

■ The *folder list window*, which shows an on-screen system of folders for storing items. The Outbox view does not have a folder list window.

■ The *item list window*, which lists items, such as cover pages and sent or received faxes.

■ The *display area window*, which provides detailed information about the item highlighted in the item list window.

This chapter tells you how to customize the on-screen appearance and contents of each of the three parts of WinFax PRO's document windows. This chapter also tells you how to customize the WinFax PRO toolbar.

Using Folders

In many of its views, WinFax PRO uses the visual metaphor of folders for organizing and storing items. The following views use folders:

- The *Send Log*, which stores sent messages.

- The *Receive Log*, which stores received messages.

- The *Attachments window*, which stores libraries of items, such as previously sent or received faxes, that you can use in future faxes.

- The *Cover Pages window*, which stores both the cover pages that come with WinFax PRO and the cover pages you create.

- The *Phonebooks window*, which stores the phonebooks where you list the recipients for your messages.

> **Note**
>
> One commonly used view, the Outbox, does not use folders because its contents are transitory. After WinFax PRO sends items in the Outbox, they move automatically to the Send Log. Also, you cannot create subfolders for phonebooks. While WinFax PRO calls individual phonebooks *folders*, they don't contain archived information such as sent faxes. As a result, you cannot nest telephone "folders."

Folders, a familiar metaphor, provide great flexibility for categorizing and storing items. You can create a system of folders that works the way you work.

Some users create folders for messages about specific tasks or job functions. For example, one folder may store messages about a departmental budget, and another series of folders may store messages about specific projects. Others users may keep a series of folders based on time. For example, each folder may represent a week's worth of messages. Some users may set up their system of folders based on different products or different sales regions.

WinFax PRO folders also are flexible because you can *nest* them. That is, besides containing messages, folders also can contain additional folders, or *subfolders*. The top-level folders can represent broad categories, and the subfolders can store messages that relate to subtopics of the main category.

For example, you can have a folder structure for your Send and Receive Logs like the one in figure 5.1.

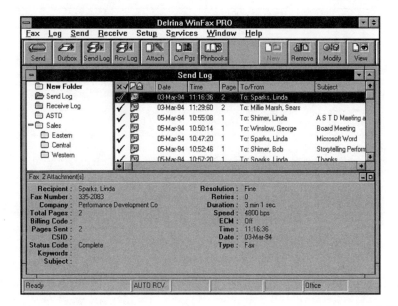

WinFax PRO Basics

Fig. 5.1
You can create structures of folders and sub-folders for the Send and Receive Logs.

Adding Folders

The procedure for creating new folders in each of the views is similar but not identical. Because the nature of the items stored in folders differs from view to view, the nature of the folders themselves is somewhat different. Another reason for the slightly different procedures is that the menu bar changes to reflect the currently active document window.

Specifically, the second menu bar item from the left changes as you change active views. You change active views either by clicking the view to which you want to switch in the toolbar, or by selecting the view you want in the **F**ax menu.

Table 5.1 shows you the name of the second menu bar item from the left in different contexts.

Table 5.1 Second Menu Bar Items in Different Views.	
Active View	**Second Menu Bar Item**
Outbox	**O**utbox
Send Log	**Lo**g
Receive Log	**Lo**g
Attachments window	**A**ttachment
Cover Pages window	**C**over Page
Phonebooks window	Phone**b**ook
View Fax window	**E**dit
No active view	**S**end

To delete a folder in any view, highlight the folder in the folder list window by clicking it once. Then press the Del key. You also can choose the main menu bar item for the active view (such as **A**ttachments or Phone**b**ooks), and then choose **R**emove. When prompted to confirm that you want to remove the selected folder, click the Yes button.

Caution

When you delete a folder, WinFax PRO does not delete the items in the folder from your hard disk. However, before you delete a folder, move the items to another folder. Otherwise, your items will not be stored in a folder and you must add them to other folders in a separate operation. To move items, drag them from the item list window that displays the contents of the folder, and then drop the items onto another folder in the folder list window.

The next several sections describe how to create new folders for the different WinFax PRO views.

Creating Send Log and Receive Log Folders

You undoubtedly will use the folders you create in the Send and Receive Logs more often than the folders you create in other views. That is why it is a good idea to create a series of folders and subfolders for these logs; multiple folders make it easy to find previously sent or received messages. Folders you create can contain both sent and received messages.

To create a new folder for the Send and Receive Logs, follow these steps:

1. Make the log window active by clicking either the Send Log or Recv Log buttons in the toolbar. Or you can click the log window if it already is open.

2. Double-click the folder called *New Folder*. The New Archive Folder dialog box appears (see fig. 5.2).

Fig. 5.2
The New Archive Folder dialog box is where you create new folders for the Send and Receive Logs.

3. In the New Archive Folder dialog box, type a name for the folder in the Folder Name text box. Folder names can contain up to 40 characters.

4. Optionally, type a file name for the folder in the File Name text box. By default, WinFax PRO uses the first eight characters of the folder name as the file name.

5. Determine whether you want the new folder to be a top-level folder or a subfolder stored within a top-level folder. Click either the Top Level or Subfolder Of button. If you select the Subfolder Of button, WinFax PRO displays all top-level folders in the window below. Highlight the top-level folder in which you want to place your new subfolder.

6. Choose OK.

If you made your new folder a top-level folder, the new folder appears at the same level as the Send and Receive Log folders. If you made your new folder a subfolder, WinFax PRO displays the new folder below and to the right of the top-level folder to which you attached the new folder.

Tip
In all views, there are two additional ways to create a new folder. Press the Ins key, or, with the mouse pointer in the folder list window, click the right mouse button to display a menu. From that menu, choose New.

Note

WinFax PRO only lets you nest one level of subfolders. That is, you can create a subfolder within a top-level folder, but you can't create a subfolder within another subfolder.

Read Chapter 11, "Using the Send and Receive Logs," for more information about using Send Log and Receive Log folders for archiving messages.

Creating New Attachments Folders

In WinFax PRO, you designate previously sent and received faxes or other images and files as *attachments*. Attachments enable you to include in new faxes the contents of previously sent or received faxes, saving you time and trouble. You also can create entirely new faxes from scratch using attachments. Because you can designate a practically unlimited number of items as attachments, you may want to keep track of them by using a series of folders.

To create a new folder for attachments, follow these steps:

1. Make sure that the Attachments document window is active.

2. Double-click the folder named *New Folder*. Or highlight a folder and then, from the **A**ttachment menu, choose **N**ew. WinFax PRO displays the New Attachment Folder dialog box (see fig. 5.3).

Fig. 5.3
This is the New Attachment Folder dialog box, where you create new folders for attachments.

3. Type a name for the new folder in the **F**older Name text box.

4. Click the **T**op-Level button if you want to create a top-level folder, or click the **S**ubfolder Of button if you want to create a subfolder located within an existing folder.

   If you create a subfolder, highlight the name of the folder you want to contain the subfolder.

5. Choose OK.

Your new folder or subfolder appears in the folder list window of the Attachments document window.

Creating New Phonebooks

Multiple phonebooks help you stay organized—especially if you are a heavy fax user. One phonebook, for example, can list the numbers of sales prospects, and another phonebook can list vendors with whom you work. Or, if you both fax and use electronic mail, you can keep a separate phonebook for each activity. In most cases, you will find the specific names you need faster and easier with multiple phonebooks. Chapter 6, "Using Phonebooks," discusses using phonebooks in greater detail.

When you create a new phonebook folder, you actually are creating the phonebook itself. You can think of phonebook folders in WinFax PRO as traditional manila folders into which you drop many individual pieces of paper with names and fax phone numbers.

You can create new phonebooks from scratch, or by using database files or existing phonebooks. This section tells you how to create new phonebook folders from scratch. Read Chapter 6, "Using Phonebooks," to learn how to create new phonebook folders from database files or existing phonebooks.

To create a new phonebook from scratch, follow these steps:

1. Make sure that the Phonebooks document window is active.

2. Double-click the folder named *New Phonebook/Group*. Or highlight a folder and then, from the **P**honebooks menu, choose **N**ew. WinFax PRO first displays the New Phonebook/Group dialog box (see fig. 5.4).

3. Click the **P**honebook button.

Fig. 5.4
This is the New
Phonebook/Group
dialog box, where
you start the
process of creating
new phonebooks.

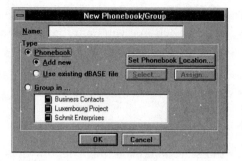

4. Type a description of the new phonebook in the **N**ame text box. Your description can contain up to 40 letters or numbers.

5. If you want to store the phonebook file in a location other than \WINFAX\DATA, which is the default, click the Set Phonebook **L**ocation button. WinFax PRO displays the Set Phonebook Location dialog box (see fig. 5.5).

Fig. 5.5
Determine a file
name and location
for storing your
phonebook.

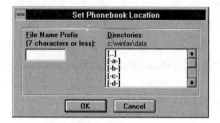

Tip
To share your
phonebook with
other network
users, save the
phonebook on a
shared network
drive. Read Chap-
ter 18, "Using
WinFax PRO in
Other Programs,"
for more informa-
tion about using
WinFax PRO on a
network.

6. Because WinFax PRO stores each phonebook in a separate file on your hard disk, you may type a file name as long as seven characters in the **F**ile Name Prefix text box. This step is optional. By default, WinFax PRO uses the first seven letters of the phonebook name.

7. In the **D**irectories list box, select a directory in which you want to store the phonebook. The default directory is \WINFAX\DATA. Click OK when you finish the New Phonebook/Group dialog box.

8. Choose OK to return to the New Phonebook/Group dialog box. In that dialog, choose OK to create your new phonebook.

Chapter 6, "Using Phonebooks," discusses creating and using phonebooks in greater detail.

Creating New Cover Page Folders

WinFax PRO makes creating custom cover pages so simple that you can have many different cover pages for different types of faxes. For example, you can have different cover pages for faxing information about different products. Similarly, you can have another series of cover pages for collecting past due invoices.

If you keep different cover pages for more than one purpose, it is a good idea to store them in a series of folders.

1. Make sure that the Cover Pages document window is active.

2. Double-click the folder named *New Folder*. Or highlight the folder and then, from the Cover Page menu, choose **N**ew. WinFax PRO displays the New Cover Page Folder dialog box (see fig. 5.6).

Fig. 5.6
The New Cover Page Folder dialog box is similar to the New Archive Folder dialog box.

3. Type the name of the new folder in the **F**older Name text box.

4. Decide whether the folder will be a top-level folder (by clicking the **T**op Level button) or a subfolder (by clicking the **S**ubfolder Of button).

   If you are creating a subfolder, in the window below the buttons, highlight the top-level folder in which you want to place your new folder.

5. Choose OK.

Read Chapter 7, "Creating and Managing Cover Pages," for more information about creating and using cover pages.

Modifying Folders

You can modify the name of a folder and its location as a top-level folder or subfolder. To do this, follow these steps:

1. Highlight the folder you want to modify.

2. Choose the menu item that is appropriate for the active document window. For example, if the Send or Receive Log window is active, choose **L**og. If the Attachments window is active, choose **A**ttachments.

Tip

You can view the dialog box for modifying folders by highlighting the folder you want to modify, clicking the right mouse button, and choosing **M**odify from the menu that appears.

3. In the menu, choose **M**odify. If you are viewing the Send and Receive Logs, WinFax PRO displays the Modify Archive dialog box. Choose **M**odify Folder.

   For all views, WinFax PRO displays a dialog box that is similar to the one you used to create the folder.

4. Optionally, change the name of the folder in the **F**older Name text box (called the **N**ame text box for phonebooks).

5. Optionally, either make a subfolder a top-level folder or make a top-level folder a subfolder. To do this, click either the **T**op-Level button or the **S**ubfolder Of button.

   If you are converting a top-level folder to a subfolder, highlight the top-level folder in which you want to place the subfolder. Remember, phonebook folders are always top-level folders. You can't make a phonebook folder a subfolder.

6. Choose OK.

> **Note**
>
> Even though they appear as folders, the Send Log and Receive Log are so essential to the operation of WinFax PRO that deleting or modifying them would be dangerous. Therefore, WinFax PRO won't enable you to change or delete them.

Changing the Appearance and Contents of Views

Each WinFax PRO document window has three parts: the folder list window, the item list window, and the display area window. WinFax PRO enables you to customize the appearance of those windows and the contents of the item list and display area windows. The following sections tell you how.

Changing Window Size

Use your mouse to change the size of the folder list window, the item list window, or the display area window. In all views, you can move the horizontal border above the display area window. In all views except the Outbox window (which doesn't have a folder list window), you can move the vertical border between the folder and item list windows.

To change window size, follow these steps:

1. Decide which section of the document window you want to make larger or smaller.

2. Position the mouse pointer over the border of that window until the pointer changes to a special cursor with two arrows pointing out from the center.

3. Hold down the left mouse button.

4. Drag the mouse, moving the border to increase or decrease the size of the window.

5. When the window is the size you want, release the mouse button.

You can minimize the display area window entirely. Below and to the right of the item list window are two buttons. Click the left button to eliminate the display area window (making the item list window larger). Click the right button to restore the display area window.

Customizing the Item List View

WinFax PRO lists items such as cover pages and sent or received faxes in the item list window. In all views, you can determine what information WinFax PRO displays in the item list window. You also can determine the order in which the information appears.

The information WinFax PRO can display in the item list window varies from view to view. For example, in the Send and Receive Logs, you can display virtually all information about faxes. That information ranges from the recipient's name to billing code information to the length of the transmission time. In the Cover Page view, your choices are fewer: you can display only the file name for the cover page and a description.

Although the information WinFax PRO displays in the item list window varies, the process for adding and deleting different types of information is the same for all views. To do this, follow these steps:

1. Place the mouse pointer over the column headings in the item list window.

2. Click the right mouse button. A list containing all the types of information that WinFax PRO can include in that particular item list window appears (see fig. 5.7). Checked items already appear in the item list window.

Fig. 5.7
The menu lists the types of information you can include in the item list window.

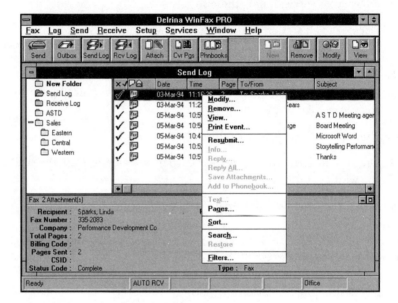

3. To add a type of information to the item list window, highlight the unchecked item in the list. To eliminate a type of information from the list window, highlight the checked item.

4. Repeat the process until WinFax PRO displays precisely the information you want.

You can further customize the item list window by changing the order in which the information appears and the width of the columns that display information.

To change the order of information in the item list window, position the mouse pointer over the column heading you want to move. Hold down the left mouse button and drag the mouse pointer to another location at the top of the item list window. Drop the column of information you selected into a new location by releasing the left mouse button.

In addition to changing the order of information columns, you can change the width of the columns. The procedure for changing the width of columns is similar to the procedure for changing the size of the various windows within views, as discussed previously in this chapter. To do this, follow these steps:

1. Position the mouse pointer over either the left side or the right side of the column heading.

2. When the mouse pointer changes to a two-arrow cursor, hold down the left mouse button.

3. Drag the mouse to either widen the column or make it narrower.

4. When the column is the width you desire, release the left mouse button.

As figure 5.8 shows, making columns narrower squeezes more information onto the screen. Making columns wider displays less information but makes the information easier to read.

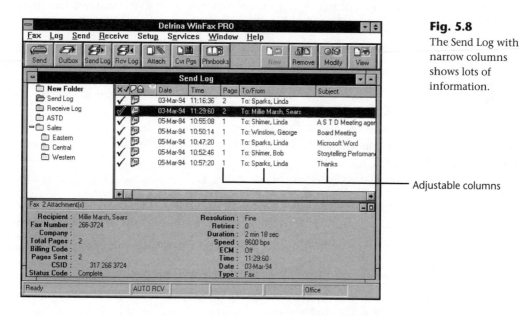

Fig. 5.8
The Send Log with narrow columns shows lots of information.

Customizing the Default Display Area Window

By default, WinFax PRO displays text-based information in the display area window. The information provides details about the item highlighted in the item list window. This section tells you how to change the appearance of the default display area window and the order of information. The next section tells you how three of the views enable you to change the information WinFax PRO displays.

WinFax PRO displays different information, of course, depending on the type of item listed. The information displayed for sent or received faxes, for example, includes information about time and date of transmission and similar information. Obviously, this information is different from, and not relevant for, cover pages.

You can't change the contents of the default display area windows. You can, however, change the order in which the information appears. WinFax PRO also enables you to add either spaces or lines between lines of information.

To change the position of a line of information in the display area window:

1. Position the mouse pointer over the line of information you want to move.

2. Hold down the left mouse button. Notice that when you hold down the mouse button, a light-colored outline appears around the information.

Tip
To make the display area easier to read, group related items together. Then add divider rules and blank lines to separate the groups.

3. Holding down the left mouse button, drag the mouse until the pointer is over the location at which you want to locate the line of information.

4. Release the left mouse button. The information line is in its new location.

You also can add and subtract divider rules and blank lines between the information (see fig. 5.9). First click the information line above which you want the rule or blank line. Then click your right mouse button, and a menu appears. From the menu, choose either **A**dd Divider Rule or A**d**d Blank Line.

To delete a divider rule or blank line, click the item, using the left mouse button. Then click the right mouse button. In the menu that appears, choose **R**emove Rule/Blank.

Changing the Display Area Window

In three WinFax PRO views—the Outbox, the Attachments view, and the Send and Receive Logs—you can change the contents of the display area window. Table 5.2 describes the different types of displays, and lists the views for which they are available.

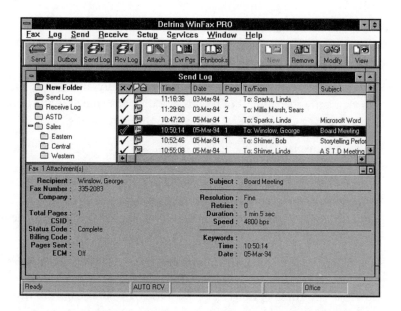

Fig. 5.9
Adding divider rules and blank lines makes the display area window easier to read.

WinFax PRO Basics

Table 5.2   Additional Information Displays for Send and Receive Logs, Outbox, and Attachments views.

Display	Description	Available Views
Information	Default; shows available information about the item	All views
Thumbnail view	Shows thumbnails of item	Send/Receive Logs, Outbox, Attachments view
Fax view	Displays the fax itself	Send/Receive Logs; Outbox

There are two ways to change the type of information WinFax PRO displays in the display area window. You can choose the **W**indow menu, and then choose either Display **I**nformation, Display **T**humbnails, or Display **F**ax View. Or you can position the mouse pointer anywhere over the display area window and click the right mouse button. The menu that appears contains the same set of options.

Customizing the Fax View

You can further customize the display area window when it displays the full image of the fax. You can make the displayed fax larger or smaller, and you can display different pages of multiple-page faxes.

To make the fax image appear larger or smaller in the display area window, choose **Z**oom from the **W**indow menu. A submenu appears with the following options:

- **1**00 Percent displays the fax at its full size. Typically, this means you can view only a small part of the fax at a time and must use the horizontal and vertical scroll bars to navigate through the fax.

- **5**0 Percent displays the fax at half its normal size.

- **2**5 Percent displays the fax at one-fourth its normal size.

- Fit Si**d**es sizes the fax so that its entire width appears in the display area window. Usually, you'll still need to use the vertical scroll bar to view the entire fax.

- Full **P**age fits the entire image of the fax into the display area window.

You also can access these options by clicking the right mouse button while the mouse pointer is anywhere over the display area window. A menu appears, displaying the options.

You can view different pages in a multiple-page fax by choosing the **W**indow menu, and then choosing Ne**x**t Page or Pre**v**ious Page. The same options are available by clicking the right mouse button to display a menu.

> **Note**
>
> To quickly switch to a mode in which you can view, annotate, or apply optical character recognition to a fax, double-click the fax image in the display area window. For more information about viewing faxes, read Chapter 14, "Viewing and Annotating Faxes."

Customizing the Toolbar

The toolbar enables you to accomplish common tasks with the click of a button. For example, by simply clicking a toolbar button you can view the Send and Receive Logs or send a fax. WinFax PRO displays the same toolbar in all views.

To customize the toolbar, choose **T**oolbar from the Setu**p** menu. The Toolbar Setup dialog box appears (see fig. 5.10).

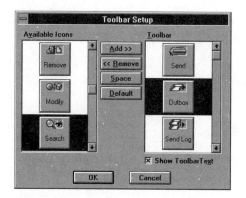

Fig. 5.10
The Toolbar Setup
dialog box is where
you customize the
toolbar.

To add a new button to the dialog box:

1. Highlight the button you want to add in the Available Icons list box.

2. In the Toolbar list box, highlight the button above which you want the
    new button to appear.

3. Click Add.

To remove a button, highlight it in the Toolbar window and click Remove.

To make the toolbar more attractive and easy to use, insert spaces between
groups of related buttons. To do that, highlight the button in the Toolbar list
box above which you want the space to appear. Then click the Space button.
A space appears above the icon in the dialog box with the word Space in the
middle (see fig. 5.11). The space appears to the left of the icon you selected in
the toolbar.

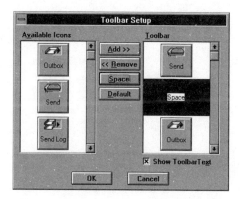

Fig. 5.11
A space appears in
the Toolbar list box.

Tip
Use the Toolbar
Setup dialog box
to add buttons to
the default toolbar
for tasks you per-
form frequently.
Eliminate buttons
for tasks you
rarely do.

To return the toolbar to the original WinFax PRO toolbar, click the **D**efault button. To display descriptive text on each button, select the Show Toolbar Text check box.

When you finish configuring the toolbar, click OK.

From Here...

This chapter and the ones preceding it helped you install WinFax PRO and set it up to work the way you do. The rest of the book tells you how to use WinFax PRO for your everyday work. You may find the following chapters of specific interest:

■ Chapter 8, "Sending Faxes," tells how to use WinFax PRO for transmitting faxes to others.

■ Chapter 9, "Receiving Faxes," discusses using WinFax PRO to receive faxes that others send to you.

■ Chapter 12, "Assembling Faxes from Many Sources," tells how to use attachments to create or enhance the faxes you send.

■ Chapter 11, "Using the Send and Receive Logs," describes how to use these logs for storing sent and received messages.

Part II

WinFax PRO in Everyday Operation

Chapter 6

Using Phonebooks

In this chapter, you learn how to do the following:

- Create new phonebooks that contain fax numbers and electronic mail addresses

- Create new phonebooks from existing database files and WinFax PRO phonebooks

- Add, delete, and import information

- Create groups of recipients

WinFax PRO's phonebooks are where you store the names and other information about the people to whom you want to send faxes, network electronic mail (e-mail) messages, and even computer files. If you send messages to lots of people, WinFax PRO enables you to maintain multiple phonebooks so that you can keep related fax phone numbers together.

Similarly, you can create groups of recipients for your messages. This enables you to easily send the same message to all members of the group.

This chapter tells you all about phonebooks and how to create, modify, and manage them. It also tells you how to create groups of recipients.

Starting To Use Phonebooks

To display WinFax PRO's Phonebook view, click the Phnbooks button in the toolbar. You also can choose Phonebooks from the Fax menu.

WinFax PRO uses the folder metaphor for storing phonebook information. WinFax PRO displays each phonebook in the folder list window of the Phonebooks view (see fig. 6.1). A phonebook icon appears to the left of each phonebook folder name.

Fig. 6.1

The Phonebook view displays each phonebook.

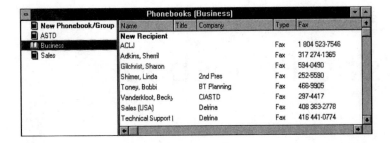

Chapter 5, "Customizing WinFax PRO," showed you how to create new phonebook folders. However, creating the phonebook folder is just the first step. After you create the phonebook folder, you must add and modify phonebook entries, also called *records*. Phonebook records include a variety of information about the recipients of your messages.

You can fill new phonebook folders either by creating new phonebook records, or by moving existing records to the new phonebook. The following sections describe both procedures.

Moving and Copying Phonebook Records

You can move existing phonebook records from one phonebook to another. To do that, follow these steps:

1. Make the Phonebooks window the active view by either choosing **F**ax **Ph**onebooks, or by clicking the Phnbooks button in the toolbar.

2. In the folder list window, double-click the phonebook containing the records you want to move.

3. Click the specific phonebook record and hold down the left mouse button.

4. Drag the phonebook record to the folder in the folder list window to which you want to move it.

5. When the mouse pointer is over the folder to which you want to move the record, an outline appears around the folder name. When that happens, release the left mouse button to drop the phonebook record into the new phonebook.

The above steps move phonebook records. That is to say, when you finish, the record no longer exists in its original phonebook folder, only in its new phonebook folder. You also can copy records so that the record remains in both its original folder and its new folder.

The procedure for copying phonebook records is nearly identical to that for moving them, with one exception. When you hold down the left mouse button over a specific phone record, also hold down the Ctrl key. Continue holding down the Ctrl key until you drop the phonebook record in its new folder by releasing the mouse button. When you finish, the phonebook record will be located in both the old and new phonebook folders.

Creating New Records

To add a new record, follow these steps:

1. From the **F**ax menu, choose P**h**onebooks, or click the Phnbooks toolbar button.

2. Choose the phonebook to which you want to add the entry. To do this, in the folder list window double-click the phonebook folder you want. WinFax PRO displays any names you already added to that phonebook in the item list window.

3. Double-click the New entry in the item list window to display the New Recipient dialog box.

4. Alternatively, from the Phone**b**ook menu, choose **N**ew, or click the New button in the toolbar. A blank New Recipient dialog box appears (see fig. 6.2).

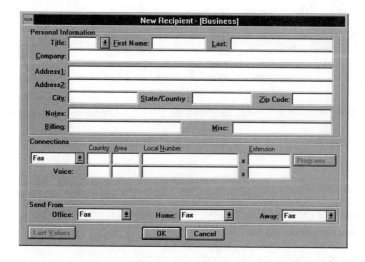

Fig. 6.2
You use the New Recipient dialog box to add new names into phonebooks.

Everyday Operation

To modify an existing phonebook record, double-click the entry in the item list window. You also can highlight the entry by clicking it once and then clicking the Modify button in the toolbar. Or highlight the entry, click the right mouse button, and then choose **M**odify from the drop-down menu.

If you modify an existing record, the Modify Recipient dialog appears. The Modify Recipient dialog box is identical to the New Recipient dialog box with one important exception: WinFax PRO displays the information you previously provided about the recipient.

Note

WinFax PRO uses the information you place in the New Recipient or Modify Recipient dialog boxes in other parts of the program. For fax recipients, WinFax PRO dials the number you provide. Creating cover pages is another good but less obvious example of how WinFax PRO uses this information. When you create cover pages, you can insert special codes, called *variables*, that automatically insert various types of information. Much of the information you can insert in cover pages is the information you enter in the New Recipient or Modify Recipient dialog boxes. Read Chapter 7, "Creating and Managing Cover Pages," for information about creating new cover pages and using variables in cover pages.

The next several sections walk you through the process of using the New Recipient and Modify Recipient dialog boxes.

Adding Personal Information

The top half of the New Recipient dialog box, the Personal Information area, is where you add information about the recipient of the fax, electronic mail message, or computer file (see fig. 6.3).

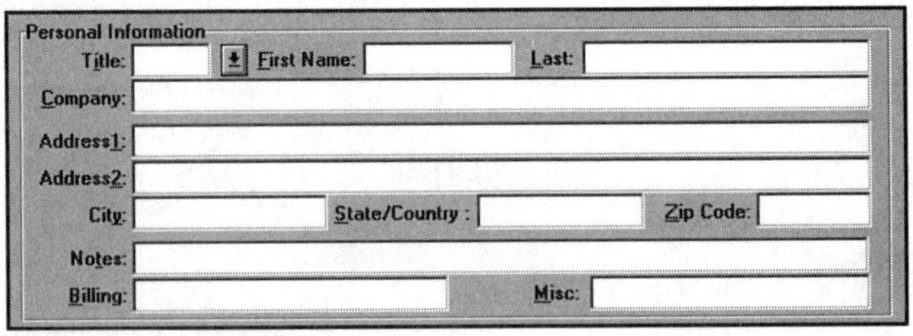

Fig. 6.3
You add information in the Personal Information area.

Fill in the following text boxes in the Personal information area:

- Title is for the recipient's title, which can be entered or selected from the drop-down list.

- First Name is for the recipient's first name.

- Last is for the recipient's last name.

- **C**ompany is for the recipient's company.

- **A**ddress **1** is for the recipient's street address, or the company's street address.

- **A**ddress **2** is for the recipient's street address if a second line is needed.

- Cit**y** is for the recipient's city.

- **S**tate/Country is for the recipient's state.

- **Z**ip Code is for the recipient's ZIP code.

- No**t**es is for brief notes about the fax recipient. You can type as many as 89 characters in the **N**otes text box. This text box is optional. Use the No**t**es text box for specialized information. Examples of such information include departmental codes or mail stop numbers if your recipient organization has a centralized fax service.

- **B**illing is for internal codes for charging the fax call to a specific department. Some organizations are strict about charging all phone calls to the appropriate department. Entering a billing code is particularly useful if you work in one department but do work on behalf of another department.

- **M**isc is for any information that isn't appropriate in the other fields. You can enter as many as 35 characters in the **M**isc. field.

> **Note**
>
> You must enter a fax or electronic mail address and at least a first name, a last name, or a company before WinFax PRO adds the record to the phonebook. However, because WinFax PRO can automatically insert all the information in the Personal Information window in cover pages, it's a good idea to fill in all the text boxes in this section of the dialog box.

Tip
You can sort your Send Log to group together all faxes billed to a specific billing code. This can streamline record keeping. See Chapter 11, "Using the Send and Receive Logs," for information about using the Send Log.

II

Everyday Operation

Adding Connection Information

The next area in the New Recipient or Modify Recipient dialog box is the Connections area (see fig. 6.4). This is the area where you select the type of connection you want to make and provide specific information so WinFax PRO can make the connection.

Fig. 6.4

You enter telephone information in the Connections area in the New Recipient or Modify Recipient dialog box.

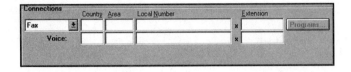

The vertical column headings are for the following information:

- **Country** is for adding the recipient's country code if he or she is in another country.

- **Area** is for the recipient's area code. For international recipients, place the recipient's city code in this text box. In most countries, rather than area codes, each city has its own code.

- Local **Number** is for the person's local telephone number. This is the telephone number you dial if you are in the same city as the recipient.

- **Extension** is for the recipient's office extension number.

The second horizontal row is for the recipient's voice telephone number. This information isn't mandatory, but it can be helpful. For example, you can include a field for the voice telephone number in fax cover pages. This is useful if there are problems with transmissions and you or somebody else must call the fax recipient to make sure that his or her fax machine is functioning properly.

In the first horizontal row, you choose the method of transmission you want WinFax PRO to make. There are two choices in the drop-down list in the upper left corner of this area: Fax and BFT. Fax refers to sending faxes as fax images as you normally would expect.

BFT stands for *Binary File Transfer*. Binary files are computer files with special formats other than plain text. Examples of binary files are files you create with your spreadsheet or word processor. BFT is one of several standards for transferring binary files from one computer to another. In this case, you transfer binary files at the same time you transfer a fax. To use BFT, the recipient also must use software and hardware that supports BFT.

If you select BFT in the Connections area, WinFax PRO uses either standard BFT or Microsoft At Work (MAW). The two protocols are similar with one exception: MAW adds various types of security to the file transfer to ensure that the file can't be used by unauthorized parties.

When you send via BFT, WinFax PRO automatically checks the capabilities of the receiving device and software. If it can accept MAW transmissions, that is what WinFax PRO automatically uses. If it can't accept MAW but can accept standard BFT transmissions, WinFax PRO uses that version of the protocol.

WinFax PRO actually supports one additional type of BFT called *Compressed BFT*. This is a special version of BFT that works only with other users of WinFax PRO 4.0. When you use this method, WinFax PRO automatically compresses the file before it is sent. By compressing the file so it takes less space, WinFax PRO can conduct the file transfer even faster.

You don't set up this type of transfer in the New Recipient (or Modify Recipient) dialog box, though. Rather, you select this method at the last minute from the Send dialog box. Specifically, in that dialog box, you select Schedule. WinFax PRO displays the Schedule/Modify Events dialog box. In that dialog box, select Compressed BFT from the Send By drop-down list.

Caution

BFT isn't a particularly widely used standard. If your recipient doesn't use software that supports the BFT standard, you must use a more generalized data communications software package, which typically supports a wide variety of other file transfer protocols.

Tip

Compressed BFT is the preferred method of communicating with somebody who also uses WinFax PRO, because it is fastest.

Caution

You may need different phone numbers for different modes of transmission. For example, the phone number for a recipient with a traditional fax machine will almost certainly be different than the telephone number you use with the BFT protocol for transmitting binary files between fax modems.

Choose the mode of transmission that is appropriate for the recipient. Then enter the appropriate telephone information about the recipient in the first row of text boxes.

Note

Read Chapter 16, "Different Ways to Send and Receive," for more information about BFT, MS At Work, and WinFax BFT transmissions.

II

Everyday Operation

If you choose BFT, WinFax PRO adds the MS At Work Alias text box to the Connections area. If you intend to transmit using MAW, type the recipient's At Work alias in the text box. If you aren't sure of the alias, ask your system administrator.

If you choose to transmit normal faxes, WinFax PRO dims, or makes unavailable, the Programs button. However, if you choose BFT, the Programs button is available. Clicking this button displays the Programs Available dialog box (see fig. 6.5).

Fig. 6.5

The Programs Available dialog box is where you select programs that are available on your recipient's computer.

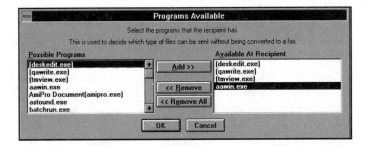

The Programs Available dialog box tells WinFax PRO which software it will interact with at the other end of your connection—at the receiving end. The recipient's software must support Microsoft At Work or the BFT protocol if that is how you send information. WinFax PRO often operates more efficiently if it knows the specific program the recipient is using.

The **P**ossible Programs list window lists all the main program files on your computer. If a program on your computer also is on your recipient's computer—and if those programs support a particular type of transmission—use this dialog box to tell WinFax PRO about them. Obviously, your recipient may use programs that you don't have on your computer but that support BFT or At Work. In this case, you still can use WinFax PRO, but it may not be as efficient.

The names in the **P**ossible Programs list window aren't the names of the programs themselves, such as Word for Windows or dBASE IV. Rather, the list window contains the names of the files on your hard disk that are the main files for running your programs. For example, the main file for the Ami Pro word processor is AMIPRO.EXE.

To add a program file to the list of possible programs with which WinFax PRO interacts, click the file once in the **P**ossible Programs list box to highlight it. Then click the **A**dd button. The program file you selected appears in the Available at Recipient list box. To remove program files from the Available at Recipient list window, click the **R**emove button or the R**e**move All button to remove all programs. When you finish adding programs to the Available at Recipient window, choose OK.

Adding an E-Mail Address

Like a traditional letter, an electronic mail message requires you to provide an address. If you plan to communicate with the recipient via electronic mail, enter his or her e-mail address in the third row of the Connections area of the New Recipient or Modify Recipient dialog boxes.

Choose Mail from the drop-down list. Then type the recipient's e-mail address in the text box to the right. You may need to ask the recipient or the mail system administrator for the correct e-mail address. Or you can find the recipient's e-mail address by clicking Fin**d**. This causes WinFax PRO to display the address book from your network e-mail system. Use that dialog box to find the recipient's address and click OK. Note that the dialog box varies according to the network e-mail package you use.

To add an e-mail address even faster, simply select the phonebook you want in the folder list window by double-clicking it. Then select Phone**b**ook New From Mai**l**. WinFax PRO will display your phonebook from your e-mail system. Select the name or names you want to add and click OK. WinFax PRO adds those names to the selected phonebook.

Setting Default Transmission Methods

You can set WinFax PRO to send messages to the recipient via one method if you are in one location and via another method when you change locations. You do this in the Send From area of the New Recipient and Modify Recipient dialog boxes (see fig. 6.6).

Fig. 6.6
The Send From area is where you determine the method of transmission from different locations.

Chapter 4, "Configuring WinFax PRO," showed you how to set up different dialing settings for your home, your office, and a third location, which WinFax PRO calls "Away." The settings described are helpful, for example, if you require special codes to dial out of your phone system at the office, but not when you use WinFax PRO from home.

Everyday Operation

As discussed in Chapter 4, you make these settings in the User Setup dialog box, which you access by selecting **U**ser from the Setu**p** menu.

You also use those settings again in the Send From area of the New Recipient or Modify Recipient dialog boxes. This is where you choose how you want to transmit your message depending on your location. For example, you can tell WinFax PRO to communicate with a particular recipient via e-mail when you are at the office but via fax when you work at home.

There are three drop-down lists in the Send From area: Home, Away, and Office. Select the method of transmission you want to use with this particular recipient from each drop-down list.

If you want to return the New Recipient dialog box to its last-saved settings, click Last **V**alues. When you finish the New Recipient or Modify Recipient dialog box, choose OK. WinFax PRO adds the record you created or modified to the phonebook.

Viewing and Deleting Entries

If you simply want to view the contents of a phonebook record, highlight the record in the item list window. WinFax PRO displays the phonebook record information in the display area window. You also can double-click a phone entry. WinFax PRO displays the Information dialog box, which is identical to the Modify Recipient dialog boxes, except you can't change any information.

To delete individual phonebook entries, highlight the entry in the item list window and press the Del key. You also can click the Remove button in the toolbar.

For an even faster method of deleting entries when you have more than one, follow these steps:

Tip
You can highlight more than one entry in the item list window. To do this, first highlight one item. Then hold down the Ctrl key or the Shift key and click additional items.

1. Highlight the entries you want to delete.

2. Position the mouse pointer over the entries. Hold down the left mouse button and drag the mouse so that the pointer is over the Remove button in the toolbar.

3. When the pointer is over the Remove button, it changes to a pointer over a stack of pages. When that happens, release the mouse button.

4. WinFax PRO displays a message that asks whether you want to delete the records. Choose OK to delete them.

Importing and Exporting Phonebooks

You can create a new phonebook from other phonebooks, including phonebooks from previous WinFax versions. You also can use database files to create your phonebooks. This exchange of information goes in both directions: You can add WinFax PRO phonebook files to database files created by other programs.

When you create phonebooks from other phonebooks or from database files, you *import* those other files. WinFax PRO enables you to import files that are compatible with the dBASE database program, including files created by previous versions of WinFax PRO.

When you prepare a WinFax PRO phonebook so that other programs can use them, you *export* the phonebook. The following sections describe the importing and exporting process.

Creating New Phonebooks from Existing Files

To create a new phonebook using either an existing WinFax PRO phonebook file or a database file created by another program, follow these steps:

1. From the **F**ax menu, choose **Ph**onebooks to display the phonebook view. Or, click the Phnbooks toolbar button.

2. Highlight any phonebook in the folder list window by clicking it once.

3. Select Phone**b**ook, **N**ew. WinFax PRO displays the New Phonebook/ Group dialog box (see fig. 6.7). You also can display this dialog box by double-clicking New Phonebook/Group in the folder list window.

Fig. 6.7
Import phonebook information in the New Phonebook/ Group dialog box.

4. Type a name for the new phonebook in the **N**ame text box. The name you type appears as the name of the phonebook folder in the folder list window.

5. Click the **U**se Existing dBASE File button.

6. Choose **S**elect. WinFax PRO displays the Select Phonebook/Database File dialog box (see fig. 6.8).

Fig. 6.8
Use the Select Phonebook/ Database File dialog box to create a new phonebook from an existing file.

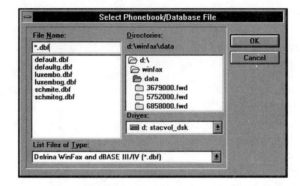

7. In the Dri**v**es drop-down list, select the drive on which you stored the existing file. In the **D**irectories window, select the directory. Select the name of the File in the File **N**ame window.

8. When you finish the Select Phonebook/Database File dialog box, click OK to return to the Add Phonebook/Group dialog box.

Tip
Use database files to create phone- books. If, for ex- ample, you keep a database of sales contacts, you can use that database to create your WinFax PRO phonebook rather than keying in all the names manually.

You are now ready to link database fields; this action is discussed in the next section.

Linking Database Fields

You aren't done after you've selected the file you want to use to create your new phonebook. You must link the database fields in the external file to the matching fields in WinFax PRO. For example, this means that you must link the First Name field in the database or phonebook file to the similar field in the WinFax PRO phonebook.

> **Note**
>
> In database parlance, a *field* is an individual bit of information. For example, First Name would be a field containing an individual's first name. All the fields about a single entity—in this case, a person—create a *record*. Each database file contains a series of records, all of which have the same fields.

To link the fields of the external phonebook or database file with those in WinFax PRO, follow these steps:

1. In the New Phonebook/Group dialog box, choose Assi**g**n. WinFax PRO displays the Data Field Assignment dialog box (see fig. 6.9).

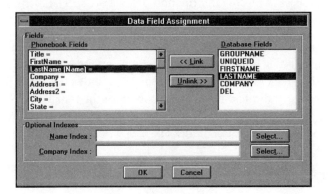

Fig. 6.9
This is the Data Field Assignment dialog box before assigning is complete.

The **P**honebook Fields list box contains all the fields in WinFax PRO phonebooks. The **D**atabase Fields list box contains the names of all the fields in the database or phonebook file you are using to create the new phonebook.

2. Highlight a field in the **P**honebook Fields list window by clicking it once.

3. Highlight the corresponding field in the **D**atabase Fields list window.

4. To assign the database field to a phonebook field, click the **L**ink button. Continue to link each corresponding field.

When you finish, WinFax PRO displays linked fields in the **P**honebook Fields window. It does this by placing the names of both fields together in the window with an equal sign between them (see fig. 6.10).

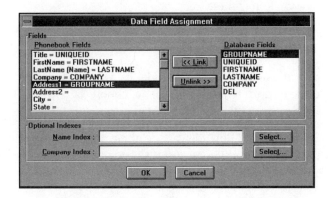

Fig. 6.10
This is the Data Field Assignment dialog box after you linked fields in the external database to WinFax PRO phonebook fields.

II

Everyday Operation

If you make a mistake, unlink a field by highlighting it in the **P**honebook Fields list window and clicking **U**nlink.

The Data Field Assignment dialog box has two additional options, but those options require some expertise in databases to use. Databases use indexes to speed the process of finding information. *Indexes* are special files that list the contents of each record and its precise location in the database.

At times, particularly in networked situations, you will want to use a preexisting index file. It may be particularly useful to use an index of names or use an index of companies. To do so, type the name of an index file in the **N**ame Index or **C**ompany Index text boxes at the bottom of the Data Field Assignment dialog box. If you are not sure about the index names, click the appropriate Select button and use the Select Index File dialog box to find the file name.

Caution

If you do not know about indexes and when and why you should share them, don't use this option. If you want more information about using database indexes, contact either your organization's network manager or your database manager.

When you finish the Data Field Assignment dialog box, click OK to return to the New Phonebook/Group dialog box. Then click OK to close the New Phonebook/Group dialog box. The newly imported phonebook appears in the folder list window.

Importing Files into Existing Phonebooks

The previous section told you how to create new phonebooks by using existing files. You also can add to existing phonebooks by importing records from databases or from other phonebooks.

To import records, follow these steps:

1. From the **F**ax menu, choose **Ph**onebooks. Or click the Phnbooks toolbar button.

2. Highlight the phonebook in the folder list window to which you want to add the records. From the **F**ax menu, choose **I**mport. WinFax PRO displays the Import Phone Records dialog box.

3. Choose the format of the file you are importing in the For**m**at drop-down list. The Import Phone Records dialog box changes depending on the format of the file you choose.

The next series of steps for importing phonebooks, ASCII, and dBASE-compatible files are covered separately in the following three sections.

Importing Phonebook Files

If you import phonebooks saved in either CAS, Lotus Organizer, WinFax PRO 3, WinFax for Networks, WinFax PRO 4, or WinFax LITE formats, the Import Phone Records dialog box changes as shown (see fig. 6.11).

Fig. 6.11
This is the dialog box for importing records from already-existing phonebooks.

After you choose one of those formats in the For**m**at drop-down list, click the **S**elect button to select the specific file. WinFax PRO displays the Import File Name dialog box. In that dialog box, follow these steps:

1. Choose the drive you want in the Dri**v**es drop-down list.

2. Choose a directory in the **D**irectories list window by double-clicking it. Files for the directory you choose appear in the File **N**ame list box.

3. Highlight the file you want to import by clicking it once, and then choose OK. The file you selected appears in the File text box of the Import Phone Records dialog box.

4. Choose OK. WinFax PRO imports the file into the phonebook you selected. When it finishes, it displays a message box telling you how many records it imported. Click OK to clear the message box and the new records appear in your phonebook.

Importing ASCII Database Files

To import a database file saved in ASCII format, choose ASCII from the For**m**at drop-down list. The Import Phone Records dialog box expands (see fig. 6.12).

The Options window of the dialog box has two purposes:

■ To determine the WinFax PRO phonebook fields that accept information from the external file.

■ To determine the character used to separate individual fields and records in the external ASCII file.

II

Everyday Operation

Fig. 6.12
This is the Import
Phone Records
dialog box for
importing ASCII
files.

If you do not want WinFax PRO to insert information in specific phonebook
fields, highlight the fields in the Field **L**ist list window and choose the **D**elete
button. If you change your mind later, choose the **A**dd button. WinFax PRO
displays the Add Field dialog box (see fig. 6.13). Highlight the name of
the fields that you want to add back to the list of phonebook fields.
Then choose OK.

Fig. 6.13
Use the Add Field
dialog box to add
back a phonebook
field you have
deleted.

The fields in the Field **L**ist list box must also be in the same order in which
the fields in the ASCII file are listed. Use the left mouse button to drag the
fields into the desired position.

When you save database information in ASCII format you must separate—or
delimit—each field from the next. You also must delimit each record from the
next. The most common way to delimit fields is to place a comma between
each field in the ASCII record. The most common way to delimit each record
is to place a carriage return between each record.

To import a database file in ASCII format, follow these steps:

1. In the Import Phone Records dialog box, Choose ASCII from the
For**m**at drop-down list.

2. Type the name of the ASCII file you are importing in the Import From
File text box. If you are not sure of the file name, click **S**elect and select
the file from the Import File Name dialog box.

3. In the Field **L**ist window, which lists WinFax PRO phonebook fields, delete any fields that do not match the fields in the ASCII file you are importing. Do that by highlighting the field and clicking **D**elete. If you make a mistake and want to add a field back in, click **A**dd and select the field from the Add Field Dialog box.

4. If necessary, change the order of field names to match the order of the fields in the ASCII file. Do that by highlighting a field name, holding down the left mouse button and dragging the field to a new position in the Field **L**ist window.

5. In the **F**ield Delimiter window, choose the delimiter in the incoming file that separates each field within a record. The default is a comma. You also can choose tab or designate your own delimiter.

6. In the **R**ecord Delimiter window, choose the delimiter in the incoming file that separates each record. The default is a carriage return. You also can choose a line feed delimiter or designate your own.

7. Choose OK to import the records into your phonebook.

Note

If you are not sure of the delimiter between records or fields in the file you are importing, the defaults usually work. If they don't, load the incoming file in a text editor and view it yourself. An example of a text editor is the Edit program that comes with MS-DOS versions 5.0 and greater.

Importing dBASE Files

If you choose dBASE III/IV format in the For**m**at drop-down list, the Import Phonebook Record dialog box appears.

Note

You need not use the dBASE database program to save files in dBASE format. Most database and spreadsheet programs can save files in the dBASE format.

II

Everyday Operation

Complete the following steps to import the dBASE data:

1. Type the name of the dBASE file you want to import in the File text box, or click **S**elect to use the Import File Name dialog box to choose the file.

   WinFax PRO examines the dBASE file you select and displays that file's fields in the **I**mport Fields list window. It displays the normal WinFax PRO phonebook fields in the Phonebook **F**ields list window.

2. Link the dBASE fields that you import to matching fields in WinFax PRO. For example, you must link the First Name field in the database file to the First Name field in the WinFax PRO phonebook. This procedure is identical to the one described previously in the "Linking Database Fields" section of this chapter, which described how to create new phonebooks from database records.

3. To link fields, highlight a field in the **P**honebook Fields list window by clicking it once. Then highlight the corresponding field in the Import Fields list window. To assign the database field to a phonebook field, choose the **L**ink button.

   Alternatively, you can link the fields by using the mouse to drag the fields in the **I**mport Fields list box to the corresponding fields in the **P**honebook Fields list.

   When you finish this process, WinFax PRO displays linked fields in the **P**honebook Fields window. The names of both fields appear together in the window with an equal sign between them.

4. After you link all the fields you want to import, choose OK. WinFax PRO adds the records in the dBASE file to the phonebook.

> **Note**
>
> After you import information into phonebooks, you still may need to edit individual records. For example, some of the recipients you added to your phonebook may have e-mail addresses that were not included in the file you imported.

Exporting Phonebook Files

The previous sections told you how to import information into phonebooks. You can reverse that process and export WinFax PRO phonebooks for use by other programs. For example, you can incorporate your WinFax PRO phonebook records into a database file. WinFax PRO enables you to export your phonebooks either in ASCII format or the format of WinFax 3 and WinFax for Networks 3.

Start the process of exporting in either format by selecting **E**xport from the **F**ax menu. WinFax PRO displays the Export Phone Records dialog box. However, that dialog box changes, depending on the format to which you are exporting. The next two sections describe how to export to WinFax and ASCII formats.

Exporting Phonebooks in WinFax Format

To export a phonebook in WinFax format, follow these steps:

1. Choose WinFax Pro 3 or WinFax for Networks 3 from the For**m**at drop-down list (see fig. 6.14).

Fig. 6.14
This is the Export Phone Records dialog box for exporting phonebooks in WinFax format.

2. In the File text box, type the drive, path, and name of the file to which you want to export your phonebook record. If you aren't sure, choose the **S**elect button and use the Export File Name dialog box to find a directory or file name to which you want to export your phonebook.

3. Choose OK. WinFax PRO exports the phonebook.

Exporting Phonebooks in ASCII Format

To export a phonebook in ASCII format, follow these steps:

1. Choose the ASCII option from the For**m**at drop-down list. WinFax PRO displays the Export Phone Records dialog box (see fig. 6.15).

Fig. 6.15

This is the Export Phone Records dialog box for exporting phonebooks in ASCII format.

2. Type the drive, path, and name of the file to which you want to export your phonebook record. If you aren't sure, choose the **S**elect button and use the Export File Name dialog box to find a directory or file name to which you want to export your phonebook.

3. If you want to delete any records from the export, highlight them in the Field **L**ist list window and click **D**elete. If, for example, you share your phonebook with somebody in another department, they may not need your billing codes, and you should delete them before exporting your phonebook.

4. In the **F**ield Delimiter window, choose a delimiter to separate one field from the other in the exported ASCII file. Typically, this delimiter is a comma, which is the default setting. However, you also can choose a Tab delimiter or specify your own. To specify your own delimiter, choose the Other check box and type your delimiter in the text box to the right.

5. In the **R**ecord Delimiter window, choose a delimiter to separate one record from the other in the exported ASCII file. Typically, this delimiter is a carriage return, which is WinFax PRO's default. You also can choose a form feed or set your own delimiter.

Caution

Unless you have specific instructions to the contrary, use the default delimiters for fields and records. These are the delimiters most programs expect when they import text files.

---

6. Select the String in **Q**uotes check box if the program that will import your phonebook file expects field information in quotes.

7. When you finish, choose OK. WinFax PRO exports the information in your phonebook to the file you selected.

If you deleted a record from the export process and want to add it back, choose the **A**dd button. WinFax PRO displays the Add Field dialog box. Highlight the name of the field that you want to add back and choose OK.

You also can change the order of records as they appear in the exported file. To do that, choose the record you want to move in the Field **L**ist list window and hold down the left mouse button. Notice that the mouse cursor changes. While the left mouse button is still pressed down, drag the cursor. When the cursor appears in the position in the Field **L**ist list window where you want the field located, release the mouse button. WinFax PRO places the field in its new position.

> **Note**
>
> Change the position of fields in the exported ASCII file if you know that the program will import the phonebook expects the fields in a particular order. Check the program documentation to find out if that is the case.

Phonebook Groups

Creating groups is an excellent way to automate the process of sending the same message to multiple individuals. Say that you have fifty preferred customers. This is a group to whom you would want to regularly send updates about your products. You can place those fifty customers in a group and send them product updates at the same time.

This section tells you how to create and modify groups. Read Chapter 6, "Using Phonebooks," for more information about using groups when sending faxes.

Creating Groups

To create a group, follow these steps:

1. Highlight a phonebook or an already-existing group folder in the folder list window, and then choose the New button in the toolbar. Or from the Phone**b**ook menu, you can choose **N**ew. WinFax PRO displays the New Phonebook/Group dialog box (see fig. 6.16).

Tip
You can include both fax and e-mail recipients in groups. That way, all group members will receive your message, no matter what method of transmission they require.

II

Everyday Operation

Fig. 6.16
You use the New
Phonebook/Group
dialog box to
create a group.

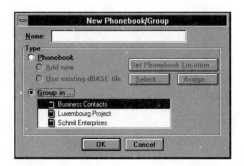

Tip
Display the New
Phonebook/Group
dialog box fast by
highlighting a
phone-book folder
and clicking the
right mouse but-
ton. From the
menu, choose
New.

2. In the Add Phonebook/Group dialog box, enter a group name in the
Name text box. The name can contain up to 31 characters.

3. Choose the **G**roup In button, and then click the name of the
phonebook for which the group will become a subfolder.

4. Choose OK. Your new group appears as a subfolder to the folder you
selected. Notice, though, that instead of a telephone book icon next to
the name of the group, which WinFax PRO applies to phonebook folders, there is an icon of a book and a person walking (see fig. 6.17).

Fig. 6.17
WinFax PRO
displays groups in
the folder list
window.

Tip
Group folders
always appear
as subfolders to
the phonebook
folder. If you're
confused,
create a
phonebook
called *Groups*
and place all
group folders
under the
Groups tele-
phone folder.

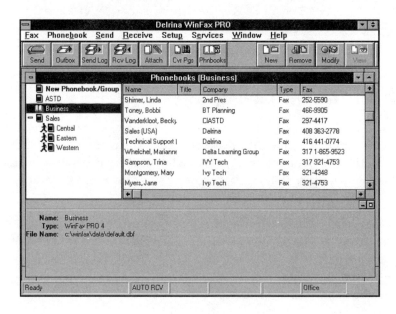

Viewing and Hiding Group Folders

A plus sign appears to the left of the folder if the folder has subfolders (in this case, group folders) that you can't see. If you can see the group folders, a minus sign appears to the left of the top-level phonebook folder.

To hide group folders, click the minus sign to the left of the phonebook folder, or highlight the top-level folder by clicking it once. From the Phonebook menu, choose Collapse Folder.

To view group folders, click the plus sign to the left of the phonebook folder. Or highlight the top-level folder by clicking on it once. From the Phonebook menu, choose Expand Folder.

Modifying and Adding to Groups

Newly created group folders are empty. You must add names to the group in order for it to be useful.

To copy names to a group, follow these steps:

1. Double-click the phonebook folder containing the names you want in the group.

2. From the item list window for that phonebook folder, highlight a name you want to add to a group folder by clicking it once. Hold down the left mouse button.

3. Drag the mouse until the pointer is over the group folder in the folder list window.

4. Notice that when you move the pointer over the group folder, the pointer changes to a pointer over a page. When this happens, release the left mouse button. This drops the name you selected into the folder.

Choose more than one name in the item list window by highlighting one name, holding down the Ctrl key, and then clicking additional names. With the mouse pointer over any one of the highlighted names, hold down the left mouse button, drag the pointer to the group folder, and release the mouse button. WinFax PRO drops all the names into the group folder.

The only modifications you can make to group folders are to change their names and to delete them. To change the name of a group folder, highlight the folder, and then click the Modify button in the toolbar. You also can choose Modify from the Phonebook menu, or click the right mouse button and choose Modify from the menu that appears.

II

Everyday Operation

With any method, WinFax PRO displays the Modify Group dialog box (see fig. 6.18).

Fig. 6.18
Change the name of group folders with the Modify Group dialog box.

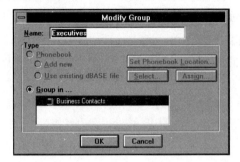

Type the new name for your folder in the **N**ame text box, and then choose OK.

To delete a group folder highlight the folder in the folder list window. Click the Remove button in the toolbar, or choose **R**emove from the Phone**b**ook menu. You also can press the Del key, or click the right mouse button and choose **R**emove from the menu that appears. When the message box appears asking if you are sure you want to delete the group, choose OK.

Searching Through Phonebooks

As you add names to your phonebooks, it may be difficult to find precisely the names you want. WinFax PRO's search capabilities help you find specific names.

Tip
You don't need to type complete information in the Search Records dialog box. You can type part of a name. For example, if you type *Schmit* in the **C**ompany text box, WinFax PRO finds all records for Schmit Enterprises and Schmit Leasing.

To search through a WinFax PRO phonebook for specific records, follow these steps:

1. With the phonebooks view active, select the phonebook through which you want to search by clicking it in the folder list window.

2. From the Phone**b**ook menu, choose **S**earch. You also can click the right mouse button and choose **S**earch from the menu that appears. WinFax PRO displays the Search dialog box (see fig. 6.19).

3. The Search dialog box is nearly identical to the New Recipient or Modify Recipient dialog boxes. When you enter information in a text box, WinFax PRO searches for all phonebook records that match what you typed. For example, you can type a specific last name in the **L**ast text box or a company name in the **C**ompany text box.

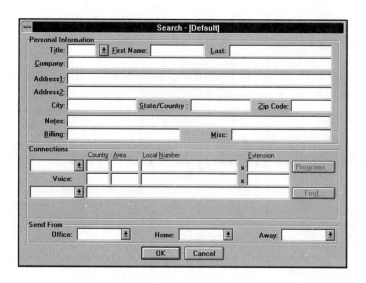

Fig. 6.19
This is where to search for phone records.

4. When you finish entering search information, choose OK. WinFax PRO searches for the information you requested and displays all the records it finds in a new item list window (see fig. 6.20).

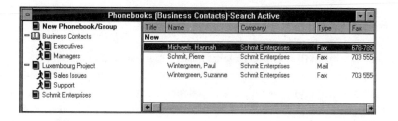

Fig. 6.20
WinFax PRO displays found records in an item list window.

You can perform the following operations on the found records:

■ Delete all the records you found by highlighting them and choosing **R**emove from the Phone**b**ook menu, or by clicking the Remove button in the toolbar. When a message box asks if you are sure you want to delete the records, choose OK.

■ Send a message to some or all the recipients you found. Highlight the recipients to whom you want to send a message. Then, with the mouse cursor over a highlighted record, hold down the left mouse button and drag the cursor to the Send button in the toolbar. When you release the left mouse button, the Send Fax window appears with the names you selected in the Recipient List list window. Read Chapter 8, "Sending Faxes," for more information about sending faxes.

II

Everyday Operation

■ Drag selected items to another phonebook or group folder in the folder list window to add the records to those folders.

To eliminate the item list of found records and restore the item list for the highlighted phonebook, choose Restore from the Phonebook menu. You can't save the results of a search, other than placing the search results in a folder.

Sorting Phonebook Contents

You can sort phonebooks so that WinFax PRO groups together related information. You can sort either on the basis of the recipient's name or company. When you sort the item list window by name, WinFax PRO sorts on the basis of last name, starting with the beginning of the alphabet. When you sort on the basis of company, WinFax PRO also starts at the beginning of the alphabet.

Tip
With the mouse pointer over an item in the item list window, click the right mouse button and choose a sort option from the menu or click the Name or Company heading to sort by that heading.

To sort by name, in the Phonebooks view, choose Sort by Name from the Phonebook menu. To sort by company, choose Sort by Company from the Phonebook menu. The type of sort that is in effect has a check next to it in the Phonebook menu.

Optimizing Phonebooks

The files that hold the phonebook information are actually database files. If you've ever worked with databases, you know that in the process of adding, deleting, and modifying records, the files fill up with outdated information. They also can become positioned on your hard drive so that WinFax PRO can't access them efficiently. Both problems slow down access to your records.

Tip
Periodically optimize your phonebooks even if you don't notice any decrease in performance. Regular optimization ensures that your phonebook files always operate efficiently.

To solve this problem, highlight the phonebook that is operating inefficiently by clicking it once in the folder list window. Then from the Phonebook menu, choose Optimize. WinFax PRO starts a process that essentially rebuilds your phonebook.

During the optimization process, WinFax PRO displays a message box telling you the status of the optimization process. If your phonebook file is small, this message box won't display for long.

Printing Phonebooks

You may want to print a phonebook to take with you when you travel, or to give it to somebody else. To print a phonebook, follow these steps:

1. Highlight the phonebook in the folder list window by double-clicking it, or highlight any item in the item list window.

2. From the **F**ax menu, choose **P**rint. WinFax PRO displays the Print dialog box (see fig. 6.21).

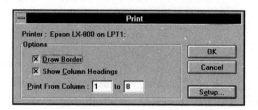

Fig. 6.21
Set up printing
your phonebook
in the Print dialog
box.

3. The currently selected printer is displayed at the top of the dialog box. To select another printer, click S**e**tup. WinFax PRO displays the Printer Setup dialog box. Click the printer you want to use and click OK to return to the Print dialog box.

4. Select the **D**raw Border check box if you want to print with a border around your phonebook.

5. Select the Show **C**olumn Headings check box if you want to print with column headings.

6. Select the range of columns you want to include in your printout in the **P**rint From Column text boxes.

7. Click OK to print your phonebook.

Using PIM Phonebooks

Personal Information Managers (PIMs) are a popular type of software. These programs enable you to keep all the information you need in a single place, such as your schedule and your phonebook. Among the better known PIMs are Lotus Organizer, PackRat, and Ecco.

Some PIMs enable you to access their phonebooks directly from WinFax PRO. These phonebooks appear as phonebook folders in WinFax PRO. You can use individual names from these phonebooks when you address messages. However, you can't modify them from within WinFax PRO. Nor can you add names from those phonebooks to groups.

II

Everyday Operation

You typically set up this capability when you install your PIM. Check with your PIM vendor to see if you can access phonebooks directly from WinFax PRO. For more about this capability, see Chapter 18, "Using WinFax PRO in Other Programs."

Troubleshooting

I get an error message when I start importing a database file.

WinFax PRO can import database files that are in the dBASE format. It also can import database files saved in ASCII format and also other WinFax phonebooks. Make sure that the file you import is in one of the formats that WinFax PRO supports. If you can't import a text file, it may have been saved using different delimiters than you specified in the Import Phone Records dialog box. Load the text file in an editor to determine which delimiter separates individual fields. Typically, commas delimit fields, but the exporting program may have used a different delimiter.

My import proceeded normally, but the information appears in the wrong columns of my phonebook item list window. For example, there are names where there should be phone numbers.

You made an error linking fields during the import process. You must delete the phonebook and start the import process again. This time, correctly assign the fields of the file you are importing with the appropriate fields in WinFax PRO.

It takes a long time to find names in my phonebook.

Optimize the phonebook by choosing **O**ptimize from the Phone**b**ook menu. This step removes outdated information in your phonebook, which can slow down operation. It also can move the phonebook file on your hard drive so that WinFax PRO can access it more efficiently.

I use a phonebook from my personal information manager. Every time I try to edit a phonebook entry, I get an error message.

While vendors of personal information managers (PIMs) can create their products so that you can access their phonebooks directly from WinFax PRO, you cannot alter the phonebook entries from WinFax PRO. Instead, you must load your PIM and change your phonebook from there.

From Here...

This chapter showed you how to set up and manage phonebooks. Now that you have this skill, you can more easily use the rest of WinFax PRO's features. You may want to read the following chapters for more information:

- Chapter 8, "Sending Faxes," shows you how to use phonebook entries when you transmit faxes.

- Chapter 10, "Using WinFax PRO for Electronic Mail," shows you how to use phonebook records to send e-mail.

- Chapter 16, "Different Ways to Send and Receive," shows you even more ways to use phonebook records to send messages with WinFax PRO.

II

Everyday Operation

Chapter 7

Creating and Managing Cover Pages

In this chapter, you learn to do the following:

- Manage your cover pages in the Cover Pages window.

- Navigate WinFax PRO's Cover Page Designer.

- Create new cover pages.

- Add variables that insert information into cover pages.

- Manage your folder of cover pages.

- Use quick cover pages.

Cover pages for faxes provide basic information about the fax. The information can include your name and number, the subject of the fax and the number of pages in the fax. It also can include a message to the recipient describing the rest of the fax transmission. Many fax transmissions consist of just a cover page with basic information and a brief note.

However, fax cover pages can provide more than just basic information. They can convey an important message, such as a sales message, or they can be humorous. Also, you can customize cover pages with your organization's logo or use drawings to turn them into digital greeting cards.

Chapter 8, "Sending Faxes," shows you how to attach cover pages to fax transmissions and how to fill in cover pages. This chapter shows you how to create cover pages and how to manage your folder of cover pages.

Regular and Quick Cover Pages

WinFax PRO uses two types of cover pages: regular cover pages and quick cover pages. Regular cover pages can be customized using WinFax PRO's Cover Page Designer. They can contain graphic images and lines between the various elements of the cover page (see fig. 7.1).

Fig. 7.1
This example of a cover page with a graphic design includes variables that allow you to insert information.

Both types of cover pages also include special variables that automatically insert information. For example, one WinFax PRO variable automatically inserts the total number of pages in the fax transmission. Another variable automatically inserts the subject of the fax, which you enter in the Send Fax dialog box.

Tip
Quick cover pages are simpler, so they transmit faster than regular cover pages. This saves long distance charges. Chapter 8, "Sending Faxes," describes how to use quick cover pages.

However, quick cover pages cannot be customized as much. The six variables of a quick cover page include the following basic information and cannot be changed:

■ Fax recipient's name.

■ Your name.

■ Subject of the fax.

■ Number of pages in the fax.

■ Time of the fax transmission.

■ Date of the fax transmission.

Figure 7.2 shows a sample quick cover page.

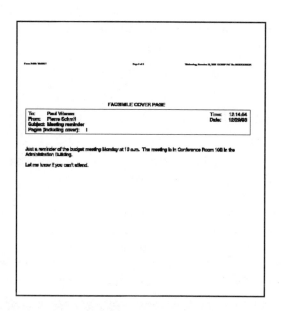

Fig. 7.2
Quick cover pages
are much simpler
than regular cover
pages.

The Cover Pages Window

Store and manage cover pages in the Cover Pages window (see fig. 7.3). To
view the Cover Pages window, click the Cvr Pgs button in the WinFax PRO
toolbar, or choose **F**ax, Cover P**a**ges.

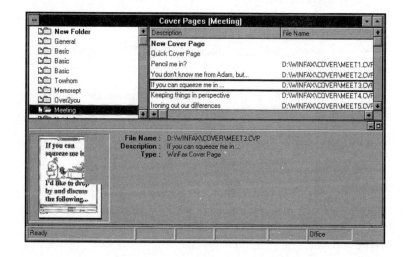

Fig. 7.3
Manage your cover
pages in the Cover
Pages window.

II

Everyday Operation

Like the Send and Receive Logs and the Attachments Window, the Cover Pages window has three windows in it:

- The folder list window displays folders and subfolders for storing cover pages.

- The item list window displays information on the cover pages in the selected folder.

- The display area window lists additional information and provides a thumbnail image of the cover page.

You can store related cover pages in folders. You also can place folders within folders. For example, a folder named Business Cover Pages can have subfolders named Sales Confirmations and Late Payment Notices. Chapter 5, "Customizing WinFax PRO," shows you how to create new folders and subfolders in the various views, including the Cover Pages window.

> **Note**
>
> Every folder in the Cover Pages window has a quick cover page. This makes it easy to select quick cover pages and to designate one as your default cover page.

Managing Cover Pages

In addition to providing an organized way to store cover pages, folders make it easy to perform many management functions on cover pages. Specifically, you can copy or move cover pages among folders or delete cover pages from folders.

To move a cover page from one folder to another, follow these steps:

1. Double-click the folder containing the cover page you want to move. WinFax PRO displays the contents of the folder in the item list window.

2. In the item list window, click the cover page you want to move and hold down the left mouse button.

3. Drag the mouse until the mouse pointer is over the folder to which you want to move the cover page. The mouse pointer changes to look like a sheet of paper.

4. Release the left mouse button. The cover page now is in the folder you chose.

When you copy a cover page, it remains in both its original folder and the folder to which you copy it. The process is similar to moving a cover page, but with one exception: Hold down the Ctrl key as you drag the cover page.

To delete a cover page, highlight the cover page in the item list window. Then press the Del key. You also can choose Co**v**er Page **R**emove. Alternatively, hold down the left mouse button and drag the cover page to the Remove button in the WinFax PRO toolbar. When it is over the Remove button, the mouse pointer turns into an icon that looks like a sheet of paper. Release the mouse button.

With any deletion method, WinFax PRO asks whether you are sure you want to delete the cover pages. If you are sure, click **Y**es. Click **N**o to keep the cover page.

WinFax PRO comes with a folder of cover pages and several folders for managing this cover page folder. However, as described in Chapter 5, "Customizing WinFax PRO," you can also add and delete folders as you want and create your own cover pages.

Viewing Cover Pages

View a cover page by double-clicking it in the item list window. WinFax PRO displays the cover page in the Cover Page Designer. In the Cover Page Designer, you can simply view the cover page, or you can modify it. Later sections of this chapter discuss the Cover Page Designer in detail.

View thumbnails of all the cover pages in a folder by choosing Co**v**er Page, **V**iew All Thumbnails. WinFax PRO displays the Cover Page Thumbnails window (see fig. 7.4).

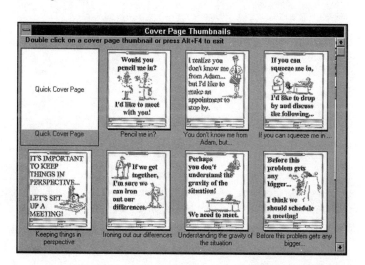

Tip
To select multiple cover pages in the item list window, highlight one cover page by clicking it. Then hold down the Ctrl key and highlight additional cover pages.

II

Everyday Operation

Fig. 7.4
View thumbnail images of all cover pages in a folder in the Cover Page Thumbnails window.

To exit the Cover Page Thumbnails window, either double-click any thumbnail, or press Alt+F4.

Modifying and Searching for Cover Pages

As you will learn, when you create a cover page, you give it a description. Modify the description of the cover page at any time by highlighting the cover page in the item list window of the Cover Pages window. Then either choose Co**v**er Page **M**odify, or click the Modify button in the toolbar. WinFax PRO displays the Modify Cover Page dialog box (see fig. 7.5).

Fig. 7.5
Modify cover page information in the Modify Cover Page dialog box.

Tip
To quickly display the Modify Cover Page dialog box, click the cover page in the item list window, click the right mouse button, and choose **M**odify.

You can either modify the description of the cover page or change the cover page file that goes with the description. To modify the description of the cover page, type the new description in the **D**escription text box. Descriptions can be as long as 59 characters.

You also can change the cover page file that goes with the description. Type the new drive, path, and file name for the cover page in the **F**ile Name text box. If you are not sure of the file name, click the **S**elect button, and WinFax PRO displays the Select Cover Page dialog box (see fig. 7.6).

Fig. 7.6
Select a new cover page file in the Select Cover Page dialog box.

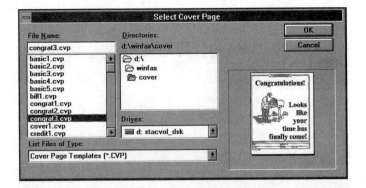

> **Note**
>
> WinFax PRO assigns cover page files the CVP file extension. By default, WinFax PRO places cover pages that come with the program in the \WINFAX\COVER subdirectory.

Select the drive where you stored the cover page file in the Dri**v**es drop-down list. Then select the directory where you stored the cover page file in the **D**irectories list window. Files with the CVP file extension in the drive and directory you choose appear in the File **N**ame list box. Click once on the file you want.

A thumbnail image of the cover page appears on the right side of the dialog box. When you find the cover page you want, click OK to return to the Modify Cover Page dialog box. The new file name is in the **F**ile Name text box. Click OK to put the changes into effect.

To change the contents of the cover page, click the **E**dit button in the Modify Cover Page dialog box. WinFax PRO displays the cover page in the Cover Page Designer. Other sections of this chapter describe the Cover Page Designer and how to use it.

Search for a specific cover page by selecting Co**v**er Page Searc**h**. WinFax PRO displays the Search Cover Pages dialog box (see fig. 7.7).

Fig. 7.7

Find a specific cover page with the Search Cover Pages dialog box.

II

Everyday Operation

To find a specific cover page, follow these steps:

1. Type as much of the cover page description as you can in the **D**escription text box.

2. If you want WinFax PRO to search for the cover page description with the precise combination of uppercase and lowercase letters you typed in the **D**escription text box, select the **C**ase Sensitive check box.

3. If you know only a part of the description, select the **M**atch Anywhere check box. Otherwise, you must type the entire description in the **D**escription text box.

4. Choose **S**earch.

WinFax PRO searches for cover pages that match the description you typed and displays found cover pages in the item list window of the Select Cover Page dialog box. To restore the normal item list window, select Cover Pages Res**t**ore.

Modifying Quick Cover Pages

In later sections of this chapter, you will learn how to create and modify regular cover pages, affix graphic images and geometric shapes, and achieve other artistic effects. However, there are only a few options for modifying quick cover pages.

To modify your quick cover page, make the Cover Pages window your active view. In the item list window, double-click the Quick Cover Page entry. Alternatively, click once on the Quick Cover Page entry and click the Modify button in the toolbar. WinFax PRO displays the Modify Quick Cover Page dialog box (see fig. 7.8).

Fig. 7.8

Set up your quick cover page in the Modify Quick Cover Page dialog box.

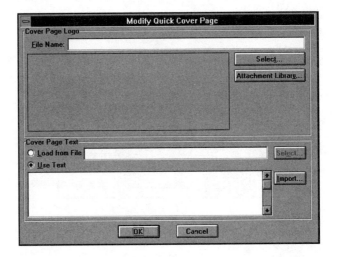

Tip

To attach a logo to a quick cover page, have someone send you a fax containing only that logo. Then type the file name in the File Name text box.

You can attach an image to a quick cover page, but it must be an already-existing WinFax PRO fax. To add the fax image to the quick cover page, type the drive, path, and name of the fax file in the File Name text box. If you are not sure of the location or file name of the fax image, click the Select button and select a file from the Open dialog box.

Whether you use an attachment or another fax image file, you can view a thumbnail of the fax by selecting the Display Logo check box in the Modify Quick Cover Page dialog box. The thumbnail appears below the File Name text box.

You also can insert pre-set text into the quick cover page. To use text from a specific file, select the Load From File button. Then type the name of the text file in the text box. If you are not sure of the file name, click Select. WinFax PRO displays the Open dialog box, where you find and select a text file.

> **Note**
>
> Remember that the file containing text for your quick cover page must be in ASCII format, not the format of a word processor or other application.

Type pre-set text directly into the Modify Quick Cover Page dialog box by activating the **U**se Text button. Click in the text box beneath the button, and then type the text. When you finish modifying your quick cover page, click OK.

Starting the Cover Page Designer

Use the Cover Page Designer to view and modify existing cover pages and create new cover pages. You can access the Cover Page Designer from several places in the WinFax PRO interface.

To create a new cover page, do one of the following:

- When the Cover Pages window is the active view, double-click New Cover Page in the item list window. In the New Cover Page dialog box that appears, click **D**esign.

- When the Cover Pages window is active and you highlighted a specific cover page in the item list window, choose Co**v**er Page **N**ew. Click **D**esign in the New Cover Page dialog box.

- In the WinFax PRO 4 program group in Program Manager, click the Cover Page Designer icon.

Any of these options loads the Cover Page Designer. In the Cover Page Designer, choose **F**ile **N**ew. WinFax PRO displays the New Cover Page dialog box (see fig. 7.9).

Fig. 7.9
Start the process of creating a cover page with the New Cover Page dialog box.

In the P**a**ge Size drop-down list, select a paper size for your new cover page (see fig. 7.10). If you select Custom, two boxes appear, where you select the page height and the unit of measurement you want to use.

II

Everyday Operation

Fig. 7.10
Select a custom page height in the New Cover Page dialog box.

After you select the paper size for the cover page, choose OK to return to Cover Page Designer.

> **Note**
>
> When you use a non-standard size for your cover page, remember to change the page size for the rest of the fax. Do that in the WinFax Driver dialog box, which you access by choosing Setup Program. In the Program Setup dialog box, click the WinFax Driver button. Chapter 4, "Configuring WinFax PRO," discusses the WinFax Driver dialog box.

Tip
Save long-distance charges by using a half-page-sized cover page. This lessens the length of time it takes to transmit the cover page.

In addition to creating new cover pages, you can use the Cover Page designer to modify existing cover pages. You start that process from the item list window of the Cover Page view. To modify an existing cover page, do one of the following:

■ Double-click the cover page you want to change in the item list window of the Cover Pages window. WinFax PRO displays the Cover Page Designer and the specific cover page you selected.

■ In the Send dialog box, click Cover. In the Select Cover Page dialog box that appears, highlight the cover page you want to edit and click Design.

■ Highlight a cover page in the item list window of the Cover Pages window and click the View button in the toolbar.

■ Highlight a cover page in the item list and click the right mouse button. Select View from the menu that appears.

■ In the WinFax PRO 4 program group in Program Manager, click the Cover Page Designer icon. After Cover Page Designer loads, choose File Open. Select the cover page you want to modify in the Open Cover Page dialog box, and choose OK.

Note

You can't change the page size of an existing cover page. You can only determine the page size when you start the cover page creation process.

Navigating Cover Page Designer

Whether you create a new cover page or modify an existing cover page, WinFax PRO loads the Cover Page Designer (see fig. 7.11).

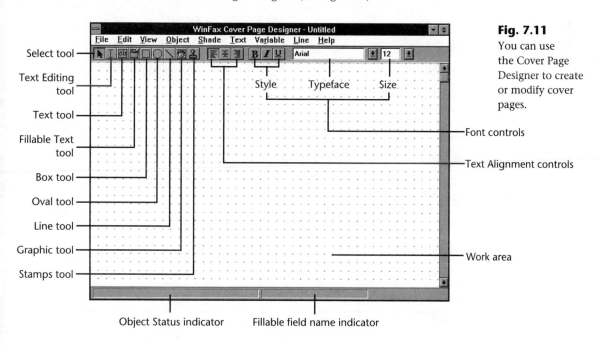

Fig. 7.11
You can use the Cover Page Designer to create or modify cover pages.

In the Cover Page Designer, you can add any of the following types of objects:

- Text that you can't change after you create the cover page.

- Spaces where you can add text just before you send the fax.

- Geometric shapes such as circles, ovals, lines, and rectangles.

- Graphic images developed by other programs.

- Variables that automatically insert information into the cover page.

You can access and fine-tune these functions from the menu system. You also can access many of these functions from the toolbar. Table 7.1 describes the items in the toolbar of the Cover Page Designer.

Table 7.1 Parts of the Cover Page Designer.	
Item	**Function**
Select tool	Select an object, such as a variable, or graphic, so you can move, size and modify it.
Text Editing tool	Highlight and then modify text.
Text tool	Create areas for regular text.
Fillable Text tool	Create areas for text you add before fax transmission.
Box tool	Draw squares or rectangles.
Oval tool	Draw ovals and circles.
Line tool	Draw straight lines.
Graphic tool	Insert a graphic image created by another program.
Stamp tool	Inserts commonly used images.
Text Justification buttons	Justify text to the left, right, or center.
Text Attribute buttons	Select text attributes.
Font selection drop-down list	Select a font for text.
Font size drop-down list	Select a font size for text.

The largest part of the Cover Page Designer is the work area in which you place the elements of your cover page. Notice that, by default, there is a grid of evenly spaced dots in the work area. A later section covers setting up the work area grid.

Also of interest is the status bar at the bottom of the Cover Page Designer window. The status bar provides details on the objects you select in the work area.

As with most windows, use the vertical and horizontal scroll bars to move around the work area.

Setting Up Cover Page Designer

There are several items to configure in the Cover Page Designer before you start creating your cover page. The next several sections describe how to set up Cover Page Designer.

Setting a Unit of Measure

It is helpful to set up the unit of measure you use when creating your cover page.

To do that, choose **F**ile Preferences. WinFax PRO displays the Cover Page Preferences dialog box (see fig. 7.12).

Fig. 7.12
Set up the unit of measurement in the Cover Page Preferences dialog box.

The Cover Page Preferences dialog box has only one function: determining the unit of measure you use while creating your cover page. Most North American users prefer inches, while most European users prefer either millimeters or centimeters. Graphic artists, however, may prefer units of measure more commonly used in their field: picas, a traditional unit of measure; or pixels, the unit of measure for computer-generated graphics. Select a unit of measure from the **U**nit of Measure drop-down list, and choose OK.

Setting Up the Grid

WinFax PRO provides a grid to make it easier to locate and line up objects in the cover page. The grid appears as a series of evenly spaced dots in the work area of the Cover Page Designer.

Set up the grid by selecting **V**iew **G**rid Setup. WinFax PRO displays the Grid Setup dialog box (see fig. 7.13).

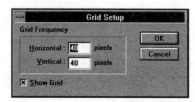

Fig. 7.13
Set up the grid in the Grid Setup dialog box.

In the Grid Setup dialog box, determine whether you want Cover Page Designer to display the grid. To turn off the grid, deactivate the **S**how Grid check box and choose OK.

Determine the space between dots in the grid with the two Grid Frequency settings. Set the horizontal space between grid points in the **H**orizontal text box and vertical space between grid points in the **V**ertical text box.

> **Note**
>
> No matter what unit of measure you set in the Cover Page Preferences dialog box, Cover Page Designer measures the space between grid points in pixels. A pixel is a single dot on-screen. The image that you view is made up of a large number of pixels.

When you finish setting up your grid, choose OK.

One other important item to determine is whether you want objects you insert in the cover page to snap to grid points. This is helpful for evenly aligning objects you insert in the cover page. When you tell the Cover Page Designer to snap objects to the grid points, you cannot locate objects between grid points.

To tell Cover Page Designer to snap objects to the grid, choose **V**iew S**n**ap to Grid. This is a toggle; when you choose the S**n**ap to Grid option, a check appears next to it in the menu. When the check appears, you deactivate the option by selecting the item again in the menu.

Setting Up Graphics

Two options in the **V**iew menu determine how quickly the Cover Page Designer works. Those options are Sho**w** Graphics and F**a**st Display.

As with the S**n**ap to Grid option, these two options are toggles. After you choose them, a check appears next to them in the menu. When deactivated, no check appears.

Graphic images take longer to display on-screen than text, lines, circles, or boxes. If you choose Sho**w** Graphics, Cover Page Designer shows graphic images. While this slows down Cover Page Designer somewhat, it usually is easier to design your cover page when you can see all the elements, including graphics.

When you hide the graphics, Cover Page Designer still displays a box the size of the graphic image (see fig. 7.14). You can still move and shape the box as if the graphic image were visible.

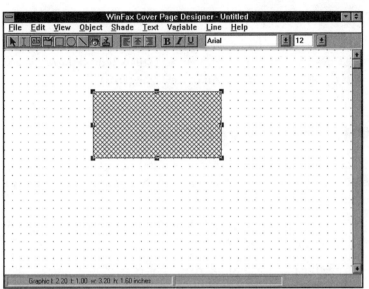

Fig. 7.14
If you choose to
hide an image
from view, Cover
Page Designer
shows a box
representing the
graphic image.

The Fast Display option determines how quickly and with how much accuracy Cover Page Designer displays graphic images. When you select Fast Display, Cover Page Designer displays images faster, but the images aren't as complete. When you deactivate this option, Cover Page Designer shows more details of the graphic image, but takes more time to display them.

Changing the View

You sometimes may want to change the amount of the cover page that the Cover Page Designer displays on-screen. The **V**iew menu has several options for that:

- **1**00% displays the cover page on-screen in its full size. You won't be able to view the entire cover page at the same time. Use the horizontal and vertical scroll bars to move around within the cover page work area.

- **5**0% displays the cover page on-screen at half its real size. This enables Cover Page Designer to show more of the cover page, but you still may need to use the vertical and horizontal scroll bars to move through the work area.

- **2**5% displays the cover page at one-fourth its real size. In most cases, this option displays the entire cover page on-screen.

Tip
When you import
a graphic image,
position it and size
it as you wish.
Then switch off the
Sho**w** Graphics
option to speed
operation of Cover
Page Designer.

Tip
In most cases,
the F**a**st Display
option provides
a happy medium
between speed and
accuracy.

■ Fit in Window displays the entire cover page on-screen.

■ Fit Sides positions the cover page on-screen so that its width fits into the Cover Page Designer window. You still will need the vertical scroll bars to view the entire length of the cover page.

Setting Up Cover Pages

When you create cover pages, you add objects, such as geometric shapes, variables, text, or graphic images. This procedure usually requires the following steps:

1. Select the object you want to add to the cover page from either the menus or the toolbar.

2. Change the position and size of the object as appropriate.

3. Modify the object by adding elements such as text, shading, or changing the weight of lines.

4. Add more objects as appropriate.

The next several sections cover how to modify all cover page objects. Subsequent sections tell you how to add and modify specific types of objects.

Moving and Sizing Cover Page Objects

While each of the cover page objects you add is different, all objects but lines are similar in one important way: they appear on-screen surrounded by boxes. You move and change the size of all object boxes the same way.

To view the object and the box that surrounds it, click the Select tool in the Cover Page Designer toolbar. This enables you to select an object by clicking on it. (The Select tool is the far left button in the toolbar and has an image of an arrow.)

After you click the Select tool, click once on the object. The box around the object appears. Also, handles, or dark blocks, appear in each corner of the object box and along the vertical and horizontal edges (see fig. 7.15).

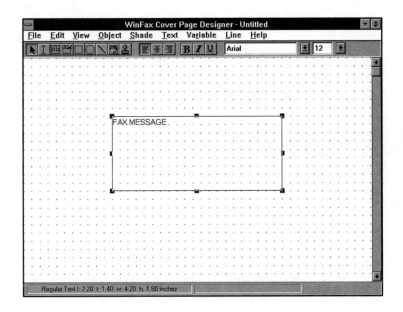

Fig. 7.15
A box with
handles surrounds
the regular text.

When Cover Page Designer displays the object box's handles, you can do any of the following:

- Move the box and its contents to another location. Click anywhere within the box and hold down the left mouse button. Drag the mouse and the box moves. When you move the box to the location you want, release the left mouse button.

- Change the size of the box. Position the mouse pointer over one of the handles. When the mouse pointer turns into a two-headed arrow, hold down the left mouse button and drag the mouse in one of the directions of the arrow. This makes the box larger or smaller.

> **Note**
>
> When you use a handle in the corner of the box, you can change the vertical and horizontal size of the box at the same time.

- Remove the box and its contents from the work area. With the handles of the box showing, choose **E**dit Cu**t** to delete the object but place it in the Windows clipboard. Once in the clipboard, paste the object back into the work area by choosing **E**dit **P**aste. Delete the box without saving it to the Windows clipboard by choosing **E**dit **D**elete or by pressing the Del key.

- Change the formatting of the contents of the box. This procedure changes with different types of objects. The following sections describe how to add and modify the different types of objects.

- Change or eliminate the borders of the box surrounding the object. The next section describes this process.

> **Note**
>
> Lines don't have boxes. However, when you click on a line, handles still appear at each end. You then can perform the functions just described on the line, except for changing the box border.

Changing Borders

You can change the type of border around an object and change the weight of the border or line. To change the type of border, follow these steps:

1. Click once on the object so the handles appear.

2. Select **O**bject Bor**d**er. A dialog box from which you can select the following options appears:

   - **N**one—no border around the object. Even with no border, handles appear when you click on the object.

   - **S**quare—places a square or rectangle around the object. This is the default border.

   - **R**ound—places a square or rectangle with rounded corners around the object.

To change the weight of a box's lines, click on the object so that handles appear, and select **L**ine. The top part of the Line menu displays several weights of lines. The bottom part of the menu displays different types of arrows you can affix to lines (see fig. 7.16).

Select the line weight you want for the box, and Cover Page Designer applies it.

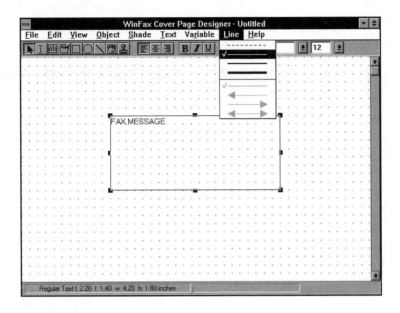

Fig. 7.16
Select border and
line weights in the
Line menu.

Changing Box Shading

You also can change the shading of all types of boxes. Select the box by clicking it, and then choose the **S**hade menu. This menu provides four shading
options:

■ **W**hite Transparent creates a white background. It also enables you to
see objects you positioned behind the box (see fig. 7.17).

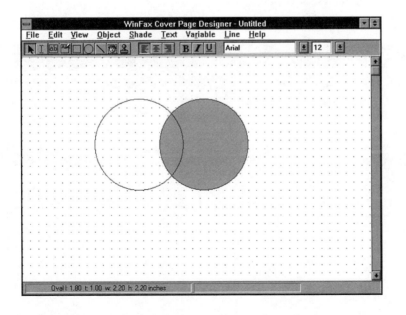

Fig. 7.17
The **W**hite
Transparent setting
lets you see objects
behind the current
object.

■ White **O**paque creates a white background but does not enable you to see objects behind it (see fig. 7.18).

Fig. 7.18
The White **O**paque setting prevents you from seeing objects behind the current object.

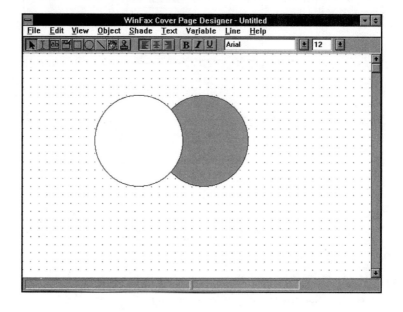

Tip
To create a shadowed box, create a black box and place a similarly sized White **O**paque box in front of it, but positioned off to the side.

■ **B**lack makes the inside of the box black. You can't see text or other objects inside the black box unless the text within the box is white. Choosing white as a text color is discussed later in this chapter.

■ **G**ray makes the inside of the box gray. You can see text and other objects inside the gray box (see fig. 7.19).

Note

These shading settings also apply to geometric shapes you add to the work area. A later section of this chapter tells you how to add geometric shapes.

Note

When you designate a gray or black box for a graphic image, Cover Page Designer only turns the part of the box gray or black that doesn't contain the image.

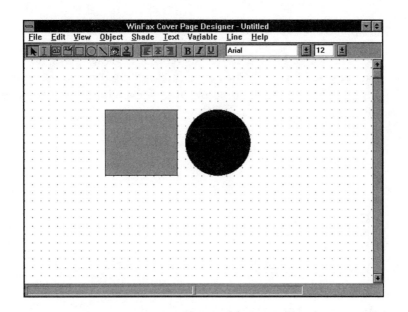

Fig. 7.19
A gray box and
a black circle.

Positioning and Selecting Multiple Objects

Cover Page Designer enables you to place objects in front of other objects.
This capability is handy for creating graphic effects like shadowed boxes,
which were described earlier.

You can control whether Cover Page Designer displays layered objects in the
background or the foreground. To place an object in front of other objects,
select the object and then choose **O**bject, Bring to **F**ront. To place an object
behind other objects, choose **O**bject, Send to **B**ack.

You also can select more than one object at a time. When you do this,
the box and handles appear around all the objects you select.

There are two methods for selecting multiple objects:

- Select one object by clicking it. Hold down the Shift key and click any
  other objects you want to select.

- Choose **O**bject, **S**elect All. This selects all objects in the work area.

You can take many of the same actions on multiple objects that you take on
single objects. For example, you can move multiple objects as a group, delete
or copy objects, or change shading and line weights.

II

Everyday Operation

Adding Objects

The previous sections discussed how Cover Page Designer works, how to set it up and navigate through it. The next several sections discuss how to add and modify cover page objects. Specifically, they tell you how to add and modify the following:

- Variables
- Regular text
- Fill-in text
- Graphics
- Geometric shapes
- Lines

Adding and Modifying Variables

Variables automatically place information into cover pages. In Chapter 4, "Configuring WinFax PRO," you read about variables used in another context: your fax header, or the information at the top of each page of your fax transmission.

Variables in cover pages are convenient because they insert different information each time you send a fax, depending on conditions. In simple terms, they are called variables because they represent information that varies from instance to instance, such as the date or the recipient's name. The information in variables comes from many parts of WinFax PRO.

Variables appear on-screen as codes. When you send the fax, WinFax PRO replaces the code with the information the code represents. For example, if the variable code is for the current time, WinFax PRO inserts the time in the cover page.

Table 7.2 lists the variables, their symbols, the information they provide, and also, the source of the information in WinFax PRO.

Table 7.2   Variable Fields and Sources of Information.

Variable Name	Symbol	Function	Source of Information
Recipient Name (First and Last Names)	@R	Adds recipient's full name	Send Fax dialog box
Recipient First Name	@F	Recipient's first name	Phonebook

Variable Name	Symbol	Function	Source of Information
Recipient Last Name	@L	Recipient's last name	Phonebook
Recipient Title	@E	Recipient's title	Phonebook
Recipient Fax Number	@X	Fax number of recipient	Phonebook
Recipient Company Name	@C	Recipient's company	Phonebook
Recipient Address 1	@V	Recipient's address, first line	Phonebook
Recipient Address 2	@W	Recipient's address, second line	Phonebook
Recipient City	@I	Recipient's city	Phonebook
Recipient State	@J	Recipient's state	Phonebook
Recipient ZIP Code	@Z	Recipient's ZIP code	Phonebook
Date	@D	Date of the transmission	Your PC's system clock
Time	@T	Time the transmission starts	Your PC's system clock
Total Number of Pages	@N	Number of pages in fax including cover	The fax file
Subject	@U	Subject of the fax	Send Fax dialog box
Sender Name	@S	Your name	User Setup dialog box
Sender Company	@Y	Your organization's name	User Setup dialog box
Sender Fax Number	@A	Your fax number	User Setup dialog box
Sender Voice Number	@H	Your voice number	User Setup dialog box
Notes Field	@O	Notes about recipient	Phonebook

Everyday Operation

(continues)

Table 7.2 Continued			
Variable Name	**Symbol**	**Function**	**Source of Information**
Misc Field	@M	Miscellaneous information about recipient	Phonebook
Billing Code	@B	Billing code for recipient	Phonebook

To add a variable to the work area, select the item you want from the Variable menu. Cover Page Designer adds the variable to the work area in a box. To add a variable to a text box, click in the text box and then select the variable from the Variable menu.

The next figure shows an example of a variable. In this case, the variable is the **R**ecipient Name variable, which displays the recipient's first and last name (see fig. 7.20).

Fig. 7.20
A newly added variable.

Variable field

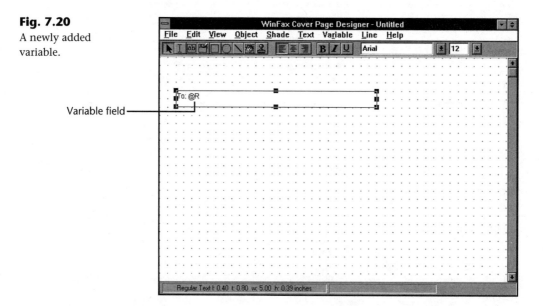

As with all objects you add to cover pages, you can move boxes containing variables and change their borders and shading. You also can change the font, font size, and attributes of the text of variables. The next section describes that process.

Adding and Editing Regular Text Objects

Regular text is text you insert in the cover page that you can't change when you send a fax. To add regular text:

1. Click the Text tool in the toolbar. The Text tool is the third button from the left. When you click the Text tool, the mouse pointer changes to a cross cursor. Use the cross cursor to draw the box within which you will add text.

2. Position the cross cursor where you want to locate the upper left corner of the text box and hold down the left mouse button.

3. Drag the mouse down and to the right across the work area to create the text box you want.

> **Note**
>
> Don't worry if you don't initially draw the text box precisely as you want.
> You can always move the text box, as described earlier in this chapter.

4. Release the left mouse button. When you do, a blinking cursor appears inside the box (see fig. 7.21).

5. Type the text you want.

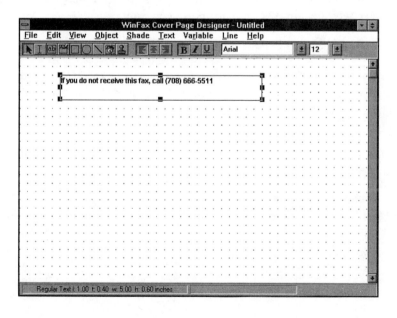

Fig. 7.21
A text box with text.

II

Everyday Operation

Select a font, font size, and attributes before you start typing or at any time after you start typing. To do so, choose **T**ext **F**ont. Cover Page Designer displays the Font dialog box (see fig. 7.22).

Fig. 7.22

Select font, font style, and size in the Font dialog box.

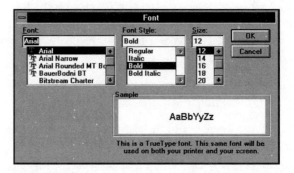

In the Font dialog box, follow these steps:

1. Select the font you want from the **F**ont list.

2. Select the attribute you want from the Font St**y**le drop-down list.

3. Select the font size from the **S**ize drop-down list.

4. Cover Page Designer displays an example of the font combination you choose in the Sample area. Repeat steps one through three until you get precisely the font, size, and attributes you want.

5. Choose OK when you complete your selections.

If you know the font, size, and attributes you want, you can set them from the toolbar. Type a font or select it from the drop-down list in the Font selection box. Similarly, select a font size from the list to the right of the font selection box.

To change a style attribute, click the buttons for bold, italic, or underline in the toolbar. You also can select these attributes from the **T**ext menu.

To set the justification for the text in the text box, click the left, center, or right justification buttons in the toolbar. You also can select these justification options from the **T**ext menu.

Note

The text characteristics you select apply to all text within the text box. Also, justification is in relation to the box itself, not the entire cover page. If, for example, you select left justification, Cover Page Designer left-justifies the text within the box, no matter where the box is located.

You can set the text characters to be either black or white. White characters are best if you shaded the text box black or gray. To designate white characters, choose **Text W**hite Text.

To designate black characters, choose **Text B**lack Text. Use black text when you have either white or gray background for the text box.

To change type characteristics at any time, click the Text Editing tool in the toolbar; then click the text box you want to edit. The mouse pointer becomes an I-beam text cursor, similar to those in most word processors.

You must select specific text to change fonts, font size, or attributes. Position the text cursor at the beginning of the text you want to select and hold down the left mouse button. Drag the mouse until you highlight all the text you want to change. Then follow the procedures for changing fonts, font size, attributes, and color.

Note

You don't need to highlight specific text in a text box to change justification or text color. Simply select the text box and then select the justification or text color you want.

Cover Page Designer includes a spell checker for text objects. To use it, highlight the text you want to check. Then choose **Text Sp**elling. Cover Page Designer starts the spell checker (see fig. 7.23).

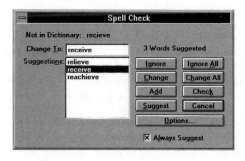

Fig. 7.23
Check the spelling of selected text in your cover page with the Spell Check dialog box.

If the spell checker finds a word that isn't in its dictionary, the word is listed at the top of the spell checking window. It offers suggestions in the Suggestions list box (if you either click **S**uggest or select the A**l**ways Suggest check box). The word you highlight in the Suggestions list box appears in the Change **T**o text box, which you can edit.

The other options in the spell checker are as follows:

- **I**gnore—ignores the current instance of the misspelling. Changes to **R**estart when spell checking is complete.

- Ignore **A**ll—ignores all instances of the misspelling.

- **C**hange—changes the current misspelling to the one suggested. Changes to **D**one when spell checking is complete.

- C**h**ange All—changes all similar misspellings.

- .A**d**d—adds the supposedly misspelled word to the spell checker's custom dictionary.

- Chec**k**—checks the specific word you've typed in the Change To text box.

- Cancel—cancels the spelling operation.

Click the **O**ptions button to view various options for the spell checker. The options include the ability to use different dictionaries, which is useful if you aren't using English or need a specialized dictionary, such as one containing medical terms. The custom dictionary contains words you have added to it by choosing the **A**dd button in the Spell Check dialog box.

Tip

Use variables in regular text boxes to create "personalized" messages in cover pages. Insert the variable codes as shown in Table 7.2. For example, typing **Dear @R,** inserts the recipient's name after the word "Dear."

In addition, you can use the Spelling Options dialog box to tell the spell checker to ignore words that are:

All in capitals

Proper nouns

Run-on words

Abbreviations

Choose OK to save changes to the Spelling options and return to the Spell Check dialog box. When the spell check is complete, choose **D**one or Cancel to close the dialog box.

Adding and Modifying Fill-in Text

A fill-in text object is similar to a regular text object described in the previous section with one exception. While regular text boxes are unchangeable when you are sending faxes, you add information to fill-in text areas when you send the fax. You fill in this information with the Cover Page Filler, which is described in Chapter 8, "Sending Faxes."

Fill-in text areas are appropriate for the message section of a cover page. You also can use them for any other information you want to add to a cover page for which there isn't a variable.

To add a fill-in text area, follow these steps:

1. Click the Fillable Text tool in the toolbar (the fourth tool from the left).

2. Drag your mouse across the work area to create the fill-in text area (see fig. 7.24). You can resize the box at any time by dragging the box's handles with your mouse.

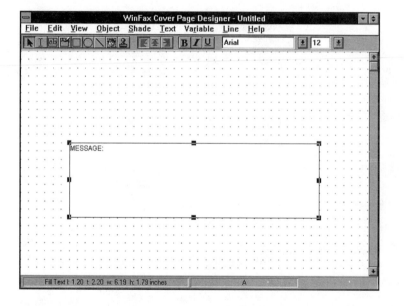

Fig. 7.24
A fill-in text area.

3. Type text into the fill-in area that won't change, such as a description of what the box contains. Modify fonts, shading, and borders just as you would a regular text box.

Caution

The layout of fill-in text areas varies depending on the information you place in them. As a result, it is best not to use variables in fill-in text areas to create personalized cover pages. Using variables in fill-in text areas can cause strange spacing in the fax message.

Changing the Fill-In Order

When you use the Cover Page Filler for filling in cover pages before sending the fax, you move from one fill-in text area to another by pressing your tab key. By default, you move from one fill-in area to another in the order they were created.

You can, however, change the order in which you fill in information in fill-in text areas by selecting **O**bject Tabbing **O**rder. Cover Page Designer then displays the Tabbing Order dialog box (see fig. 7.25).

Fig. 7.25
Change the order of fill-in text areas with the Tabbing Order dialog box.

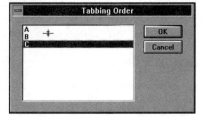

The Tabbing Order dialog box lists fill-in text areas in the order in which you added them. Cover Page Designer gives the text boxes letter names that correspond to that order.

To change the order in which you complete fill-in text areas, highlight the variable you want to change and hold down the left mouse button. Notice that the mouse pointer changes to a cursor with a horizontal line and two arrows facing each other.

While holding down the mouse button, drag your mouse until the mouse pointer is over the new position. Then release the left mouse button. The order of the fill-in text areas should reflect your change.

Adding and Modifying Graphics

You can place a graphic image anywhere in the cover page. This is useful for adding a corporate logo to the cover page or adding an appropriate graphic to make the cover page fit a specific theme. For example, you could add a graphic image of a stork for a cover page announcing a birth.

To add a graphic image, click the Graphic tool in the toolbar. This is the eighth button from the left; it contains a face. Click where you want the graphic to appear. Cover Page Designer displays the Graphic Attributes dialog box (see fig. 7.26).

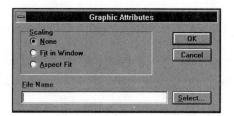

Fig. 7.26
Select a graphic and determine its attributes in the Graphic Attributes dialog box.

In the Graphic Attributes dialog box, you both select the graphic file you want to insert and determine how it appears. In the scaling section of the dialog box, determine how you want Cover Page Designer to handle the graphic image. This is an important selection because the image likely won't fit precisely into the box you create for it. Your three choices are:

■ **N**one. The image will be the same size in Cover Page Designer as it was in the original application. However, if it is bigger than the box for the graphic, you won't be able to see parts of it.

■ **Fi**t in Window. Cover Page Designer fills the graphic box with the image. However, the image may appear distorted and out of proportion.

■ **A**spect Fit. Cover Page Designer essentially redraws the object so that it retains its original proportions. However, the image may become smaller than it was originally and, in fact, may be smaller than the graphic box.

After selecting scaling for the graphic image, type the drive, path, and file name for the image in the **F**ile Name text box. If you do not know the drive, path, or file name, click the **S**elect button. Cover Page Designer displays the Select Graphic dialog box (see fig. 7.27).

II

Everyday Operation

Fig. 7.27
Preview and select
a graphic image in
the Select Graphic
dialog box.

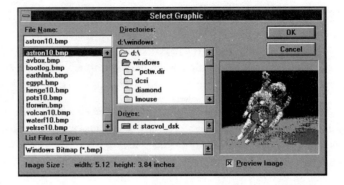

As with similar dialog boxes, select a drive in the Dri**v**es drop-down list and a directory in the **D**irectories list box. Also, select the type of file you want to import in the List Files of the **T**ype drop-down list. This drop-down list contains all the types of graphic file formats that you can import into Cover Page Designer.

Each format has a specific file name extension. Table 7.3 lists the formats that you can import into Cover Page Designer and the file name extension of those formats.

Table 7.3 Formats and File Extensions.	
Format	**File Extension**
Windows Bitmap	BMP
Windows Metafile	WMF
TIFF	TIF
PC Paintbrush	PCX
GEM Image	IMG
GEM Metafile	GEM
Mac Paint	BIN
Encap Postscript (Encapsulated Postscript)	EPS
Gr Interchange Format (Graphics Interchange Format)	GIF
WinFax PRO fax	FXS

After you select a format, drive, and directory, the Select Graphic dialog box displays the files in the **F**ile Name text box and list window. Highlight the image file you want. To preview it, select the **P**review Image check box. The image displays in the window. Choose OK to return to the Graphic Attributes dialog box.

After you select the image, choose OK. Cover Page Designer places the image in a box in the work area, as shown in the next figure (see fig. 7.28).

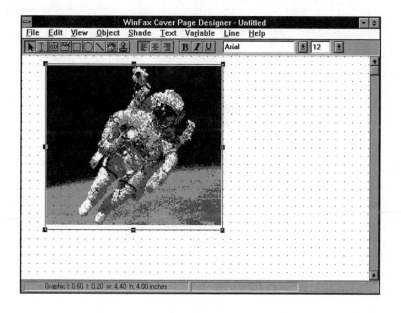

Fig. 7.28
An image inserted into a cover page.

Move, delete, or change the weight of the border as you would any object. Also, if the image is smaller than the box, you can shade the non-image portion of the box.

You can also return to the Graphic Attributes dialog box to change the scaling. Using the Select tool, double-click the graphic box.

Inserting Commonly Used Images

Cover Page Designer enables you to speed the process of inserting images you commonly use. Cover Page Designer calls commonly used images *stamps*.

To add a stamp to the work area, choose **O**bject S**t**amps. The mouse pointer turns into a pointer that looks like a hand stamp. Then click in the work area where you want to place the image. Cover Page Designer displays the Stamps dialog box (see fig. 7.29).

Tip
Corporate logos are an obvious use of graphic images in cover pages. However, you also can use the logos of specific products for faxes to sales prospects.

Fig. 7.29
Keep frequently
used images in the
Stamps dialog box.

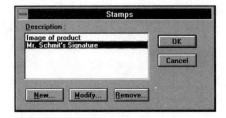

Click once on the description of the image and then choose OK. Cover Page Designer places the image in the work area.

To add a new image to the Stamps dialog box, click the **N**ew button. Cover Page Designer displays the New Stamp dialog box (see fig. 7.30).

Fig. 7.30
Add new images
in the New Stamp
dialog box.

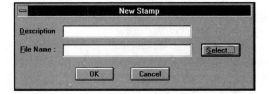

In the **D**escription text box, type a description for the stamp. In the **F**ile Name text box, type the drive, path, and file name of the image. If you are not sure of the drive, path, or file name, click the **S**elect button. Cover Page Designer displays the Select Graphic dialog box, which is discussed in the preceding section.

Tip
Keeping digitized
versions of your
signature on file
makes it easy to
add your signature
when creating
cover pages and
annotating faxes,
as discussed in
Chapter 14, "View-
ing and Annotat-
ing Faxes."

Select a file in the Select Graphic dialog box and choose OK. The file appears in the **F**ile Name text box. Choose OK in the New Stamp dialog box, and Cover Page Designer adds the description of the image to the **D**escription list box in the Stamps dialog box.

To modify the file name or description of the image, click **M**odify. Cover Page Designer displays the Modify Stamp dialog box, which is virtually iden-tical to the New Stamp dialog box. Change either the description or the file name and choose OK.

To remove an image from the Stamps dialog box, click once on the descrip-tion of the image and click the **R**emove button. Cover Page Designer asks if you are sure you want to remove the image. If you are sure, choose OK.

When you have finished making changes in the Stamps dialog box, choose OK.

Adding and Changing Geometric Shapes

You can add circles, ovals, squares, and rectangles to the work area. To add circles or ovals, click the oval tool in the toolbar. Then hold down the left mouse button and drag the mouse. Determine the shape and size of the circle or oval by where you drag the mouse. To make a perfect circle, hold down the Shift key while dragging the mouse. When you've created the precise size and shape you want, release the mouse button (see fig. 7.31).

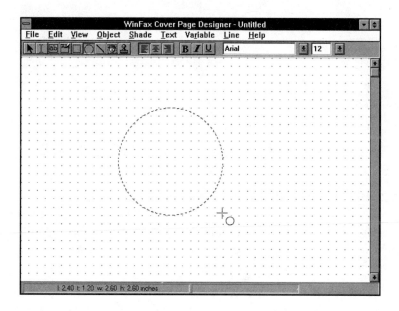

Fig. 7.31
Creating a circle in the work area.

As with other objects, you can move, copy, delete, resize, or shade circles and ovals by selecting them and then selecting the appropriate option. Previous sections of this chapter told you how to modify objects.

Note

Circle and oval objects don't have visible boxes around them as do other types of objects. However, when you click on them, handles still appear.

The process for creating squares or rectangles is nearly identical. Click the Box tool in the toolbar and create the shape in the work area by dragging your mouse (see fig. 7.32). To make a perfect square, hold down the Shift key while dragging the mouse.

Fig. 7.32
Creating a square
in the work area.

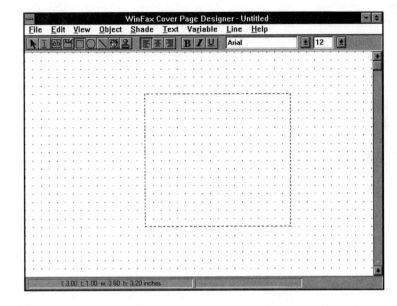

Tip
Add text to geo-
metric shapes and
overlap shapes
and lines to create
custom designs
and logos.

Adding and Modifying Lines

Lines are like two-dimensional geometric shapes. Create them the same way
you create circles, ovals, squares, and rectangles. Click the Line tool in the
toolbar and then drag the mouse pointer across the work area to create the
line you want.

There are a few differences between lines and other geometric shapes. First,
lines are not in boxes as are other objects. However, like boxes, you can increase the weight of lines and even turn lines into one-headed or two-headed
arrows.

To change the line weight of lines, select the line by clicking the Selection
tool in the toolbar and then clicking on the line. As with other objects,
handles appear at the ends of the line. Then choose **Line**. The **Line** menu
displays different line weights and styles of arrows (see fig. 7.33).

Fig. 7.33
Use the **Line** menu
to choose different
weights for lines.

In the **Line** menu, choose the line weight or arrow style you want.
Cover Page Designer applies your selection to the line.

To move a line after you draw it, click the line once so that handles show at each end. Position the mouse cursor directly over the line and hold down the left mouse button. Drag the line to the new position. To make a perfectly straight line, hold down the Shift key while dragging the mouse.

To make the line longer or shorter, select the line and position the mouse pointer over one of the handles. When the mouse pointer turns into a cross with a line in the lower right corner, hold down the left mouse button and drag the line to make it longer or shorter or to change its angle in the work area.

Troubleshooting

I created and then used a new cover page. However, the recipient told me that the cover page was a half page, not a full page as I wanted.

Before you created your cover page, you created a half-page cover page. You forgot to designate the new cover page as a full-page cover. You can't change the size of a cover page after you create it.

I inserted a graphic image in Cover Page Designer. However, all I see is a box with cross-hatched lines.

In Cover Page Designer, choose **V**iew. If there isn't a check mark next to the Sho**w** Graphics menu item, click it with your mouse. This will display the graphic image.

I used a large font for part of a cover page I created. However, when I send the fax or print it on a printer, it comes out jagged.

Either Windows or WinFax PRO doesn't support the font size you specified. Modify the cover page in Cover Page Designer using a different font or, if necessary, a smaller font size.

I created a cover page with fill-in areas. When I fill in the cover page before sending a fax, WinFax PRO doesn't let me fill in the areas in order.

When you created the cover page, you didn't insert the fill-in areas in order. To set the order for filling in these areas, start Cover Page Designer and load the cover page. Then choose **O**bject **T**abbing Order. Use the Tabbing Order dialog box, described in the section, "Changing the Fill-In Order," to change the order in which you fill in the areas.

II

Everyday Operation

Saving and Printing Cover Pages

When you finish a new cover page in the Cover Page Designer, choose **F**ile **S**ave to save it. If you modified an existing cover page, either save it or choose **F**ile Save **A**s. This saves a new version of the cover page without eliminating the old version. Cover Page Designer displays the Save Cover Page dialog box (see fig. 7.34).

Fig. 7.34
The Save Cover Page dialog box.

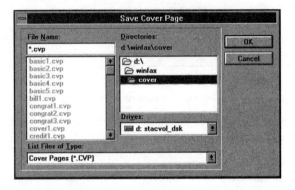

Tip
To examine your cover page, create a fax using it but schedule a later transmission. Then, from the Outbox, print the fax or view it by double-clicking on it.

In the Save Cover Page dialog box, select a drive and path for your cover page. By default, WinFax PRO places cover pages in the \WINFAX\COVER subdirectory. Type a file name in the **F**ile Name text box. Make sure to use the CVP file extension—WinFax PRO can't use your cover page unless it has that file name extension.

After you save a new cover page, you still must place it in the cover page folder in the Cover Page window. Display the Cover Page window by clicking the Cvr Pgs tool in the toolbar.

Double-click the folder or subfolder in which you want to place the cover page. WinFax PRO displays the cover pages already stored in that folder in the item list window. In the item list window, double-click New Cover Page. WinFax PRO then displays the New Cover Page dialog box (see fig. 7.35).

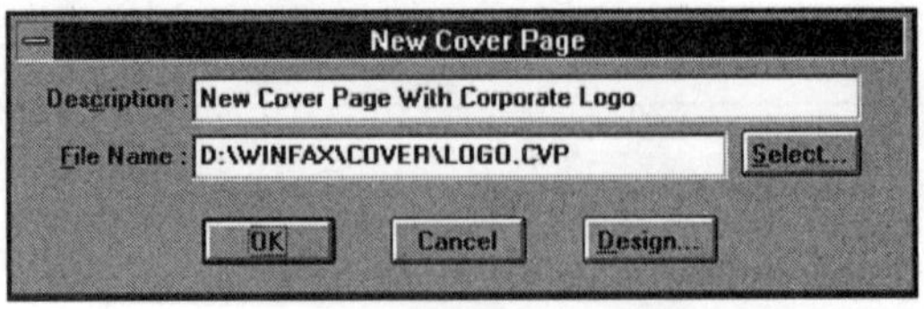

Fig. 7.35
Add a cover page to a folder in the New Cover Page dialog box.

Type a description for the new cover page Description text box. In the File Name text box, type the drive, path, and file name for the cover page in the File Name dialog box.

If you forget the name of the cover page, click the Select button and select the cover page from the Cover Page Templates dialog box. Choose OK and the drive, path, and file name appear in the File Name text box in the New Cover Page dialog box. Choose OK. WinFax PRO adds the cover page to the folder.

Designating a Default Cover Page

To designate a cover page as the default, select the cover page in the item list window of the Cover Pages window. Then choose Cover Page Set Default. Notice that the cover page listing in the item list window turns blue to designate its status as the default.

> **Note**
>
> You also can highlight a cover page in the item list window, click the right mouse button and select Set Default from the menu that appears.

To make sure that you always use a cover page, choose Cover Page Always Use Cover Page. This means that WinFax PRO automatically selects the option in the Send Fax dialog box to use a cover page. Unless you tell WinFax PRO otherwise, it automatically uses the default cover page you designated.

Adding a Cover Page with OLE

Besides using the Cover Page Designer, WinFax PRO provides yet another method for creating and using cover pages. This method uses a capability of Windows called *Object Linking and Embedding (OLE)*.

OLE is an advanced capability that enables you to embed files created by other programs in your current application. For example, use OLE to embed a graphic image in a word processing document. Then, when you double-click that image, you can edit the image in the original application.

Similarly, you can create a cover page in another application that supports OLE and use the cover page in WinFax PRO. This is a handy alternative if you don't like using WinFax PRO's Cover Page Designer.

II

Everyday Operation

There are, however, several disadvantages to using OLE to create cover pages. First, it is complicated to use because it involves the use of multiple applications.

Second, you can't use WinFax PRO's variables or its text fill-in areas in cover pages you create in other applications. You can, however, use variables that the application supports. Most full-fledged word processing programs (like Microsoft Word for Windows and Lotus Ami PRO) have their own sets of variables you can use.

Third, using OLE can be a slow and cumbersome process, particularly if you don't have a powerful PC. That's because it requires WinFax PRO to load the other application to create and modify cover pages and also to use them when you send faxes. This adds another step to the process of sending faxes.

Still, OLE enables you to use applications with which you are familiar to create cover pages. And, depending on the application you use, your other application may be more powerful and flexible than Cover Page Designer.

The four different types of OLE provided by WinFax PRO can all be accessed through the Cover Page menu when the Cover Page window is active.

The OLE Template Option

The first OLE option is the Template option. The Template option retrieves an existing file and embeds it. It also shows the Insert Object from File dialog box. You start in WinFax PRO and use another application to create the cover page. This option uses a file already created by another application (see fig. 7.36).

Fig. 7.36
Use the Insert Object from File dialog box to retrieve an existing file.

> **Note**
>
> The applications listed when you display the Insert New Object dialog box will undoubtedly be different than those listed in the figure.

When you install applications, they tell Windows whether they support OLE. The Insert New Object dialog box lists all the applications you use that support OLE. In the Object Type dialog box, select the application in which you want to create the cover page and click OK.

WinFax PRO and Windows launch that application. Create your cover page in the other application. When you finish, use that application's File Save As function (not the regular Save function) before you close the application. When you close the application, you automatically return to WinFax PRO.

WinFax PRO displays its Save As dialog box so you can save the cover page in WinFax PRO's cover page format. Select a drive and path for your cover page (remembering that, unless you tell it otherwise, WinFax PRO saves cover pages in the \WINFAX\COVER subdirectory). The cover page will appear at the end of the item list window for the folder that was active when you created the OLE cover page.

Begin modifying the OLE cover page as you would a normal WinFax PRO cover page. Do that by highlighting the cover page in the item list window and clicking the Modify button in the toolbar. WinFax PRO displays the Modify Cover Page dialog box. Click the **E**dit button.

Rather than loading Cover Page Designer, however, WinFax PRO and Windows load the application that created the cover page. Modify the cover page using your other application. You can't use Cover Page Designer to modify cover pages you create with this method.

The OLE Insert Option

The second OLE option is the Insert option. This enables you to use another application to create a cover page. To use this option, choose Co**v**er Page **O**LE **I**nsert. WinFax PRO displays the Insert New Object dialog box.

To use this option, follow these steps:

1. Choose Co**v**er Page **O**LE **I**nsert. WinFax PRO displays the Insert New Object dialog box from which you select the file you want (see fig. 7.37).

Everyday Operation

Fig. 7.37
The Insert New
Object dialog box
allows you to
easily access and
insert objects.

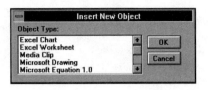

2. Select a drive in the Dri**v**es drop-down list and a directory in the **D**irectories list box.

3. In the List Files of **T**ype drop-down list, select the application you want. The files created by that application appear in the **F**ile Name list box.

4. In the **F**ile Name list box, click the file you want and then choose OK.

From this point, the operation is similar to the Template option described in the previous section. WinFax PRO and Windows load the file in your other application. Make any changes you want to the file. Use that application's **F**ile Save As command to save the file. Then exit the application.

WinFax PRO asks you to name the file as a cover page using the CVP file name extension. Give the cover page a file name and WinFax PRO inserts it in the currently active cover page folder.

When you select this cover page, WinFax PRO and Windows loads the other application and the cover page. You can then make any changes you want to the cover page and close the application. WinFax PRO will proceed with the fax transmission process.

The Link OLE Option

The third OLE option is the Link option. This option creates a direct link to the application you use to create a cover page.

In the application, copy the cover page to the Windows clipboard. With the application still open, return to WinFax PRO and make the Cover Pages window the active window. Choose Co**v**er Page **O**LE **L**ink in WinFax PRO.

WinFax PRO displays its Save File As dialog box. Save the file as a cover page with the CVP file extension. WinFax PRO adds the new cover page to the currently active cover page folder. To modify the cover page, double-click it in the cover page folder.

The Paste OLE Option

WinFax PRO's final OLE option is the Paste option. With this option, you copy a cover page from another application to the Windows clipboard. However, unlike the other options, the application need not support OLE for this option to work.

Open your application and either create the cover page or load a cover page file (or edit a previously created cover page). Then copy the cover page to the Windows clipboard.

Back in WinFax PRO, make the Cover Pages window the active window. Then choose Co**v**er Page **O**LE **P**aste. WinFax PRO displays its File Save As dialog box, in which you provide a name for the cover page using the CVP file name extension. WinFax PRO places the new cover page in the currently selected folder.

If you copied the information from an application that supports OLE, WinFax PRO treats the cover page as it does the other options. In other words, when you want to modify it, WinFax PRO and Windows load the application that originally created the cover page.

Similarly, when you select this cover page when sending a fax, WinFax PRO also loads the application. Make any changes you want to the contents of the cover page, and exit the application. WinFax PRO then proceeds to send your fax.

If the application from which you pasted the cover page does not support OLE, WinFax PRO makes Cover Page Designer the application you use to modify the cover page.

Tip

OLE is a complex function. To learn more about it, read the Windows user's guide and the documentation for your application.

Troubleshooting

I created a cover page in another application and used Object Linking and Embedding (OLE) to bring it into WinFax PRO. Now, however, I can't edit the cover page with Cover Page Designer.

You can't use Cover Page Designer to edit cover pages that you embed in WinFax PRO with most types of OLE. Rather, you must edit the cover page in the application.

From Here...

Now that you know how to create and manage cover pages, you might want to review the following chapters:

- Chapter 5, "Customizing WinFax PRO," discusses how to create folders and subfolders in the various WinFax PRO views, including the Cover Pages window.

- Chapter 8, "Sending Faxes," explains how to send faxes. It includes information on attaching a cover page to the faxes you send and using the Cover Page Filler for fill-in text areas.

- Chapter 18, "Using WinFax PRO in Other Programs," provides more ideas on how to connect WinFax PRO and other applications.

Chapter 8
Sending Faxes

In this chapter, you learn how to do the following:

- Send faxes from within WinFax PRO.

- Send faxes from other applications.

- Select fax recipients and groups.

- Attach cover pages to faxes.

- Use attachments with your faxes.

- Schedule faxes for later transmission.

- Resubmit and forward existing faxes.

Although WinFax PRO can send and receive electronic mail and binary files, it is, at its heart, a program for sending and receiving faxes. WinFax PRO is particularly noteworthy because it makes sending faxes simple, yet gives great flexibility about how and when to send faxes.

This chapter describes how to send faxes. It also describes many options that WinFax PRO provides for sending faxes.

Starting the Faxing Process

Not surprisingly, you start the process of sending a fax by creating your message. Do this either in WinFax PRO itself, or in any Windows program that can print documents.

Chapter 2, "How WinFax PRO Works," describes how WinFax PRO uses a special piece of software called a *driver* to print your fax on a remote fax machine. This printing process is similar to printing a document on a printer, with one major exception: rather than sending the information to the printer, WinFax PRO sends it to your fax modem. Your fax modem, in turn, sends the fax to the remote fax machine.

This is how WinFax PRO works, regardless of whether you start the process from an application or from WinFax PRO itself. The next several sections, however, describe the specific procedures for starting the faxing process from your applications and from WinFax PRO.

Faxing from Your Application

As stated previously, you "print" your fax on other fax machines and fax modems by selecting the WinFax PRO printer driver and printing as you normally would. This, in turn, means that you can create fax documents with normal software applications—such as your word processor, database, or spreadsheet—and start the fax process directly from the applications.

For example, you can create a business proposal in your word processor, and add charts, graphs, images, or other elements. You can fax it to all your recipients without ever leaving your chair to go down the hall and use the traditional fax machine.

There are only a few simple requirements for sending faxes from within your software applications:

■ You must properly install WinFax PRO.

■ You must properly install and turn on your fax modem. Read Chapter 1, "Installing WinFax PRO," for information about installing WinFax PRO and your fax modem.

■ You must set up WinFax PRO to work with your specific fax modem. Read Chapter 4, "Configuring WinFax PRO," for information about setting up WinFax PRO to work with specific modems.

■ Your application must print using normal Windows printing processes. To determine whether your application can print, open the application's **F**ile menu. If there is a **P**rint option, you can use WinFax PRO.

Note

Virtually all Windows applications can print. However, many Windows utilities—or tools for enhancing your Windows environment—don't have printing capabilities.

Create a document in your application as you normally would; you don't need to load WinFax PRO before starting this process.

Selecting the WinFax Driver

When it is time to send your document, make sure that the WinFax driver is the active printer driver. To check the active printer driver, select the option in your application's File menu for switching printers.

The name of the option for switching printers is different in different applications. However, in many applications, the option is File, Print Setup. In other applications, you select a printer by selecting File, then, selecting the Print option. In the application's printing dialog box, there is an option for setting up your printer. If you can't find this option, check your application's documentation.

Wherever you find the option for changing printers, the Print Setup dialog box appears. This dialog box appears different in different applications, but the essence of the dialog box remains the same: It lists available printer drivers (including the WinFax driver), and enables you to fine-tune the driver. Figure 8.1 shows the Windows default Printers dialog box.

In the printer selection dialog box (in this case, the Windows Printer dialog box that you access from the Windows Control Panel), double-click the WinFax driver. This loads the WinFax driver and makes it the default driver for all Windows operations. Then click the control menu box. Procedures vary with printer setup dialog boxes you access from various applications.

To modify the method in which the WinFax PRO driver works, click **S**etup in the Windows Printer dialog box. (Some applications call this button the Options button.) No matter what the application calls the button, however, the WinFax Driver Setup dialog box is accessed (see fig. 8.2).

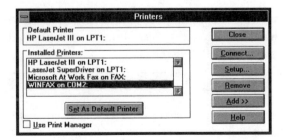

Tip

Distribute newsletters and marketing brochures by faxing directly from your desktop publishing software. This adds immediacy to these documents. Schedule transmissions after the phone rates go down.

Tip

If you can't find the option for changing printers (or if your application doesn't have one), change printers by clicking the Printers icon in the Windows Control Panel.

Fig. 8.1

Change printer drivers in the Printers dialog box.

Everyday Operation

Fig. 8.2

Adjust how
WinFax PRO sends
your fax in the
WinFax Driver
Setup dialog box.

In the WinFax Driver Setup dialog box, you can change the size of the page
that WinFax PRO sends, the page orientation, and the resolution at which it
sends your faxes. Read Chapter 4, "Configuring WinFax PRO," about using
the WinFax Driver Setup dialog box.

When you complete the WinFax Driver Setup dialog box, choose OK. Then
click the control menu box of the Printer dialog box (or the equivalent button in your application's printer setup dialog box).

You now can start the faxing process from your application. Choose **F**ile and,
in most applications, **P**rint. Many applications display a dialog box that con-
trols such elements as the number of copies and the range of pages you want
to print. Complete that dialog box as you would for any printing operation,
and click OK.

This process loads WinFax PRO and displays the Send dialog box (see fig. 8.3).
The Send dialog box is the WinFax PRO control center for sending faxes.

Most of this chapter is about using the various options in the Send dialog
box. Read the rest of this chapter to learn how to set up the various aspects of
sending faxes, such as scheduling the fax.

Caution

Remember to switch your printer driver back to your normal printer driver when you
finish sending your fax. If you don't, when you start to print a document, you start
the fax process instead.

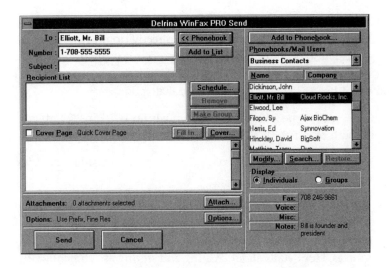

Fig. 8.3
The Send dialog
box is the control
center for sending
faxes.

Automatically Using the WinFax Driver

Some applications save you the trouble of switching printer drivers to send faxes. One way to do this is to use a special macro included with WinFax PRO for that particular application. The macro places a special menu option in the application for sending faxes. Also, some application vendors added similar capabilities so that you can simply click a menu option for sending faxes, instead of switching printer drivers.

WinFax PRO comes with macros for several popular applications such as Microsoft Word for Windows, Lotus Ami Pro, and leading spreadsheet programs. Typically, these macros add a special item in the File menu of these applications for WinFax PRO.

When you use these included macros, the macro automatically switches to the WinFax driver and starts WinFax PRO's fax transmission process. When WinFax PRO completes the transmission, the macro automatically switches the printer driver back to your normal driver.

Application vendors can add this capability directly to their programs so you don't even have to run a macro. Check with the vendor to see if this capability has been added to your application. Read Chapter 18, "Using WinFax PRO in Other Programs," to learn how to set up the macros that come with WinFax PRO.

II

Everyday Operation

Sending from WinFax PRO

In addition to being able to send your fax directly from within your application, you can also begin the transmission process directly from within WinFax PRO itself. To do this, click the Send button on the toolbar, or choose **S**end **F**ax. WinFax PRO displays the Send dialog box.

When you initiate the faxing process from within WinFax PRO, there are two options, both of which this chapter discusses in detail:

■ You can send only a cover page. This is good for sending brief fax messages.

■ You can assemble a fax from existing files, which WinFax PRO calls attachments. This chapter tells you how to add attachments to a fax before sending it. Read Chapter 12, "Assembling Faxes from Many Sources," for details about creating and storing attachments within WinFax PRO.

Whether you start the faxing process from an application or from within WinFax PRO, the processes from this point forward are virtually identical. The remainder of this chapter describes that process.

Troubleshooting

When I try to send a fax from my application, it prints on my printer.

Change the printer driver from your normal driver to the WinFax PRO driver. (An earlier section of this chapter describes the process.)

Selecting Recipients

As stated previously, the Send dialog box is the control center for sending faxes. It uses information collected from several other parts of WinFax PRO, including your system of phonebooks (discussed in detail in Chapter 6, "Using Phonebooks").

You obviously can't send a fax until you select recipients. If it is not already visible in the Send dialog box, display phonebook information by clicking the Phonebook button. The phonebook information appears on the right side of the Send dialog box (see fig. 8.4).

Fig. 8.4
Phonebook
information as it
appears in the
Send dialog box.

Using Phonebooks from the Send Dialog Box

From the Send dialog box, you can access most of the phonebook functions available in the Phonebooks application window. This section gives you a tour of the phonebook options available from the Send dialog box. Read Chapter 6, "Using Phonebooks," for details about creating and modifying phonebooks and phonebook entries.

The elements of the phonebook area of the Send dialog box are as follows:

■ The Add to Phonebook button enables you to add a phonebook entry to the phonebook you selected. Clicking the Add button displays the New Recipient dialog box for adding a phonebook record.

■ The Phonebooks/Mail Users drop-down list. Switch among phonebooks by using the Phonebooks/Mail Users drop-down list. Note that WinFax PRO automatically adds a phonebook called Mail Users, which you can access from this drop-down list only. This selection displays your electronic mail phonebook from your network electronic mail program. Read Chapter 10, "Using WinFax PRO for Electronic Mail," for more information about how to send and receive electronic mail.

■ The Name and Company list box. WinFax PRO displays the names and companies contained in the phonebook you select in this list box.

■ The Modify button displays the Modify Recipient dialog box. When you click this button, you can edit the phonebook record highlighted in the Name and Company list box.

■ The **S**earch button displays the Search dialog box so that you can search for specific records in the currently selected phonebook. WinFax PRO displays the records you find with this dialog box in the **N**ame and Compan**y** list box.

■ The Restore button restores the **N**ame and Company list box to its original state before you search for specific records. This button only becomes active after you conduct a search.

■ The Display area provides two buttons so that you can determine whether WinFax PRO displays individual names (**I**ndividuals) or phonebook groups (**G**roups) in the **N**ame and Compan**y** list box.

The bottom part of the phonebook area of the Send dialog box changes based on whether you view individuals or groups. When you view individuals, WinFax PRO displays four different items of information from that particular recipient's phonebook record.

To change the information WinFax PRO displays, position the mouse pointer directly over the item you want to change and click the left mouse button. WinFax PRO displays a menu listing all the information display options (see fig. 8.5).

Fig. 8.5
The menu for selecting information that appears
in the Send dialog
box.

Repeat the same process for all four items until WinFax PRO displays precisely the information you want.

If you display groups, the bottom part of the phonebooks area changes to a Members list box with all members of the group selected in the Groups list box.

> **Note**
>
> Although WinFax PRO displays group member names in the Members list box, you cannot select individual names from this box.

Selecting Individual Recipients

If you know the recipient's name and fax phone number, type them directly into the **T**o and N**u**mber text boxes in the upper left corner of the Send dialog box. If you don't know the recipient's name and fax phone number, follow these procedures:

1. In the P**h**onebooks/Mail Users drop-down list, select the phonebook from which you want to select recipients. The names and companies of the recipients in the phonebook you select appear in the **N**ame and Compan**y** list box below.

   > **Note**
   >
   > To display the names of individuals, make sure that you select the **I**ndividuals button below the **N**ame and Compan**y** list box.

2. Highlight the name in the **N**ame and Compan**y** list box by clicking it once. WinFax PRO displays the name and fax phone number in the upper left corner of the Send dialog box.

3. If the recipient is an electronic mail recipient, a drop-down list appears to the left of the **T**o text box in the Send dialog box. From the drop-down list, select from the following two options:

   - *To* enables the recipient to receive the fax normally.

   - *cc* sends a copy of the fax that you send to the To recipient. For copies, WinFax PRO doesn't change any variable information in the fax cover page to reflect the copy recipient.

4. Click the Add to **L**ist button at the top of the Send dialog box. This adds the recipient's name to the **R**ecipient List box.

5. Repeat the process until all the recipients you want are in the **R**ecipient List box.

II

Everyday Operation

Tip
To add recipients, you can double-click the recipient's name in the phonebook **N**ame and Company list box, or drag the name from the list box and drop it in the **R**ecipient List box.

In the **R**ecipient List box of the Send dialog box, WinFax PRO displays the recipient's name, the type of transmission, and the time when the transmission is scheduled (see fig. 8.6).

Selecting Groups

The process of selecting groups to receive your fax is similar to the process of selecting individuals to receive your fax:

1. At the bottom of the phonebook area of the Send dialog box, click the **G**roups button. WinFax PRO displays the names of all groups you create.

2. Click once on the group to which you want to send your message. Notice that WinFax PRO now displays the name of the group in the **T**o text box in the upper left corner of the Send dialog box.

3. Click the Add to **L**ist button. WinFax PRO adds the group to the **R**ecipient List box.

Fig. 8.6
The **R**ecipient List box displays the recipients of your message.

As with individual names, you can speed the process of adding groups to the **R**ecipient List in two ways: double-click the group name in the Groups list box, or drag it from the Groups list box to the **R**ecipient List box.

Managing the Recipient List

At any time before you send the fax, you can add, delete, or modify entries in the recipient list.

Tip
To remove multiple entries, highlight one entry, hold down the Ctrl key, and click more entries. This quickly removes entries from the **R**ecipient List box.

To delete an entry from the recipient list, highlight the entry by clicking it once. Then click the Remo**v**e button to the right of the **R**ecipient List box.

You also can use your mouse to drag the entry out of the recipient list and drop it anywhere else. As you drag the name out of the recipient list, notice that the mouse pointer turns into a garbage can. With the garbage can visible, release the mouse button. WinFax PRO eliminates the name from the recipient list. Note that this process does not remove the recipient's name from the phonebook.

To modify a recipient's information, click the entry once in the **R**ecipient List area. The recipient's name and phone number appear in the text boxes above the recipient list. You can change the spelling of the name, or, if the recipient receives electronic mail, whether he or she will receive an original message or a copy. Click Add to **L**ist to add the revised name to the recipient list, and remove the old entry from the list with the Remo**v**e button. Note that this does not change the original phonebook entry for the recipient.

You also can create a new phonebook group from entries in the **R**ecipient List area. To create a group from the recipient list, highlight the recipients you want, and then click the Ma**k**e Group button. In the Make Group dialog box that displays, type the name of the group. Then select the phonebook that you want the group to be included in and click OK. WinFax PRO adds the group to your phonebook system. Read Chapter 6, "Using Phonebooks," for more information about phonebook groups.

Tip

Creating a group from the **R**ecipient List is useful if you assemble many individual recipients and want to make the individuals a permanent group.

Everyday Operation

Troubleshooting

I searched for a name in my phonebook, but couldn't find it.

Remember that searches only explore the phonebook that you select in the **Ph**onebooks/Mail Users drop-down list. Chances are that you stored the recipient in another phonebook.

I sent the same fax to somebody twice, but didn't intend to.

You accidentally placed the recipient's name in the **R**ecipient List area twice. Or you may have added a recipient who also is part of a group to which you are sending a fax. These mistakes are relatively easy to make, particularly if you use the shortcut method of double-clicking names in the list box of the Phonebooks section of the Send dialog box. Before you send a fax, make sure the names in the recipient list are precisely the way you want them.

Adding a Subject

After you select recipients for your fax, type a subject for the fax in the Subject text box.

Typing a subject isn't mandatory, but it is helpful. You can use variables to automatically place the subject of the fax into the cover page, a process described in Chapter 7, "Creating and Managing Cover Pages." Also, you can search for archived faxes on the basis of subject. Finally, you can display the subject of the fax in the item display area window of the Send Log, as described in Chapter 11, "Using the Send and Receive Logs." This enables you to find faxes faster and to understand the nature of each item in the Send Log, Receive Log, or Outbox.

Scheduling and Modifying Faxes

By default, WinFax PRO sends the fax when you complete the Send dialog box and click Send. However, to schedule a fax for later transmission, click the Schedule button. WinFax PRO displays the Schedule/Modify Events dialog box (see fig. 8.7). In addition to scheduling faxes, this dialog box also enables you to change the method of fax transmission, change archival information such as keywords, or add a level of security to your fax transmission.

Fig. 8.7
Schedule transmissions and modify events in the Schedule/Modify Events dialog box.

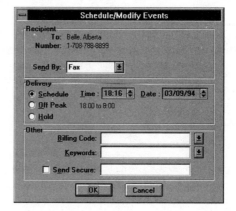

Scheduling Fax Transmissions

The Recipient List area designates recipients to whom you are immediately sending faxes with the word "Now." You can, however, schedule WinFax PRO to send faxes at a later time. This is useful for at least two reasons. You can:

- Save long distance charges by scheduling fax transmissions when phone rates are lowest.

- Schedule the transmission of non-urgent faxes later, so you don't tie up your fax modem. This is useful in either high-volume faxing situations or with networked fax modems.

After you add the individual and group recipients to the recipient list, highlight those that you want to schedule for a later transmission time and click the Schedule button. Fill in the Delivery area of the Schedule/Modify Events dialog box (see fig. 8.8).

Fig. 8.8
The Delivery area for scheduling faxes.

To schedule the transmission of a fax at a specific time, follow these steps:

1. Click the **S**chedule button.

2. In the **T**ime text box, enter a specific time of day that you want to transmit the fax. Either type the time in the text box, or use the up and down arrows to select a time.

3. Enter a transmission date in the **D**ate text box. Again, either type the date in the text box or use the up and down arrows to select a date.

To send a fax for transmission during off-peak hours, select the Off Peak button. Define specific off-peak hours in the User Setup dialog box, which you access by choosing Setu**p U**ser. Chapter 4, "Configuring WinFax PRO," discusses the User Setup dialog box in detail. Off-peak can mean anything you like, but typically, it refers either to when the phone rates go down, or when there is less faxing traffic to tie up modems or networks.

To hold the fax so you can schedule transmission for another time, select the **H**old button. Holding a fax is similar to scheduling a fax for later transmission. Both selections send the fax to the Outbox. However, WinFax PRO transmits faxes you schedule for later transmission; held faxes are not transmitted, and remain in the Outbox until you schedule them for transmission.

Changing the Transmission Method

Use the Schedule/Modify Events dialog box to change the method of transmission for selected recipients. Do this in the Recipient area of the dialog box (see fig. 8.9).

Say that normal faxing is the default transmission method for messages you send to a colleague in a branch office. If your colleague is away from the office, but carries a notebook computer, she can check for electronic mail messages. In that case, you would want to switch from a fax transmission to an electronic mail transmission.

Tip
Use the Hold option for time-sensitive faxes. For example, you can prepare a fax announcing a price change and hold it until you receive final approval for the change.

II

Everyday Operation

Fig. 8.9
Change the
method of
transmission in
the Recipient area.

Change the type of transmission with the Se**n**d By drop-down list in the
Recipient area of the Schedule/Modify Events dialog box.

> **Note**
>
> Changing the transmission method in the Schedule/Modify Events dialog box
> doesn't affect the default transmission method. It only affects the transmission for a
> single message.

Modifying and Securing the Fax Information

The Schedule/Modify Events dialog box also can be used to change or add
keywords or billing information, and to add security to the fax transmission.
Make changes or add keywords in the Other area of the dialog box (see
fig. 8.10).

Fig. 8.10
Change fax
information or
security in the
Other area of the
Schedule/Modify
Events dialog box.

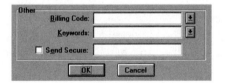

Add or modify billing code information directly in the **B**illing Code box.
To access billing codes that you previously used, click the down arrow.

Add or modify keywords for the fax directly in the **K**eywords box; you can
also click the down arrow to access other keywords you used.

You also can use the Schedule/Modify Events dialog box to add security to
the transmission process. Specifically, you can tell WinFax PRO to transmit
only if the receiving fax modem or fax machine has a specific station
identifier.

When two fax machines or fax modems connect, they exchange a wide variety of information about themselves and how they expect to transmit the
fax. (Read Chapter 2, "How WinFax PRO Works," for more details about
how the faxing process works.) Among the information the fax machines
exchange are their station identifiers.

Enter the station identifier you expect on the other end of the connection, in the Schedule/Modify Events dialog box. If the station identifier of the remote fax doesn't match the identifier number you provided, WinFax PRO tells your fax modem not to make the connection.

To select this capability, check the Send Secure check box. Type the remote fax machine's station identifier in the text box to the right.

After making all your changes to the Schedule/Modify Events dialog box, click OK.

Managing Scheduled and Held Faxes

When you schedule transmissions for a later date or hold faxes for later disposition, WinFax PRO sends them to the Outbox. In the Outbox, you can manage and modify pending faxes (see fig. 8.11).

Access the Outbox by clicking the Outbox button on the WinFax PRO toolbar, or by choosing Fax Outbox.

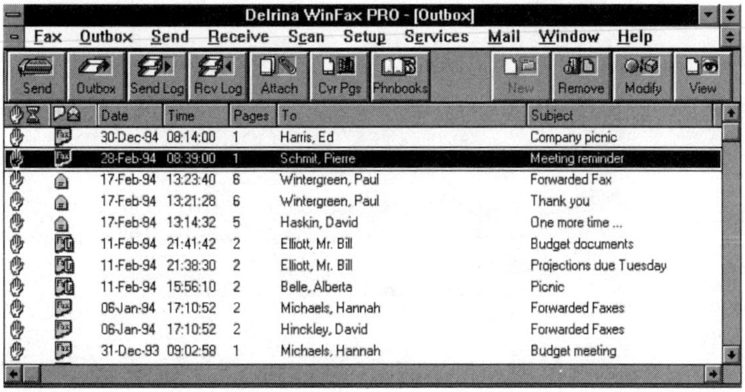

Tip

Use the Send Secure option when people move in their organization. Because workers often change fax machines when they change offices or duties, this option ensures that you send faxes only to the recipient's current machine.

Fig. 8.11
The Outbox is where WinFax PRO stores messages that it hasn't yet sent.

The Outbox is similar to other views, such as the Send Log or the Phonebooks view, with one exception: It doesn't have a folder list box. Folders are not relevant in the Outbox because they archive information. However, pending messages are only temporary; after you send them, they move to the Send Log.

Notice that in the Type column of the item list view, held faxes and scheduled faxes have different icons. Held faxes have a hand with an open palm; scheduled faxes have an hourglass icon.

II

Everyday Operation

Tip
Quickly access the options described in the following sections by high-lighting an item in the item list box of the Outbox and clicking the right mouse button. Select the option you want from the menu that appears.

You can manage held or scheduled faxes in several ways. The next few sections describe these management activities.

> **Note**
>
> You can customize the item list box and the item display area window of the Outbox. Read Chapter 5, "Customizing WinFax PRO," for more information about customizing WinFax PRO's views, including the Outbox.

Modifying Pending Fax Information

Modify basic information for held and scheduled faxes by selecting **O**utbox **M**odify. WinFax PRO displays the Modify Scheduled Event dialog box (see fig. 8.12).

Fig. 8.12
You can modify held or scheduled events in the Modify Scheduled Event dialog box.

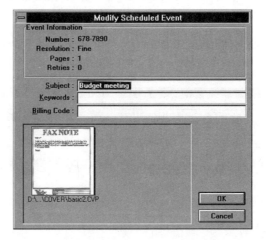

WinFax PRO displays basic information about the fax at the top of the Modify Scheduled Event dialog box. A thumbnail of the fax is also displayed at the bottom of the dialog box.

Add or modify the subject in the **S**ubject text box. Add or modify keywords in the **K**eywords text box. You also can add or modify billing information in the **B**illing Code text box. When you finish, click OK.

Holding, Releasing, and Sending Pending Faxes

Change the status of held or scheduled faxes by sending or deleting them. You also can schedule held faxes and hold scheduled faxes.

To delete a pending or scheduled message, choose **O**utbox **R**emove. A dialog box asks whether you are sure you want to eliminate the message. If you are sure, click Yes.

Release a held fax by highlighting it in the item list box of the Outbox and then selecting **O**utbox Re**l**ease. When you release a held fax, WinFax PRO sends it.

When WinFax PRO completes the transmission, it places the previously held fax in the Send Log. If you release a fax and cancel the transmission before completion, the fax goes to the Send Log as an uncompleted transmission. Read Chapter 11, "Using the Send and Receive Logs," to learn more about using the Send Log.

To change a held fax to a scheduled fax, to change the scheduled transmission time of a scheduled fax, or to hold a scheduled fax, highlight the fax in the item list box and select **O**utbox Res**c**hedule. WinFax PRO displays the Schedule dialog box (see fig. 8.13), which is similar to the Delivery area in the Schedule/Modify Events dialog box.

Fig. 8.13
The Schedule dialog box that you access from the Outbox enables you to change the message delivery schedule.

The three options in the Schedule dialog box are as follows:

- **S**chedule is for scheduling a fax for transmission at a specific time. Set the specific time in the **T**ime text box and the specific date in the **D**ate text box.

- **O**ff Peak tells WinFax PRO to send the fax during the next off-peak period, which you set up in the User Setup dialog box.

- **H**old puts the fax on hold and displays it in the Outbox.

Another method of converting a scheduled fax to a held fax is to highlight the scheduled fax and choose **O**utbox **H**old. This method eliminates any scheduling and places the fax in the Outbox as a held fax. To convert all scheduled faxes to held faxes, choose **O**utbox **H**old All.

Changing the Recipient

To change the recipient of a pending fax, choose **O**utbox Change **D**estination. WinFax PRO displays the Change Destination dialog box (see fig. 8.14).

Fig. 8.14

Change the recipient of pending faxes with the Change Destination dialog box.

Type the new recipient's name in the **T**o text box and the new recipient's number in the Nu**m**ber text box. If you are not sure of the name or number, click the **S**elect button. WinFax PRO displays the Select Recipient dialog box (see fig. 8.15).

Fig. 8.15

Change the recipient for held or scheduled faxes in the Select Recipient dialog box.

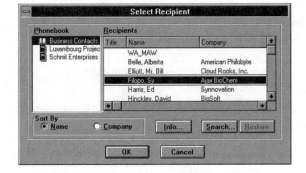

In the Select Recipient dialog box, WinFax PRO displays phonebooks and groups in the **P**honebook list area. Recipients are displayed in the R**e**cipients area.

In the Sort By area of the dialog box, select the **N**ame button to sort the Re-cipients area by name, or select the **C**ompany button to sort by company. To view information about a highlighted recipient, click the **I**nfo button. WinFax PRO displays the Information dialog box, which contains all phonebook information about the recipient.

To search for specific recipients, click the **S**earch button. WinFax PRO dis-plays the Search dialog box, which is like an empty New Recipient dialog box used for creating a new phonebook record. Chapter 6, "Using Phonebooks," describes how to use the New Recipient dialog box for creating new phonebook records.

Fill in the information for which you are searching in the appropriate areas of the Search dialog box. When you finish, click OK. WinFax PRO places all the recipients it finds in the Recipients list area of the Select Recipient dialog box. Select a single recipient and click OK to return to the Change Destination dialog box. To change the recipient of the message, click OK in the Change Destination dialog box.

Viewing and Annotating Pending Faxes

As with faxes in the Send Log and Receive Log, you can view faxes from the Outbox to review their contents. When you do this, WinFax PRO loads the View window.

Reviewing contents is a common use of the View window; it also is relatively simple. The View window includes tools for annotating faxes, which is useful when you have to comment on a fax and return it or forward it to another recipient. You can add text in any font supported by your Windows configuration, and also add graphic images.

To view a fax, double-click it in the item list box of the Outbox. You also can click the right mouse button on the item and choose **V**iew from the menu that appears. WinFax PRO displays the fax in the Viewer window (see fig. 8.16).

Tip

You can hold faxes till approval or last-minute changes. Annotate faxes in the View window to make last-minute changes, or show changes to recipients.

Fig. 8.16
View pending faxes in the Viewer window.

Read Chapter 14, "Viewing and Annotating Faxes," for details about how to use the tools of the View window.

Filtering the Outbox

You can change the fax events that WinFax PRO displays in the item list box. Choose **O**utbox **F**ilter. WinFax PRO displays the Filter Scheduled Events dialog box (see fig. 8.17).

Select the **S**cheduled check box to have WinFax PRO display scheduled faxes. Select the **H**eld check box to display all held faxes.

Fig. 8.17
The Filter Scheduled Events dialog box is for controlling the contents of the Outbox.

The Show **G**roups check box tells WinFax PRO how to display held or scheduled group fax transmissions. If you check the Show **G**roups check box, WinFax PRO shows the held or scheduled group transmission in a single line in the item list box. If you don't check this option, WinFax PRO displays all members of the group as separate recipients in the item list box.

The advantage of showing groups is that it takes up less space in the Outbox. The advantage of showing the individual faxes within a group is that you can act on them as individual faxes. In other words, you can break individual faxes out of their group and send, delete, or modify them.

After you set the filter options you want, choose OK.

Troubleshooting

I accidentally released a held fax. Before the transmission started, I canceled it, but the event disappeared from the Outbox. How do I get it back?

WinFax PRO placed the fax in the Send Log. To move it back to the Outbox, switch to the Send Log, highlight the fax in the Send Log, right-click, and choose Resubmit. WinFax PRO displays the Send dialog box. Click Schedule and select the Hold button and choose OK. Finally, click the Send button at the bottom of the dialog box. WinFax PRO places the fax in the Scheduled Events view.

Using Cover Pages

A cover page is the first page sent when you transmit a fax. Cover pages aren't mandatory, but they often provide important information regarding the fax. For example, cover pages typically state who the fax is to, who it is from, the subject of the fax, and the total number of pages. You also can add brief messages to a cover page.

Chapter 7, "Creating and Managing Cover Pages," tells you how to create and manage WinFax PRO cover pages. This section tells you how to affix cover pages to faxes you send from the Send dialog box. As with phonebook functions, you can manage and even edit cover pages from the Send dialog box.

Adding and Selecting a Cover Page

To add a cover page to your fax, select the Cover **P**age check box in the Send dialog box. Until you tell it otherwise, WinFax PRO uses the cover page you designated as the default page. Chapter 7, "Creating and Managing Cover Pages," tells you how to designate a cover page as the default cover page.

To use a cover page other than the default, click the **C**over button. WinFax PRO displays the Select Cover Page dialog box (see fig. 8.18).

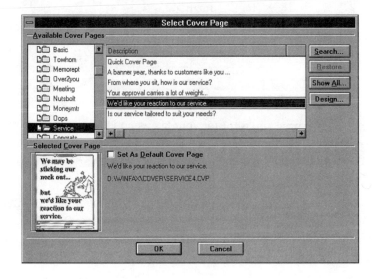

Fig. 8.18
Pick a cover page for your fax in the Select Cover Page dialog box.

II

Everyday Operation

In the left corner of the **A**vailable Cover Pages area, WinFax PRO displays your cover page folders. In the window to the right of the folder list box, WinFax PRO displays the description and file names of cover pages in the selected folder.

In the Selected **C**over Page area at the bottom of the dialog box, WinFax PRO displays both a thumbnail of the cover page and information about the cover page.

To view thumbnails of all the cover pages in the folder, click the Show **A**ll button. WinFax PRO displays thumbnails of all the cover pages in the Cover Page Thumbnails window (see fig. 8.19).

Fig. 8.19
The Cover Page Thumbnails window shows all the cover pages in the selected folder.

To select the cover page you want for your fax when viewing the All Cover Pages window, double-click it. To select a cover page from the Select Cover Page dialog box, highlight it in the item list box and click OK. Either way, you will return to the Send dialog box.

To designate a cover page as the default cover page, highlight it in the item list box of the Select Cover Page dialog box. Select the Set As **D**efault Cover Page check box and click OK. WinFax PRO differentiates the default cover page in the item list box by coloring it blue.

You can change the cover page for your fax at any time until you send the fax from the Send dialog box. You cannot, however, change the cover page after you schedule or hold a fax; nor can you change the cover page when you resend or forward faxes from the Send or Receive Logs.

Caution

When changing cover pages, be careful about switching from a cover page with text fill-in sections to a cover page without text fill-in sections. WinFax PRO transfers any message you write in the fill-in area to the other cover page—only if the other cover page has a fill-in section. If the other cover page doesn't include a fill-in section, you will lose your message.

Searching for Cover Pages

WinFax PRO enables you to find a cover page if you know at least some of the contents of its description. To search for a cover page by description follow these steps:

1. Click the **S**earch button in the Select Cover Page dialog box. WinFax PRO displays the Search Cover Pages dialog box (see fig. 8.20).

Fig. 8.20
The Search Cover Pages dialog box.

2. Type as much of the cover page description as you can in the **D**escription text box.

3. Select the **C**ase Sensitive check box if you want WinFax PRO to search for the description with the precise combination of upper- and lower-case letters you typed in the **D**escription text box.

4. Click OK.

WinFax PRO searches for cover pages that match the description you entered. WinFax Pro lists the found cover pages in the Description list area of the Select Cover Page dialog box.

To eliminate the list of found cover pages and restore the normal list of cover pages for the selected folder, click the **R**estore button.

Filling In Cover Pages

There are two ways to fill in your cover page. If the cover page has a text fill-in field, WinFax PRO displays a text fill-in area beneath the **C**over Page check box. If your cover page uses variable fields and you only need to write a note to the fax recipient, it is easier to use this text fill-in area.

> **Note**
>
> If the cover page you selected does not include a text fill-in field, WinFax PRO does not display the fill-in area in the Send dialog box.

If you want to type your note directly into the cover page, click the **F**ill In button in the Send dialog box. WinFax PRO displays the Cover Page Filler window (see fig. 8.21) in which you can type directly into any text fields in the cover page.

Fig. 8.21

Fill in your cover page in the Cover Page Filler window.

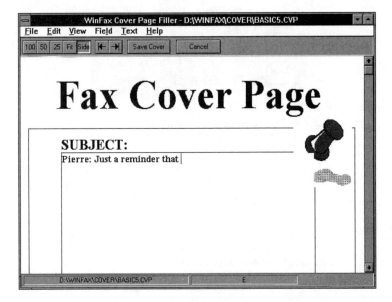

The Cover Page Filler provides a number of features to help you edit your cover page message. Editing options include cutting and pasting, the ability to change fonts, and a spell-checker. It does not have drawing annotation tools, or the ability to add graphics.

The Cover Page Filler toolbar (see fig. 8.22) makes several of the options quickly available—particularly the options for scaling the view of the cover page. It also includes arrows to go to the next or previous fill-in area and for saving the cover page after you fill it in.

Fig. 8.22
The Cover Page Filler toolbar provides tools for viewing and navigating cover pages as you fill them in.

Access the rest of the options in the Cover Page Filler's menus. Table 8.1 lists some of the key features of the Cover Page Filler, the location of the features in the menus, and a description of what the features can do. Because Cover Page Filler is a subset of features described previously in the Cover Page Designer, the following table is not exhaustive; rather, it lists key capabilities available to you in the Cover Page Filler.

Table 8.1   Menu Options in the Cover Page Filler.

Option	Menu Location	Description
Send Fax	**F**ile	Saves the changes you made to the cover page for use with your fax and returns to the Send dialog box.
Cancel	**E**dit	Cancel fill-in and return to Send dialog box.
Cu**t**	**E**dit	Cuts highlighted text and places it in clipboard.
Copy	**E**dit	Copies highlighted text and places it in clipboard.
Paste	**E**dit	Pastes contents of clipboard to current cursor location.
Delete	**E**dit	Removes highlighted text.
100%	**V**iew	Shows cover page at full size.
50%	**V**iew	Shows the cover page at 50% its normal size.
Fit in Window	**V**iew	Fits the entire cover page in the Cover Page Filler window.
F**i**t Sides	**V**iew	Sizes the cover page so that it fits the entire Cover Page Filler window horizontally.

(continues)

II

Everyday Operation

	Menu	
Option	Location	Description
Show Graphics	**V**iew	Displays all graphics that are part of the cover page.
F**a**st Display	**V**iew	Speeds up display by not showing graphics.
First Field	Fie**l**d	Moves the insertion point to the first field in the cover page.
Last Field	Fie**l**d	Moves the insertion point to the last field in the cover page.
Left Justify	**T**ext	Left-justifies selected text.
Bold	**T**ext	Boldfaces selected text.
Font	**T**ext	Leads to the Font dialog box for changing font of the filled-in message.
Spelling	**T**ext	Spell-checks filled in text.

Table 8.1 Continued

Using a Quick Cover Page

WinFax PRO makes available what it calls quick cover pages to speed the process of sending faxes. A quick cover page is faster to send because it is simpler than a normal cover page. A quick cover page has just six fields (To, From, Subject, Pages, Time, Date), which are not changeable. Also, it doesn't include graphic images, which take longer to change into a fax image and transmit.

Chapter 7, "Creating and Managing Cover Pages," describes quick cover pages and how to designate them as a default cover page. You can always switch to a quick cover page, and even designate it as a default cover page, from the Send Fax window.

To use a quick cover page from the Send Fax window, click the **C**over button. In the Select Cover Page dialog box, select Quick Cover Page from the Description list box and click OK. Each cover page folder includes the Quick Cover Page option. Designate the quick cover page as the default by checking the Set as **D**efault Cover Page check box.

Adding Attachments

Attachments are files that you add to faxes. When you send a fax, WinFax
PRO incorporates the contents of the file into the fax. For example, you can
attach the word processing file of an old memo to provide background information for a new fax. When you send a message using electronic mail or a
transmission such as BFT, WinFax PRO sends the attachment as a computer
file. Read Chapter 10, "Using WinFax PRO with Electronic Mail" and Chapter
16, "Other Ways to Send and Receive," for more information about those
options.

Chapter 12, "Assembling Faxes from Many Sources," describes attachments
and the Attachments view in detail. The following section tells you how to
find and view attachments from the Send dialog box and how to add them to
faxes.

Finding, Viewing, and Using Attachments

Add attachments to faxes from the Send dialog box by clicking the
Attach button. WinFax PRO displays the Select Attachments dialog box
(see fig. 8.23).

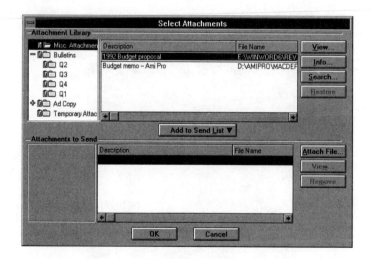

Fig. 8.23
Add attachments
to your faxes from
the Select Attach-
ments dialog box.

The top half of the dialog box, the Attachment Library area, displays all the
attachments you created. The far left window displays your attachment folders, and the list box to the right lists the attachments in the folder you select.

Tip
Annotate faxes to emphasize important topics with an arrow or a comment you add to the fax, particularly with attachments of older documents used as background information for newer documents.

To view the attachment, click the **V**iew button. If the attachment is a fax, WinFax PRO displays the fax in the Viewer window. Alter and annotate the fax attachment in the Viewer window as you would annotate any fax in the Send or Receive Logs or Outbox. Read Chapter 14, "Viewing and Annotating Faxes," for information about annotating faxes.

If the attachment is a binary file—or a file you create with another program—and you click **V**iew, WinFax PRO tries to load that program and then the specific file listed as an attachment.

However, WinFax PRO only does this if the type of file you selected has a Windows association with a specific application. For example, when you install the Word for Windows word processor, that program's installation tells Windows to associate files with the DOC file extension with Word for Windows. Then, when programs like WinFax PRO load a file with the DOC file extension, Windows knows to automatically load Word for Windows.

If an association does not exist for the file you are trying to view, WinFax PRO cannot load it. Also, WinFax PRO won't be able to attach that file to your fax. Read your Microsoft Windows user's guide or Que's *Using Windows 3.1* to learn how to create associations.

For information about the attachment, click **I**nfo. WinFax PRO displays the Attachment Information message box (see fig. 8.24).

Fig. 8.24
View information about an attachment in the Attachment Information message box.

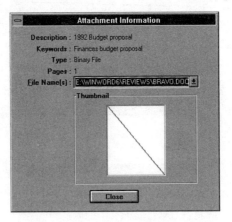

The Attachment Information message box lists basic information about the attachment, such as its file name and description, and a thumbnail of the attachment if it is a fax. If the attachment is another kind of file, like a binary file, the thumbnail window is blank except for a diagonal line through it.

To search for attachments in the folder you selected in the folder list box, click the **S**earch button. WinFax PRO displays the Search Attachments dialog box (see fig. 8.25).

Fig. 8.25
Find attachments with the Search Attachments dialog box.

Type the description for the attachment in the **D**escription text box. Type keywords in the **K**eywords text box and type a file name for the attachment in the **F**ile Name text box. You need not fill in all the text boxes. You can search by typing information in only one of the text boxes.

Select the **C**ase Sensitive check box if you want WinFax PRO to search for information with precisely the combination of lower- and uppercase letters that you typed in the text box. Select the **M**atch Anywhere check box to find information even if you typed only partial information about the attachment in the text boxes.

Tip
The **M**atch Anywhere option helps if you aren't certain about information in the text boxes. If the attachment description is "Fax to Joe," type "Joe" in the **D**escription text box to find it.

> ### Caution
>
> The search dialog box does not accept wild cards such as the asterisk (*). This means that you can't search for all attachment files with the DOC file extension by typing ***.DOC** in the **F**ile Name text box. Instead, simply type **DOC** in the text box.

WinFax PRO displays found attachments in the item list box of the Select Attachments dialog box. You can view those attachments, examine information about them, or attach them to the fax. To restore the normal item list box for the selected folder, click **R**estore.

To use an attachment, highlight it in the list box of the Attachment Library area of the Select Attachments dialog box, and then click the Add to Send **L**ist button. The attachments appear in the list box at the bottom of the Select Attachments dialog box, in the Attachments to Send area.

To view the attachment you selected, click the **V**iew button. To remove the attachment from the item list box, click **R**emove. When you finish designating attachments, click OK.

Last-Minute Attachments

You can add an attachment from the Select Attachments dialog box, even if it isn't in your system of attachment folders. This enables you to add attachments at the last minute without using the Attachments window.

To add an attachment, follow these steps:

1. Click the **A**ttach File button. WinFax PRO displays the Select Attachment Files dialog box (see fig. 8.26).

Fig. 8.26
Select more attachments from the Select Attachment Files dialog box.

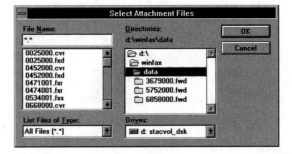

2. Select the drive in which you store the file in the Dri**v**es drop down list.

3. Select the directory in which you store the file in the **D**irectories list box.

4. Select the specific file you want to attach in the File **N**ame list box. Click the file you want to add.

5. Click OK. The file you selected appears in the list box of the Attachments to send Area of the Select Attachments dialog box.

After you select the files you want as attachments, click OK at the bottom of the Select Attachments dialog box. If an attachment already was a fax image, WinFax PRO adds it to the fax. If the attachment was a binary file and you are sending a fax, WinFax PRO turns it into a fax image when you actually send the fax. If you are using any other method of transmission, WinFax PRO sends the file as a binary file without first turning it into a fax.

Creating Attachments from Application Files

You can create attachments in WinFax PRO directly from other applications by creating a document and starting the fax transmission process. When WinFax PRO displays the Send dialog box, however, instead of adding recipients, a cover page, and attachments, click the **M**ake Attachment button at the bottom of the dialog box. WinFax PRO displays the Create Attachment dialog box (see fig. 8.27).

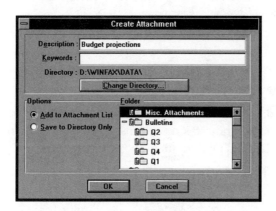

Fig. 8.27
Add attachments in the Create Attachment dialog box.

At the top of the Save to File dialog box are the **D**escription and **K**eywords text boxes. In these text boxes, enter any information you want for the attachment.

To change the directory in which WinFax PRO stores the attachment, click the **C**hange Directory button. WinFax PRO displays the Directories dialog box. In this familiar-looking dialog box, select the drive and directory in which you want to store the attachment in the Dri**v**es drop-down list and the **D**irectories list box. After you finish, click OK.

At the bottom of the Create Attachment dialog box, select the **A**dd to Attachment List button to add the attachment to a specific folder. Select the folder in the **F**older list box to the right. Otherwise, WinFax PRO adds the attachment to the currently selected folder. Select the **S**ave to Directory Only button to save the attachment but not place it in a folder.

When you finish, click OK. WinFax PRO acts momentarily as if it is starting to send the fax, but it actually creates an image of the file and stores it as an attachment.

II

Everyday Operation

Troubleshooting

WinFax PRO didn't send an attachment that I made to a fax.

Chances are that the attachment was a binary file and that there is no Windows association for that file. Associations tell Windows and applications, such as WinFax PRO, about the application that created the file. If no association exists, you cannot view or send the attachment. Read the Microsoft Windows user's guide for more information about associations and how to create them.

Setting Send Options

There is only one more stop in the Send dialog box before you actually send the fax. To change various faxing options, click the **O**ptions button. WinFax PRO displays the Send Options dialog box (see fig. 8.28).

Fig. 8.28
Change various options in the Send Options dialog box.

Tip
The Use **P**refix setting is handy when you visit a customer and want to send a fax. If the customer's organization requires a special dial prefix, use this option so you won't have to change your defaults.

Any options you set in the Send Options dialog box apply only to the current fax transmission. To change options permanently, use the various setup options available from the Setu**p** menu. Read Chapter 4, "Configuring WinFax PRO," for information about setting up WinFax PRO options.

The options available in the Send Options dialog box are as follows:

■ Use **P**refix for adding a special dial prefix to get an outside line for sending the fax. Type the dial prefix in the text box, or use the drop-down list to access dial prefixes you previously used.

- Preview/Annotate tells WinFax PRO that you want to view the fax in the Viewer before you send it. This enables you to make last minute annotations to the fax. When you close the viewer, WinFax PRO asks if you would like to send the fax. To send the fax, click OK. Read Chapter 14, "Viewing and Annotating Faxes," for information about annotating faxes.

- Send Failed Pages Only sends pages of failed fax transmissions that WinFax PRO did not successfully send. For example, if you try to send a ten page fax and the connection broke after WinFax PRO sent eight pages, selecting this option sends the remaining two pages only.

- Delete Pages After Send deletes the fax file after you send it. This is useful if you send the same fax to many recipients and don't want all the different faxes to fill up your hard disk.

- Registered Receipt (Mail) is for sending electronic mail messages. If you check this option, your electronic mail system notifies you when the recipient reads the message you send. Read Chapter 10, "Using WinFax PRO for Electronic Mail," for more information about this subject.

The Broadcast area is only available if you are using the special Delrina service: Fax Broadcast. Chapter 16, "Different Ways to Send and Receive" describes this services.

To adjust Microsoft At Work settings, click the **At** Work button. Read Chapter 16, "Different Ways to Send and Receive," for information about MS At Work.

Sending the Fax

To review the broad steps of sending faxes, follow these steps:

1. Set up WinFax PRO correctly. Chapter 4, "Configuring WinFax PRO," discusses setting up WinFax PRO to work correctly in your situation.

2. Create your message either in another application or in a WinFax PRO cover page.

3. Select recipients for your fax by clicking on them and then clicking Add to List. Or drag recipient names from the **N**ame and Compan**y** list box to the **R**ecipient List box.

4. Add a subject to the fax in the Subject text box.

5. If necessary, schedule the fax for later transmission or hold it until you are ready to send it. Do that by clicking the Schedule button. This displays the Schedule/Modify Events dialog box.

Tip
Use WinFax PRO
to send out notices
of special sale
offers of a brief
duration. The
immediacy of
faxes makes
WinFax PRO
particularly useful
for this sort of
application.

6. Select and add a cover page. by clicking Cover. Fill in the cover page if necessary, either in the fill-in text box or by clicking Fill In. This displays the Cover Page Filler

7. Add any attachments to the fax by clicking Attach. This displays the Select Attachments dialog box.

8. Fine-tune sending options in the Send Options dialog box. This displays the Send Options dialog box.

When you complete these steps, you are ready for the final step: Click the Send button in the Send dialog box. WinFax PRO then begins the process of actually sending the fax.

Monitoring and Stopping Faxes

During the transmission process, WinFax PRO displays the WinFax PRO Status dialog box (see fig. 8.29), which displays the status of the call.

Fig. 8.29
The WinFax PRO Status information box displays up-to-date information about the transmission.

The status message box provides the following information:

■ *Operation* describes what the fax modem is doing at the present moment. To better understand the fax transmission process and some of the messages WinFax PRO displays in this line, read Chapter 2, "How WinFax PRO Works."

■ *Identifier* lists the station identifier of the recipient's fax machine or fax modem.

■ *Current Page* lists how much of the current page WinFax PRO has transmitted.

- *Destination* lists the recipient's name.

- *Fax Number* lists the recipient's fax number.

- *Page* lists the current page number and the total number of pages in the transmission.

- *Speed* lists the transmission speed of the fax in bits per second (bps).

Note

Do not be alarmed if the transmission speed is less than the maximum speed specified for your modem. As described in Chapter 2, "How WinFax PRO Works," fax devices can slow down the transmission speed if the line is not completely clear of interference. Also, the receiving fax machine may not be able to handle the speeds at which your fax modem can operate. In such cases, most fax modems automatically reduce their speed to match the speed of the slower device.

At any time during the transmission process you can end the transmission by clicking the Cancel button at the bottom of the WinFax PRO Status message box. When you do this, the transmission appears in the Send Log as an unsent message.

The Send Log

After you send a fax, WinFax PRO stores information about it in the Send Log (see fig. 8.30). As discussed in Chapter 3, "Starting and Navigating WinFax PRO," the Send Log has three windows:

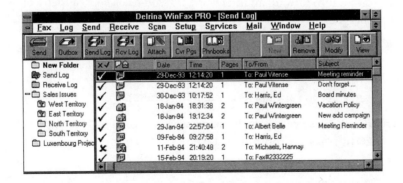

Fig. 8.30
The Send Log.

- The folder list box, which displays folders in which you can store sent faxes.

■ The item list box, which lists sent faxes and information about the faxes.

■ The item display area window, which provides additional information about the faxes.

The Send Log works in conjunction with the Receive Log in that you can create a series of folders in which you can store either sent or received faxes. The Send Log serves as a hub for managing sent faxes and also is the place from which you can initiate a variety of actions. Among these actions are resending or forwarding faxes, which the next section discusses. Read Chapter 11, "Using the Send and Receive Logs," for more information about managing sent faxes in the Send Log.

> **Note**
>
> While this chapter is specifically about sending faxes, the Send Log also stores information about other kinds of messages, such as electronic mail messages, that you can send using WinFax PRO.

Resending and Forwarding Messages

You can either resend faxes you previously sent or forward faxes you have received to new recipients. This is useful in several circumstances:

■ You want to resend a fax that WinFax PRO did not successfully transmit.

■ You want to forward an interesting fax you received to a friend or colleague.

■ The recipient lost the fax you originally sent him or her and asks you to resend it.

To forward a fax you already received, follow these steps:

1. With the Receive Log as the active view, choose **L**og For**w**ard. WinFax PRO displays the Forward dialog box.

2. In the Forward dialog box, WinFax PRO displays thumbnails of all the pages in the fax.

3. To forward all pages, select the All **P**ages check box.

4. To forward only selected pages, deactivate the All **P**ages check box. Hold down the Ctrl key and click the thumbnail image of each page

you want to send. When you have selected a page, a line appears around the thumbnail image.

5. In the After Forward/Route area of the dialog box:

- Select the **K**eep Event button to keep the message, all related files, and the notation of the message in the Receive Log.

- Select the Delete **I**mage Files (Keep Event) button to delete the message file but keep the event in the Receive Log.

- Select the Dele**t**e Event and Image Files button to delete both the files and the notation of the message in your Receive Log.

When you finish the Forward dialog box, click OK. WinFax PRO then displays the Send dialog box, from which you can select the recipients to whom you want to forward the fax.

Read Chapter 11, "Using the Send and Receive Logs," for more information about using the Send Log and Receive Log.

Note

Forwarding faxes in this case merely sends an existing fax to somebody else. This is different from *automatic forwarding*, which involves setting up WinFax PRO to automatically send incoming faxes to a pre-specified fax device. For more about automatic forwarding, read Chapter 17, "WinFax PRO Away from the Office."

Resubmitting messages you already sent is a similar process: From the Send Log, choose **L**og Res**u**bmit, or click the right mouse button and choose Resubmit. WinFax PRO displays the Send dialog box. To immediately resubmit the message, click Send. You also can add recipients, add a new cover sheet or edit the old cover sheet if it has text fill-in areas. After you complete the Send dialog box, click Send to resubmit your fax.

Note

You also can set WinFax PRO to automatically resend faxes if the transmission fails because of a bad connection or other technical problem. As discussed in Chapter 4, "Configuring WinFax PRO," do this in the Fax/Modem Setup dialog box, which you access by selecting Setu**p** **F**ax/Modem. Select the number of times you want WinFax PRO to try resending the fax Di**a**l Retries text box and the time (in seconds) between retries in the **R**etry Every text box.

Troubleshooting

I did everything described in this chapter, but I still can't connect with the other fax machine.

Chances are that the problem is with your WinFax PRO configuration. Read Chapter 4, "Configuring WinFax PRO," about setting up WinFax PRO. Pay particular attention to the section on setting up your modem. Most likely, you need to select another modem type or adjust your initialization or reset strings. There also is a small chance that the receiving modem is an old-fashioned modem with which WinFax PRO can't communicate. Read Chapter 2, "How WinFax PRO Works," to learn more about the different types of standard fax machines.

I sent a fax to a group. When I finished, a fax for one of the recipients appeared in the Send Log with a red X, indicating that WinFax PRO did not successfully send it.

Few people watch the entire transmission process. Chances are that the recipient's fax number changed or you had some other error in the phonebook. Or, if you used the Secure Send option, his or her remote station identifier may have changed. Check with the recipient for the correct number and station identifier.

When I transmit faxes from my word processor, I also send a page of information about the word processing file. Where does this come from and how can I stop it?

Many word processors enable you to print summary information about the file at the same time you print the file itself. Because faxing with WinFax PRO is essentially a printing operation, WinFax PRO unwittingly includes this information page with the fax if that is how you set your word processor. Read your word processor's documentation to learn how to print without the page of summary information.

From Here...

This chapter taught you all the steps necessary to send a fax message. For even more information, read the following chapters:

- Chapter 9, "Receiving Faxes," tells you what to do to prepare to receive faxes.

- Chapter 10, "Using WinFax PRO for Electronic Mail," gives you specifics about using WinFax PRO to send and receive electronic mail messages.

- Chapter 11, "Using the Send and Receive Logs," provides in-depth information about how to manage messages you send and receive.

■ Chapter 16, "Different Ways to Send and Receive," discusses WinFax PRO's other transmission methods, such as the ability to transfer binary files and to use the Microsoft At Work series of protocols.

■ Chapter 17, "WinFax PRO Away from the Office," tells you how to shape WinFax PRO to work efficiently when you take it on the road.

II

Everyday Operation

Chapter 9

Receiving Faxes

In this chapter, you learn how to do the following:

- Set up WinFax PRO to receive faxes automatically.

- Use WinFax PRO to manually receive faxes.

- Automatically receive notice of received faxes.

- Automatically print received faxes.

- Convert fax images into text you can edit.

As you learned in Chapter 8, "Sending Faxes," sending faxes is a multistep task. In contrast, receiving faxes is much simpler. Even though actually receiving faxes is an easy process, WinFax PRO gives you many options during the fax reception and enables you to determine what it does with the faxes when it receives them.

Chapter 4, "Configuring WinFax PRO," provided general details about setting up WinFax PRO to receive faxes. This chapter goes into more depth about receiving faxes, and what you can do with faxes immediately after receipt.

Getting Ready to Receive Faxes

Previous chapters discussed how the faxing process works and how to get ready to receive faxes. To summarize, the steps in receiving a fax are as follows:

1. *Install WinFax PRO.* Chapter 1, "Installing WinFax PRO," told you how.

2. *Install your fax modem properly and switch it on.* Read your fax modem documentation to learn how.

3. *Load WinFax PRO.* Do that by double-clicking the WinFax PRO icon in Program Manager or by loading Windows with the command **WIN C:\WINFAX\FAXMNG.EXE**. Change this last command as appropriate if you installed WinFax PRO on a different drive and directory.

4. *Set options relating to WinFax PRO and receiving faxes.* Chapter 4, "Configuring WinFax PRO," told you how to do that. This chapter provides more details.

One setup option determines whether WinFax PRO receives faxes automatically or whether you must start the process manually. If you decide to automatically receive faxes, WinFax PRO automatically initializes the fax modem when you load the program. After the brief initialization process (described in Chapter 2, "How WinFax PRO Works"), WinFax PRO receives the faxes without your intervention.

Tip
To use a program such as a general communications program when automatic reception is active, choose **R**eceive **A**utomatic Receive. This deactivates automatic reception. Choose the same menu option again to reactivate.

> **Caution**
>
> If you activate automatic reception, WinFax PRO prevents other programs—such as a general communications program you use for logging on to bulleting—from using your communications port.

If you decide to manually receive faxes, WinFax PRO only receives faxes when you tell it to. In that case, when you hear the telephone ring and know it is a fax call, choose **R**eceive **M**anual Receive Now. WinFax PRO goes through the initialization process and then begins to receive the fax.

If you don't select automatic reception and somebody tries to send you a fax, WinFax PRO won't start the fax reception process until you choose **R**eceive **M**anual Receive Now.

To set WinFax PRO to automatically receive faxes, choose Setu**p** **R**eceive. WinFax PRO displays the Receive Setup dialog box (see fig. 9.1).

> **Note**
>
> You use the Receive Setup dialog box for several setup options discussed in this chapter.

When you select the **A**utomatic Reception check box in the Receive Setup dialog box, WinFax PRO automatically answers the phone and starts receiving the call.

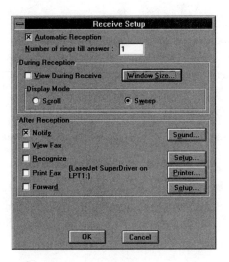

You also must determine how many times the phone rings before WinFax PRO answers the call and starts the receiving process. Type the number of rings in the **N**umber of Rings Till Answer text box. The default is one ring.

What Happens During Reception

Chapter 2, "How WinFax PRO Works," discussed the faxing process. To briefly review:

1. The sending fax machine (or fax program like WinFax PRO) converts the document to a graphical image composed of a series of dots. This process is called *rasterization*.

2. The sending fax device dials the receiving fax device. The receiving device can be either a fax modem or a normal fax machine.

3. The two fax machines communicate with a series of tones to determine how the sending device sends and the receiving device receives the fax.

4. The sending device starts sending the fax image, one page at a time.

5. The receiving device reassembles the fax image into a graphic image.

6. The sending device tells the receiving machine that it is finished. The two devices then end the connection and hang up.

Tip

If you select automatic reception, AUTO RCV appears in the status bar. The status bar doesn't tell you, however, when automatic reception is not selected.

Tip

If you use the same phone line for voice and fax, use manual reception. If you use automatic reception, your voice callers hear the fax tone.

II

Everyday Operation

After receiving a fax, WinFax PRO saves it as an image file. WinFax PRO initially places that fax in your Receive Log, where you can place it in any folder in your log window. Read Chapter 11, "Using the Send and Receive Logs," to learn more about using your Send Log and Receive Log for archiving and retrieving previously received faxes.

This process is simple enough. But WinFax PRO also gives you many options about what happens during the reception process and immediately afterward. The next several sections review those options.

Monitoring the Progress of Received Faxes

You may find it useful to monitor the progress of incoming faxes so that you know how far along the process is and whether WinFax PRO encounters any problems during the reception process.

To view the progress of incoming faxes, choose Setu**p P**rogram. In the Program Setup dialog box, select the Displa**y** Call Progress check box. Then click OK.

When you select this option, WinFax PRO displays a status message box whenever it receives a fax (see fig. 9.2).

Fig. 9.2
WinFax PRO
displays the status
of incoming calls.

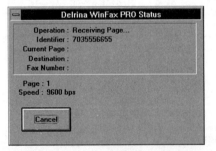

> **Note**
>
> The Display Call Progress setting also pertains to viewing the progress of faxes you send. In fact, WinFax PRO uses a nearly identical message box when it sends and when it receives faxes.

The elements of the Status box are as follows:

- *Operation* describes the current part of the reception process. For example, when the fax devices begin the process of connecting, the word Training appears in the Operation line. As WinFax PRO receives the fax, the information in this line says Receiving, and may describe more specifically what it is receiving, such as Receiving Page.

- *Identifier* shows the station identifier of the sending fax. A station identifier is a unique identification for fax machines or fax modems. Read Chapter 4, "Configuring WinFax PRO," to learn more about station identifiers.

- *Current Page* does not show information about incoming faxes. For outgoing faxes, it displays the percentage of the current page that WinFax PRO sent.

- *Destination* does not show information about incoming faxes. For outgoing faxes, it shows the recipient's station identifier.

- *Fax Number* does not show information about incoming faxes. For outgoing faxes it shows the recipient's fax number.

- *Page* shows the page number of the incoming fax.

- *Speed* shows the speed at which the transmission occurs.

Viewing Faxes During Reception

You can view the incoming fax as WinFax PRO receives it much as you view a paper fax coming out of a traditional fax machine. But in ordinary circumstances, there is no reason to view the incoming fax. In fact, there is a good reason *not* to do it.

Drawing a graphical image on-screen requires a lot of your computer's processing power. It also requires lots of the power of your video adapter. When you view a fax during reception, your computer must devote much of its processing and video capabilities to displaying the fax.

As a result, all other functions for which you use your computer slow down or stop when WinFax PRO displays the incoming fax. So unless you have an overwhelming need, don't use this option when receiving faxes.

II

Everyday Operation

> **Caution**
>
> You can't disable or stop this capability during reception. If you don't want this capability, make sure you switch it off before you start receiving faxes.

Although this option is not often useful, there still will be times when you are in a hurry to view the fax and you are not using your computer for any other purpose. If that is the case, viewing the fax during reception may be useful.

To activate viewing capabilities during reception, follow these steps:

1. From the Setu**p** menu, choose **R**eceive. WinFax PRO displays the Receive Setup dialog box. Select the **V**iew During Receive check box.

2. Determine the size of the window in which you view the incoming fax by clicking the Window **S**ize button. Adjust the size of the window that appears, as you would any window. This window displays the incoming fax. When you finish, close the window by double-clicking the control menu box in the upper left corner.

Tip

Although both methods require lots of computer resources, S**w**eep requires fewer resources than S**c**roll, so your PC operates more efficiently during reception.

3. Next, determine the way you want WinFax PRO to display the incoming fax. If you select the S**c**roll button, lines are added to the bottom of the fax one after the other, emulating the way a paper fax comes out of a traditional fax machine. S**w**eep paints the incoming fax image from top to bottom.

4. When you finish setting up how you want to view faxes during reception, choose OK in the Receive Setup dialog box.

Receiving in the Background

One strength of the Windows operating environment is that it enables you to do multiple operations at the same time. This capability is called *multitasking,* which means that you can work in your word processor at the same time WinFax PRO receives (or sends) a fax. Note, however, that this capability works only when Windows operates in *Enhanced mode.*

Windows automatically starts in Enhanced mode (unless you tell it otherwise) if you have a sufficiently powerful computer. Specifically, you need a computer based on the 40386 processor (or greater) and at least 4M of random-access memory.

To determine whether you are in Enhanced mode, in Program Manager, choose **H**elp **A**bout. The message box tells you the mode in which your computer is running. Read your Windows user's guide for more information about running in Enhanced mode.

If your computer and Windows support Enhanced mode, you don't need to do anything special to start multitasking. With one application doing something, simply start and use your other applications as you normally would. For example, when WinFax PRO receives a fax, you can start and use your word processor or spreadsheet.

Note

You can also describe the way WinFax PRO receives faxes as you use other applications by saying that WinFax PRO is "working in the background." That is, as you use your word processor, spreadsheet, or database, WinFax PRO still works behind the scenes.

Caution

As stated previously, if you view faxes as you receive them, you may not be able to do other tasks in WinFax PRO—even in Enhanced mode. Viewing during receipt requires so many of your computer's resources that you typically won't be able to do any other tasks.

Be careful to close all unnecessary applications as your PC multitasks. Leaving applications open in Windows uses memory and other computer resources. If you run out of these resources, your system can lock up, requiring a reboot and resulting in a possible loss of data in applications.

After You Receive the Fax

After WinFax PRO receives the fax, it places information about the fax in the Receive Log. You can initiate a wide variety of actions on any received faxes from the Receive Log, including viewing the fax, modifying basic information such as keywords, and initiating the process of turning the fax image into editable text.

The next several sections, however, don't tell you about the actions you can initiate at any time from the Send and Receive Logs. Rather, they tell you about actions WinFax PRO can automatically take right after receiving a fax.

II

Everyday Operation

Notifying You of Received Faxes

One basic WinFax PRO activity is to notify you after it receives faxes, which is useful if you are multitasking. A message box appears in your application and a sound is played, telling you that WinFax PRO received a fax (see fig. 9.3).

Fig. 9.3
WinFax PRO
notifies you after
it receives a fax.

To make sure WinFax PRO notifies you after it receives faxes, choose Setu**p** **R**eceive. Select the Notif**y** check box.

You can set WinFax PRO to play a sound when it displays the notification dialog box. Click the S**o**und button. WinFax PRO displays the Sound dialog box (see fig. 9.4).

Fig. 9.4
Select the sound
that notifies you
about received
faxes in the Sound
dialog box.

Tip
Notification is
particularly
useful if you
turned off your
modem's
volume in the
Modem Setup
dialog box, or
if your modem
is not near
enough for
you to hear.

In the Sound dialog box, you can use WinFax PRO's default sound, or you can select your own sound file. To use WinFax PRO's default sound, select the WinFax **G**enerated button.

To select your own sound file, select the **W**ave File button. WinFax PRO can play waveform files, which have the WAV file extension. After you select the **W**ave File button, type the drive, path, and name of the file in the text box.

If you do not know the drive, path, or file name of the WAV file, click the **S**elect button. Then use the Select Wave File dialog box to find and select the sound file (see fig. 9.5).

In the Select Wave File dialog box, select a drive in the Dri**v**es drop-down list and a directory in the **D**irectories list window. File names appear in the File **N**ame list window. Select the file you want; then click OK.

Whether you select your own wave file or use WinFax PRO's default notification sound, you can hear the sound by clicking the **T**est button.

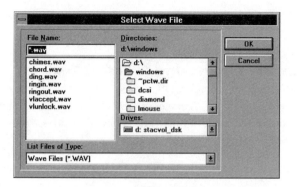

Automatically Viewing Received Faxes

You can view faxes immediately after they arrive by activating the View Fax
check box in the Receive Setup dialog box. With this option active, WinFax
PRO displays a Viewer window containing the newly received fax
(see fig. 9.6).

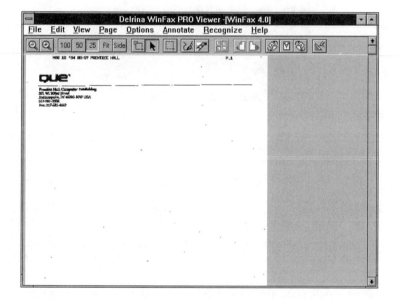

As with any viewed fax, you can annotate and add graphics to faxes you view
immediately on receipt. Read Chapter 14, "Viewing and Annotating Faxes,"
which discusses annotating faxes.

You also can view faxes at any time by double-clicking them in the Send and Receive Logs.

Automatically Converting Faxes to Text

You can set WinFax PRO to automatically convert incoming faxes into editable text by using *optical character recognition* (OCR). OCR enables WinFax PRO to convert the fax file so your word processor or other applications can edit it instead of keeping the fax file as an image.

To have WinFax PRO automatically apply OCR to incoming faxes:

1. From the Setup menu, choose **R**eceive. The Receive Setup dialog box appears.

2. Select the **R**ecognize check box.

3. Set parameters for the automatic recognition by clicking the Se**t**up button. WinFax PRO displays the Recognize Setup dialog box (see fig. 9.7).

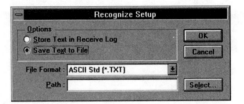

4. Select either the **S**tore Text in Receive Log button or the Save Te**x**t to File button.

   ■ To access the converted fax document from the Receive Log, select the **S**tore Text in Receive Log button.

   ■ To automatically save the recognized text to a separate file that you can open from another application, select the Save Te**x**t to File button.

5. In the F**i**le Format drop-down list, select a file format in which you want to store the converted text. Most applications can import ASCII format. However, ASCII files can't include formatting, such as bold-faced characters. If you find your application, select it in the drop-down list. Then, in the **P**ath text box, type the drive and path where you want WinFax PRO to save the file.

6. If you aren't sure of the drive and path in which you want to store the file, click Select. WinFax PRO displays the Directories dialog box. Select a Drive in the Drives drop-down list and a directory in the **D**irectories list window. Click OK to return to the Recognize Setup dialog box.

7. Choose OK.

Like viewing a fax during reception, the OCR process requires lots of your computer's resources, slowing down other operations. Usually, it is easier for those who receive lots of faxes to initiate the OCR process later, on faxes in the Receive Log or in the archive files.

When you recognize faxes at a later time, WinFax PRO loads the fax in the Viewer window, and also gives you greater control over the recognition process. For more information about recognizing faxes in this way, read Chapter 15, "Converting Faxes to Text."

Printing On Receipt

WinFax PRO can automatically print incoming faxes after it receives them. In this way, WinFax PRO acts like a traditional fax machine, giving you a paper copy of the fax.

To set up WinFax PRO to print on reception, follow these steps:

1. From the Setu**p** menu, choose **R**eceive. In the Receive Setup dialog box, select the Print **F**ax check box. Your default Windows printer appears to the right of this option.

2. To change the printer to which you want to send incoming faxes, click the **P**rinter button. WinFax PRO displays the Printer Setup dialog box (see fig. 9.8).

Tip
If the fax contents are more important than the fax image, set WinFax PRO to automatically apply OCR to the incoming fax. Converted text files take less disk space than do fax images.

Fig. 9.8
Select a printer in the Printer Setup dialog box.

The Printer Setup dialog box lists all printers for which you installed Windows printer drivers, including WinFax PRO. To add or delete printers, use the Windows Control Panel. For information about the Windows Control Panel and specific ways to add or delete printers from Windows, read the Windows user's guide.

3. Select the printer you want. Then choose OK.

You also can print sent or received faxes at any time from the Send and Receive Logs. For information about printing from the Send and Receive Logs, read Chapter 11, "Using the Send and Receive Logs."

Automatic Forwarding

One of WinFax PRO's more advanced features includes its ability to automatically forward faxes to other numbers.

The capability is a boon for travelers. Automatically forwarding faxes, for example, enables you to have faxes sent to your hotel when you are traveling, so you can use them when you arrive. Read Chapter 17, "WinFax PRO Away from the Office," for a more in-depth discussion about this feature.

You also can forward faxes to other recipients from the Send and Receive Logs at any time—read Chapter 11, "Using the Send and Receive Logs."

Troubleshooting

My connection breaks before WinFax PRO finishes receiving the fax. Similarly, sometimes, the two fax devices never make the initial connection.

The problem is probably either a bad phone line or incompatibilities between your fax modem and the sending fax modem. If this problem occurs infrequently, chances are that the problem is compatibility. If it occurs with a variety of senders, you either have a faulty phone line, or your settings in the Modem Setup dialog box are wrong. Read Chapter 4, "Configuring WinFax PRO," for more information about setting up your modem.

The speed displayed in the Status message box for incoming faxes is slower than the maximum speed that my fax modem can handle.

There are several possible solutions to this problem. First, your fax device may handle higher speeds than the sending device can handle. In those cases, the fax devices agree to send the fax at a slower speed. This feature is helpful and is not a problem. Rather, it ensures that fax devices with different capabilities can still communicate.

Another possibility is that there is interference on the phone line. This is another time when the fax machines agree to send the faxes at a slower speed. To determine whether this is the problem, listen to the phone line. If line interference is particularly bad, you hear static. To solve this problem, call a telephone repairperson.

The third possibility is that there is an incompatibility between your fax modem and the sending fax device. Class 2 fax devices are particularly susceptible to these problems because they are not based on an agreed-upon standard. Read Chapter 2, "How WinFax PRO Works," for more information about the different types of faxes.

If the problem persists, check your modem settings by choosing Setu**p** **F**ax/Modem. Make sure that you selected the correct modem type. Also, check with your fax modem's documentation to make sure the initialization and reset strings listed in the Modem Setup dialog box are correct.

Make sure the communications port to which you attached your modem is operational, too. You do that in the Modem Setup dialog box (which you access by choosing Setu**p** **F**ax/Modem). Select a communications port in the **P**ort drop-down list, and click **T**est. If the test finds that the communications port is not functioning properly, try another port or consult your PC's documentation.

I can view faxes as they arrive, but I can't do anything else with my computer.

Viewing faxes during reception often requires virtually all your computer's resources, even on relatively fast computers. Usually, viewing faxes during reception is not necessary. To switch off this capability, from the Setu**p** menu, choose **R**eceive. Then deactivate the **V**iew During Receive check box.

I did not set WinFax PRO to view faxes during reception, but I still can't do anything else with my computer during reception.

Make sure that you loaded Windows in Enhanced mode. You can only do multiple things with your computer at the same time, known as multitasking, if you load Windows in Enhanced mode. If you have a sufficiently powerful computer, Windows loads automatically in Enhanced mode. This requires at least a computer based on the 40386 processor and 4M of random-access memory. If your computer does not meet these requirements, Windows starts in other modes (called either Real mode or Standard mode) that don't support multitasking.

To determine whether you are in Enhanced mode, in Program Manager, choose **H**elp **A**bout. The message box tells you the mode in which you are running. Read your Windows user's guide for more information about running in Enhanced mode.

My system sometimes locks up when WinFax PRO receives a fax while I am doing something else with my computer.

Even if you have adequate hardware for multitasking, each task still uses up memory and oor simply leave too many applications open at the same time—

(continues)

> (continued)
>
> you will run out of resources and run the risk of crashing. To prevent this problem, close all unnecessary applications.
>
> I set WinFax PRO to automatically convert incoming faxes to the format of my word processor, but they don't appear when I open my word processor.
>
> You must load a converted file into your word processor, as you would any file. As part of the automatic OCR process, you set a drive and path for converted files. In your word processor, load the file from that directory.

From Here...

This chapter told you how to receive faxes and how to set up several options for handling faxes immediately after receipt. You also can use some of the functions described in this chapter at a later time, from other parts of WinFax PRO. For more information, you may want to read the following:

- Chapter 11, "Using the Send and Receive Logs," tells you about the actions you can initiate directly from the Send Log and Receive Log.

- Chapter 15, "Converting Faxes to Text," tells you how to use OCR capabilities after you receive faxes. When done at a later time, WinFax PRO gives you more control over the OCR process.

- Chapter 14, "Viewing and Annotating Faxes," gives you details about using the Viewer window to annotate fax images.

Chapter 10

Using WinFax PRO
for Electronic Mail

In this chapter, you learn how to do the following:

■ Create and send network electronic mail with WinFax PRO.

■ Receive network electronic mail with WinFax PRO.

■ Reply to and forward electronic mail messages.

■ Store and manage electronic mail messages.

Much of this book concerns using WinFax PRO for sending and receiving faxes. However, WinFax PRO handles messages other than faxes. This chapter discusses how to use WinFax PRO for what may be the most common type of messages other than faxes: network-based electronic mail, also known as *e-mail*.

About Electronic Mail

These days, computer networks are common in even relatively small organizations. Networks connect desktop computers and make it easy for many users to share resources such as printers. Networks also make it easy to share specially licensed applications and information.

Network e-mail programs are one way users who have connected their PCs to computer networks can exchange information and files. Like traditional mail, e-mail messages consist of words. However, instead of putting the message in a paper envelope and placing the envelope in a mailbox, you address an e-mail message to one or more persons connected to the network.

An e-mail message can be virtually any type of correspondence among people in organizations. Such correspondence can range from notifying people about a meeting or after-work gathering to exchanging memos and reports.

In addition to simple written messages, you can include files with an e-mail message. The file can be a word processing or spreadsheet file or a graphic image. In fact, it can be any computer file, including the files needed to run programs. The recipient can read the words you send, and use the files, too. These files are called *attachments*.

Note that e-mail attachments are both similar to and different from fax attachments. E-mail messages are similar because they start out as computer files, sometimes called *binary files*. Binary files can be either the files created by applications or the applications themselves.

But when you transmit standard faxes, WinFax PRO converts binary files to fax images and sends them as normal faxes. With e-mail, however, the files remain binary files and WinFax PRO transmits them as such. Read Chapter 12, "Assembling Faxes from Many Sources," for more information about attachments.

Note

Standard faxing is the most common way to send and receive faxes. However, WinFax PRO also provides additional methods for sending faxes—Binary File Transfer, Microsoft At Work, and a proprietary WinFax PRO method. When you use those methods, you send computer files as files, not as fax images. Read Chapter 16, "Different Ways To Send and Receive," for information about those methods.

About E-Mail Software

There are many commercially available e-mail products. Typically, this software has two elements:

- An element for the network administrator—the person who manages your network—for establishing who uses e-mail and how the network transmits and stores e-mail messages. Sometimes this part of the software is called the *back end* because it works behind the scenes to do the technical work of managing, transmitting, and distributing e-mail.

- An element for all the individual users of e-mail. Like WinFax PRO, this software typically has logs for sent and received e-mail messages. It also includes address books for e-mail recipients and a method for creating e-mail messages. Sometimes, this part of the software is called the *front end* because it is the part of the e-mail process that is up front—or the part that most end-users use.

Typically, the back end part of the product breaks network users into groups—sometimes called *workgroups*. For administrative purposes, the back end program assigns workgroups to a *post office*.

Much like usual post offices in cities and towns, an e-mail post office collects mail going out from workgroup members and distributes it—to other workgroup members or to other post offices, if appropriate. It also collects mail coming in to workgroup members and distributes it.

> **Note**
>
> *Post office* is a commonly used term, but not all e-mail programs use it. We use it here because it describes well what the e-mail software does. Your e-mail program may use another term.

Why Use WinFax PRO for E-Mail?

WinFax PRO can't act like a post office. However, for many popular e-mail packages, it can replace the normal front-end software that individuals use for sending, receiving, and managing e-mail messages.

To simplify sending and receiving e-mail, WinFax PRO uses several elements with which you already are familiar—phonebooks and the Send and Receive Logs. You create entries for e-mail recipients in a phonebook by using the same dialog box that you use for creating fax recipients. You manage attachments to e-mail messages by using the Attachments window. E-mail messages you receive appear in the Receive Log and those you send appear in the Send Log.

There are several advantages to using a single program for faxing and using e-mail messages:

- You must learn only one program, not two, if you both fax and use e-mail.

- You can use the same phonebook for fax and e-mail recipients.

- You can send fax and e-mail messages at the same time.

- You can store fax and e-mail messages in the same place.

II

Everyday Operation

Getting Started with WinFax PRO

There are only a few things you need before you start using WinFax PRO to manage, send, and receive your e-mail:

- You must be connected to a network. Your network administrator will describe how.

- The network administrator must enable you to send and receive electronic mail.

- You must have access to a copy of the front-end part of the e-mail package designed for individual users (not the part for network administrators).

- You must log on to your network by using the procedures required by your specific type of network. Your network manager can tell you how to do this.

- You must know how to log in to your e-mail system. This procedure is separate from logging in to your network. Your network administrator will tell you how to do this.

- You must have WinFax PRO properly installed and running on your computer. Chapter 1, "Installing WinFax PRO," tells you how.

You optionally can log on to your e-mail system before you use WinFax PRO to manage e-mail messages. As the next section discusses, however, you also can log on from within WinFax PRO.

Also, to work with WinFax PRO, your e-mail system must support one of two standards used for e-mail systems: Microsoft Application Programming Interface (MAPI) and Vendor Independent Messaging (VIM). These are two of the most widely accepted standards for determining how, in a technical sense, a network system manages and routes e-mail messages.

Tip
If you are not sure whether your e-mail package supports one of these standards, ask your network administrator.

Many—but certainly not all—electronic mail programs support one of these standards. For example, Microsoft Mail supports the MAPI standard and cc:Mail supports the VIM standard.

Setting Up WinFax PRO for E-Mail

After your system administrator sets you up to send and receive e-mail, it is simple to switch to WinFax PRO as your front-end software for sending, receiving, and managing your messages. If you already know how to use your organization's e-mail software, you should be able to switch easily to WinFax

PRO. That's because, with its system of folders and subfolders, WinFax PRO already looks and acts like many e-mail products.

To set up WinFax PRO to work with your e-mail system, choose Setu**p M**ail. WinFax PRO displays the Mail Setup dialog box (see fig. 10.1).

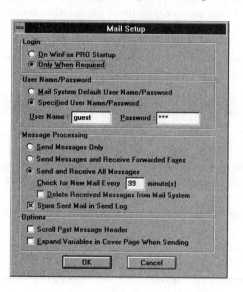

Fig. 10.1
Set up e-mail in the Mail Setup dialog box.

In the Login area of the dialog box, tell WinFax PRO when you want it to log in to your network e-mail system. Your options are the following:

- *O*n WinFax PRO Startup automatically connects to your e-mail system when you start WinFax PRO.

- Only *W*hen Required connects WinFax PRO to your e-mail system only when you take an action such as sending an e-mail message or checking to see whether you received any messages.

In the User Name/Password area, set up the name and password you want WinFax PRO to use to access your network e-mail system. The options are as follows:

- *M*ail System Default User Name/Password tells WinFax PRO to apply your user name and the password that you and your network manager set up for normal use of the e-mail system.

- Speci*f*ied User Name/Password tells WinFax PRO to use another user name and password. If you select this option, type the user name in the **U**ser Name text box and the password in the **P**assword text box.

Tip
Occasional e-mail users should select the Only **W**hen Required option. Regular users select the **O**n WinFax PRO Startup option automatically to get ready to use WinFax PRO with e-mail.

Tip
Use Specified
User Name/
Password to
check messages
from somebody
else's PC. Or a
secretary could
check for mes-
sages for the
boss.

Tip
Select **S**end
Messages Only
if you occasion-
ally send the
same messages
to both fax and
e-mail recipi-
ents but rely on
another e-mail
front end for
day-to-day e-
mail operation.

Tip
Use the Send
and Receive All
Messages op-
tion to fully
utilize WinFax
PRO as your
network e-mail
front end.

In the Message Processing area of the Mail Setup dialog box, determine the specific types of messages you want WinFax PRO to handle:

■ *Send Messages Only* tells WinFax PRO that you will use it only to send messages. If you select this option, you can't use WinFax PRO to receive e-mail messages. Rather, you must use another e-mail front end.

■ *Send Messages and Receive Forwarded Faxes* sets up WinFax PRO to enable you to send mail and to receive faxes forward, via electronic mail, from other WinFax PRO users.

> **Note**
>
> This book is about the version of WinFax PRO for individual users. Even the single-user version has many network capabilities such as the ability to send and receive e-mail. However, a special version of WinFax PRO has additional network capabilities. For example, it has enhanced capabilities to handle large volumes of faxes generated by multiple users. Check with your network manager to learn more about the special version of WinFax PRO specifically for networks.

■ *Send and Receive All Messages* tells WinFax PRO to send and receive all messages. As with the previous option, type a number in the *Check for New Mail Every Minute(s)* text box if you select this option.

■ If you choose to use WinFax PRO to receive e-mail, it can check your e-mail system periodically for new messages. Tell it how frequently you want it to do that by typing a number in the *Check for New Mail Every Minute(s)* text box.

■ *Delete Received Messages from Mail System* deletes messages from the e-mail system and also from WinFax PRO when you remove them from the Send and Receive Logs. If you don't select this check box, the message remains in the network e-mail system. This means that even if you delete the message from WinFax PRO, you can access the message from another e-mail front end.

■ Selecting the *Store Sent Mail in Send Log* check box stores sent mail messages only in WinFax PRO's Send Log, not your normal e-mail front end.

The Options area of the Mail Setup dialog box includes two check boxes that determine how e-mail messages appear when you display messages in the display area window of the log window:

- *Scroll Past Message Header* displays only the message itself when you use display e-mail messages in the display area window of the log window. Otherwise, WinFax PRO also displays the header information, which includes the sender's name, the subject, and similar information.

- *Expand Variables in Cover Page When Sending* inserts variable information in e-mail messages rather than codes you used to represent the variables. Chapter 7, "Creating and Managing Cover Pages," describes how to use variables to insert information like the recipient's name. If you select this option, WinFax PRO translates the variable fields in e-mail messages you create when you use the Send dialog box. If you don't activate this field, the variables appear as codes in the e-mail.

Tip

Make sure you select this check box if you send form e-mail letters from the Send dialog box. This option doesn't work if you use the Compose Mail Message dialog box.

> **Note**
>
> A later section of this chapter, "Creating and Sending E-Mail Messages," discusses using both the Send Fax and Compose Mail dialog boxes for sending e-mail messages.

Logging Into E-Mail

Before you use WinFax PRO to send and receive e-mail messages, you must log into your network and then log into your e-mail system. You must log into your network before starting WinFax PRO, but you can log into your e-mail system from WinFax PRO.

To log into your e-mail system directly from WinFax PRO, choose **M**ail **L**ogin. If you haven't yet logged into the network, WinFax PRO displays a message similar to the one in the next figure (see fig. 10.2). The precise message depends on your network and e-mail system.

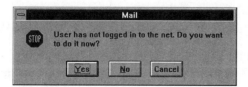

Fig. 10.2
WinFax PRO displays a message if you aren't logged into your network.

If you already logged into your network, WinFax PRO displays a dialog box very similar to the one your e-mail system uses for logging in. Figure 10.3 shows the Log In dialog box for Microsoft Mail.

Fill in the Log In dialog box and click OK.

Fig. 10.3
Log into your
network with the
Log In dialog box.

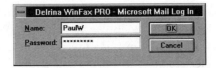

> ## Caution
>
> Your network or e-mail system may limit the number of errors you can make when you try to log on. For example, you may only get two attempts. If you type the wrong password or user name twice, the network or e-mail package stops the process. Check with your network administrator for more details.

Adding E-Mail Phonebook Entries

You can use the regular WinFax PRO phonebook or your e-mail system's phonebook for addressing messages. Depending on your network and e-mail system, you can use one phonebook or both.

To add a name to your e-mail system's phonebook, use the procedures described in the user's manual for your e-mail front end. To add an e-mail recipient to WinFax PRO's normal e-mail phonebook, follow the instructions provided in Chapter 6, "Using Phonebooks"—but with a couple of exceptions.

To briefly review, you can create a new WinFax PRO phonebook record by following these steps:

1. Make the Phonebooks document window the active view.

2. Double-click the New Recipient entry at the top of the item list window of the Phonebooks view. WinFax PRO displays the New Recipient dialog box (see fig. 10.4).

3. Enter information as appropriate in the New Recipient dialog box.

   This procedure is identical (so far) to the procedure for adding new fax recipients. However, in addition, you must enter an e-mail address for the recipient in the Mail line of the Connections area of the dialog box.

4. Mail addresses can be complicated. To make sure that you enter the correct e-mail address, click the Fin**d** button. WinFax PRO displays the address book from your e-mail package. Figure 10.5 shows an Address dialog box for MS Mail.

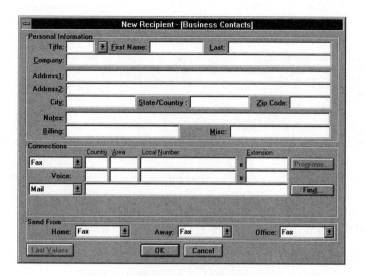

Fig. 10.4
Create new e-mail
addressees in
WinFax PRO in
the New Recipient
dialog box.

Fig. 10.5
Find an e-mail
recipient in the
Address dialog
box—in this case
the address book
from MS Mail.

II

Everyday Operation

5. Select a name in the top list box of the dialog box and click the **A**dd
   button. The name appears in the Entry For This Phone Record list box
   at the bottom.

6. Choose OK and WinFax PRO adds the e-mail address in the New
   Recipient dialog box.

> **Note**
>
> The dialog varies, depending on the e-mail product you use. This procedure
> describes how to add a name from an MS Mail electronic mail system. The
> dialog box you see may be different from the dialog box described here.

7. Complete the New Recipient dialog box and choose OK.

Troubleshooting

I can't get into my organization's e-mail system.

Talk to your organization's network administrator. Make sure that you know the correct procedures for logging on to the network and then logging on to the e-mail system.

Sending and Receiving E-Mail Messages

Tip
WinFax PRO automatically creates a special phonebook containing only e-mail recipients, who also appear in normal phonebooks. But if you send only e-mail, this special phonebook is faster to use.

After you add e-mail recipients to your phonebook, you can send e-mail messages to those people using WinFax PRO. You also can use WinFax PRO to receive e-mail messages from anybody on your organization's computer network. The following sections tell you how.

Creating and Sending E-Mail Messages

You can use one of two methods for creating e-mail. The first method is probably more familiar because it involves using WinFax PRO's Send dialog box, described in Chapter 8, "Sending Faxes." This method is most useful for sending the same message using multiple methods of transmission, such as e-mail and faxes.

1. Click the Send button in the WinFax PRO toolbar. Alternatively, choose **S**end **F**ax. In either case, WinFax PRO displays the Send dialog box.

2. Select the phonebook you want from the Phonebooks drop-down list.

3. Select the recipients you want.

Tip
The Send dialog box is best for providing special treatment for e-mail messages, such as scheduling them for later transmission.

4. Type your message in the cover page fill-in area of the Send dialog box.

5. Add attachments and set options as appropriate.

6. Choose Send to send the e-mail or place it in the Outbox if you scheduled it for later transmission.

The other method for creating and sending e-mail messages is faster, but you only can use it for e-mail.

1. Choose **M**ail C**o**mpose. WinFax PRO displays the Compose Mail dialog box (see fig. 10.6).

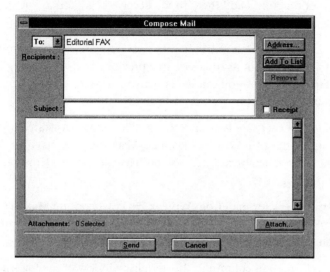

Fig. 10.6
Create e-mail messages in the Compose Mail dialog box.

2. To select recipient addresses, click the A**dd**ress button. WinFax PRO displays the address list from your e-mail application. Select the addresses you want and choose OK. The names you selected appear in the **R**ecipients list box. Or if you know the recipient's address, type it in the text box at the top of the dialog box; then click Add **T**o List.

3. Click Re**m**ove to remove a name from the **R**ecipients list.

4. Type a subject for the message in the Sub**j**ect text box.

5. If you want a receipt when the recipient reads the message, select the Rece**i**pt check box. A receipt is simply a notification that the recipient received the message.

6. Type the message in the text fill-in box below the Sub**j**ect text box.

7. To attach a file, click **A**ttach. WinFax PRO displays the Select Attachment dialog box. Select attachments and click OK to return to the Compose Mail dialog box. (Read Chapter 12, "Assembling Faxes from Many Sources," for instructions on how to use the Select Attachments dialog box.)

8. When you complete the Compose Mail dialog box, choose Send. WinFax PRO sends your e-mail message.

Receiving and Viewing E-Mail

WinFax PRO does not automatically gather e-mail messages from your system's post office and add them to the Receive Log. Rather, you must tell WinFax PRO to check for new mail.

To briefly review, you first must log into your network. Then you must log into your e-mail system. As discussed in a previous section, "Setting Up WinFax Pro for E-Mail," you can log directly into your e-mail system by using your standard e-mail front end, or you can log in using WinFax PRO.

After you log in, there are two ways to check for e-mail. As stated in a previous section, "Setting Up WinFax PRO for E-Mail," you can have it check for your e-mail automatically at intervals you select. You select this option in the Mail Setup dialog box.

You also can check for mail from WinFax PRO by choosing **M**ail Retrie**v**e Mail. WinFax PRO checks your e-mail system for new mail and adds any new mail—and attachments to the mail—to your Receive Log.

The Type information column in the item list window of the log window represents e-mail with an envelope icon. If the icon is an open envelope, it means you already read the e-mail message. If the envelope appears closed, it means that you haven't yet read the message.

Manage sent and received e-mail messages the same as you manage sent and received faxes. You can keep them in the Send and Receive Logs or drag them from the item list window to a folder that you create. Read Chapter 11, "Using the Send and Receive Logs," for more information about folders.

View an e-mail message the same way you view a fax message. You can either double-click the message in the item list window, or click the View button in the toolbar. However, you view e-mail messages in a different window than the one you use for viewing fax messages. You view e-mail in the Mail Message Contents window (see fig. 10.7).

View the text portion of the e-mail message in the **N**otes box. You cannot edit the text in the **N**otes box. You can, however, copy text to the Windows clipboard. To do that, follow these steps:

Tip

Pasting is handy when responding to e-mail. It enables you to place the precise words in the received e-mail into your message and then respond to them.

1. Use your mouse to highlight text.

2. Press Ctrl to copy the text to the Windows clipboard.

3. Paste the text into your Windows application by using the normal procedures for pasting into that application.

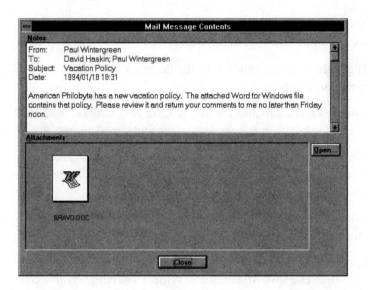

Fig. 10.7
View e-mail messages in the Mail Message Contents window.

Beneath the **N**otes area is the **A**ttachment area, which displays all attachments to the e-mail message. Open an attachment either by double-clicking it or by clicking it once and clicking the **O**pen button. When you finish viewing the e-mail message, choose Close.

A faster way to view the contents of e-mail messages is to view them in the display area window of the Send and Receive Logs. Choose **W**indow Display **M**essage after you highlight an e-mail message in the item list window. If you highlighted a fax in the item list window, choose **W**indow Display **F**ax View.

When you display e-mail messages in the display area window of the Send and Receive Logs, WinFax PRO displays icons representing attachments. The icons are from the application that created the attachment. To view the attachment, double-click the icon in the display area window.

Saving Attachments and Addresses

WinFax PRO enables you to save both the addresses of the people who send you e-mail messages, and any attachments they sent you.

To save addresses, follow these steps:

1. Make the Phonebooks view active by clicking the Phnbooks button in the toolbar, or by selecting **F**ax **Ph**onebooks.

2. Select the phonebook to which you want to add the recipient by double-clicking it.

3. Make the Receive Log active by clicking the Rcv Log button in the toolbar or by selecting **R**eceive **L**og.

4. Highlight the e-mail address in the Receive Log that you want to add to your phonebook.

5. Choose **L**og Add to Phone**b**ook. WinFax PRO displays the New Recipient dialog box with the sender's name and e-mail address filled in.

6. Fill in any other information you want to in the New Recipient dialog box, such as the person's fax number. Click OK to add the address to your phonebook.

If somebody sends you an e-mail message that includes an attachment, you also can save that attachment. To do that, follow these steps:

Highlight the e-mail message with the attachment in the Receive Log, and then select **L**og Sa**v**e Attachments. WinFax PRO displays the Save Attachments dialog box (see fig. 10.8).

Fig. 10.8
Save received
e-mail attach-
ments in the Save
Attachments
dialog box.

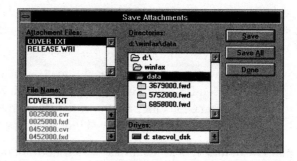

In the Save Attachments dialog box, follow these steps:

1. In the A**t**tachment Files list window, select which part of the received attachment to save. You can click as many parts of the message as you want.

2. Save all the parts of the message listed in the A**t**tachment Files list window by clicking Save **A**ll. If you click this button, you needn't follow steps 3 through 6.

3. In the File **N**ame dialog box, type a name for the attachment.

4. In the Dri**v**es drop-down list, select the drive on which you want to store the attachment.

5. Select a directory for storing the attachment in the **D**irectories list window.

6. Click **S**ave. WinFax PRO saves the files with the names you selected.

7. Click **D**one to return to the Receive Log.

If you want to add your new attachments to an attachment folder, you're not done. To add the file to the attachment library, follow these steps:

1. Make the Attachments window active by clicking the Attach button on the toolbar, or by choosing **F**ax A**t**tachments.

2. Double-click the folder in which you want to place the new attachment.

3. Double-click New Attachments in the item list window. Alternatively, choose **A**ttachment **N**ew. WinFax PRO displays the New Attachments dialog box.

4. Type a description of the new attachment in the **D**escription text box.

5. Enter the drive, directory, and name of the new attachment in the **F**ile Name text box. If you don't remember the file name, click **S**elect. WinFax PRO displays the Select Attachment dialog box.

6. Select the drive, directory, and file name for the attachment in the Select Attachment dialog box. Click OK to return to the Select Attachment dialog box.

7. If you want, add keywords for the attachment in the **K**eywords text box.

8. Click OK to return to the Attachments window. WinFax PRO adds your new attachment to the folder you selected.

Read Chapter 12, "Assembling Faxes from Many Sources," for more information about attachments.

Replying To and Forwarding E-Mail

As with any message, at times you must reply to an e-mail message or forward it on to somebody else. To forward a message:

1. Select the e-mail message to forward in the item list window of the Send and Receive Logs.

2. Choose **M**ail For**w**ard. WinFax PRO displays the Compose Mail dialog box as described in the previous section, "Creating and Sending E-Mail Messages." There is one exception, however: The dialog box displays the contents of the e-mail message.

II

Everyday Operation

3. Choose **A**ddress to select the people to whom you want to forward the e-mail message. WinFax PRO displays the address book from your e-mail program. When you finish selecting addresses, return to the Compose Message dialog box.

4. Choose **A**ttach to add any attachments to the e-mail message.

5. Choose Send to forward the e-mail message.

The process for replying to e-mail messages is similar. To reply to the person who sent the e-mail message to you:

1. Choose **M**ail Repl**y**. WinFax PRO displays the Compose Mail dialog box, which displays all information, including the sender's address and the message.

2. Above the original message, type your response.

3. Add new recipients by clicking the **A**ddress button. Select the new recipients in the address book that WinFax PRO displays.

4. Add new attachments by clicking the **A**ttach button. WinFax PRO displays the Select Attachments dialog box. Read Chapter 12, "Assembling Faxes from Many Sources," for more information about attachments and using the Select Attachments dialog box.

> **Note**
>
> A reminder: When you attach an item to a normal fax, WinFax PRO transmits it as a fax image. When you attach an item to an e-mail message, WinFax PRO transmits it as a normal computer file that the recipient opens with his or her applications.

5. When you finish adding addresses and attachments and typing your response, choose Send. WinFax PRO sends the e-mail response.

You also can automatically respond to all persons associated with an e-mail, including the sender and other recipients. To do that, choose **M**ail Reply **A**ll. Then follow the instructions you would use for replying only to the sender.

Tip

Keep the original message if you respond to specific points. Otherwise, eliminate the original message before you reply by highlighting it and pressing the Del key.

Troubleshooting

After sending an e-mail message, I get a message from the system administrator saying that the message couldn't be delivered.

Most e-mail systems notify you when you enter the wrong address for the recipient and the system couldn't deliver the message. Find the correct address and resend the message.

I know a colleague just sent me an e-mail message, but WinFax PRO doesn't display it. What's wrong?

WinFax PRO polls your e-mail system for new messages periodically. You set the frequency for this polling in the Mail Setup dialog box, which you display by selecting Setup **M**ail. Chances are that you set the interval for too long a period of time and WinFax PRO simply hasn't looked for the message yet. Either set the interval for a shorter period of time, or choose **M**ail Retrie**v**e Mail.

From Here...

This chapter told you how to use WinFax PRO for sending, receiving, and managing e-mail messages. For related information, you may want to read the following:

- Chapter 6, "Using Phonebooks," tells you how to create phonebook entries in WinFax PRO, including entries for those to whom you want to send e-mail.

- Chapter 11, "Using the Send and Receive Logs," describes how to manage all messages you send and receive, including e-mail messages.

- Chapter 12, "Assembling Faxes from Many Sources," tells you how to create attachments that you can add to e-mail messages.

- Chapter 16, "Different Ways to Send and Receive," describes several other methods of transmitting messages using WinFax PRO.

II

Everyday Operation

Chapter 11

Using the Send and Receive Logs

In this chapter, you learn how to do the following:

- Navigate the Send and Receive Logs.

- Archive messages.

- Search for archived messages.

- Filter folders to determine what WinFax PRO displays.

- Sort the contents of the Send and Receive Logs.

WinFax PRO stores the messages you send and receive in the Send and Receive Logs. Because these logs automatically store your messages, they also serve as the hub for many WinFax PRO activities.

The Send and Receive Logs store more than just faxes. WinFax PRO stores all messages, no matter the medium used to send or receive them, in the Send and Receive Logs. These logs store binary files that you transfer with WinFax PRO and electronic mail messages, in addition to faxes.

The Send Log and Receive Log appear in the log application window. You also can add a series of folders to the log window for archiving your messages. A well-designed system of folders makes it easy to store and find older messages. You also can place folders in other folders for more detailed categorization of messages.

Chapter 8, "Sending Faxes," showed you how to send and receive faxes. This chapter tells you how to get the most out of the log window. Read Chapter 10, "Using WinFax PRO for Electronic Mail," to learn how to send and receive electronic mail messages. Read Chapter 16, "Different Ways to Send and Receive," to learn how to send and receive binary files.

A Guided Tour

Like several other views in WinFax PRO, the log window has three windows in it (see fig. 11.1).

Fig. 11.1
The Send and Receive Logs have three windows.

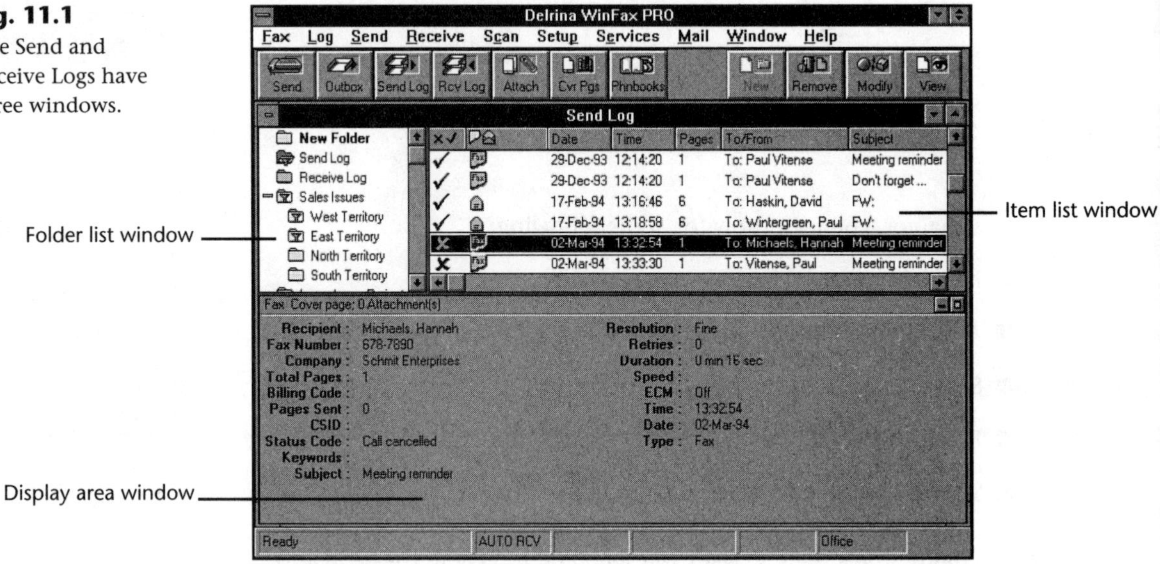

- The *folder list window* lists the Send Log, Receive Log, and the other folders (and subfolders) where you store messages.

- The *item list window* lists the messages you send and receive. You can customize the information contained in the item list window. You also can customize the order in which WinFax PRO displays the information, the width of the columns of information and the shading of the columns.

- The *display area window* displays information about the message. There are three ways to view information in the information window: text information (as shown in the previous figure), thumbnails of the fax highlighted in the item list window, or a view of the actual fax itself.

Read Chapter 5, "Customizing WinFax PRO," to learn how to customize the three windows of the Send and Receive Logs.

The Send Log and the Receive Log are separate folders in the log application window. These folders differ from the folders and subfolders you create in three fundamental ways:

■ You cannot delete either the Send Log or Receive Log.

■ You cannot change their names.

■ WinFax PRO automatically places sent or received messages in the Send Log or Receive Log. You must manually copy or move messages to other folders.

When you send a message, WinFax PRO automatically places it in the Send Log. When you receive a message, WinFax PRO automatically places it in the Receive Log. WinFax PRO places a dark check in the Status column for messages it successfully sends or receives. It places a red x in the Status column for messages that it unsuccessfully sends or receives.

Viewing Log Information

WinFax PRO displays a wealth of information in both the item list window and the display area window. Although you can't change the information displayed in the display area window, you can determine the information WinFax PRO displays in the item list window.

In the item list window, WinFax PRO displays information in columns.

To add or delete information from the item list window, follow these steps:

1. Position the mouse pointer above the column headings.

2. Press the right mouse button. A menu appears, listing the information WinFax PRO can display in the columns (see fig. 11.2).

Fig. 11.2
Select the information you display in the item list window from this menu.

Tip

Avoid including too much information in the item list window, which makes it difficult to read. Most people don't need to know all the information WinFax PRO offers.

3. To set a specific type of information to appear in the item list window, highlight the item in the menu. A check appears next to types of information that WinFax PRO displays in the item list window. To eliminate a type of information from the item list window, select a checked item.

Table 11.1 lists the information you can place in the item list window.

Table 11.1 The information you can display in the item list window.	
Information item	**What it tells you**
Status	Whether transmission or receipt was successful (green check) or unsuccessful (red X).
Type	Type of transmission (such as fax or e-mail).
Date	Date of transmission.
Time	Time of transmission.
Pages	Number of pages in transmission.
To/From	Whether you sent or received message, and name of recipient or sender.
Subject	Subject of message.
Keywords	Keywords you added to messages you sent.
Billing	Billing information for messages you sent.
Speed	Speed at which receipt or transmission occurred.
Pages Sent/Recv	Number of pages in message.
Company	Company of message recipient.
Retries	Number of times WinFax PRO had to retry sending message.
Duration	Time it took to send or receive message.
Resolution	Resolution at which WinFax PRO sent or received fax.
Remote CSID	Recipient's or sender's station identifier.
Status Code	Disposition of transmission (such as whether it was completed or aborted).
Number	Recipient's telephone number.
ECM	Whether WinFax PRO used Error Correcting mode.

Note

Read Chapter 5, "Customizing WinFax PRO," to learn how to change the position, width, and on-screen shading of the information columns. Chapter 5 also tells you how to change the order of information displayed in the display area window.

About Folders

You could keep all messages in the Send and Receive Logs. However, it soon would become difficult to keep track of specific messages. Folders and subfolders provide an organized method for storing messages in the Send and Receive Logs. They are at the heart of WinFax PRO's system of *archiving* messages.

WinFax PRO's folders have several important characteristics:

- When you move a fax item from the Send Log or Receive Log to a folder, WinFax PRO automatically compresses it to save disk space. WinFax PRO does not compress items in the Send Log or Receive Log.

- Your system of folders can classify and subclassify information, as you do on your job. For example, salespeople can have a Sales folder and have subfolders for messages about each different product. Or they could have subfolders for messages to and from specific sales prospects.

- You can store sent and received items in the same folders. This means you can store related items together, whether you sent or received them.

- You can store different types of messages in folders, such as faxes, electronic mail, and binary file transmissions.

- You can further classify and subclassify messages by affixing keywords and descriptions to them. This enables you to search for related information.

Copying, Moving, and Removing Messages

WinFax PRO enables you to copy and move messages among folders. Copying and moving messages are similar procedures with one important difference. Moving an item from one folder to another means it resides only in the

II

Everyday Operation

Tip
To take the greatest advantage of WinFax PRO's archiving capabilities, think through your system of folders. Also, expect to refine your folder system over time.

destination folder. Copying a file means it resides both in its original folder and in the destination folder.

Moving and copying messages from one folder to another is a simple matter of dragging and dropping. To move an item from one folder to another, follow these steps:

1. In the folder list window, select the folder or subfolder containing the item you want to move.

2. Select the item or items in the item list window.

3. Hold down the left mouse button.

4. With the left mouse button held down, drag the mouse until the mouse pointer is over the destination folder or subfolder. When it is over a folder or subfolder, notice how the mouse pointer changes to a cursor resembling a sheet of paper.

5. Release the mouse button. WinFax PRO displays the Archive Log Records dialog box. The two options in this dialog box are the following:

   ■ **S**ave Pages with Event saves both the file and the notation of the message in the new folder.

   ■ Save **A**ttachments saves any attachments included with either electronic mail messages or the use of Binary File Transfer, WinFax BFT or Microsoft At Work. Chapter 10, "Using WinFax PRO for Electronic Mail," describes the former and Chapter 16, "Other Ways to Send and Receive," describes the latter.

> **Note**
>
> You can set WinFax PRO to not display this dialog box. To do that, select Setu**p P**rogram **L**og. WinFax PRO displays the Log Setup dialog box described in Chapter 4, "Configuring WinFax PRO." In that dialog box, activate or deactivate the Display Archive Options for Move/Copy check box to display or repress the display of this dialog box.

To copy the item, follow the same steps with one addition: Hold down the Ctrl key when you drag the mouse. When you finish, the item is in both its old folder and its new folder.

To move or copy multiple items, select a message in the item list window. Hold down the Ctrl key and click additional items. You can drag all selected items to the new folder at the same time. To select multiple consecutive items, select the first item, hold down the Shift key, and then click the last item you want to select.

> ### Note
>
> You can copy and move transmissions that WinFax PRO both successfully sent or received and those that were not successful.

WinFax PRO places pending transmissions—those you either scheduled for later transmission or put on hold for later disposition—in the Outbox. As a result, you can't place them in folders or subfolders until you send them. Read Chapter 8, "Sending Faxes," for information on sending messages and understanding the Outbox.

> ### Troubleshooting
>
> *I dragged a message to a new folder, and now the message isn't in its original folder.*
>
> When you drag a message to a new folder, you move it from one folder to another. You also can copy messages so that they appear both in their original folder and also in the new folder. To copy the message, hold down the Ctrl key as you drag the message to the new folder.

Expanding and Collapsing Folders

Chapter 5, "Customizing WinFax PRO," describes how to create new folders and subfolders. After you create subfolders, WinFax PRO enables you to display them in the folder list window or hide them from view.

When WinFax PRO displays subfolders, a minus sign appears to the left of the top-level folder in the folder list window. Subfolders appear below and indented to the right of top-level folders. When a top-level folder has subfolders that WinFax PRO hides, a plus sign appears next to the folder.

The fastest way to display or hide subfolders is to click on the plus or minus sign beside the top-level folder. When you click once on the plus sign next to a top-level folder, the folder's subfolders become visible. When you click the minus sign, WinFax PRO hides the subfolders.

Alternatively, you can display subfolders by highlighting the top-level folder and choosing **Log Expand** Folder. To hide subfolders, choose **Log Collapse** Folder.

Archiving Messages

When you place a message in a folder, you actually *archive* that message. In WinFax PRO, archiving means storing the message for later use. It also means that WinFax PRO automatically compresses the message so that it takes less space.

Archiving is a simple act that requires only moving or copying the message from the Send Log or Receive Log to a folder. Also, it is useful (but not mandatory) to add descriptive information to the item, such as a subject and keywords, when you archive it.

WinFax PRO also provides additional support for managing archived messages. When you place an item in a folder, WinFax PRO automatically compresses it so that it takes less storage space on your hard drive. WinFax PRO doesn't compress items listed in the Send Log or Receive Log.

Tip
WinFax PRO can prompt you for keyword and billing information when you send messages. Choose Setu**p P**rogram, and then select the Pr**o**mpt for Keywords/ Billing Code.

Another part of the archiving process is affixing information to messages to describe them and make them easier to search for. Specifically, you can affix a subject, keywords, and billing information to messages.

The next section describes how to add and modify the information you affix to sent or received messages.

Modifying Items

As you probably know by now, many of WinFax PRO's capabilities rely on information about items. Some information comes from the conditions and status of the message, such as the time of day you sent or received it, or the number of pages. You provide other information, such as a subject for the message, keywords, and billing information.

You can't modify the information that describes the state of the fax, but you can always modify the information you create. To do so, highlight the item in the item list window and choose **Log Modify**. Alternatively, click the right mouse button and choose **Modify** from the menu that appears.

However you do it, WinFax PRO displays the Modify Record dialog box (see fig. 11.3).

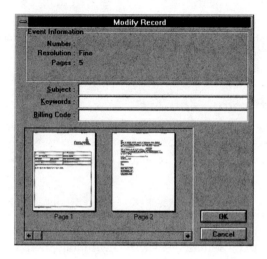

Fig. 11.3
Modify information about an item in the Modify Record dialog box.

The Modify Record dialog box displays basic information about the item in the Event Information area at the top of the dialog box and a thumbnail image of the item (if it is a fax) at the bottom.

In the middle are three text boxes for information on the item. If you previously entered information about the item, it appears in the text boxes. If you haven't provided information, the text boxes are empty.

In either case:

Type a new subject or modify the previous subject in the **S**ubject text box.

Type new keywords or modify existing keywords in the **K**eywords text box.

Type new billing information or modify old information in the **B**illing Code text box.

Note

If the message is only a quick cover page, you won't be able to view it.

When you finish the Modify Record dialog box, choose OK.

Tip
View and annotate faxes by double-clicking the thumbnail image at the bottom of the dialog box. Read Chapter 14, "Viewing and Annotating Faxes," to learn how to annotate faxes.

II

Everyday Operation

Searching For and Deleting Messages

When your folders and Send and Receive Logs start to fill up, it becomes difficult to find the messages you want. WinFax PRO enables you to search for specific messages and to delete items and folders. You can also use filters to display only the information you want. The following sections describe searching for, deleting, and filtering information.

Searching through Folders

When you search for specific messages, you search either for the information you added (such as keywords), or for information on the status of the message (such as transmission date). To search for specific messages, follow these steps:

1. In the folder list window, select the folder through which you want to search.

2. Either select **Log** Searc**h**, or click the right mouse button while the mouse pointer is over the folder name and select Searc**h** from the menu that appears. WinFax PRO displays the Search Log dialog box (see fig. 11.4).

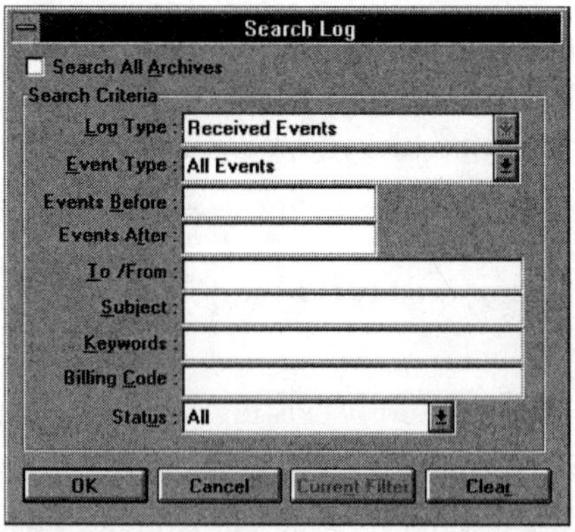

Fig. 11.4

Search for messages with the Search Log dialog box.

3. The Search Log dialog box enables you to search either on the basis of information you added, or information on the status of the message. Fill in the appropriate information in the text boxes or, in some cases, from drop-down lists.

4. To search through all folders, select the Search All **A**rchives check box. Deactivate the check box if you only want to search in the currently selected folder.

5. To clear the Search Log dialog box and start over, click Clea**r**.

6. When you finish, choose OK.

After you complete the Search Log dialog box and click OK, WinFax PRO conducts the search, and displays the items it finds in the item list window. Act on those items as you would items in a normal window.

To restore the normal item list window, choose **L**og Res**t**ore, or click the right mouse button and choose Res**t**ore from the menu.

The search fields in the Search Log dialog box are as follows:

- **L**og Type. This selection specifies the type of item you want to search for. From the drop-down list, select whether to search through Sent Events, Received Events, or both types of events. This selection applies only to folders. When searching through either the Send Log or Receive Log, WinFax PRO automatically makes the selection for you.

- **E**vent Type. The options in this drop-down list are All Events, All Unread Messages, Faxes, Mail Messages, Unread Faxes, and Unread Mail.

- Events **B**efore. WinFax PRO searches for items sent or received before the date you type in this text box. Use the date format that you set in the Windows Control Panel.

- Events **A**fter. WinFax PRO searches for all items sent or received after the date you specify in this text box.

- **T**o/From. Type either the recipient's or sender's name.

- **S**ubject. Type subject of the message.

- **K**eywords. Type any keywords that you affixed to the message.

- Billing **C**ode. Type any part of the billing code you affixed to the item.

- Stat**u**s. From the drop-down list select among All, Completed, or Failed.

> **Note**
>
> You can search on the basis of partial entries in the Search Log dialog box. For example, to find all messages to or from John, Johnson, and Johannson, type **Joh** in the To/From text box.

Tip

Use the Events **B**efore and Events **A**fter text boxes to set date ranges. Search for messages between 12/31/93 and 4/1/94 to find messages from the first three months of 1994.

Tip

Consistency in the three types of user-created information makes it easier to classify and find messages. For example, always use the keyword Acme, Inc. in the keyword field, not Acme, Inc. or AI.

II

Everyday Operation

Searches can be very broad or very specific. An example of a broad search is to select all fax messages in the **E**vent Type drop-down list and not type information in any other text boxes. This search finds all faxes. A more specific search is to ask for completed faxes to a person named Smith sent before a specific date.

Filtering Folder Contents

Searches are one-time events. After restoring the item list window to its normal contents, the results of the search no longer apply.

Filters are like searches, except that you name and save them and apply them to folders at any time. To create a filter, choose **L**og **F**ilters. WinFax PRO displays the Log Filters dialog box (see fig. 11.5).

Fig. 11.5
Filter the contents of your Send and Receive Logs with the Log Filters dialog box.

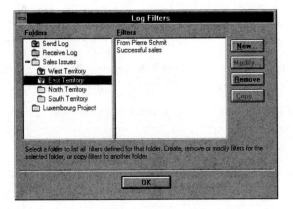

The Log Filters dialog box has two windows. The Folders window lists folders, and the **F**ilters window lists the filters available for the folder you highlight.

To create a new filter, follow these steps:

1. In the Folders window, select the folder to which you want to apply the filter.

2. Click the **N**ew button. WinFax PRO displays the New Filter dialog box. The New Filter dialog box is similar to the Search Log dialog box used when searching for specific items (see fig. 11.6).

3. Type a name for the filter in the **F**ilter Name text box.

4. Fill in the remaining text boxes as appropriate. Fill in as many or as few of the text boxes and drop-down lists as appropriate.

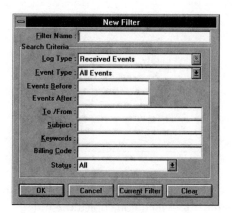

Fig. 11.6

You create filters with the New Filter dialog box.

To clear information in the New Filter dialog box, click the Clear button. To insert the parameters for the most recently used filter, click on the Current Filter button. When you finish the Search Log, choose OK to return to the Log Filters dialog box. WinFax PRO displays the name of the new filter in the Filters window.

When you finish the New Filter dialog box, choose OK. Notice that WinFax PRO displays a funnel in the folder icon for the folder in the Folders window of the Log Filters dialog box. Choose OK. When you return to the log window, notice that a funnel also appears in the folders icon in the folder list window.

To modify a filter, choose Log Filters to display the Log Filters dialog box. Select a filter from the Filters list window, and choose Modify. WinFax PRO displays the Modify Filter dialog box, containing current information for the filter. Make any changes to the filter and choose OK. Then click the OK button in the Log Filters dialog box.

To copy a filter so that it applies to another folder, follow these steps:

1. Highlight the filter in the Log Filters dialog box.

2. Click the Copy button. WinFax PRO displays the Copy Filter to Archive dialog box, which shows your folders (see fig. 11.7).

3. In the Copy Filter to Archive box, click the folder to which you want to copy the filter.

4. Choose OK.

Tip

To copy the filter to more than one folder, hold down the Ctrl key and click on the additional folders.

II

Everyday Operation

Fig. 11.7
Copy filters using
the Copy Filter to
Archive dialog
box.

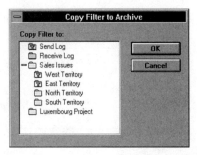

After returning to the Log Filters dialog box, notice that funnels now appear in the icons of the folder to which you copied the filter.

To delete a filter from the selected folder, select the filter in the **F**ilters window and click the **R**emove button. Note that you only remove the filter from the current folder, not from all folders to which the filter has been copied.

When you finish the Log Filters dialog box, click the OK button.

Deleting Messages and Folders

To delete messages from a folder, highlight the messages you want to delete. Then either press the Del key or choose **L**og **R**emove. WinFax PRO asks whether you are sure you want to delete the selected records. If you are sure, click OK. WinFax PRO displays the Delete Log Records dialog box, which provides several options for deleting items (see fig. 11.8).

Fig. 11.8
The Delete Log
Records dialog box
is where you
delete items from
the Send and
Receive Logs.

A log record consists of the following three parts:

- The message file.

- The reference to the message in the folder or log.

- Any attachments to the fax.

WinFax PRO provides three options in the Delete Log Records dialog box related to the parts of a record:

- To delete the message file but keep a record of the message in your log, select the **D**elete Pages (Keep Event) check box.

- To delete attachments to the fax, select the Delete **A**ttachment check box.

- To delete all evidence of the message—the log entry, fax file, and attachments—select no check boxes. Simply choose OK.

To delete an entire folder, highlight it in the folder list window. Then either press the Del key or select **L**og **R**emove. WinFax PRO asks if you are sure you want to remove the folder. If you are sure, choose **Y**es.

Troubleshooting

I searched for information by typing information into two text boxes in the Search Log dialog box. I know there are messages in my folder containing the information I typed, but WinFax PRO doesn't find them.

When you type information in more than one text box of the Search Log dialog box, WinFax PRO only finds messages that contain both pieces of information. For example, if you put Jones in the To/From text box in the Search Log dialog box and Budget in the Subject box, WinFax PRO only finds messages to or from Jones about the budget. If you didn't send any messages about budgets to Jones, WinFax PRO finds nothing. To ensure that you find the information, search for only one term or the other.

I know there are more items in a particular folder, but WinFax PRO doesn't display them.

You probably left a filter in effect. To eliminate the filter, position the mouse pointer over the folder. Click the right mouse button. From the menu that appears, click No Filter.

Sorting Items

Sorting provides a different way to view information in a folder. Unlike the results when you search or apply a filter, when you sort the contents of a folder, all items appear in the item list window in the sort order you specify.

II

Everyday Operation

To sort a single column of information in the item list window, click on the column heading. WinFax PRO sorts the items in the item list window on the basis of the contents of that column.

For example, if you click the Date column, WinFax PRO lists the messages in the item list window by the date of transmission, with the oldest transmissions first. If you click on the To/From column heading, WinFax PRO lists received (From) messages first and lists the senders in alphabetical order. It lists the sent (To) messages next with recipients listed in alphabetical order.

To reverse the order of sorts, hold down the Alt key, and then click the column heading. If, for example, you use this method to sort on the basis of date, WinFax PRO places the most recent messages first in the Date column and the sent messages first in the To/From column.

Figures 11.9 and 11.10 show the same folder sorted by the To/From column and by the Date column.

Fig. 11.9

This item list window is sorted by the To/From column.

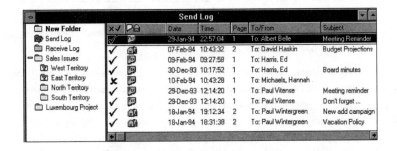

Fig. 11.10

This item list window is sorted by date.

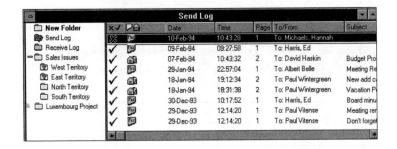

You can fine-tune sorting even more by selecting **Log Sort**. WinFax PRO then displays the Sort Log dialog box (see fig. 11.11).

Fig. 11.11
Sort the log with
the Sort Log dialog
box.

The Sort Log dialog box is a more powerful way to sort than clicking on column heads. When you use the Sort Log dialog box, you can do the following:

- Sort on three columns. This is done by designating a column for the primary sort and as many as two additional columns for secondary sorts. For example, your primary sort can be by date. A secondary sort on the To/From column sorts all messages from the same day on the basis of recipient or sender.

- Determine more easily whether the sort is in ascending or descending order.

- Specify whether WinFax PRO should apply the sort whenever you start the program.

To use the Sort Log dialog box, follow these steps:

1. Select the field on which to base your primary sort in the **1**st Key drop-down list.

2. Select either the **A**scending or **D**escending buttons.

> **Note**
>
> Ascending order starts at the beginning and moves to the end. For example, ascending order starts with A. It also starts with the earliest date or first number. Descending order starts with Z and goes backward. It also starts with the most recent date or last number.

3. Optionally, you can repeat the process for the **2**nd Key. Select None from the drop-down list if you don't want to sort on a second column.

4. Optionally, you can repeat the process for the **3**rd Key. Select None from the drop-down list if you don't want to sort on a third column.

5. When you finish the Sort Log dialog box, click Apply.

II

Everyday Operation

> **Note**
>
> Read Chapter 5, "Customizing WinFax PRO," to learn how to customize the appearance of the item list window.

Printing Logs and Faxes

You will sometimes want to print either your log or a message in the log. For example, if you travel to a client's office, you may need to carry copies of all messages you exchanged with the client. Or perhaps all you need is a record of the messages. In either case, WinFax PRO makes it easy to print the logs and to print messages after you send or receive them.

Whether you print logs or specific messages, select and set up the printer by choosing **F**ax, Printer **S**etup. WinFax PRO displays the Printer Setup dialog box (see fig. 11.12).

Fig. 11.12

Select and set up your printer from the Printer Setup dialog box.

> **Note**
>
> You only need to select a printer if you plan to use a printer different from your default Windows printer. Read the Windows user's guide for more information on selecting default printers for Windows applications.

Select your printer driver in the **P**rinter list box. To set up the printer driver, click **S**etup. WinFax PRO displays the standard setup dialog box for your printer driver. Each printer has a different Setup dialog box. You also can access the Printer Setup dialog box from the Windows Control Panel.

After you set up your printer, choose OK in the printer's setup dialog box. Then choose OK in WinFax PRO's Printer Setup dialog box.

To print a fax, choose **F**ax or (electronic mail message), Print Eve**n**t. WinFax PRO displays the Print Fax dialog box (see fig. 11.13).

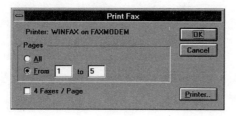

Fig. 11.13
Before printing a fax, complete the Print Fax dialog box.

To print all pages in the fax, select the **A**ll button. To print only a range of pages, select the **F**rom button. Type a range of pages in the next two text boxes. To print miniature versions of your fax so that four fax pages appear on a single printed page, select the 4 Fa**x**es/Page check box.

When you finish the Print Fax dialog box, choose OK. WinFax PRO prints your fax.

To print the current log or folder, choose **F**ax, **P**rint Log. WinFax PRO displays the Print dialog box. Choose from the Options area the way that you want the log to look. Select the **D**raw Border check box to enclose the printed log and its headings in boxes. Select the Show Column Headings check box to show the column headings. Designate the range of columns to print by entering the column position numbers in the **P**rint From Column text boxes. Choose OK to print.

Exporting Logs

To keep archive records of your messages without storing the actual messages, export logs from WinFax PRO and import them into other applications, such as database programs.

To export the Send Log, Receive Log or folder, select the folder list window. Then choose Fax Export. WinFax PRO displays the Export Log dialog box for exporting in ASCII format (see fig. 11.14).

To export the log, follow these steps:

1. Type the name of the file to which you will export the log in the **E**xport To text box.

2. To find an existing file to which you can export the log, click the **S**elect button. This displays the Export File Name dialog box (see fig. 11.15).

Tip
By exporting logs, you track heavy message traffic without overloading your logs and folders. If you are a heavy WinFax PRO user, periodically export your logs to a database.

Everyday Operation

II

Fig. 11.14
The Export Log dialog box is the control center for exporting logs.

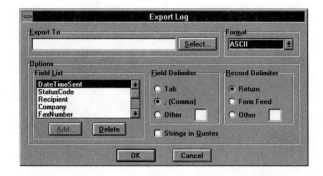

Fig. 11.15
Select an existing file for exporting in the Export File Name dialog box.

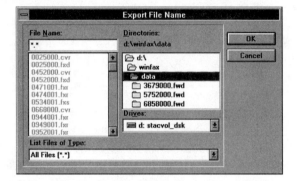

3. If necessary, use the Drives drop-down list, the Directories list window, and the File Names text box and list window to find the file to which you want to export your log.

4. Click OK in the Export File Name dialog box to return to the Export Log dialog box.

5. WinFax PRO displays all fields in the Field List list box. Delete fields you don't want to export by clicking the Delete button. Add fields you deleted by clicking the Add button and selecting the previously deleted fields from the Add Field dialog box.

6. Change the order of fields in the Field List list box by clicking on a field, holding down the left mouse button, and dragging the field to a new location. With mouse pointer over the new location, release the mouse button.

Caution

You must export the log fields in the order expected by your other application. Otherwise, the process of importing the information into your database or other application could fail.

---

7. Select a delimiter between fields in the **F**ield Delimiter area of the dialog box. Commas are the default—and most commonly used—delimiter, but you can designate tabs or your own delimiter.

8. Select a delimiter between records in the **R**ecord Delimiter area of the dialog box. Return is the default—and most commonly used—delimiter, but you also can designate Form Feed or your own delimiter.

9. To place the contents of fields in quotes (which some databases require), select the **S**trings in **Q**uotes check box.

10. When you finish the Export Log dialog box and are ready to export your log as an ASCII file, click OK. WinFax PRO informs you when it completes the export process. Click OK.

The process for exporting in dBASE IV format is even simpler. When WinFax PRO first displays the Export Log dialog box, select dBASE IV from the For**m**at drop-down list. WinFax PRO changes the appearance of the Export Log dialog box (see fig. 11.16).

Type the drive, path, and name of the file in the **E**xport To text box. To find an existing file to which you will export your log, click **S**elect and use the Export File Name dialog box.

After entering the name in the Export To text box of the Export Log dialog box, click OK. WinFax PRO exports your log in dBASE format and tells you when it completes the operation. Click OK.

Tip
Read the documentation for your database or other application to learn the precise format and delimiters it expects when importing ASCII files.

Fig. 11.16
The Export Log dialog box is used to export files in dBASE format.

II

Everyday Operation

> **Troubleshooting**
>
> *I exported my log, but I can't import it into my database program.*
>
> Chances are that you used a delimiter to separate records that your database doesn't support. Most database programs—and other applications that can import database files—support comma-delimited ASCII files. When you export log records from WinFax PRO, comma-delimited ASCII is the most common format. If that doesn't work, exporting in dBASE format also is a good bet. Most database applications import dBASE files.

Saving Received Attachments

If you receive a message with binary files as attachments, you can save those attachments to a file. This enables you to use the attachments later for messages of your own.

To save a message's attachments, highlight the message in the Receive Log. Then choose **F**ax Sa**v**e Attachments. WinFax PRO displays the Save Attachments dialog box, which lists the attachments attached to the message.

> **Note**
>
> You receive binary attachments with electronic mail messages, and also with faxes that you received using the Binary File Transfer, Microsoft At Work, and Compressed BFT methods of transmission. For more information about those methods, read Chapter 16, "Different Ways to Send and Receive."

From Here...

This chapter showed you how to get the most out of the Send and Receive Logs. For more information, you might want to read the following chapters:

- Chapter 12, "Assembling Faxes from Many Sources," tells you how to manage and use attachments.

- Chapter 16, "Different Ways to Send and Receive," describes how to use WinFax PRO for network and public electronic mail, and how to send and receive binary files.

- Chapter 18, "Using WinFax Pro in Other Programs," tells you how to use WinFax PRO as a "front end" for electronic mail programs and how to connect WinFax PRO with other programs.

Part III

Power Faxing with WinFax PRO

Chapter 12

Assembling Faxes from Many Sources

In this chapter, you learn to do the following:

- Navigate the Attachments window.

- Designate faxes and files as attachments.

- Add attachments to faxes.

Attachments are an excellent way to extend the reach of WinFax PRO. An *attachment* is a file that you include with a message that you send. For example:

- An architect attaches a drawing for a building addition to a price quote. He sends the quote and drawing via fax to a customer.

- An accountant attaches a spreadsheet file to a report on the tax ramifications of a client's business deal. She sends the spreadsheet and report via Binary File Transfer.

- An executive attaches a memo and spreadsheet concerning last year's budget to a new memo regarding this year's budget. He sends the two memos and spreadsheet via electronic mail to all managers.

Attachments enable you to assemble messages from files created in virtually any Windows program; this greatly extends the usefulness of WinFax PRO. You can add multiple attachments created by multiple applications to a single message. This chapter tells you how to designate and use attachments, and how to navigate the attachments window.

How Do Attachments Work?

WinFax PRO takes its fax images and data files created in other applications, such as a word processor, and turns them into attachments. WinFax PRO refers to data files created in other applications as *binary file attachments*; faxes used as attachments are referred to as *fax attachments*.

Whether you use fax images or binary files as attachments, store them in the Attachments window. Assign attachments to messages in the Send dialog box. For more information about sending faxes, read Chapter 8, "Sending Faxes."

When you send a fax, WinFax PRO converts the binary file into a fax image and transmits the fax image as it usually would. For more information about the faxing process, read Chapter 2, "How Faxing Works."

If you send a message with any other method—as an electronic mail message, or by using the Microsoft At Work (MAW) or Binary File Transfer (BFT) methods—WinFax PRO transmits the file as a binary file, much the same as you download or upload a file from a bulletin board service.

For BFT, MAW, and electronic mail transmissions, you can use any file on your hard drive as an attachment. For fax attachments, you can create an attachment from any fax you have either sent or received. You also can create an attachment from any data file for any program for which a Windows *association* exists.

In Windows terminology, an *association* is the connection between a file name extension and a specific application. For example, when you install Word for Windows, that application tells Windows that any documents it creates will have the DOC file name extension, which means that certain actions involving DOC files occur automatically. If you use the Windows File Manager, for example, and double-click a file with a DOC file name extension, Windows automatically knows to launch Word for Windows and load that specific file.

Most Windows applications automatically set up associations during the installation process. Because an association exists, WinFax PRO knows the name of the application that created the binary file attachment. Then, behind the scenes, it works with that program to create a fax image of the contents of the file and includes it with the fax as an attachment.

Using the Attachments Window

WinFax PRO's Attachments window is similar to the Send and Receive Logs and other windows in that it has three windows in it:

- The *folder list window* lists the folders and subfolders that you create for storing attachments.

- The *item list window* lists the attachments in the folder you select and basic information about each attachment.

- The *display area window* displays either information about the attachment or a thumbnail of the attachment, if it is a fax image. If the attachment is a binary file, rather than a thumbnail image of the attachment, WinFax PRO displays an icon representing the application that created the attachment (see fig. 12.1).

Folder list window

Item list window

Display area window

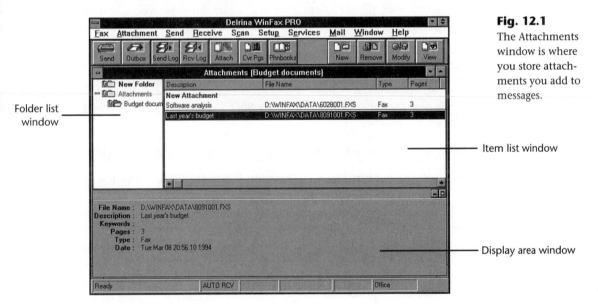

Fig. 12.1

The Attachments window is where you store attachments you add to messages.

Related attachments are stored in a system of folders that you devise. You can create as many folders as you want, and even place folders in other folders to subclassify your attachments. For example, you could name one attachment folder "Memos," and in it place subfolders called "Budget memos," "Product memos," and "Personnel memos."

Power Faxing

III

To review how to navigate the Attachments window, follow these steps:

1. Open a folder by double-clicking it in the folder list window.

   WinFax PRO displays the items within the folder you select in the item list window.

2. Begin the process of acting on a specific item—for example, viewing, copying, or deleting an attachment—by clicking the item in the item list window.

3. Move attachment items by dragging them from the item list window to other folders in the folder list window.

4. Copy attachment items by holding down the Ctrl key and dragging them to other folders.

You can customize the three windows in the Attachments view. Specifically, you can:

- Hide or display all subfolders in the folder list window.

- Change the information displayed in the item list window.

- Change the order in which WinFax PRO displays the information in the item list window.

- Sort the contents of specific column headings in the item list window.

- Display either text-based information in the display area window or thumbnail images of the item if they are regular faxes. If the attachment is a binary file, WinFax PRO displays an icon representing the application that created the file.

Designating Attachments

There are three common ways to create attachments:

- Use a scanner to scan documents and designate them as attachments. Chapter 13, "Scanning Faxes," describes how.

- Start the process of sending a fax from another application but use the Send dialog box to designate the item as an attachment. Chapter 8, "Sending Faxes," describes the process.

- Designate a new fax or binary file from the Attachments window. The following section describes how.

To designate a new attachment while in Attachments view, follow these steps:

1. Double-click the New Attachment item in the item list window. (Alternatively, choose **A**ttachment **N**ew.) WinFax PRO displays the New Attachment dialog box (see fig. 12.2).

Fig. 12.2
Designate new attachments in the New Attachment dialog box.

2. Type a description of the attachment in the **D**escription text box.

3. Type the drive, path, and file name for the attachment file in the **F**ile Name text box. If you are not sure of the drive, path, or file name, click the **S**elect button. WinFax PRO displays the Select Attachment dialog box (see fig. 12.3).

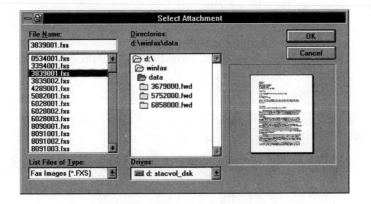

Fig. 12.3
Find attachments to add in the Select Attachment dialog box.

4. In the List Files of **T**ype drop-down list of the Select Attachment dialog box, select the type of file you want to find.

5. In the Drives drop-down list, select the drive where you stored the file.

6. Select the directory where you stored the file in the **D**irectories list area.

7. Select the file from the File **N**ame list box. A thumbnail image of the file appears in the viewing area.

III

Power Faxing

8. Choose OK and return to the New Attachment dialog box.

9. Add keywords for the attachment in the **K**eywords text box. You use keywords to help find attachments.

10. Choose OK. WinFax PRO adds the attachment to the currently selected folder.

> **Note**
>
> If you add faxes as attachments, you only add one fax page at a time as an attachment. WinFax PRO doesn't add multiple page faxes as single attachments.

Adding and Deleting Folders

If you use lots of attachments, your system of folders is important for keeping track of them all. As with other views, you can create a series of folders for attachments. You also can create subfolders, or folders within folders, to help you further categorize your attachments.

To create a new attachment folder, follow these steps:

1. Make sure the Attachments window is active. If you are not sure whether it is the active window, click the Attach button in the WinFax PRO toolbar.

2. Double-click the New Folder icon in the folder list window. WinFax PRO displays the New Attachment Folder dialog box (see fig. 12.4).

Fig. 12.4

Create new attachment folders with the New Attachment Folder dialog box.

3. Type a name for the folder in the **F**older Name text box. This name will appear in the folder list window.

4. Determine whether the folder is a top-level folder or a subfolder. If it is a top level folder, click the **T**op Level button.

5. If the folder is to be a subfolder, click the **S**ubfolder Of button. WinFax PRO displays the top level folders in the display window. Click the top level folder in which you want to place the new folder.

6. Choose OK to return to the Attachments window. WinFax PRO displays your new folder.

> ### Note
>
> New folders added to the Send and Receive Logs are archival folders. As you learned in Chapter 11, "Using the Send and Receive Logs," when you move faxes to archival folders, WinFax PRO automatically compresses them to save disk space. WinFax PRO does not compress attachments.

To modify an existing folder, select the folder in the folder list window by clicking it once, and then choose **A**ttachment **M**odify. You can also click the right mouse button and choose **M**odify from the menu that appears. WinFax PRO displays the Modify Attachment Folder dialog box.

The Modify Attachment Folder dialog box is identical to the New Attachment Folder dialog box with one exception: It contains information about the folder. Change the information in this dialog box and choose OK to return to the Attachments window.

You can determine whether or not a folder has subfolders by on-screen hints.

■ A folder containing subfolders, which are visible on-screen, has a minus sign to the left of the folder name in the folder list window.

■ A folder containing subfolders, which are hidden on-screen, has a plus sign to the left of its name in the folder list window.

■ A folder with no subfolders has neither a plus nor minus sign to the left of its name.

The plus and minus signs are *toggles*. If you click the sign once, they toggle, or switch, to the other state. For example, if you click a plus to the left of a folder, all its subfolders become visible on-screen, and the plus turns into a minus. If you click a minus, the subfolders become hidden and the minus turns into a plus.

III

Power Faxing

Alternatively, you can select a folder and choose either the **A**ttachment Expand/**C**ollapse Folder to show or hide subfolders.

Modifying Attachments

As with messages, cover pages, and phonebooks, you can modify attachment information to help in archiving and locating attachments.

Modifying the Description

To modify the information you affix to attachments, select the attachment to modify and choose **A**ttachment **M**odify. WinFax PRO displays the Modify Attachment dialog box, which is identical to the New Attachment dialog box except that it contains information previously filled in about the item.

Change any information you want and click OK. WinFax PRO displays the new information in the item list window.

Deleting the Attachment

To remove an attachment, select the attachment in the item list window and choose **A**ttachment **R**emove. WinFax PRO asks you to confirm that you want to modify the attachment. If you are sure, click **Y**es.

Viewing and Modifying the Attachment

Whether you use a fax or a file as an attachment, you can view it at any time. To view the attachment, follow these steps:

1. Select the attachment to view by clicking it once.

2. Choose **F**ax **V**iew. Alternatively, click the View button on the toolbar.

If the attachment is a fax, WinFax PRO displays it in the Viewer. In addition to viewing faxes, you also can use the Viewer to annotate faxes by drawing on them and adding graphic images. For more information about using the Viewer, read Chapter 14, "Viewing and Annotating Faxes."

If the attachment is a binary file, WinFax PRO automatically launches the application that created the attachment and loads the attachment file. Use the application that created the attachment to view and modify the attachment.

Searching for Attachments

As your folders begin to fill up with attachments, it becomes time-consuming to find precisely the attachments you want. To solve that problem, use WinFax PRO's searching capabilities.

To search for an attachment, follow these steps:

1. Make sure the Attachments window is the active view by clicking the Attach button on the toolbar, or by choosing **F**ax A**t**tachments.

2. Choose **A**ttachment Searc**h**. WinFax PRO displays the Search Attachments dialog box (see fig. 12.5).

Fig. 12.5
Find attachments with the Search Attachments dialog box.

3. Type the description of the attachments for which you are looking in the **D**escription text box.

4. Type keywords that describe the attachment in the **K**eywords text box.

5. Type a file name for the attachment in the **F**ile Name text box.

6. Select the **M**atch Anywhere check box if you are entering only partial information in any of the text boxes. If you don't select this check box, you must enter the information precisely as you entered it when you created the attachment.

7. Select the **C**ase Sensitive check box to have WinFax PRO search for information with the precise combination of lower- and uppercase letters that you typed in the text boxes.

8. Choose OK to begin the search.

III

Power Faxing

> **Note**
>
> If you place information in more than one text box of the Search Attachments dialog box, WinFax PRO finds only attachments that meet all the search criteria, not the criteria on one line or another. In other words, typing information in multiple text boxes narrows the search so that WinFax PRO finds fewer items rather than expanding the search to find more.

WinFax PRO places the attachments it finds in the item list window of the Attachments window. You can act on those items as you would on any items in the item list window. For example, you can drag found attachments to folders or delete them.

Tip

Create a new folder in the folder list window and fill it by searching for appropriate items. Drag the items you find to the new folder.

To return to the full list of items in the item list window, choose **A**ttachment Res**t**ore. Remember, however, that after you restore a search, the search results are gone. To get the search results again, you must search again.

Displaying Information about Attachments

Chapter 5, "Customizing WinFax PRO," describes how to add new columns of information to item list windows, how to change the order of columns, and how to sort the contents of item list windows. To briefly review how to add types of information to item list windows:

1. Position the mouse pointer over a column heading in the item list window.

2. Click the right mouse button. A menu displays the types of information available. A check mark to the left of an information type informs you that WinFax PRO already is displaying that type of information.

3. To add a type of information, click an information type that does not have a check mark next to it.

4. To eliminate a type of information type, click an information type that has a check mark next to it.

Although this procedure is the same for the display area window in all views, the types of information you can place in the item list window vary among views.

Table 12.1 lists the types of information you can display in the item list window of the Attachments window.

Table 12.1 Information available in the item list window of the Attachments window.	
Item	**Description**
Description	The description you typed when you created the attachments.
File name	The file name of the attachment.
Type	The type of attachment, such as fax or binary.
Pages	The number of pages in the attachment.
Keywords	The keywords you typed when you created the attachment.
Date	The date you sent or received the fax attachment or the last date you modified the binary attachment.

To switch the type of information shown in the display area window so that it shows thumbnails, choose **W**indow Display **T**humbnails. To switch back to viewing text-based information in the display area window, choose **W**indow Display **I**nformation.

Adding Attachments to Messages

Attachments are added to messages just before you send the message. Read Chapter 8, "Sending Faxes," to learn more about sending fax messages. Read Chapter 10, "Using WinFax PRO for Electronic Mail," to learn how to add attachments to electronic mail messages. Read Chapter 16, "Different Ways to Send and Receive," to learn about using WinFax PRO to send electronic mail and binary files.

In any of these cases, you add attachments from the Send dialog box. When you add attachments from the Send dialog box, follow these steps:

1. Click the **A**ttach button near the bottom of the Send dialog box. WinFax PRO displays the Select Attachments dialog box (see fig. 12.6).

III

Power Faxing

Fig. 12.6
Select attachments
for transmission
in the Select
Attachments
dialog box.

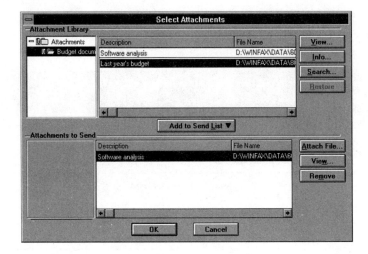

Tip
Select multiple
attachments by
selecting one
attachment,
holding down
the Ctrl key,
and selecting
additional
attachments.

2. In the folder list in the Attachment Library area, select the folder containing the attachment you want to add.

3. In the item list in the Attachment Library area, select the specific item you want to add.

4. Click the Add to Send List button to add the attachments to the message. WinFax PRO places the attachments in the item list in the Attachments to Send area of the dialog box. View thumbnails of the attachment on the left side of the Attachments to Send area.

5. Repeat the process to collect all the attachments you want.

Tip
For faster
method, click
attachments in
the Attachment
Library area.
Hold down the
left mouse
button and
drag the attach-
ments to the
item list win-
dow of the
Attachments
to Send area.

6. Choose OK to return to the Send dialog box. Below the cover page fill-in window of the Send dialog box, WinFax PRO lists the number of attachments and attachment pages you added.

Setting Attachment Order

Most people need control over the order in which WinFax PRO sends attachments in faxes. WinFax PRO sends faxes in the following order:

■ The cover page, if any, that you designate in the Send dialog box.

■ The main body of the fax you send.

■ Any attachments you designate. WinFax PRO sends attachments in the order you set in the Attachments to Send area of the Select Attachments dialog box.

To change the order in which WinFax PRO sends attachments in the item list area of the Attachments to Send area of the Select Attachment dialog box, follow these steps:

1. Position the mouse cursor over the attachment you want to move.

2. Hold down the left mouse button. The regular mouse pointer changes to a horizontal line with arrows pointing up and down.

3. Drag the pointer to the new position and release the mouse button. WinFax PRO reorders the attachments and displays the new order in the item list area of the Attachments to Send area.

Additional Capabilities

The Select Attachments dialog box has several additional capabilities that you may find useful.

■ The dialog box has two buttons for viewing attachments. To view the attachment, in the Attachment Library area, click **V**iew. To view an attachment in the Attachments to Send area, click Vie**w**. If the attachment is a fax, WinFax PRO displays it in the Viewer. If it is a binary file, WinFax PRO loads the application that created it and loads the attachment file itself.

■ To view information about the attachment, click **I**nfo. WinFax PRO displays the Attachment Information window, which displays information about the attachment and also a thumbnail image of fax attachments (see fig. 12.7).

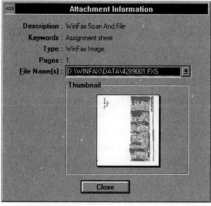

Fig. 12.7
View information about the attachment in the Attachment Information window.

■ To find specific attachments, click **S**earch. WinFax PRO displays the Search Attachments dialog box described in a previous section of this chapter, "Searching for Attachments." WinFax PRO displays the results of the search in the item list window of the Attachment Library area. To restore the item list display, click the **R**estore button.

■ You can attach files that you haven't yet designated as attachments. To do so, click the **A**ttach File button. WinFax PRO displays the Open dialog box discussed in the "Designating Attachments" section of this chapter. Use the Open dialog box to select attachments to add to the item list window of the Attachments to add area.

Troubleshooting

I know I have an attachment somewhere, but I can't find the folder in which I put it.

You probably placed the attachment in a subfolder that is not currently visible to you. In the folder list window, look for top level folders with a plus sign to the left of the folder names. A plus sign indicates that the folder has subfolders in it. Click the plus sign once to view the subfolders.

I attached several items to faxes, but they didn't transmit in the order I wanted.

You can change the order of fax attachments in the item list area at the bottom of the Send Attachments dialog box. To review how to change the order, see the section of this chapter, "Setting Attachment Order."

I attached a file created by one of my other applications to a fax, but WinFax PRO wouldn't transmit it via fax.

The application probably doesn't have the correct Windows association for its data files. WinFax PRO can't attach files to faxes if an association doesn't exist. Read the Windows user's guide to learn more about creating associations.

Transmitting Attachments

WinFax PRO handles attachments differently, depending on the method of transmission. This section provides some background about how WinFax PRO transmits attachments.

If you transmit a message using traditional fax transmission methods, WinFax PRO simply adds fax attachments to the fax message. It converts binary attachments to fax images and adds them to the fax message.

> **Note**
>
> WinFax PRO only converts binary files to fax images if a proper Windows association exists between the file type and the application that created it. A previous section of this chapter, "How Do Attachments Work?" explains associations. If no association exists, WinFax PRO is unable to send the attachment.

If you use either Microsoft At Work (MAW), Binary File Transfer (BFT), or transmit directly to another WinFax PRO 4 user, WinFax PRO transmits all information, whether it is a fax or attachment, as a binary file. The recipient's software reconstructs the entire transmission either as fax images or as binary files. Read Chapter 16, "Different Ways to Send and Receive," to learn more about BFT and MAW transmissions, and about transmitting to another WinFax PRO user.

From Here...

This chapter told you how to add attachments to messages and how to transmit those attachments with the messages. For more information, you might want to review the following chapters:

- Chapter 8, "Sending Faxes," tells you how to use the Send dialog box for sending faxes.

- Chapter 13, "Scanning Faxes," tells you how to create attachments from scanned documents.

- Chapter 15, "Viewing and Annotating Faxes," tells you how to use Viewer. When using Viewer, you can view and annotate faxes and fax attachments.

- Chapter 14, "Different Ways to Send and Receive," tells you how to use Microsoft At Work (MAW) and Binary File Transfer (BFT) to exchange messages and attachments.

III

Power Faxing

Chapter 13

Scanning Faxes

In this chapter, you learn how to do the following:

- Set up WinFax PRO to work with your scanner.

- Send faxes using your scanner.

- Scan items and save them as attachments files.

Scanning and faxing are natural partners because they work in a similar way. Both scanning and faxing covert a page into an image composed of a series of dots, called *pixels*; this conversion process is called *rasterization*.

Scanners don't work by themselves; you use scanners with other programs. For example, graphic artists scan photos or other images and use an image editing program to edit the image and prepare it for insertion into documents. Others scan documents into an optical character recognition (OCR) program to convert a scanned page so that it is editable.

Similarly, you can scan documents and send those pages with WinFax PRO. This, in effect, makes WinFax PRO act like a traditional fax machine. You also can scan documents and save them as attachments that you add to future faxes. This chapter describes how to use scanners in conjunction with WinFax PRO.

Getting Ready to Scan

Tip
If you buy a scanner, make sure you know whether it is TWAIN compliant. Low-cost scanners are less likely to comply with the TWAIN standard.

WinFax PRO works scanners that are *TWAIN compliant.* Established by scanner developers and software vendors, TWAIN is a standard that makes it easier to initiate scanning from within programs.

You must, of course, make sure that you properly install and set up your scanner. Read your scanner's documentation to learn how to do that.

To work with WinFax PRO, your scanner must support the type of images that WinFax PRO sends. Specifically, it must be able to do the following:

■ Support black-and-white or gray scale images.

■ Support a resolution of 200 dots per inch (dpi) by 200 dpi.

If you have a color scanner, set it to black and white or gray scale. Similarly, set the resolution at which the scanner operates at 200 dpi by 200 dpi. Do that with the software that accompanied your scanner.

> **Note**
>
> Many hand-held scanners are TWAIN compliant, but won't work well with WinFax PRO. That's because most documents require more than one pass of the hand-held scanner to capture the entire page. Unlike image editing programs, WinFax PRO cannot piece together the images acquired in multiple scanning passes. If you use a hand-held scanner, stitch together your pages with an image editing program. Then send the pages by printing them with the WinFax PRO driver from the image editing program.

To designate a scanner to use with WinFax PRO, select Scan Select Scanner. WinFax PRO displays the Select Source dialog box (see fig. 13.1).

Fig. 13.1
Select a scanner in the Select Source dialog box.

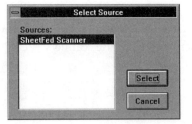

Even if only one scanner name is listed in the Select Source dialog box, highlight the name and click the Select button. If you properly set up your scanner, that selection should enable you to start scanning from WinFax PRO.

Starting the Scanning Process

WinFax PRO enables you to either send a fax of a document you scan, or save the scanned document as an attachment. Start either process by placing the page you want to scan into the scanner.

To scan the page and send it as a fax, choose Scan Scan and Send. To scan the page and save it to a file, choose Scan, Scan and File.

The following two sections explain each of these options in detail. However, whichever option you choose, WinFax PRO displays the Scanner dialog box, where you adjust various settings relating to the scanning process (see fig. 13.2).

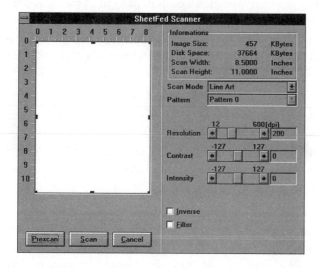

Fig. 13.2
Adjust the scanning process from the Scanner dialog box.

The Scanner dialog box isn't a WinFax PRO dialog box. Rather, this dialog box, which WinFax PRO loads, is provided by the scanner manufacturer. So the same dialog box displays when you use the scanner with other applications.

> **Note**
>
> The dialog box used in this chapter is a typical dialog box with typical settings. It may not, however, be the same as the Scanner dialog box you see. Because TWAIN is a standard, the contents of dialog boxes provided by different scanning software are usually similar. We discuss this particular dialog box because it is typical, not because it includes all the options you may see. If this section does not explain an option in the dialog box you see, consult your scanner's documentation.

III

Power Faxing

> **Note**
>
> Because the Scanner dialog box is not a WinFax PRO dialog box, selecting options may be different in the dialog box you use. For example, some dialog boxes use buttons instead of the check boxes used in this dialog box. Similarly, some dialog boxes use drop-down lists instead of the slider bars used in this dialog box.

The left side of the Scanner dialog box is for selecting the size of the image. Leave the page size as the same size you specified in the WinFax Driver dialog box discussed in Chapter 4, "Configuring WinFax PRO." (For North American users, that page size typically is 8 1/2 by 11 inches.)

To change the page size to match a custom page size you set in the WinFax Driver dialog box, click the handles along the edges of the window and hold down your left mouse button. Then drag the mouse to change the page size. Notice that the information in the upper right corner of the dialog box changes as you change the size of the page. The information includes the precise page size measurements.

In the Scan Mode drop-down list, select the mode in which you want the scanner to work. This particular Scanner dialog box is for a gray scale scanner, so the options are Line Art, Halftone, 16 Gray Scales, and 256 Gray Scales. Any of those settings works with WinFax PRO. If you use a color scanner, do not scan the image in color.

The Pattern drop-down list determines the patterns used for black-and-white and gray scale images. *Patterns* refer to the arrangement of pixels in the scanned image, which emulate different shades of gray. Each scanner has its own options. Read your scanner manual to learn what those options are.

Select the resolution for the scanned image with the Resolution slider bar. Remember to select a resolution no higher than 200 dpi.

The contrast slider bar determines the contrast between light and dark parts of the image. Contrast settings are not important for black-and-white and halftone settings, although they are important when scanning gray scale images.

The Intensity slider bar determines the intensity of black or gray parts of the image.

Leave the **I**nverse check box deactivated to scan the image normally. To reverse blacks and whites in the image, which makes the image look like a photographic negative, select the **I**nverse check box.

Select the **F**ilter check box to filter out extraneous markings and other "noise" from the scanned page.

To see what the page will look like after you scan it, click the **P**rescan button. WinFax PRO displays an image of the page in the page size window.

In the Scanner dialog box, adjust the page size to match the size of the image. If you do this, however, remember to also change the page size in the WinFax Driver dialog box. To start the scanning process in earnest, click the **S**can button.

The next two sections describe scanning and faxing, and scanning and saving the image to file.

Sending Faxes from the Scanner

To send the fax directly from the scanner, follow these steps:

1. Make sure your page is in the correct position in the scanner.

2. From the Scan menu, choose Scan, **S**can and Send.

3. Fill in the dialog box, as described in the previous section.

4. When you finish the Scanner dialog box, click the **S**can button. Your scanner then scans the image. Most scanners display a message box telling you the progress of the scanning process.

5. After scanning each page, WinFax PRO asks whether you want to scan another page. Click the **Y**es button if you want to scan another page.

6. Repeat the process until you scan all the pages of your document.

7. After scanning your final page, when WinFax PRO asks whether you want to scan another page, click the **N**o button. WinFax PRO displays the Send dialog box.

In the Send dialog box, notice that WinFax PRO designates the subject of the fax as WinFax Scan And Send. You can, of course, change the subject as you want.

From this point forward, the process of sending the fax is identical to sending a fax from your application or starting the faxing process from within WinFax PRO. Read Chapter 8, "Sending Faxes," for more information about the sending process.

III

Power Faxing

Scanning Attachments

Besides scanning and faxing, you also can scan pages and save them as attachments to be used at a later time. To do that, follow these steps:

1. From the Scan menu, choose Scan and File.

2. Proceed with the scanning process as described in previous sections of this chapter.

3. After you scan the last page and WinFax PRO asks whether you want to scan another page, click No. WinFax PRO displays the Create Attachment dialog box (see fig. 13.3).

Fig. 13.3
Scan and save documents as attachments in the Create Attachment dialog box.

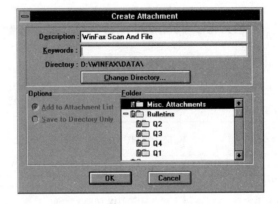

In the Create Attachment dialog box, follow these steps:

1. Type a description for the attachment in the Description text box.

2. Add keywords in the Keywords text box.

3. By default, WinFax PRO stores attachments in the \WINFAX\DATA subdirectory. To select another directory, click the Change Directory button. WinFax PRO displays the Directories dialog box (see fig. 13.4).

Fig. 13.4
Change the directory where you store attachments in the Directories dialog box.

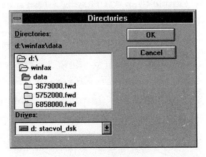

4. In the Directories dialog box, select a drive from the Drives drop-down list. Select a directory from the **D**irectories list box.

5. When you finish the Directories dialog box, choose OK. WinFax PRO displays the new directory beneath the **K**eywords text box of the Create Attachment dialog box.

6. Select the **A**dd to Attachment List button if you want to add the attachment to a folder.

7. Select the **S**ave to Directory Only button to save the scanned document as an attachment file, but not place it in a folder.

8. If you selected the **A**dd to Attachment List button, select the folder in which you want WinFax PRO to store the attachment in the **F**older window.

When you finish the Create Attachment dialog box, choose OK. If you elected to display the new attachment in a folder, the new attachment appears in that folder in the Attachments window.

Tip
Scan corporate logos, save as attachments and add to quick cover pages. When you scan, make sure the page size of the scanned image is as small as possible.

Troubleshooting

I can't get WinFax PRO to work with my scanner.

WinFax PRO only supports TWAIN compliant scanners. Chances are that if WinFax PRO doesn't work with your scanner, it isn't TWAIN compliant.

If your scanner is TWAIN complaint, reinstall the driver and any other files that came with your scanner. Then try using them with WinFax PRO again.

When I start the scanning process from WinFax PRO, I see a dialog box different from the one described in this chapter.

The scanner's software, not WinFax PRO, determines the dialog box you see after you start the scanning process. The Scanner dialog box discussed in this chapter is typical of other Scanner dialog boxes, but is not identical to other dialog boxes.

I scanned a document and saved it as an attachment, but I don't see it anywhere in my folders.

You probably selected the **S**ave to Directory Only button in the Create Attachment dialog box. You can either rescan the document or, in the Attachments window, select **A**ttachment, **N**ew and add the scanned file into a folder. Read Chapter 12, "Assembling Faxes from Many Sources," for more information about attachments.

I scanned a document and sent it as a fax. However, the document arrived at my recipient's fax software upside down.

You fed the document through the scanner upside down. This means you should feed the top of the document through the scanner first instead of the other way around.

III

Power Faxing

From Here...

This chapter told you how to use a scanner with WinFax PRO. To review some of the issues discussed in this chapter, you may want to read the following:

■ Chapter 8, "Sending Faxes," tells you how to send faxes and use the Send dialog box.

■ Chapter 12, "Assembling Faxes from Many Sources," describes attachments and how to manage them.

Chapter 14

Viewing and Annotating Faxes

In this chapter, you learn how to do the following:

- Navigate the WinFax PRO Viewer.

- View sent, received, and pending faxes.

- Enhance the way faxes appear on-screen.

- Add lines, arrows, and geometric shapes to faxes.

- Add graphic images such as signatures to faxes.

- Export faxes to other graphic formats.

In WinFax PRO, you will frequently view faxes you send, receive, or schedule. Often, though, you must do even more: You must mark or comment on faxes and return them to the sender or forward them to others.

You can accomplish both these tasks in the WinFax PRO Viewer. Viewer's ability to annotate faxes means that you need not print them before you comment on them or sign them. Instead, you can add text, freeform designs, geometric shapes, and graphic images to received faxes.

In addition, the Viewer is where you convert faxes into text your other applications can edit. This process is called *optical character recognition (OCR).*

This chapter describes how to use the WinFax PRO Viewer to view and annotate faxes and to convert faxes to editable text. The next chapter, "Converting Faxes to Text," describes the third function for which you use Viewer: starting the optical character recognition process to convert fax images to editable text.

Viewing Faxes

The Viewer actually is a separate program. You usually start Viewer from within WinFax PRO. With a fax item highlighted in the Send and Receive Log, Outbox, and Attachments windows, start Viewer (and automatically view a selected fax) by one of the following methods:

■ Choose **F**ax **V**iew.

■ Select a fax and click the View button in the toolbar.

■ Double-click an item in the item list window.

■ Click an item, and then click the right mouse button. From the menu that appears, choose **V**iew.

Also, you can load the Viewer by clicking its icon in the WinFax 4 program group in Program Manager. Whichever method you use, WinFax PRO loads the Viewer and the item you selected. At this point, you are in *Viewing mode*, as opposed to *Annotation mode*, which later sections of this chapter discuss (see fig. 14.1).

Fig. 14.1
The Viewer window is where you view faxes.

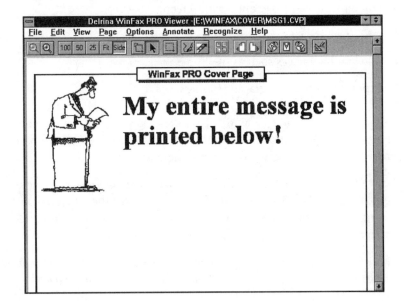

Loading a New Fax

If you start Viewer from the Send or Receive Log, Attachments, or Outbox windows, it automatically displays the selected fax. If you start Viewer from Program Manager, it does not display a fax. You can, however, display a fax or even an image saved in the PCX graphics format. The PCX format is a popular graphics format used by the Paintbrush program, which comes with Windows.

To display a fax or PCX image, follow these steps:

1. Choose **F**ile **O**pen. WinFax PRO displays the Open File for Viewing dialog box (see fig. 14.2).

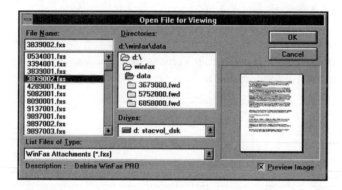

Fig. 14.2
Select a fax or bit-mapped image to view in the Open File for Viewing dialog box.

2. In the List Files of **T**ype drop-down list, select the type of file to view. Select from the following:

   ■ Attachments

   ■ Sent Faxes

   ■ Received Faxes

   ■ All items

   ■ PCX Files

3. Select the drive where you stored the files in the Dri**v**es drop-down list.

4. Select the directories where you stored the files in the **D**irectories list window.

III

Power Faxing

Tip

Because WinFax PRO gives fax files difficult-to-understand numbered file names, it saves time to preview faxes before you load them into the Viewer.

Note

By default, WinFax PRO places all sent and received faxes and attachments in the \WINFAX\DATA subdirectory.

5. Select a specific file to view in the File **N**ame list box.

6. Select the **P**review Image check box to view a thumbnail of the image you select in the File **N**ame list window.

7. When you finish the Open File for Viewing dialog box, click OK. Viewer loads the selected file.

Tip

Select multiple faxes to load into the Viewer by holding down the Ctrl key and clicking more than one file name.

Viewer has a toolbar for both viewing faxes and for annotating them. However, when you start Viewer, it is in View mode and displays only the Navigation toolbar (see fig. 14.3).

Fig. 14.3

The toolbar helps you navigate through Viewer.

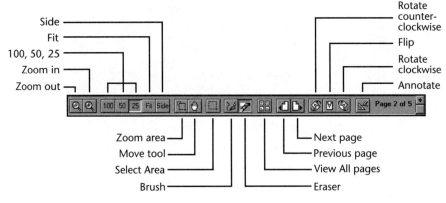

Tip

Hiding the toolbar provides a little more room for viewing faxes.

If you prefer, hide the toolbar as you view faxes. To do that, choose **V**iew Hide **T**oolbar. To display the toolbar, choose **V**iew Show **T**oolbar.

Table 14.1 lists the navigation toolbar buttons, what they do, and where in the menu system you can find the same functions.

Table 14.1 Buttons in the Toolbar for Viewing Mode.

Button	Function	Menu Location
Zoom out	Zooms out to fit more on screen	N.A.
Zoom in	Zooms in for detailed view	**V**iew **Z**oom In

Button	Function	Menu Location
100	Zooms to 100% of fax size	**V**iew **1**00%
50	Zooms to 50% of fax size	**V**iew **5**0%
25	Zooms to 25% of fax size	**V**iew **2**5%
Fit	Fits entire page on-screen	**V**iew **Fi**t in Window
Side	Fits fax width on-screen	**V**iew **Fi**t Sides
Zoom area	Draws area for zooming in	**V**iew **Z**oom In
Move tool	Enables moving image in window	N.A.
Select area	Select portions of fax for editing	N.A.
Brush	Draw freeform lines	N.A.
Eraser	Erase any part of fax image	N.A.
View All Pages	Views thumbnails of all pages	**V**iew **A**ll Pages
Previous Page	Views previous page	**P**age **P**revious Page
Next Page	Views next page	**P**age **N**ext Page
Rotate 90 Degrees Counterlockwise	Rotates current page 90 degrees counterclockwise	**O**ptions **R**otate Current Page Co**u**nterclockwise 90
Flip	Rotates current page 180 degrees	**O**ptions Rotate Current Page **F**lip 180
Rotate 90 degrees clockwise	Rotates current page 90 degrees clockwise	**O**ptions **R**otate Current Page **C**lockwise 90
Annotation tool	Opens and closes Annotation mode	**A**nnotate **S**how and **A**nnotate **H**ide

Viewer divides the tools for viewing faxes into the following types:

- Tools that determine the size of the fax image on-screen.
- Tools for determining the orientation of fax pages.
- Tools for simple annotation. The next three sections discuss these viewing options.
- Tools that move you from page to page.

Determining On-Screen Page Size

The on-screen size of fax pages is important because sometimes you must view an entire page, and sometimes you must view a part of a page in detail.

From the toolbar or menus, you can choose to view the fax at 100% of its regular size (**View 1**00%), fifty percent of its normal size (**View 5**0%), or twenty-five percent of its normal size (**View 2**5%).

You also can set Viewer to fit each page's width in the work area (**View Fit** Sides), or to view a full page in the work area (**View Fit** in Window).

> **Note**
>
> Depending on the size of the page, the twenty-five percent view and the Fit in Window view should be similar.

Figures 14.4 and 14.5 show a fax page at one hundred percent view, and the same page at the Fit in Window view, respectively.

Fig. 14.4

This is a fax page viewed at (100%) size.

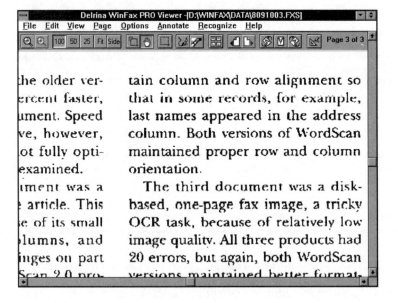

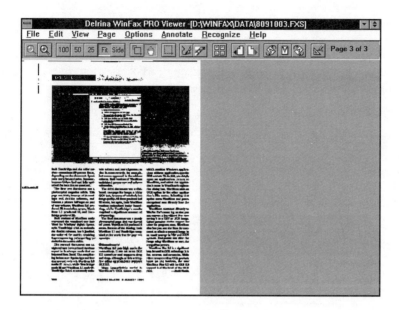

Fig. 14.5
This view shows
an entire fax page
in the window.

You also can view all the pages of a fax in thumbnail images in the same
window (see fig. 14.6). Select the View All Pages button in the toolbar, or
choose **V**iew **A**ll Pages.

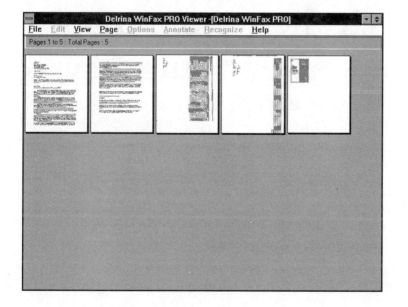

Fig. 14.6
This view shows
thumbnail images
of all pages of a
fax.

III

Power Faxing

To return to normal view, double-click any thumbnail image of a page.

Another option is to select an area of a fax page and zoom in on it. This is useful for examining fine detail of a portion of a fax. To zoom in on a specific section of a fax page, follow these steps:

1. Select the Zoom Box tool from the toolbar, or choose **View Zoom** In. Viewer displays a mouse pointer that looks like the Zoom area box.

2. Drag the pointer over the portion of the page you want to zoom in on.

3. Release the mouse button. Viewer displays a zoomed image (see fig. 14.7).

Fig. 14.7
Zoom in to view details of a small part of a page.

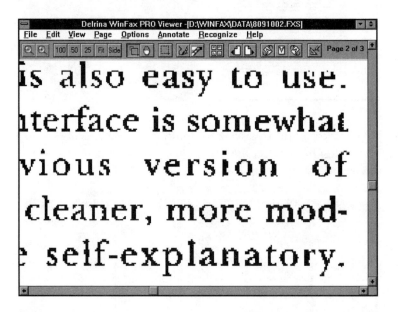

Tip
Zooming in and out is useful when you must annotate a specific part of the page. Zoom in to precisely position your annotation; zoom out to look at the entire page.

To return to a different view after you zoom in, click the desired view in the toolbar, or choose it from the **View** menu.

A variation on determining page size is using the miniature viewer, which displays a separate window over the regular fax view with a miniature view of the entire fax page. This window enables you to only view, in miniature form, the fax page. You cannot change the page in any way.

To view the miniature page, choose **View** Show **M**iniature or double-click the fax. Viewer shows the Miniature View window (see fig. 14.8).

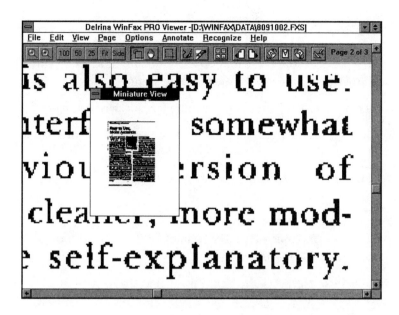

Fig. 14.8
The Miniature View
window shows a
tiny version of the
entire page.

The miniature viewer is helpful because it enables you to see the entire page
in a separate window, even if you zoom in on a portion of the page. It also is
useful as a navigation tool, enabling you to move to a different section of the
fax page.

Within the Miniature View window is a box. To view a different part of the
fax page, follow these steps:

1. Position the mouse cursor over the box.

2. Hold down the left mouse button.

3. Drag the box over the part of the fax page you want to view.

4. Release the left mouse button.

The viewed page underneath the miniature viewer shifts the selected section.

Determining Page Orientation

Changing the orientation of fax pages is useful because often, fax senders put
faxes into their fax machine upside down. To view them in WinFax PRO, you
must turn the page 180 degrees. Also, a fax page may be easier to read when
you change the orientation. This is often true when viewing images.

III

Power Faxing

You can change the orientation of individual pages, or of all the pages in the fax. To rotate the current page, choose **O**ptions **R**otate Current Page. To rotate all the pages in your fax, choose **O**ptions Rotate **A**ll Pages. In either case, Viewer displays a submenu with the following options:

- **C**lockwise 90 rotates the page or entire fax clockwise 90 degrees.

- **F**lip 180 flips the page or all fax pages 180 degrees. Use this option when somebody sends you an upside down fax.

- Co**u**nter Clockwise 90 rotates the page 90 degrees counterclockwise.

Moving to Another Page

Many faxes have multiple pages. The simplest of the Viewer's tools, the Next Page tool, moves you to a different page.

To view the next page, click the Next Page tool in the toolbar. Alternatively, choose **P**age **N**ext Page. To move back a page, click the Previous Page button in the toolbar, or choose **P**age **P**revious Page.

To jump to a specific page number, choose **P**age, **G**o To Page. WinFax PRO displays the Go To Page dialog box (see fig. 14.9).

Fig. 14.9

Jump to a specific page in the Go To Page dialog box.

This simple dialog box states how many pages are in the fax. Type the number of the page you want to view in **P**age text box and click OK. If you made any changes to your current fax page, WinFax PRO asks whether you want to save them. Choose **Y**es to save, **N**o to revert to the way the page was originally. Then the Viewer displays the page you designated.

You also can jump to a different page when viewing thumbnail images of all pages of a fax. When viewing thumbnails of all pages, double-click the page you want, and Viewer displays it.

> **Note**
>
> If you view a fax stored in an archive folder, remember that WinFax PRO compresses each page of a multiple page fax separately. As a result, it may take some time before it appears in Viewer, as WinFax PRO expands the compressed fax.

Enhancing Fax Quality

Viewer provides two ways to enhance the quality of the fax image. These methods are not mutually exclusive; you can use them in conjunction with each other.

Enhanced view enables you to view images on-screen with gray scales. Ordinarily, faxes are in black or white—that is, each pixel that makes up the image is either a black pixel or a white pixel.

Enhanced view enables you to view pixels of various shades of gray, which provides greater detail. This option is just for viewing images on-screen; it does not enable you to print or transmit faxes in gray scale.

> **Note**
>
> Enhanced view doesn't change anything if you are viewing faxes. That's because faxes already are in black and white. Rather, Enhanced view is useful only when viewing items that already are gray-scale images, such as images of photographs or artwork.

To view an image in Enhanced view, choose **V**iew **E**nhance View. Viewer redraws the image on-screen, using gray scales.

The clean up fax option cleans up the random black dots and specks that appear in received faxes. These specks, which shouldn't be part of the fax, occur because of faulty transmission lines and other problems in the transmission process. Typically, this problem is most pronounced around the edges of fax pages.

To clean up the fax, choose **E**dit **C**leanup. Viewer displays the Cleanup Fax dialog box (see fig. 14.10).

Fig. 14.10

Clean up random dots in received faxes with the Cleanup Fax dialog box.

In the Cleanup Fax dialog box, do the following:

1. In the **A**rea area, decide to clean up the entire page, only the section that you are viewing on-screen, or selected area.

2. In the **D**egree area, determine whether you want Viewer to clean up only larger, more obvious specks (Light) or smaller, less obvious specks (Heavy). The default setting is Medium.

3. When you finish the Cleanup Fax dialog box, click OK.

Viewer displays an information box displaying the progress of the fax clean up. If you watch the fax during this process, you can see the cleanup process work.

> **Caution**
>
> Sometimes the cleanup fax option "cleans" narrow lines. If your fax has fine lines, such as lines that define the borders of a table, use the Light setting in the Cleanup Fax dialog box.

Viewer has one final setting that affects how the fax appears on-screen. That setting inverts the colors of the fax, creating an effect similar to photographic negatives. To apply this effect to your fax, choose **V**iew In**v**ert Display.

Simple Annotation

Viewer provides two elementary annotation tools for Viewing mode: the Brush and the Eraser. The Brush enables you to draw freehand on a fax. The Eraser deletes freehand drawings, as well as anything else on the page.

To use the Brush tool, follow these steps:

1. Click the Brush tool button in the toolbar. The mouse pointer turns into a pointer that looks like a paintbrush with a cross cursor.

2. Position the cross cursor on the page where you want to start drawing.

3. Hold down the left mouse button.

4. Drag the mouse pointer across the screen as you would move a brush.

5. When you finish, release the mouse button.

To change the thickness of the line you draw with the Brush tool, choose **O**ptions **B**rush Width. Viewer displays a submenu with lines of varying thickness (see fig. 14.11).

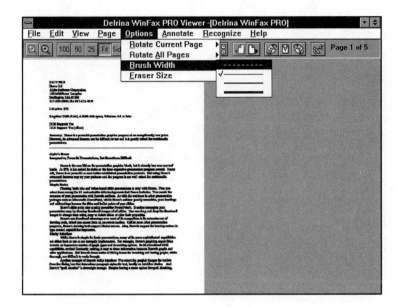

Fig. 14.11
Select line thickness
in the Brush Width
menu.

Your subsequent brush drawings use the thickness you select.

The Eraser tool enables you to erase anything in the fax image. You can erase brush drawing marks or the contents of the fax itself.

To select the Eraser, click the Eraser tool in the toolbar, which is an icon showing a pencil eraser. The mouse pointer turns into a square. To erase something, position the square over the item and hold down the left mouse button. Drag the mouse, and Viewer erases whatever is under the path of the square pointer (see fig. 14.12). You can undo your most recent erasure by selecting **E**dit **U**ndo.

Caution

Be careful using the Eraser tool; it erases everything in its path.

As with the Brush tool, you can change the thickness of the Eraser tool. To do that, choose **O**ptions **E**raser Size. Viewer displays a submenu showing differ-ent sized squares. Select the desired Eraser size. Viewer applies that size to future erasers.

III

Power Faxing

Fig. 14.12

Use the Eraser tool to erase information from faxes.

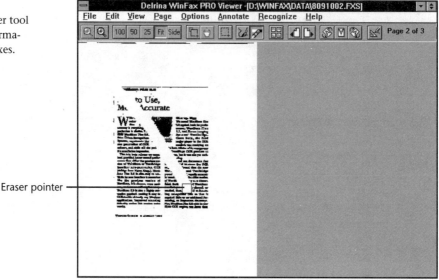

Eraser pointer

Tip

Use the smaller eraser sizes for finer detail while erasing. For example, if you don't want to disturb information right next to the item you must erase, use a smaller eraser.

Troubleshooting

When I view a fax I received, it is upside down.

That means the sender sent it upside down. To make the current page appear right side up, choose **O**ptions **R**otate Current Page **F**lip 180. To flip all pages of the fax, choose **O**ptions Rotate **A**ll Pages **F**lip 180.

When I view or print a fax I received, it has lots of black dots that weren't in the original document.

Those dots occur during transmission because of interference in the phone line. To clean up your fax, in the Viewer, choose **E**dit **C**leanup. This process eliminates many of those small dots.

Annotating Faxes

The ability to annotate faxes before sending them is important. It enables you to affix graphic images or explanatory text to the fax. You can annotate faxes you receive, faxes that you forward to others, or faxes stored in the Outbox.

Entering Annotation mode is a simple matter of clicking on the Annotation tool in the Viewer toolbar. Or choose **A**nnotate **S**how. Either action shows the Annotation toolbar on-screen (see fig. 14.13).

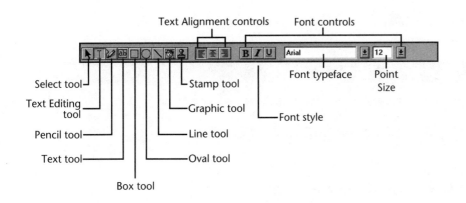

Fig. 14.13
The Annotation
toolbar gives you
fast access to many
annotation
capabilities.

When in Annotation mode, you still use the Viewer toolbar for navigating through the fax page or to other pages. Use the Annotation toolbar and the related menu options for annotating the fax.

Table 14.2 describes the buttons in the Annotation toolbar and what they do.

Table 14.2   Items in the Annotation Toolbar.

Button	Function
Select Tool	Select an object, such as a line or graphic, so you can move, size, and modify it.
Text Editing tool	Highlight and modify text.
Pencil tool	Draw freehand shapes.
Text tool	Create a box that can contain text.
Box tool	Draw squares or rectangles.
Oval tool	Draw ovals and circles.
Line tool	Draw straight lines.
Graphic tool	Insert a graphic image created by another program.
Stamp tool	Automatically inserts a pre-specified graphic image.
Text Alignment controls	Left, right, or center justify text.
Font style	Bold, italic, or underline text.
Font typeface	Select a font for text.
Point size	Select a font size for text.

III

Power Faxing

The next several sections describe how to set up Viewer and how to use it to annotate faxes.

> **Note**
>
> If you think the Viewer's annotation capabilities are similar to those in the Cover Page Designer, you're right. Although not precisely the same, the two programs share a similar interface and capabilities.

Setting Up Viewer for Annotations

When you switch to Annotation mode, the Annotation toolbar becomes visible, and two more things happen in Viewer:

- Options needed for annotations become available in the menu system. These options weren't necessary—or available—when you were in Viewing mode.

- Viewer adds a grid to help align annotation objects you add to the fax. The grid appears as a series of dots in the Viewer work area.

Setting up the Viewer for annotations is a simple matter similar to setting up Cover Page Designer as described in Chapter 7, "Creating and Managing Cover Pages."

Tip
The grid helps align annotation items such as text and shapes. Annotations are easier with the grid visible.

One set of options deals with the grid. Viewer displays a grid, but you can turn the grid display off by choosing **V**iew Show **G**rid. This menu item is a toggle: when a check appears next to it, the grid display is on. If no check is next to the menu item, the grid display is off.

Next, set up the grid arrangement by choosing **A**nnotate Grid Set**u**p. Viewer displays the Grid Setup dialog box (see fig. 14.14).

Fig. 14.14
Set up your grid in the Grid Setup dialog box.

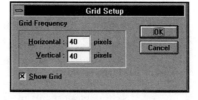

Set the distance between dots in the grid in the Grid Setup dialog box. Viewer measures the distance in pixels, no matter what you set as your unit of measurement in the Viewer Preferences dialog box.

The default grid dimensions are 40 pixels between each dot on the grid, both horizontally and vertically. To change the horizontal distance between dots, type a new number in the **H**orizontal text box of the Grid Setup dialog box. To set a new vertical distance between dots on the grid, type a new number in the **V**ertical text box.

The Grid Setup dialog box provides a second opportunity to determine whether Viewer displays the grid. To show the grid, make sure that an X appears in the **S**how Grid check box. Deactivate the check box if you don't want to use the grid.

The final grid setup option is to determine whether items snap to the grid. When you set this option, annotation objects like geometric shapes and graphic images that you add to the fax automatically line up on the nearest grid points.

To make items snap to the grid, choose **A**nnotate **S**nap to Grid. This menu item is a toggle; when the snap to grid option is active, a check appears next to the menu item. To deactivate the snap to grid option, choose the menu item when a check appears next to it.

Two final setup options determine how Viewer displays graphic images. Those options are **V**iew **S**how Graphics and **V**iew **F**ast Display.

Like the **S**nap to Grid option, these two options are toggles. After selecting them, a check appears next to them in the menu. When deactivated, no check appears.

If you choose **S**how Graphics, Viewer shows graphic images. If you don't select this option, Viewer displays a box the precise size of the graphic. Instead of the graphic, however, a line pattern displays in the box. This helps Viewer operate more quickly, because graphic images take time to draw on-screen. However, you won't be able to see your image on-screen. When you send the fax or print it, though, the image appears as you would expect.

The **F**ast Display option determines the speed and accuracy with which Viewer displays graphic images. When you choose Fast Display, Cover Page designer displays images faster, but doesn't display as many details of the image. Deactivating this option requires more time for images to display, but shows more details of the images.

Tip
The **S**nap to Grid option is a handy way to ensure a neat appearance for your annotations.

III

Power Faxing

About Annotation Objects

As stated previously, you can add geometric shapes, graphic images, text and freeform lines to faxes in the Viewer's Annotation mode. Subsequent sections of this chapter describe how to add each of those objects. Before those sections, though, you should know something about how objects work and how to manage, move, copy, and modify them.

All types of objects have *handles*. Handles appear as little black boxes. Around geometric shapes and images, handles appear in the corners of the box containing the shape or image, and also along the sides. On lines and objects drawn freeform, they appear at the ends.

> **Note**
>
> Freeform objects drawn with the Brush tool in Viewing mode do not have handles. Only freeform objects drawn in Annotation mode have handles.

You can act on any object by selecting it. To select an object, follow these steps:

1. Click the Selection tool, the first tool on the left, in the Annotation toolbar.

2. Position the mouse pointer over the object on which you want to act.

3. Click the left mouse button. The handles appear on the object you selected (see fig. 14.15).

Fig. 14.15
An example of handles—in this case, around a rectangle.

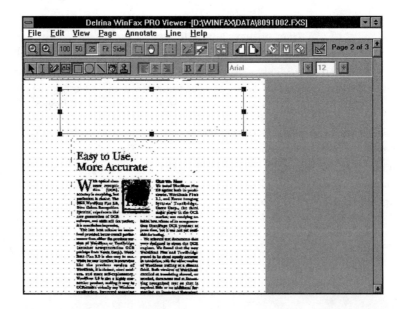

To select more than one object, select a single object. Then hold down the Shift key and select additional objects. To select all objects, repeat this process for all objects, or choose **E**dit **S**elect All.

Note

When you select multiple objects, actions you take affect all the objects you selected.

After you select multiple objects, deselect an individual object by holding down the Shift key and clicking the object. To deselect all objects, click anywhere on the work area that is not an object.

Note

Viewer does not consider items that already exist as part of the fax, such as the message, as objects.

After you select an object and its handles are visible, you can do several things with it:

- Delete the object by choosing **E**dit **C**u**t** (which places it in the Windows clipboard) or **E**dit **D**elete Object, which deletes the object but doesn't place it in the clipboard.

- Copy the object by choosing **E**dit **C**opy. This leaves the object in the work area, but places it in the clipboard so you can copy it back into Viewer.

- Paste an object saved to the Windows clipboard back into Viewer by choosing **E**dit **P**aste.

- Move the object by positioning the mouse pointer over it, holding down the left mouse button and dragging the object to a new location.

- Change the size of the object by positioning the mouse pointer over a handle. When the pointer turns into a two-headed arrow, hold down the left mouse button and drag the mouse until the object is precisely the desired size.

III

Power Faxing

> **Note**
>
> You can't change the size of an object drawn with the Pencil tool. Nor can you change the size of individual objects when you select more than one object. Rather, you must change the size of each object separately.

The Viewer keeps text and graphic objects in boxes. You move text and images by moving the boxes that contain them, using the methods just described. You also can change the size of text and graphics boxes.

You can control the type of border of the object box or shape and the shading that fills them. Viewer also enables you to place one object in front of another to create special effects.

To do that, highlight the object and choose either **E**dit Bring to **F**ront or **E**dit Send to **B**ack. The ability to place objects in front of or behind other objects is particularly helpful when used with the different types of shading that Viewer supports. The combinations of these two abilities make it possible to create special effects.

Table 14.3 describes the types of shading you can apply to the inside of boxes containing annotation objects.

Table 14.3	Different Types of Shadings You Can Apply to Shapes and Boxes.	
Type	**Menu Location**	**Behavior**
White Transparent	**A**nnotate Sha**d**e **W**hite Transparent	White background, shows items behind it.
White Opaque	**A**nnotate Sha**d**e White **O**paque	White background, doesn't show items behind it.
Gray	**A**nnotate Sha**d**e **G**ray	Gray opaque background
Black	**A**nnotate Sha**d**e **B**lack	Black opaque background

> **Note**
>
> You can't change the shading of lines or freeform objects that you draw with the Pencil tool, but you can change their thickness. Subsequent sections of this chapter describe how.

Combine the ability to place objects behind one another and the ability to choose backgrounds to create special effects, like shadowed boxes as described in Chapter 7, "Creating and Managing Cover Pages."

The ability to change backgrounds applies to the boxes that contain text and images as well as to geometric shapes. In addition to changing the background of those objects, you also can change the line weight of those boxes and also the type of box.

To change the line weight of the box surrounding text or an image, follow these steps:

1. Select the object.

2. Choose **L**ine. Viewer displays a menu containing several different line weights ranging from a simple dotted line to a heavier line weight.

3. Select the desired line weight. Viewer changes the line weight for you.

Similarly, you can change the type of box that surrounds your object. To do that:

1. Select the object.

2. Choose **A**nnotate **B**order. Viewer displays a submenu.

3. From the submenu, select among the following:

   ■ **N**one provides no border around the object.

   ■ **S**quare provides a border with angled corners.

   ■ **R**ound provides a border with rounded corners.

Adding and Modifying Text

Adding text to faxes is a good way to add comments directly on the fax before you return it to the sender or forward it to somebody else.

To add text to a fax page displayed in Viewer, follow these steps:

1. Click the Text tool in the Annotation toolbar. The mouse pointer turns into a cross cursor.

2. Position the cursor in the upper left corner of the area where you want to add the text.

III

Power Faxing

3. Hold down the left mouse button and drag the mouse down and to the right. Viewer draws a box in which you add text.

4. When the text box is the desired size, release the left mouse button.

5. Viewer displays a box with a blinking cursor inside. You can start typing your text as you normally would (see fig. 14.16).

Fig. 14.16
You place text
inside a text box.

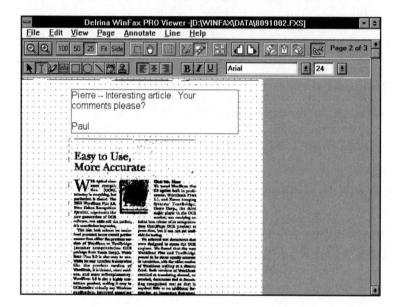

To edit and add text to an existing text box, select the text object and click the Text Editing tool in the Annotation toolbar. When the cursor appears inside the text box, you can add and edit text.

When working in a text box, you can perform most of the basic functions you would expect with a text editor. Specifically, you can cut, delete, copy, and paste text within the box. You can change fonts and font attributes, and also the justification of the text in the text box.

Editing and Justifying Text

Copying and cutting text and pasting in new text is a basic editing function. To copy, cut, or delete text while working in Viewer, follow these steps:

1. Select the text box.

2. Select the Text Editing tool from the Annotation toolbar.

3. In the text box, position the cursor at the beginning of the text you want to alter.

4. Hold down the left mouse button and drag the mouse to highlight all the text you want to alter.

5. Choose the editing option you want from the **E**dit menu. Those options are Cu**t** and **C**opy.

Cu**t** deletes the text and places it in the clipboard. **C**opy copies the text to the clipboard but leaves it in its original position. To paste previously cut or copied text at the cursor position in the text box, choose **E**dit **P**aste.

You also can justify the text within the box. To do that before you enter text into a text box, click one of the text justification buttons in the Annotation toolbar. Your choices are:

Left justified

Center justified

Right justified

To justify text you already added, click the Text Selection tool and highlight the text. Then click one of the justification buttons in the Annotation toolbar.

You also can select justification options and text types by choosing **A**nnotate **T**ext. Choose the desired option in the submenu that Viewer displays.

Changing Fonts

You can change font, font size and attributes at any time either before you enter text in a new text box or at any time afterward. To set the font, size, and characteristics before typing in a new text box:

1. Choose **A**nnotate **F**ont. Viewer displays the Font dialog box (see fig. 14.17).

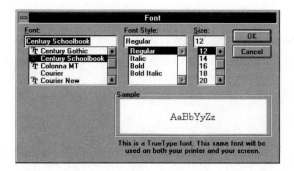

Fig. 14.17
Select annotation fonts in the Font dialog box.

III

Power Faxing

To use the Font dialog box, follow these steps:

1. Select the desired font in the Font list window.

2. Select the style in the Font Style list window. Your choices are Regular, Italic, Bold, and Bold Italic.

3. Select the font size in the Size list window.

   You can view what your selection looks like in the Sample area.

4. When you are satisfied with your font, size, and type, click OK.

5. Start typing in the text box.

To change the font of existing text, select the text box; then select the Text Editing tool. Highlight the specific text you want to change and use the Font dialog box.

One other text formatting option is to select black text or white text. In text boxes with white or gray backgrounds, use black text, which is the default. However, for text in black boxes, white text is the best choice. To designate a text color, follow these steps:

1. If you already entered text and want to change it, highlight the text.

2. Choose Annotate Text.

3. In the submenu that appears, choose either White Text or Black Text as appropriate.

Checking Spelling

When you finish adding text, you can spell-check it. To do that, follow these steps:

1. Click the Text Editing tool.

2. Select the specific text to spell check.

3. Choose Annotate Spelling. Viewer displays the Spell Check dialog box (see fig. 14.18).

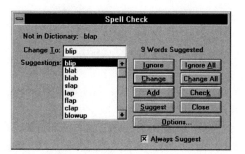

Fig. 14.18
Check spelling in
the Spell Check
dialog box.

The spell checker looks for words that are not in its dictionary. Then it either
tells you it encountered an unknown word, or suggests a correct spelling. To
have the spell checker suggest the correct spelling, click **S**uggest. To have the
spell checker automatically suggest alternative spellings, select the A**l**ways
Suggest check box.

You can type a different spelling in the Change **T**o text box, or select a spelling from the Suggestio**n**s list window. The other options in the Spell Check
dialog box are as follows:

- **I**gnore ignores the currently selected misspelling.

- Ignore **A**ll ignores the currently selected misspelling and all identical
  words in the document.

- **C**hange changes the incorrect spelling to the suggested spelling you
  select in the Suggestio**n**s list window.

- C**h**ange All changes all instances of the misspelled word to the suggested word or the word you typed in the Change **T**o text box.

- A**d**d adds either the word you typed in the Change **T**o text box or the
  word the spelling checker failed to recognize to the dictionary. In either
  case, the spell checker won't stop again when it encounters the word.

- Chec**k** checks the spelling of the word you type in the Change **T**o text
  box. If the spelling is correct, the words Spelling Approved appear to the
  right of the text box. If the spell checker does not recognize the word,
  the words Unknown Spelling appear.

- Suggest places possible correct spellings in the Suggestio**n**s list box.

- Close cancels the spelling operation.

III

Power Faxing

■ Options leads to the Spelling Options dialog box for determining how the spell checker works. Read Chapter 7, "Creating and Managing Cover Pages," for more details about setting options for the spell checker.

Adding Geometric Shapes

Viewer enables you to add rectangles, squares, circles, and ovals to faxes. These shapes are useful when you create designs, or when you want to highlight something in a fax you will resubmit or forward.

The process for creating all four shapes is essentially the same:

1. Create rectangles and squares by clicking the Box tool in the Annotation toolbar. Create circles and ovals by clicking on the Oval tool in the Annotation toolbar. In either case, the mouse pointer turns into a cross cursor.

> **Note**
>
> A circle appears in the lower right quadrant of the cross cursor if you are drawing a circle or oval. A square appears in the lower right quadrant if you are drawing a square or rectangle.

2. Position the cross cursor in the upper left corner of the work area location where you want to place the geometric shape.

3. Hold down the left mouse button and drag the mouse down and to the right. A dotted line appears in the work area, representing the shape.

4. When the dotted line is precisely the size and shape you want, release the left mouse button. Viewer replaces the dotted line with a solid red line in the actual shape.

Whether you create a square or a rectangle or a circle or an oval depends on how you drag the mouse.

As stated before, you can overlap shapes and shade them. You can select the shapes and drag them to a new position or resize them by dragging on their handles. You also can change the line weights of the geometric shapes.

Note that the handles in a circle or oval appear as though they are on an invisible rectangle surrounding the circle or oval rather than appearing on the circle itself.

Tip

If a particular paragraph is important in a fax, draw a rectangle around it to set it apart from the rest of the fax. Add text in the margins to explain why the information is special.

Tip

To simplify placement of shapes on the fax, use the grid and select the Snap to Grid option. To make a perfect square or circle, hold down the Shift key while dragging the mouse.

Adding Lines and Arrows

The ability to add lines when annotating text enables you to create odd shapes and to point to important items in the fax.

To draw a line, follow these steps:

1. Click the Line tool in the Annotation toolbar. The regular mouse pointer turns into a cross cursor.

2. Position the cursor in the work area where you want to start the line and hold down the left mouse button. To draw a perfectly straight horizontal or vertical line, hold down the Shift key.

3. Drag the cross cursor across the work area. As with geometric shapes, a dotted line represents the line as you draw it.

4. When the line is the length and in the position you want, release the left mouse button.

Move lines as you move any object. Follow these steps:

1. Click the Select button in the Annotation toolbar.

2. Click the line to select it.

3. Position the cursor directly over the line and hold down the left mouse button.

4. Drag the line to its new position and release the left mouse button.

To make the line longer, select the line and drag one of its ends straight out. Press the Shift key while dragging, if you want to keep the line straight. To change the angle of a line, select the line and drag one of the ends of the line off at an angle from the line. The other end of the line remains anchored in its current position even as the angle of the line changes.

Use multiple lines to create nonrectangular shapes like triangles. To do that, follow these steps:

1. Draw a line as you normally would.

2. With the cross cursor positioned over one of the handles of the line, draw another line.

3. Repeat the process, adding more lines and connecting them to the handles of other lines until you create the shape.

III

Power Faxing

Move the new shape by selecting one; then hold down the Shift key to select the others. Select all the lines that you used to create the shape. Then move all the lines at the same time.

To change the weight of the line, and to turn a line into an arrow, choose **L**ine. A menu drops down, showing the various weight and arrow options.

In the **L**ine menu, select the desired line weight and arrow style. The current line weight and arrow style, if applicable, have checks next to them in the menu.

Inserting Images

Graphic images can include anything from your organization's logo to a scanned copy of your signature. To add a graphic image, follow these steps:

1. Click the Graphic tool in the Annotation toolbar. The regular mouse pointer turns into a cross cursor with a graphic image in corners.

2. Position the cross cursor over the work area and drag the left mouse button. Viewer displays the Graphic Attributes dialog box (see fig. 14.19).

Fig. 14.19

Insert a graphic image with the Graphic Attributes dialog box.

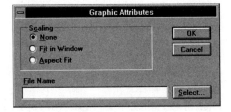

3. Type the name of the graphic file in the **F**ile Name text box.

4. If you are not sure of the name of the graphic file, click the **S**elect key. Viewer displays the Select Graphic dialog box (see fig. 14.20).

5. In the Select Graphic dialog box, select a drive from the Dri**v**es drop-down list.

6. Select a directory from the **D**irectories drop-down list.

7. Select a graphic file format from the List Files of **T**ype drop-down list.

8. Select a specific graphics file from the File **N**ame list window.

9. Select the **P**review Image check box to view a thumbnail image of the graphic.

10. After you select the image file, click OK. The name of the image file appears in the **F**ile Name list box in the Graphic Attributes dialog box.

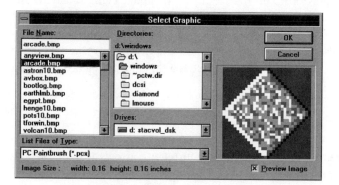

Fig. 14.20
Select the graphic to insert into the fax in the Select Graphic dialog box.

> **Note**
>
> Viewer can import nine different types of graphic image formats plus WinFax PRO fax image files.

11. Select the method you want Viewer to use for scaling the image. Scaling refers to the process of sizing the image and determining its proportions in the fax compared to the size and proportions of the image in its original form.

12. When you finish the Graphic Attributes text box, click OK.

> **Note**
>
> Remember that Viewer places graphic images in boxes with borders. Unless you tell Viewer otherwise, the borders appear around the image when you finish annotating and send the fax. If you don't want the border to appear, select the graphic item; then choose **A**nnotate **B**order **N**one.

The three scaling options are as follows:

■ **N**one. This option keeps the image the same size in the annotation as it was originally. You won't be able to see parts of the image if it is bigger than the graphics box. This is a good option if there is room in the fax to make the graphics box larger or smaller, as needed.

■ **Fi**t in Window. The entire image fits in the graphic object box. To make it fit, Viewer changes the proportions of the image, so it may appear distorted.

■ **A**spect Fit. Viewer re-creates the image to make it retain its original proportions. This may result in the image being smaller than the graphic box.

Viewer also enables you to designate graphic images you use regularly, like a corporate logo, as *stamps*. It provides a separate dialog box for rapidly inserting these images into the fax.

To add a commonly used image to the list of stamps, follow these steps:

1. Click the Stamp icon in the Annotation toolbar, or choose **A**nnotate **St**amps. The mouse pointer turns into arrows at right angles with a handstamp.

2. Click the fax where you want the stamp to appear. Viewer displays the Stamps dialog box (see fig. 14.21).

Fig. 14.21
Keep frequently used images in the Stamps dialog box.

3. Click the **N**ew button. Viewer displays the New Stamp dialog box (see fig. 14.22).

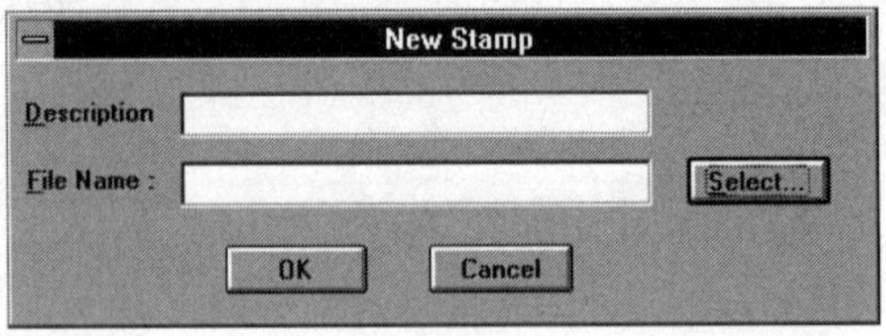

Fig. 14.22
Add new images in the New Stamp dialog box.

4. Type a description for the stamp in the **D**escription text box.

5. In the **F**ile Name text box, type the drive, path, and file name of the image.

6. If you don't know the drive, path, or file name, click the **S**elect button. Viewer displays the Select Graphic dialog box, discussed previously in this chapter.

7. Select a file in the Select Graphic dialog box and click OK. The file name of the image appears in the **F**ile Name text box.

8. Click OK in the New Stamp dialog box. Viewer adds the image to the Stamp dialog box.

To modify the file name or description of the image, click the Stamp button. In the Stamps dialog box, click **M**odify. Viewer displays the Modify Stamp dialog box, which is virtually identical to the New Stamp dialog box, except that it displays the previously entered information. Change the description or the file name and click OK.

To eliminate an image from the Stamp dialog box, click once on the description of the image in the Stamp dialog box, and click the **R**emove button.

To add a stamp to the fax while in Annotation mode, click the Stamp button in the Annotation toolbar, or choose **A**nnotate S**t**amps. Select the desired image in the Stamp dialog box and click OK. Viewer inserts the image into the fax.

Adding Freehand Drawing

Freehand drawing is useful for a variety of needs. For example, you can draw a freehand circle around a phrase in a report for emphasis, draw a freehand line from the circled phrase and add text to explain something about it.

Adding freehand drawing is simple. Follow these steps:

1. Click the Pencil tool. The regular mouse pointer turns into a brush.

2. Position the pencil where you want to begin the drawing.

3. With the left mouse button still held down, drag the mouse around the work area to create your freehand drawing.

4. When you finish drawing, release the left mouse button.

When you finish the drawing and release the mouse button, notice that Viewer places handles at each end of the drawing. By comparison, using the Brush tool capabilities when in Viewing mode does not create drawing objects with handles.

III

Power Faxing

With the handles visible, you can move, copy, and delete the freehand object. You also can change the width of the lines in the freehand object. You cannot, however, change the freehand drawing itself. After you lift your finger off the mouse button, the drawing is complete.

Manipulating the Fax Image

In addition to adding shapes, lines, drawings, and images, you can manipulate the fax image itself. This is different from other types of annotations for the following reasons:

- Other annotations add objects to faxes. Manipulating the fax changes the existing fax image.

- You can only manipulate the image when you are in Viewing mode, not Annotation mode.

- You can isolate specific parts of a fax image and do things like move them or delete them.

For any of these operations, follow these steps:

1. Click the Select area tool in the Viewer toolbar. The mouse pointer turns into a cross cursor with a dotted box.

2. Position the cross cursor in the upper left corner of the part of the fax page you want to manipulate.

3. Drag the cursor down and to the right until the dotted box surrounds the area you want to manipulate.

4. Release the mouse cursor. The dotted box surrounds the selection.

To move the selection to another part of the page, follow these steps:

1. Position the mouse pointer over the selection. The mouse cursor turns into a hand surrounded by triangular handles.

2. Hold down the left mouse button. The cross cursor turns into an icon that looks like a hand.

3. Drag the item to its new position.

4. Release the left mouse button.

Notice that the former position of the item is now blank. To move the item to a new position in the page while leaving it in its old position, use the

Select Area tool to surround the item. Then choose **E**dit Dup**l**icate. A copy of the selected area appears in the upper left corner of the View window. Drag this item to a new position.

Similarly, you can also perform the following functions after you selected a section of the fax:

- Cut the selection from the fax image and copy it to the Windows clipboard. To do that, choose **E**dit Cu**t**. After the selection is in the Windows clipboard, you can paste it into virtually any Windows application.

- Copy the selection to the Windows clipboard while keeping it in its original location. To do that, choose **E**dit **C**opy.

- Delete the selection without adding it to the Windows clipboard. Choose **E**dit **D**elete.

- Invert the selection. Choose **E**dit **I**nvert. The selection now appears with lights and darks reversed, much like a photographic negative.

- Eliminate stray dots from the selection. Choose **E**dit **C**lean up. A previous section of this chapter describes the cleaning up process.

- Save the selected section to a file. Choose **F**ile **E**xport. The next section describes how to export selected sections of faxes.

Special Uses for Annotation

WinFax PRO's annotation capabilities are powerful and can be extremely useful. Before the advent of fax modems and programs such as WinFax PRO, you would receive a paper fax, add your comments to it and fax it back. Now all these activities occur electronically, saving both time and paper.

This section lists just a few uses for WinFax PRO's annotation capabilities.

Adding Signatures

Adding a signature to a fax and returning it is a common need. If you have a scanner, scan a copy of your signature into an image editing or paint program, such as the Paintbrush program that comes with Windows. Then save the signature. If you use Paintbrush, for example, that program automatically saves the signature as a PCX file, a commonly used graphics format. Other programs offer a wide variety of other graphics format. When you must sign and return a fax, insert the image of your signature and either forward the fax or send it back to the original sender.

III

Power Faxing

Tip
Usually, it is a
good idea to
eliminate the
border around
the graphic
image box
containing a
signature. If
you don't, the
border appears
around your
signature in
the fax.

If you don't have a scanner, you still can capture your signature as an image if you have a copy of a fax you signed. If necessary, ask somebody to send you such a fax.

To capture your signature as an image, follow these steps:

1. Switch to Viewing mode.

2. Use the Select Area tool in the Viewer toolbar to surround your signature.

3. Choose **E**dit **C**opy. This copies your signature to the Windows clipboard.

4. In the Viewer, open the fax to which you must add a signature.

5. Choose **E**dit **P**aste. Viewer pastes the signature into the fax page.

6. Position the mouse cursor over the signature.

7. Hold down the left mouse button and drag the signature to the desired location.

To keep a permanent copy of the signature as a graphics file, follow these steps:

1. Use the Select Area tool to surround the signature.

2. Choose **F**ile **E**xport. Viewer displays the Export dialog (see fig. 14.23).

Fig. 14.23
Export your
signature so you
can use it in faxes
later.

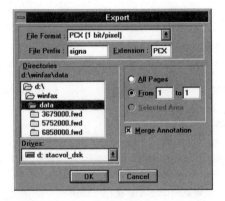

3. Select the file format in the **F**ile Format drop-down list. The available formats are as follows:

- *PCX (1 bit/pixel)*. One bit/pixel means that the exported image is in black and white.

- *TIFF (G3 Compressed)*. TIFF is a common format. Because TIFF files usually take a lot of disk storage space, Viewer compresses it to take less space.

- *FXS*. This is WinFax PRO's normal format for storing graphic images. Using this option make it easy to save the fax image as an attachment. Read Chapter 12, "Assembling Faxes from Many Sources," to learn how to create attachments.

- *BMP*. This is a common graphics format, particularly for Windows applications. For example, Windows wallpaper files are in the BMP format.

4. Select a file name of as many as five characters in the **F**ile Prefix text box. Viewer automatically places the correct file extension name for the selected image format in the **E**xtension text box.

5. Select the drive on which you will store the exported image in the Dri**v**es drop-down list.

6. Select the directory in which you will store the exported signature in the **D**irectories list window.

7. Click OK. Viewer saves your signature in a graphic format.

Adding Comments

Use Viewer to add comments to faxes you receive. Then either return them to the sender, or forward them on to others for additional comments.

Adding comments may be useful when a colleague in a different location faxes you a draft of a memo or report requiring your comments. You might also want to add comments when an advertising agency sends you initial samples of ads for your comment, for example.

Creating Maps

Create a map to your location by using Viewer's drawing tools. You can even add an arrow and text saying "Here's our building!"

III

Power Faxing

Tip
Add maps to your collection of stamps that you quickly can add to faxes.

Tip
When you fill out forms, be sure to use a typeface that transmits well. Typically, sans serif fonts, such as Helvetica, are easier to read in faxes than serif fonts such as Times New Roman.

You can add the map to a fax somebody sent you, or you can create the map from scratch and fax it right from Viewer by "printing" it to the recipient's fax machine.

Completing Forms

Sometimes you'll receive faxes containing forms you must fill out and return. Rather than printing the fax and returning the form with a standard fax machine, use the Viewer's text annotation capabilities to complete the forms. This is more legible and faster than filling out paper-based forms with pen.

Troubleshooting

I typed text into a text box, but I can't see it.

One cause of this problem is that the text color matches the background color. For example, you may have shaded the box black and used black text. To see if this is a problem, change the shading of the box by selecting Annotate Shade. The other problem might be that you made the text box too small to view the text within it. To solve that problem, select the box, and then drag its handles to make it larger.

I find it difficult to properly line up images and shapes that I add to the fax.

Use the Snap to Grid option. This option forces objects that you add to line up on the grid. To use this option, you must be in Annotation mode. Then choose Annotate Snap to Grid.

I added a graphic image to a fax, but I can't see the entire image in the image box.

You didn't choose scaling when you inserted the image. If the original image is larger than the image box into which you place it, you won't be able to see parts of it on-screen. Delete the image from the fax and reinsert it. This time, however, choose a different type of scaling for the image.

Saving Annotations

When you create annotations, the borders around boxes or the shapes and freehand lines are red. This indicates that you have not yet made the annotation changes permanent.

Before saving the fax file and annotations, you can revert to the original fax. To do that, choose **F**ile Re**v**ert. Viewer warns you that all changes will be discarded. Choose OK. This eliminates all your annotations and returns Viewer to Viewing mode.

To save the fax image and the annotations without making the annotations permanent, choose **F**ile **S**ave. The next time you load the file in Viewing mode, the annotations are not visible. When you switch to Annotation mode, however, the annotations appear.

Making the annotations permanent adds the changes to the fax image file. Viewer re-creates the image to merge your annotations in to the original fax. To do that, choose **F**ile **M**erge Annotation with Fax. Viewer warns you that you cannot undo the annotations once you take this action (see fig. 14.24).

Tip
Use the **F**ile **S**ave option to save annotations that you start but haven't yet completed.

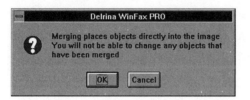

Fig. 14.24
Viewer warns you that you cannot change the fax once you complete the annotation.

If you are sure that you want to go ahead with the annotation, choose OK. Viewer re-creates the fax image incorporating your changes. As it does so, it displays a message box showing you its progress.

When Viewer finishes, the fax image includes your annotations. Notice that the lines of your annotation now appear black on-screen, the same as all other elements of the fax.

Note

The only way to undo annotations incorporated into the fax image is to use the Eraser tool in Viewer's Viewing mode.

Printing & Exporting Annotated Faxes

After you complete your annotations and incorporate them into the fax image, you have three options:

III

Power Faxing

- Send the fax to either the original sender or to another recipient. (Chapter 8, "Sending Faxes," tells you how.)

- Print the annotated fax.

- Export the fax from viewer as a graphics file.

Printing Annotated Faxes

To select a printer, follow these steps:

1. Choose File Printer Setup. Viewer displays the Printer Setup dialog box.

2. Select the desired printer.

3. To set up the printer, click the Setup button. Viewer displays the Printer Setup dialog box for the selected printer.

4. When you finish the printer-specific setup dialog box, click OK. This returns you to the Viewer's Printer Setup dialog box.

5. Click OK in the Viewer's Printer Setup dialog box.

To print the annotated fax to a regular printer, follow these steps:

1. Choose File Print. Viewer displays Print Fax dialog box (see fig. 14.25).

Fig. 14.25
Print annotated faxes with the Print Fax dialog box.

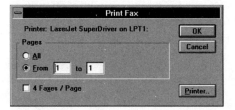

- To print all pages of the fax, select the All button.

- To print only selected pages of the fax, select the From button. Then type the range of pages in the text boxes to the right of the From button.

- To print four fax pages per printed page, select the 4 Faxes/Page check box.

- To change printers or make last minute changes to your printer setup, click Printer. Viewer displays the Printer Setup dialog box.

2. When you finish the settings, click OK. Viewer prints your fax.

Exporting Faxes

When you export the fax, Viewer saves it in one of several commonly used graphic file formats. This makes it easy to incorporate the fax into other applications.

> **Note**
>
> Most applications, such as word processors, spreadsheets, and desktop publishers, can import graphics saved in common graphic file formats. They cannot, however, import fax images in the format that WinFax PRO normally uses to save faxes.

To export the fax from Viewer, choose **F**ile **E**xport. Viewer displays the Export dialog box discussed previously in the "Adding Signatures" section of this chapter. This time, however, the Export dialog box has some additional options for exporting entire faxes.

1. Choose **F**ile **E**xport. Viewer displays the Export dialog box.

2. Select the file format in the **F**ile Format drop-down list.

3. Type a file name of as many as five characters for the fax you are exporting. Viewer automatically places the correct file extension name for the selected image format in the **E**xtension text box.

4. Select the drive on which you will store the exported image in the Dri**v**es drop-down list.

5. Select the directory in which you will store the exported image in the **D**irectories list window.

6. Select the **A**ll Pages button to save all the pages in the fax in the graphic file.

> **Note**
>
> Only the TIFF format can save multiple pages in the same file. If you save a multiple page fax in other formats, Viewer creates separate files for each page. Viewer numbers the files consecutively. For example, if you export a two page fax in BMP format and provide the file name MYDOC, Viewer names the files MYDOC001.BMP and MYDOC002.BMP.

7. Select the **F**rom button to export a range of pages. Type the page numbers to export in the text boxes to the right of the button.

Tip
Use Viewer's
export option to
export any fax,
even if you
haven't anno-
tated it or sent it.

8. Select the **M**erge Annotations check box to merge annotations into the image file if you haven't yet done so.

9. Click OK to export the file.

Troubleshooting

It takes a long time to print faxes from the Viewer.

This is a common problem when printing any image. Because images are composed of a series of dots, called pixels, Windows must process each dot to prepare it for printing and then send each dot to the printer. There's not much you can do about this problem.

I rotated a fax; then it didn't print entirely.

If you originally sent or received the fax in landscape mode (which is a normal printed page turned on its side), and you rotate it 90 degrees so it appears normal, you may cut off part of the fax or image when printing. The only way to print the entire fax or image is to print it in its page orientation.

Optical Character Recognition

This chapter described how to view faxes and how to annotate them. It does not describe the other major capability of the Viewer: applying *optical character recognition (OCR)* to faxes.

OCR is a process in which the software analyzes the contents of an image (in this case, a fax image), and converts the contents to text that your other applications can edit. While annotation enables you to add notes, shapes, and images to faxes, OCR enables you to actually edit the contents of faxes.

Viewer's OCR capabilities are useful for many reasons. For example, if somebody faxes you a contract that is under negotiation, you can apply OCR to the fax and use your word processor to make any changes.

OCR is an important part of WinFax PRO; and this book devotes a separate chapter to it. To learn how to use OCR, read Chapter 15, "Converting Faxes to Text."

From Here...

This chapter told you how to use WinFax PRO's Viewer to view, annotate, and enhance faxes. For background and more information about related activities, you may want to read the following chapters:

■ Chapter 7, "Creating and Managing Cover Pages," describes how to use the Cover Page Designer, which is similar to the Viewer.

■ Chapter 8, "Sending Faxes," tells you how to send faxes and also how to schedule them for later and hold them for later disposition.

■ Chapter 9, "Receiving Faxes," describes how to receive faxes.

■ Chapter 11, "Using the Send and Receive Logs," tells you how to use the Send and Receive logs to store information about faxes.

■ Chapter 12, "Assembling Faxes from Many Sources," tells you how to create and store attachments that you can add to faxes.

■ Chapter 15, "Converting Faxes to Text," describes how to use WinFax PRO's OCR capabilities, which you access from the Viewer.

Chapter 15

Converting Faxes to Text

In this chapter, you learn the following:

- How the OCR process works.

- How to set up WinFax PRO to do OCR.

- How to convert fax documents into editable text using OCR.

- How to convert sections of faxes into editable text.

One of WinFax PRO's most useful features is its ability to convert fax images into text that other applications can edit. The process by which this occurs is called *optical character recognition (OCR)*. This is useful in many instances such as the following:

- In contract negotiations, attorneys for both sides can fax draft contracts to each other, apply OCR, edit the contract, and fax the contract back.

- An advertising agency can fax drafts of advertising copy to a client, who then can apply OCR, edit the copy, and send the edited copy back to the agency.

- You can keep all the information in the fax when you apply OCR and save the file. Editable text takes up much less disk space than ordinary fax images.

This chapter explains how the OCR process works in WinFax PRO.

What Is OCR?

To understand OCR, think of the same document in two forms: One form is the document as you create it in your word processor. The other form is a photograph of a printed version of the same document.

The document you create in your word processor can be edited and saved on your hard disk as an editable file. That is, you can open the file and edit the words in it.

The photograph of the document can be drawn on, but you can't actually edit it. In rough terms, the fax images that WinFax PRO stores are this kind of uneditable image.

As you learned in Chapter 14, "Viewing and Annotating Faxes," you can annotate fax images by adding shapes, lines, other images, and freeform drawings. You can draw a circle around an important part of the fax, draw an arrow from the circle, and add a comment in the margin, but you cannot edit the words within the fax image.

This is where OCR comes in. OCR has been around since the late 1950s and has advanced considerably over the years. Stand-alone OCR packages are popular applications because they enable users to scan paper documents and then turn the scanned document into editable text. This process also helps eliminate paper clutter in offices.

During the OCR process, the following steps occur:

1. The user decides whether to apply OCR to the entire image or to designated sections of the image called *zones* or *areas*.

2. The OCR software examines the contents of the image or zone.

3. If the page or zone contains an image such as a photo or drawing, the OCR software does not attempt to translate it.

4. For the parts of the image containing text, the software applies rules that the OCR developer has provided to attempt to determine the identity of each letter.

5. The OCR software then uses a dictionary to examine the translated document and change words that the dictionary does not recognize. Depending on the OCR software, this occurs either automatically or interactively with the user's assistance.

6. The software saves the results of its translation in a file. The file can be either a standard ASCII text file or in the format of a designated application.

Sound simple? Well, it's not really. OCR is a complex process that must consider many variables. For example, the OCR process becomes less accurate if:

- One letter overlaps another.

- The image is skewed at an angle.

- The original document used unusual fonts.

- The fax image has a great number of random dots and other "noise" caused by line interference during transmission.

These are just a few of the problems that OCR software must overcome. Modern OCR technology can handle most of these problems with varying degrees of success.

But you need to be aware of one thing: The accuracy of the OCR process decreases as the quality of the original image decreases. The resolution—or crispness of the characters—of faxes is also much lower than the resolution of typeset pages or even of pages printed with laser printers.

A laser printer prints each character at a minimum resolution of 300 dots per inch (dpi) by 300 dpi. Resolutions of typeset documents are several times that high. But the maximum resolution of a fax transmission is 200 dpi by 200 dpi. This low resolution makes it more difficult to attain a high level of accuracy when applying OCR to fax images than when applying it to "cleaner" images such as images of typeset pages.

OCR Requirements

The preceding section describes how the OCR process works. Before you start OCR, there are some additional items you should know:

First, you need a PC that is powerful enough and has sufficient RAM to handle the OCR process. The OCR process requires at least an 80386 PC. It also requires that Windows run in *Enhanced mode.* If you have an 80386 or greater PC with at least 4M of RAM, Windows automatically runs in Enhanced mode. If you do not meet these specifications, Windows may not be able to run in Enhanced mode.

Enhanced mode is a method of running windows that enables you to run multiple operations at the same time, a process called *multitasking*. It also is a mode that enables applications to use memory more efficiently. Because the OCR process requires a lot of memory, it requires the capabilities that Enhanced mode provides.

Although Enhanced mode requires only 4M of memory, you also need additional memory resources. Specifically, you need at least 2M of available disk space for a *swap file*.

What is a swap file? During operation, programs use memory in order to function. When they finish using the memory, they make it available for use again. If a Windows program needs RAM but Windows has no more memory to give, Windows acts as though the disk is RAM. Instead of placing program information in RAM, Windows temporarily places the information in a disk-based swap file.

Read your Windows user's guide for more information about Enhanced mode, RAM, and swap files.

Caution

You cannot start OCR unless you are running Windows in Enhanced mode. Even in Enhanced mode, though, system crashes can occur if you don't have enough RAM or a large enough swap file. Make sure that you have adequate resources before using OCR.

Tip
If handwriting is on the fax you are recognizing, you will achieve better results by using manual recognition to draw recognition zones around the clean type, as discussed later in this chapter.

Certain characteristics enhance the quality of the recognition process. Specifically, better recognition results occur if:

- The sender sets the fax machine to transmit in Fine resolution. Fine resolution is 200 dpi by 200 dpi.

- There are no handwritten notes or underlining on the received fax.

- The fax uses common fonts, preferably sans serif fonts such as Helvetica or Gill Sans.

- The font size is relatively large—12 point type or greater is the best.

Setting Up Automatic OCR

Chapter 4, "Configuring WinFax PRO," describes how to set up WinFax PRO to automatically start the OCR process when it receives faxes. This is a useful option for applying OCR to all faxes you receive; however, because the OCR process requires a lot of your PC's resources, it usually is more efficient to apply OCR only to selected faxes.

To review the process of setting up WinFax PRO to automatically apply OCR, follow these steps:

1. Choose Setu**p R**eceive.

2. In the Receive Setup dialog box, select the **R**ecognition check box if you want WinFax PRO to start the OCR process automatically every time you receive a fax.

3. To set up the automatic OCR process, click the Se**t**up button to the right of the **R**ecognition check box. WinFax PRO displays the Recognize Setup dialog box (see fig. 15.1).

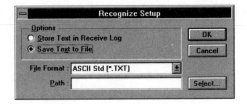

Fig. 15.1
Set up automatic OCR in the Recognize Setup dialog box.

4. Select the **S**tore Text in Receive Log button if you want to access the recognized text from the Receive Log.

5. Select the Save Te**x**t to File button to save the text to a file that you can use in other applications.

6. If you save the text to a file, choose a format for the file from the F**i**le Format drop-down list.

7. Type the drive and path in which you want to save the file in the **P**ath text box.

8. If you don't know the path, click the Se**l**ect button. Select a path from the Directories dialog box and click OK to return to the Recognize Setup dialog box.

Tip

If you don't find the format of your other application in the F**i**le Format drop-down list, select ASCII Std., is a standard ASCII text format that virtually all applications can import.

III

Power Faxing

9. Click OK to return to the Receive Setup dialog box.

10. After returning to the Receive Setup dialog box, click OK to return to WinFax PRO.

Starting the Recognition Process

The previous section reviewed how to set up WinFax PRO to automatically recognize faxes when you receive them. The rest of this chapter describes how to recognize only specific faxes you select.

Tip
Load multiple faxes into the viewer by selecting one fax, holding down the Ctrl key and selecting additional faxes.

Start the OCR process and further refine your OCR configuration in the Viewer. To learn about using Viewer to view and annotate faxes, read Chapter 14, "Viewing and Annotating Faxes."

Start the OCR process the same way you start the viewing or annotation process. Double-click a fax or an attachment in a log window and Viewer loads with the first page of the selected item visible. Alternatively, highlight a fax in the item list window and choose **Fax View**.

If you already are in Viewer, choose **File Open**. Select files in the Open File for Viewing dialog box.

When Viewer starts, it is in Viewing mode. It is from this mode—not Annotation mode—that you access WinFax PRO's OCR capabilities.

Refining Your OCR Options

As stated previously, you can set up WinFax PRO to automatically recognize faxes in the Receive Setup dialog box. However, Viewer has additional setup options for applying OCR to specific faxes.

To set up selective OCR, when you are in Viewing mode in the Viewer, choose **Recognize Setup**. Viewer displays the Recognition Setup dialog box (see fig. 15.2). While this dialog box has almost the same name as the dialog box for setting up automatic OCR, it has a different set of options.

The following several sections discuss the elements of the Recognition Setup dialog box.

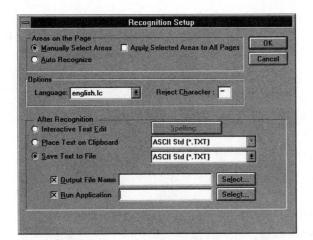

Fig. 15.2
Set up the
selective OCR
process in Viewer's
Recognition Setup
dialog box.

Determining the Areas for OCR

In the Recognition Setup dialog box, you tell Viewer to automatically apply
OCR to entire pages. Or you can tell Viewer that before the OCR process com-
mences you will designate specific zones on each page within which the OCR
process should proceed. Make this determination in the Areas on the Page
area of the dialog box.

Manually designating zones is useful for editing only parts of the fax. To tell
WinFax PRO that you will designate the zones of the fax for OCR, select the
Manually Select Areas button. To tell WinFax PRO to automatically apply
OCR to entire pages, select the **A**uto Recognize button.

If you choose to manually designate zones to recognize, you also can tell
WinFax PRO to recognize the same zones you designate on the first page on
every page. This is useful, for example, if there is a logo or other standard
item at the top and bottom of each page that you don't want to process. To
apply zones you select on the first page to all other pages of the fax, select the
Appl**y** Selected Areas to All Pages check box.

OCR Error-Checking Options

In the Options area of the Recognition Setup dialog box, determine the
language of the text in the Lan**g**uage drop-down list. The language setting
determines the rules WinFax PRO uses to recognize specific characters.

As described in the previous section, "What Is OCR?", OCR software applies
rules to each character to help translate the character. Because different languages have different characters, it is necessary to tell WinFax PRO which
language it is translating.

III

Power Faxing

Also described in "What Is OCR?": After Viewer completes the first phase of the recognition process, it uses a dictionary to check words it did not recognize. Setting the language of the document enables WinFax PRO to use the correct dictionary.

Because faxes are more difficult for the OCR process to recognize than typeset or laser-printed documents, WinFax PRO often cannot recognize every character. When this happens, it replaces the unrecognizable character with a standard character called a *reject character*.

In the Reject Character text box, type the character WinFax PRO should insert in place of characters it does not recognize. The default is the tilde (~) character. To use another character, type it in the text box.

> **Note**
>
> For normal English usage, the tilde character is a good choice because its use is rare in English. If you designate another reject character, make sure it is not a commonly used character.

Post-OCR Options

Use the After Recognition area of the Recognition Setup dialog box to determine what WinFax PRO does with the recognized text after it completes the OCR process. In this area, you determine whether to do the following:

- Interact with the process of cleaning up and completing a recognized document.

- Let much of the cleanup and completion process occur automatically and save the results to the Windows clipboard.

- Let much of the cleanup and completion process occur automatically and save the results to a file.

When the recognition process occurs automatically, WinFax PRO recognizes the page and applies the spell-checking process to recognized text without user intervention. When WinFax PRO finishes with this process, the resulting information contains words in which unrecognizable characters have the reject character.

However, to participate in the spell-checking process—much as you would when using a spell checker in a word processor—you need to select the Interactive Text Edit check box.

Selecting the Interactive Text **E**dit box helps ensure the accuracy of recognized documents. Although it does take up more of your time, it is useful because:

- The spell checker, when it runs automatically, can easily make wrong choices. For example, if a partially recognized word before spell-checking is *r~n*, the spell checker must choose between either *run* or *ran*. Interactive text editing enables you to pick the correct word.

- Many words have so many reject characters that the spell checker won't even attempt to correct them. Again, you can correct these words during the OCR process rather than trying to figure them out later.

If you choose interactive editing, you can configure how the spell checker operates by clicking the **S**pelling button. Viewer displays the Spelling Options dialog box (see fig. 15.3).

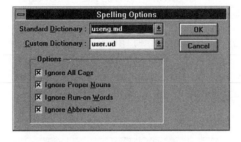

Fig. 15.3
Set spelling options for the OCR process in the Spelling Options dialog box.

In the Spelling Options dialog box:

- Select the dictionary for normal use in the Standard **D**ictionary drop-down list.

- Select any custom dictionaries from the **C**ustom Dictionary drop-down list. A custom dictionary contains specialized information. For example, you can obtain dictionaries containing words specific to your profession.

Click OK to return to the Recognition Setup dialog box.

Additional options in the After Recognition area of the Recognition Setup dialog box are available only if you selectd the **A**uto Recognize button. These options are concerned with the location of the text after WinFax PRO finishes the automatic recognition process.

Tip
If you recognize text in other languages, choose interactive text editing. This option enables you to select a language-specific dictionary for the recognition process.

Power Faxing

Select the **P**lace Text on Clipboard option to save the text to the Windows clipboard. This enables you to paste the text into other applications.

If you select the **P**lace Text on Clipboard option, also select a format for the text to be saved to the clipboard in the drop-down list to the right. The available options are:

- ASCII Standard—a version of standard ASCII text that places a carriage return at the end of each line. You may need to eliminate all carriage returns except those between paragraphs after you paste the text into your application.

- ASCII Smart—a variation of ASCII that attempts to place hard returns only between paragraphs. This prevents the hassle of having to remove inappropriately placed hard returns after pasting the text into your document.

- ASCII Stripped—a variation of ASCII that strips out all invisible characters, such as hard returns.

- Word for Windows (RTF) saves the file in Rich Text Format, which is readable by Microsoft Word and Microsoft Word for Windows. If you use either of these word processors and select this option, recognized text can retain much of the formatting in the image, such as boldface characters.

Caution

Remember that recognized text placed in the clipboard only remains there until you cut or copy something else into the clipboard. Make sure that you paste recognized text into your application as soon as you complete the recognition process.

Select the **S**ave Text to File check box to save recognized text to file. Select a file format for the file in the drop-down list to the right.

You can save the files in the formats of a wide variety of word processing, database, and spreadsheet programs. You also can select the three ASCII options previously discussed. If you don't find the name of the application you want, select one of the ASCII options.

After you select the **S**ave Text to File check box and choose a file format, select the name of the file to which you save the recognized text. **O**utput File Name is the name of the file containing the recognized text. Type a drive, path, and file name in the text box. To save the file to an existing file when you are not sure of the file name or location, click the Select button. Viewer displays the Select OCR Output File dialog box from which you select an existing file (see fig. 15.4).

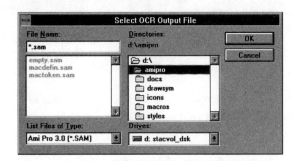

Fig. 15.4

Select a file for your recognized text in the Select OCR Output File dialog box.

In the Select OCR Output File dialog box, follow these steps:

1. Select the type of file for which you are searching in the List Files of **T**ype drop-down list. Files with different formats use different file extensions. After selecting a file type, only files with those extensions appear in the File **N**ame window.

2. Select a drive in the Dri**v**es drop-down list.

3. Select a directory in the **D**irectories drop-down list.

4. Select a specific file in the File **N**ames window.

After you complete the OCR Output dialog box, click OK to return to the Recognition Setup dialog box.

The other option enables you to immediately launch an application so that you can edit the recognized text. In most cases, the application automatically loads the recognized text.

To automatically run an application, follow these steps:

1. Select the **R**un Application text box.

2. Type the drive, path, and file name of the program you want to run.

3. If you are not sure of the drive, path, and name of the application file, click the Select button. Viewer displays the Select Application dialog box, which is similar to the Select OCR Output File dialog box discussed previously.

III

Power Faxing

4. In the Select Application dialog box, which is similar to the Select OCR Output File dialog box, select the file needed to run the application. Click OK to return to the Recognition Setup dialog box.

> **Note**
>
> The file name extension for basic files that run applications is EXE. This is the only selection in the List Files of **T**ype drop-down list.

After you complete the Recognition Setup dialog box, click OK. You return to Viewer and the fax you want to recognize.

The Recognition Process

Tip
It often doesn't make sense to recognize a cover page. Save time by using the Select Pages dialog box to recognize all pages except the cover page.

The recognition process breaks down into several relatively simple steps. You can have Viewer recognize entire fax pages automatically. You also can select the areas of pages, or zones of the page, to recognize. Finally, you can choose to edit the recognized text yourself, or let Viewer do it automatically. The next several sections describe these processes.

Selecting Pages

You can choose to recognize the currently displayed page by selecting **R**ecognize **C**urrent Page, or to recognize multiple pages by selecting **R**ecognize Select **P**ages. If you choose the latter option, Viewer displays the Select Pages dialog box (see fig. 15.5).

Fig. 15.5
Determine the pages to recognize in the Select Pages dialog box.

In the Select Pages dialog box, select the **A**ll button to recognize all pages of the fax. To recognize multiple pages, select the **F**rom button and enter a range of pages.

If you choose to recognize only the current page, Viewer switches you to Recognition mode. If you choose to select specific pages, Viewer switches you to Recognition mode after you click OK in the Select Pages dialog box.

Recognition mode includes a work area grid like the grid used in Annotation mode. Most of the fax viewing and manipulation tools available in Viewing mode are also available in Recognition mode.

When in Recognition mode, however, Viewer displays the Recognition toolbar (see fig. 15.6).

Selection tool   Order Zones tool   Recognize button

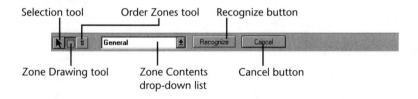

Zone Drawing tool   Zone Contents   Cancel button
drop-down list

Fig. 15.6
Select recognition options from the Recognition toolbar.

Table 15.1 describes each button in the Recognition toolbar.

Table 15.1	The Buttons in the Recognition toolbar.
Button	**Function**
Selection tool	Selects recognition area
Zone Drawing tool	Draws a zone in which recognition occurs
Order Zones tool	Changes the order in which Viewer recognizes zones
Zone Contents drop-down list	Determines type of information in a zone
Recognize button	Starts recognition
Cancel button	Cancels recognition

Tip
Fax pages must be right side up before recognition begins. People using standard fax machines often send faxes upside down. Use the rotate functions in Viewer's Viewing mode to flip the pages.

Auto Recognize

If you choose **A**uto Recognize in the Recognition Setup dialog box, the recognition process begins when you select the page or pages to recognize. Viewer displays a series of status messages telling you how far along in the recognition process it is (see fig. 15.7).

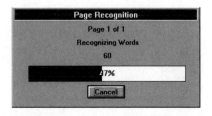

Fig. 15.7
Status messages describe how far along the recognition process is.

III

Power Faxing

When Viewer finishes the recognition process, it places the text in the Windows clipboard or in the file you designated in the Recognition Setup dialog box. If you chose the Windows clipboard, paste the recognized text into your application. If you chose a specific file format and file name, open your application and load the file.

The text in the file or clipboard consists of the words and characters that the OCR process recognized. Characters that it couldn't recognize are represented by the tilde character—or whatever reject character you designated in the Recognition Setup dialog box.

In either case, you will probably need to use a Windows application and its spell checker, if any, to clean up the text and check its spelling. As stated previously, the OCR process often is not highly accurate with faxed documents.

Recognizing Selected Areas

If you chose **M**anually Select Areas, you must select zones in each page that you want to recognize. A later section in this chapter discusses how to create zones.

After selecting zones, start the recognition process by selecting **R**ecognize **S**elected areas. Alternatively, click the Recognize button in the toolbar.

As with the automatic recognition process, Viewer displays status messages. If you chose to save the recognized text either to the Windows clipboard or to a file, Viewer returns you to Viewing mode after it finishes.

The following section describes how to proceed if you choose interactive text editing in the Recognition Setup dialog box.

Editing Text Interactively

The Interactive Text **E**dit option in the Recognition Setup dialog box enables you to work with the text immediately after Viewer recognizes it. This option has several advantages.

Specifically, you can:

■ Spell-check the document and correct errors, which is more accurate than the behind-the-scenes spell checking that occurs when you automatically save text. In those cases, if the spell checker does not recognize a word, it remains in the document and you will need to spell-check it with your other application.

Tip
Select the entire page as a zone to exclude the fax header from the recognition process and avoid the extraneous black dots along the edges caused by line interference.

Tip
When drawing zones, zoom in to see more detail of the fax. Otherwise, it is easy to draw the zone line over a line of text, which could exclude it from the recognition.

- Edit the text while still viewing the actual fax image, which is a big benefit because, when a word is poorly recognized, you can reference the word in the actual fax image.

- Apply specific fonts to the text.

- Justify sections of the text. This is useful, for example, when you want to center-justify section headings.

- Change text attributes, such as adding bold or italic text.

If you choose interactive editing, Viewer goes through the initial part of the recognition process the same as if you chose to save text to a file or to the clipboard. However, when Viewer finishes the recognition process, it splits the Viewer application window in half. The top half is the normal Viewer window and the bottom half is a window containing the converted text (see fig. 15.8).

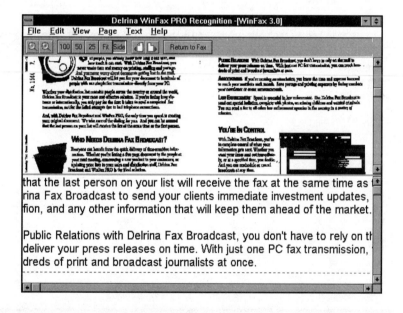

Fig. 15.8
Viewer displays converted text after the recognition process beneath an image of the fax.

Note

At any time before the recognition process actually begins, you can return to Viewer by selecting **F**ile, Return to Fa**x**.

III

Power Faxing

To change the size of the text viewing window, follow these steps:

1. Position the mouse cursor over the horizontal line dividing the two windows. The mouse pointer turns into a horizontal line cursor with two arrows pointing out.

2. Hold down the left mouse button.

3. Drag the mouse up to make the text viewing window larger. Drag the mouse down to make the text viewing window smaller.

4. Release the left mouse button.

You can edit the text that appears in the text viewing window in the same way that you edit text you insert in Annotation mode. Table 15.2 describes the actions you can take on text in the text viewing window. For more information about text editing capabilities, read Chapter 14, "Viewing and Annotating Faxes."

Table 15.2   Text Editing Actions in Interactive Editing Mode.

Action	Steps
Left-justify	**T**ext **L**eft Justify
Center-justify	**T**ext **C**enter Justify
Right-justify	**T**ext **R**ight Justify
Bold	**T**ext **B**old
Italic	**T**ext **I**talic
Underline	**T**ext **U**nderline
Normal text	**T**ext **N**ormal
Change font	**T**ext **F**ont
Check spelling	**T**ext **S**pelling

There are only a few differences between editing in text boxes in Annotation mode and editing in the text editing window. Most noticeably, you don't need to select text to perform a spell-check as you do in Annotation mode. Rather, selecting **T**ext **S**pelling starts the spell checker for all the text you recognized.

As in editing in Annotation mode, however, you must select specific text for changing fonts, adding text attributes, and justification.

Troubleshooting

My recognized text has a lot of spelling errors and words I don't recognize.
What happened?

OCR typically isn't very accurate with faxes, and its accuracy decreases as the quality of the fax decreases. For the best OCR results, ask senders to send faxes to you in Fine resolution rather than Standard resolution and to use sans serif type fonts such as Helvetica. Also, you can clean up the fax before starting the recognition process. Chapter 14, "Viewing and Annotating Faxes," describes the fax cleanup process.

Creating Zones

There are several advantages to using zones rather than selecting **A**uto Recognize. Zones enable you to recognize only the information you want. You can avoid recognizing unnecessary items such as letterhead contents or the contents of the fax header.

If you choose **M**anually Select Areas in the Recognition Setup dialog box, you must first create zones on fax pages. Viewer recognizes only the information in the zones you select.

To create zones on the page, follow these steps:

1. Click the Zone Drawing tool in the Recognition toolbar. The normal mouse pointer turns into a cross cursor.

2. Position the cross cursor in the upper-left position of the zone you want to draw.

3. Hold down the left mouse button and drag the mouse down and to the right. A dotted line box surrounds the area that you draw with your mouse.

4. When the dotted line completely surrounds the area you want to recognize, release the mouse button. A red line with handles replaces the dotted line. This is the recognition zone.

Recognition zones have several important features. The next several sections describe those features.

Sizing and Moving Zones

Just like geometric shapes in Annotation mode, recognition zones include handles (see fig. 15.9). The handles enable you to change the size of the zone and move the zone to another part of the page.

Fig. 15.9
Recognition zones include handles that enable you to manage the zones.

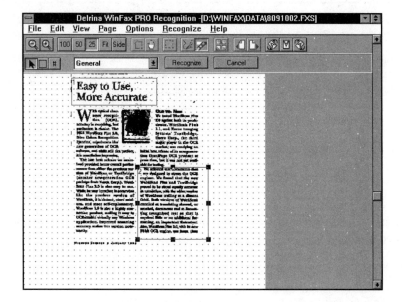

Handles on recognition zones work the same as handles on geometric shapes. To activate the handles, click the Selection tool in the Recognition toolbar and then click the zone.

To move a zone to another part of the page, follow these steps:

1. Position the mouse pointer over the zone.

2. Hold down the left mouse button.

3. Drag the zone to another part of the page.

4. Release the left mouse button.

You also can use handles to change the size of the zone. As with geometric shapes, position the mouse pointer over the handle. When the pointer turns into a two-headed cursor, hold down the left mouse button and drag the zone border to make it larger or smaller. When you finish, release the left mouse cursor.

When the handles are visible, you also can cut, copy, and paste zones. These actions occur to the zone borders and their dimensions, not the contents of the zone.

To cut or copy a zone, select the zone. Then choose **E**dit **C**opy or **E**dit Cu**t**. Both operations copy the zone to the Windows clipboard. Copying, however, leaves the zone in its original location; cutting eliminates the zone in its original location.

To paste a zone into a new location, choose **E**dit **P**aste. To delete the zone without copying it to the clipboard, choose **E**dit **D**elete.

Numbering Zones

Viewer gives each zone a number. The number, located in red in the upper-left corner of the zone, initially reflects the order in which you created the zones.

Viewer uses the numbers to determine the order in which to conduct the recognition. It places recognized text into the clipboard or a file in the determined order.

To change the order of the zones, follow these steps:

1. Click the Order Zones tool in the Recognition toolbar.

2. Click the zone you want to change to select its handles.

3. Click the zone again, and the number of the zone changes, as do the numbers in the other zones.

4. Continue clicking the zone until it contains the number you want.

5. Repeat the process, if necessary, with other zones.

Determining Zone Contents

You can designate the type of contents of zones to help Viewer do a better job of recognizing the contents. Select the zone contents in the zone contents drop-down list.

The following are the options in the zone contents drop-down list:

General
Text
Number
Money

Tip

Copying zones is useful when you want to recognize a specific section of multiple pages.

Tip

Zone ordering enables you to reconstruct documents in a new order. You can create a new document starting with information in the middle, add information from the end, and end with information from the begin-ning.

III

Power Faxing

Telephone number
Date
Time
Roman numeral

Each type of information has different rules and needs for optimizing the recognition process: Particularly in situations where fax quality is not very good, determining the information type helps minimize errors.

For example, if you designate a number zone, the OCR process won't confuse the number 5 for the letter S. When image quality is poor, this can be an easy error to make.

Troubleshooting

I set a zone, but Viewer didn't recognize all the information within it.

Chances are you placed the zone borders over lines of text, which can result in the failure to recognize those lines. Run the recognition process one more time, being careful to not place the zone borders over text you want to recognize.

Viewer is not very accurate recognizing numbers.

If you are recognizing only numbers, make sure that you select Numbers from the zone contents drop-down list. Viewer can then apply special rules that make recognition more accurate.

My recognized text comes out in strange order.

You made one of two errors: either you mistakenly renumbered the zones or you added new zones above previously designated zones. Even though the new zones are not physically the last zone on the page, Viewer numbers zones in the order you add them. Run the recognition process again, numbering the zones in precisely the order you want.

From Here...

This chapter described how to use the Viewer to convert faxes to text. For related information, you may want to read the following chapters:

■ Chapter 9, "Receiving Faxes," discusses how to receive faxes, to which you can apply OCR.

■ Chapter 14, "Viewing and Annotating Faxes," covers how to use the Viewer for these two important tasks.

■ Chapter 18, "Using WinFax PRO in Other Programs," describes how to use WinFax PRO and its capabilities with your other applications.

III

Power Faxing

Chapter 16

Different Ways to Send and Receive

In this chapter, you learn about the following:

- ■ Sending files and faxes using Binary File Transfer

- ■ Sending files and faxes to other WinFax PRO users

- ■ Sending files and faxes to Microsoft At Work devices

- ■ Setting up "alternative" capabilities

- ■ Two proprietary fax services that WinFax PRO supports

One strength of WinFax PRO 4 is that you can use it for other types of messages in addition to faxes. Chapter 10, "Using WinFax PRO for Electronic Mail," tells you how to use WinFax PRO to send, receive, and manage network e-mail. This chapter describes several advanced methods for sending and receiving information.

These advanced methods are the following:

- ■ *Binary File Transfer (BFT).* This method sends computer files and faxes to other fax modems at the same time.

- ■ *The Compressed BFT method.* This method is similar to BFT, but is an even faster way of exchanging files with other WinFax PRO 4 users.

- ■ *Microsoft At Work (MAW).* This method enables you to send and receive information to other devices that support this new standard.

- ■ *Delrina's Fax Broadcast Service.* This is a method of broadcasting multiple faxes quickly and inexpensively.

About File Transfers

Chapter 2, "How WinFax PRO Works," tells you about the generally accepted standards for transmitting faxes used by both fax modems and standard fax machines. It also tells you how the faxing process works.

To briefly review the fax transmission process:

1. Either your fax software or a standard fax machine converts each page of a document into a graphic image comprised of a series of dots.

2. The sending fax device calls the receiving fax device.

3. The two fax devices exchange a series of tones. This "communication" determines how the devices interact with each other and how they transmit and receive the fax.

4. The sending machine sends the fax image and the receiving machine receives it.

5. When the devices finish sending and receiving all the fax pages, the fax devices disconnect.

The process of using software like WinFax PRO and a fax modem to transmit or receive faxes is nearly identical to transmitting faxes between two standard fax machines. However, fax modems have an important capability that standard fax machines don't have: the ability to transfer files other than fax images.

In fact, using modems for faxing is a relatively new development. Until recently, modems were used only for transferring files and logging on to other computers, such as on-line services.

When we talk about transferring files, we usually are talking about *binary files*. A binary file is a non-text file. The information can be specially formatted word processing or spreadsheet files, or it can be computer programs.

When transferring binary files, you typically use a communications program designed specifically for that task. Such programs usually include several *file transfer protocols*.

File transfer protocols are standard methods of transmitting binary files so that both ends of the transmission—the sending modem and the receiving modem—know what to expect and the transfer can proceed without confusion. File transfer protocols include methods by which the receiving modem can be certain that all the information has arrived without being damaged or lost en route.

Until recently, these standards pertained only to traditional data transmission. However, an emerging standard enables fax modems to transmit regular computer binary files at the same time as fax images. This standard is called *Binary File Transfer (BFT),* and WinFax PRO supports it.

Using BFT

BFT is a file transfer protocol, but it is specifically for fax modems and the software that works with fax modems. It enables you to send a binary file at the same time you send a fax message.

For example, you can send a cover page explaining a detailed spreadsheet and send the large spreadsheet file at the same time. This means that you don't have to send the spreadsheet as a fax.

Some clarification is in order. First, BFT works only with Class 1 fax modems. Chapter 2, "How WinFax PRO Works," describes the different types of fax modems. If you are not sure whether your fax modem is Class 1 or Class 2, check your modem documentation.

To add to this alphabet soup of standards, BFT works in conjunction with *Error Correcting Mode (ECM).* A method first implemented in standard fax machines, ECM checks the accuracy of fax transmissions one section of a page at a time. Usually, ECM occurs behind the scenes to ensure the accuracy of fax pages and requires no intervention by the user. WinFax PRO supports ECM.

It is important to note that BFT file transfers don't work with normal faxes. Rather, in a BFT transfer, WinFax PRO transmits fax images as it normally would and transmits attachments using BFT.

Finally, you may face some confusion surrounding which type of BFT you are using. When you select a method of transmission for a recipient in the New Recipient or Modify Recipient dialog box, there is only one choice, called BFT. However, even though this choice is called BFT, it includes both regular BFT and MAW.

How can a single choice include two separate methods of transmission? The answer is simple: When you start to send the message using BFT, WinFax PRO automatically determines which type of BFT the recipient can handle and uses the appropriate type.

But what about Compressed BFT? To use this method, you must select it from the Send dialog box. To do that, click Schedule. Then select Compressed BFT from the Send By drop-down list.

III

Power Faxing

There are several advantages to sending attachments as files using BFT rather than transmitting them as regular faxes:

■ Sending binary files is faster than sending fax images.

■ To edit the file, you don't have to use OCR to convert the fax image to editable text. Rather, if the recipient has an application that can edit the binary file, all he or she has to do is load the file and edit it.

■ You can improve the performance of fax modems with slow data transmission rates. Many older fax modems transfer binary files at only 2400 bits per second, but they almost always support fax transmissions at 9600 bits per second. Because BFT file transfers occur at fax speeds, you can transfer those files at 9600 bits per second, even on older fax modems.

■ BFT enables you to transmit binary attachments that WinFax PRO ordinarily can't convert into fax images. While WinFax PRO can convert files created by most popular Windows programs into faxes, it can't convert many other types of files, such as the files needed to run programs. With BFT, you can transfer files, even if WinFax PRO can't convert them into faxes.

Setting Up Binary File Transfer

Setting up BFT is simple. Your most difficult task is to make sure that the recipient is using fax software, such as WinFax PRO 4, and hardware, such as a Class 1 modem, that supports BFT. If that is the case, select BFT as the mode of transmission for that recipient.

Select BFT either when you create a new phonebook record in the New Recipient dialog box, or when you modify a recipient record using the Modify Recipient dialog box. Remember that BFT refers to either the standard BFT transmission method or the Microsoft at Work (MAW) method and that WinFax PRO automatically determines which to use. Chapter 6, "Using Phonebooks," describes how to create phonebook entries.

To create a phonebook record using BFT, follow these steps:

1. First confirm with the recipient that she or he uses fax software that supports BFT transmissions.

> **Note**
>
> You cannot make BFT transfers with standard fax machines. BFT works only when the recipient uses a fax modem and fax software that supports it.

2. Make the phonebooks window the active window. The easiest method is to click the Phnbooks button on the WinFax PRO toolbar.

3. Double-click the New Recipient in the item list box of any phonebook.

4. Add information to the New Recipient dialog box as you normally would (as described in Chapter 6, "Using Phonebooks").

5. In the drop-down list in the first row of the Connections area of the New Recipient dialog box, select BFT as your method of transmission.

> **Note**
>
> If you are set up for use with an Intel SatisFAXion board, WinFax PRO calls the selection SatisFAXion. SatisFAXion is virtually identical to regular BFT, except that it is tuned to work specifically with the Intel SatisFAXion modem. Read Chapter 2, "How WinFax PRO Works," for more information about the different types of fax modems.

6. Click the Programs button. WinFax PRO displays the Programs Available dialog box (see fig. 16.1). This dialog box has two list boxes. The **P**ossible Programs window lists all the programs on your computer and the **A**vailable at Recipient window lists the programs on the recipient's computer.

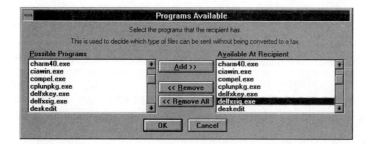

Fig. 16.1
Select programs your BFT recipient is likely to have in the Programs Available dialog box.

> **Note**
>
> The first time you use this dialog box for a particular recipient, it lists all the programs on your computer in the A**v**ailable at Recipient list window.

7. In the **P**ossible Programs list window, select the programs you think the recipient has on his or her computer.

8. After you select possible programs, click the **A**dd button. The programs you selected appear in the A**v**ailable at Recipient list window.

Tip
To select multiple programs, click the first program, hold down the Ctrl key, and click additional programs.

III

Power Faxing

> ### Note
>
> WinFax PRO does not list all programs by their commercial names. Rather, it often lists the key files needed to run the programs. That is because WinFax PRO scans your system to look for programs with the EXE file name extension, the extension usually used by primary program files.

9. Remove programs from the Available at Recipient list window by selecting the programs to remove and clicking either the **R**emove or R**e**move All buttons.

10. After you complete the Programs Available dialog box, click OK to return to the New Recipient dialog box. Complete the New Recipient dialog box and click OK to add the record to your phonebook.

Tip

If you aren't sure which programs the recipient has, or to use BFT to transfer a file even if the recipient doesn't have the program, leave all your programs in the Available at Recipient list window.

Why tell WinFax PRO which programs the recipient has on his or her computer? It often makes little sense to transfer a file if the recipient can't use the file.

In order to use the file, the recipient must have the program that created the file. If you delete a program from the Available at Recipient list window, WinFax PRO won't transmit the file using BFT. Rather, it converts the file to a fax image and sends it using regular fax transmission methods.

Finally, when setting up BFT, make sure that ECM is active. This is WinFax PRO's default setting, but to make sure that ECM is active, select Setu**p F**ax/Modem. Make sure you have not selected the Di**s**able Error Correcting Mode check box.

Tip

You usually want ECM to be active, because it ensures greater accuracy for normal fax transmissions. Deactivate only when the message box informs you during a transmission that it cannot work with the recipient's ECM.

Even if you set up a recipient for another type of transmission, such as a normal fax transmission, you can switch to a BFT recipient at any time by double-clicking that person's phonebook entry in the item list box. WinFax PRO displays the Modify Recipient dialog box, which is identical to the New Recipient dialog box with one exception: It already includes information about the recipient. Change the dialog box to a BFT transfer and click OK.

You also can change the transmission to a BFT or a Compressed BFT transmission at the last minute from the Send dialog box. To do that, click the Sche**d**ule button. WinFax PRO displays the Schedule/Modify Events dialog box (see fig. 16.2).

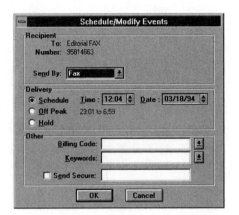

Fig. 16.2
Modify your
method of
transmission in
the Schedule/
Modify Events
dialog box.

Select a different type of transmission from the Send By drop-down list. Make any other modifications you want, and click OK to return to the Send dialog box. For more information about sending faxes, read Chapter 8, "Sending Faxes."

Note

If you set up the recipient to receive only electronic mail, it will be the only option available in the Send By drop-down list. If you still want to send the message via BFT, modify the recipient's phonebook record to include BFT transfers.

Sending with BFT

The previous section described how to set up a recipient for BFT transmissions. After setting up the recipient for BFT, proceed as though it is a normal fax transmission. Remember, though, that BFT only works with attachments—WinFax PRO still sends the regular fax as it sends any other fax. The difference is that with BFT, WinFax PRO sends the attachment as a binary file instead of converting the attachment into a fax image and sending it as a fax. As a result, in the Send dialog box, you must add at least one attachment.

You will notice three differences with BFT transmissions:

- BFT transmissions are much faster than standard fax transmissions.

- During transmission, the Status message box informs you that it is conducting a BFT transfer.

- In the Type information column of the Send and Receive Logs, and in any archive folders, BFT transmissions have a fax icon with a paper clip over it.

Tip
Because BFT transfers are so fast, this method is excellent for transmitting faxes with attachments—if your recipient's fax software and hardware supports BFT.

III

Power Faxing

During the initial phase of the modem connection when the modems exchange information about each other using tones, WinFax PRO tells the modem to see if the recipient can accept BFT. If not, WinFax PRO displays a message to that effect in the Status message box while the modems are exchanging tones. WinFax PRO then cuts off the transmission and resends the message as a normal fax.

If the recipient cannot receive BFT, you must change his or her phonebook entry to reflect that fact. Or you can have WinFax PRO automatically change the phonebook record for you when it determines that the recipient cannot receive BFT.

To have WinFax PRO automatically change the phonebook record, follow these steps:

1. Choose Setu**p P**rogram. WinFax PRO displays the Program Setup dialog box, as discussed in Chapter 4, "Configuring WinFax PRO."

2. In the Phonebook area at the bottom of the dialog box, select the Update Recipient Record for Unsupported **B**FT check box. After selecting the check box, every time you try a BFT transfer and the recipient's software doesn't support BFT, WinFax PRO automatically changes the recipient's phonebook record to transmit by standard fax.

3. Click OK to close the Program Setup dialog box.

> **Note**
>
> If your recipient can receive BFT transmissions, but you are only sending a standard fax, the transmission proceeds as it normally would.

Receiving BFT Transmissions

Receiving BFT transmissions is even simpler than sending them. You receive the transmission as you would receive a normal fax. That is, you let WinFax PRO do the work.

After receiving a BFT transmission, you treat it as any other fax transmission, with one exception. WinFax PRO displays the fax message and lists attachments in the Mail Message Contents dialog box rather than in the Viewer (see fig. 16.3).

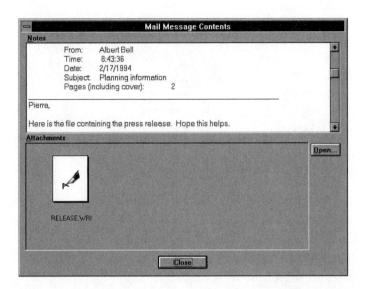

Fig. 16.3
WinFax PRO
displays received
binary file
transfers in the
Mail Message
Contents dialog
box.

Note

The Mail Message Contents dialog box is the same dialog box you use for viewing
sent and received electronic mail messages. For more about electronic mail, read
Chapter 10, "Using WinFax PRO with Electronic Mail."

The **N**otes area at the top of the dialog box displays the contents of the quick
cover page, if your sender used one. The **A**ttachments area shows thumbnail
images of each page of the fax and icons for each binary file.

View the thumbnail image of the fax by double-clicking its thumbnail. View
the contents of a binary file by double-clicking its icon or by highlighting the
fax page or binary file and clicking **O**pen.

Note

If the binary file is a program file—or the file needed to run a program—WinFax PRO
launches that program for you.

You also can save a BFT attachment to your attachments folder; highlight
the received BFT transmission in the Receive Log, and then select **L**og Sa**v**e
Attachments. WinFax PRO displays the Save Attachments dialog box (see
fig. 16.4).

III

Power Faxing

Fig. 16.4

Save attachments
you receive via
BFT in the Save
Attachments
dialog box.

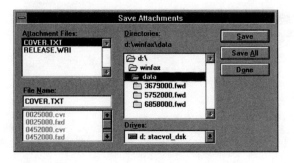

In the Save Attachments dialog box, follow these steps:

1. In the Attachment Files list box, select the part of the received transmission you want to save as an attachment. You can click as many parts of the message as you want.

2. To automatically save all the parts of the message listed in the Attachment Files list box, click Save All. If you click this button, you don't have to follow steps 3 through 6.

3. Type a file name for the attachment in the File Name dialog box.

4. Select the drive on which you want to store the attachment in the Drives drop-down list.

5. Select a directory in which you want to store the attachment in the Directories list box.

6. Click Save. WinFax PRO saves the files with the file names you selected.

7. Click Done to return to the Receive Log.

After you complete the Save Attachments dialog box, you still must add the file to the attachment library.

To add the file to the attachment library, follow these steps:

1. Make the Attachments window the active view by clicking the Attach button on the toolbar, or by choosing Fax Attachments.

2. Select the folder in which you want to place the new attachment by double-clicking it in the folder list window.

3. Double-click New Attachment in the item list box. Alternatively, choose Attachment New. WinFax PRO displays the New Attachments dialog box.

4. Enter a description of the new attachment in the **D**escription text box.

5. Enter the drive, directory, and name of the file you saved as an attachment in the **F**ile Name text box. If you cannot remember the file name, click **S**elect. WinFax PRO displays the Select Attachment dialog box.

6. In the Select Attachment dialog box, select the drive, directory, and file name for the attachment. Click OK to return to the Select Attachment dialog box.

7. Optionally, add keywords for the attachment in the **K**eywords text box.

8. When you finish, click OK to return to the Attachments window. WinFax PRO adds your new attachment to the folder you selected.

For more information about attachments, read Chapter 12, "Assembling Faxes from Many Sources."

Troubleshooting

I can't seem to complete a BFT transmission with a specific recipient.

There are three possible problems. First, your recipient may not be using software that supports BFT. Check to make sure that your recipient's software supports BFT.

Second, you may have specified the wrong modem type. Only Class 1 modems can send and receive BFT transmissions. Make sure that both you and the recipient have Class 1 modems and that they are correctly set as such in the Fax/Modem Setup dialog box. Access the Fax/Modem Setup dialog box by selecting Setu**p** **F**ax/Modem.

The third possible problem is that either you or your recipient disabled the Error Correcting Mode (ECM) in WinFax PRO, or your recipient uses software that doesn't support ECM. In WinFax PRO, choose Setu**p** **F**ax/Modem. Make sure you have not selected the Disable Error Correcting Mode check box.

Transmitting to Other WinFax PRO Users

If your recipient uses WinFax PRO 4, you can use a variant of BFT that transmits attachment files even faster than BFT. It transmits files faster because WinFax PRO compresses files, or makes them smaller before transmitting

III

Power Faxing

them. Because the files are smaller, it takes less time to transmit them. Not surprisingly, the name of the variant of BFT is Compressed BFT.

Remember that even without compression, BFT transfers information faster than a normal fax transmission. Compressed files, because they are smaller, transmit even faster. If you transmit BFT compressed files via long distance, you save both time and money.

You can't set up Compressed BFT in advance. Rather, you select it at the last minute from the Send dialog box. To do that, follow these steps:

1. Confirm with your recipient that he or she uses WinFax PRO 4. You can use this method with other WinFax PRO 4 users only.

2. In the Recipient List window, highlight the name of the recipient with whom you want to use this method.

3. Click Schedule. WinFax PRO displays the Schedule/Modify Events dialog box.

4. In the Send By drop-down list, select Compressed BFT. Note that this option is available only if you designate the recipient to receive faxes or BFT transmissions.

5. Click OK to return to the Send dialog box. Proceed by sending the message as you normally would.

Receiving messages using the Compressed BFT method is as simple as BFT transmissions; WinFax PRO does the work. The received Compressed BFT transmission appears in the Receive Log the same as any other received message. In the Type column of the Send and Receive Logs, the icon is a normal fax icon with an image of a paper clip over it.

Access the message and the binary attachments the same as you would a BFT transmission. Either double-click the message or highlight it in the item list box and click the View button on the toolbar. As with BFT transmissions, you can view the message in the Mail Message Contents dialog box, described in the previous section, "Receiving BFT Transmissions."

Caution

Do not use the Compressed BFT method if you are communicating with someone using any other kind of software. The transmission will fail.

Using Microsoft At Work

Yet another variation of BFT is Microsoft At Work (MAW). MAW is a complex series of standards and protocols that, when put together, enable various office machines, such as fax machines, fax modems, and even photocopy machines, to exchange information.

At the time of this writing, MAW standards are still under development and are not widely in use. Because these standards are powerful and reasonably well developed, some vendors, such as Delrina, are beginning to implement them. WinFax PRO 4 is actually one of the very first hardware or software products on the market to support MAW.

At the heart of MAW is BFT. In simple terms, a MAW fax transmission is a BFT transmission with various security safeguards.

For example, MAW can *encrypt* data that it transmits. Encrypting a data file alters its contents in ways that make it difficult for others to view the file. You decrypt the files using a *key*, or password. The MAW device, whether it is WinFax PRO or another device, then reassembles the file or document as it previously was.

As discussed previously, you don't differentiate between standard BFT and MAW when you create a new recipient record. Rather, WinFax PRO determines whether the recipient can accept MAW or BFT and automatically sends using the correct method.

However, unlike BFT transmissions, you will need help from your system administrator to finish setting up MAW transmissions; sending MAW requires dealing with much more than just another computer user with a fax modem.

To set up MAW, select BFT in the Connections area of the New Recipient or Modify Recipient dialog boxes. When you do, the dialog box changes by adding the At Work Alias text box at the bottom of the Connections area. Add the recipient's alias in the text box. If you are not sure of the alias, ask your system administrator.

Also, you must learn about the other devices that use MAW and about the other setup parameters in the MS At Work Setup dialog box. Access the MS At Work Setup dialog box by selecting Setup MS At Work.

If you are not absolutely certain that you are communicating with a MAW recipient—and at this point there are few of them—don't bother filling in

III

Power Faxing

the At Work Alias text box. This means that WinFax PRO will only use regular BFT. If you know that your recipient can handle MAW, contact your system administrator for help in setting it up.

About Fax Broadcast

Delrina, the developer of WinFax PRO, offers an extra-cost service to help if you send or receive large volumes of faxes. This service is particularly useful if you are in a high volume situation, but can't afford to tie up your PC or modem. The service is Fax Broadcast.

Fax Broadcast is a service by which you send a fax to a central collection point. From that central location, the Broadcast fax service broadcasts the fax to all your recipients—even hundreds or thousands of recipients.

This service obviously saves time because it takes about as long to send a fax to hundreds or thousands of recipients as it does to send a fax to a single recipient. In addition to saving time, Fax Broadcast won't tie up your phone line and modem for extended periods of time.

One other advantage of Fax Broadcast is that this centralized service for broadcasting faxes enables all recipients to receive the fax at the same time. If you use WinFax PRO and a fax modem, you must transmit the faxes sequentially, one after another.

Unless you tell WinFax PRO that you are interested in this service, the Services menu does not appear. You can designate the services to which you want to subscribe (and make the Services menu appear) by choosing **H**elp **A**bout. In the About WinFax PRO box, click **R**egister. In the registration dialog box, click Fax **B**roadcast to view dialog boxes that you must fill out to sign up for those services.

After you complete the registration dialog box, register—and, optionally, sign up for this service—by clicking **R**egister now. WinFax PRO automatically dials a special toll-free number, registers you, and signs you up for the special add-on services you selected. For more information about either of these services, call Delrina Communications Services at (800) 268-6082. After you subscribe, Delrina provides separate documentation for the services and other necessary information.

From Here...

This chapter told you about using WinFax PRO for several types of transmissions besides standard fax and electronic mail transmissions. For review, you may want to read the following:

- Chapter 6, "Using Phonebooks," describes how to create new phonebook records using the New Recipient dialog box. The New Recipient dialog box is where you determine the transmission method to a particular recipient.

- Chapter 8, "Sending Faxes," tells you how to send messages using the Send dialog box.

- Chapter 9, "Receiving Faxes," describes what happens after you receive messages.

- Chapter 12, "Assembling Faxes from Many Sources," tells you how to use attachments that you can add to messages.

III

Power Faxing

Chapter 17

WinFax PRO Away from the Office

In this chapter, you learn how to do the following:

- Automatically forward faxes.

- Call in to WinFax PRO to check for faxes.

- Use tips and tricks when traveling with WinFax PRO.

We live in mobile times, and for many people, moving from office to office and city to city is just part of the job. Also, increasingly people spend parts of their week working at home. Many of these "road warriors" carry laptop or notebook computers with them as they travel to different locations.

WinFax PRO is built to work in multiple locations. And you don't have to be piling up frequent flier miles to take advantage of the mobile capabilities of WinFax PRO. WinFax PRO is equally useful whether you travel across the country or work at home one afternoon a week.

WinFax PRO provides a rich set of features for those who work away from the office. For example, it can check for faxes you received in a previous location and forward them to your new location.

This chapter tells you how to take advantage of WinFax PRO when you are traveling.

Working in Different Locations

WinFax PRO enables you to maintain different settings for three separate locations: home, away, and office. What these locations mean, of course, is up to you. For example, home can literally mean your home, or it can mean your "home office."

The ability to designate your location is useful for several reasons:

- WinFax PRO automatically places the information from your different settings in fax headers and cover page fields. This means that you do not need to change this information when you change locations.

- You can use different methods of transmission for different locations. For example, when you are in your office, you can communicate with a coworker via electronic mail. However, when you are at home or somewhere else, you can automatically communicate with that person via fax.

- You can customize WinFax PRO to dial out of different phone systems from different locations. For example, in the office you may need to dial 9 to get an outside line. Obviously, you wouldn't need to do this at home.

The next two sections describe how to set up different locations, including how to set up WinFax PRO so that it automatically uses different transmission methods for different locations.

Setting Your Location

Tip

Use commas in the prefix to create pauses. Each comma pauses the dialing process for one second. Many phone systems need pauses to operate correctly after dialing a prefix.

Set up the characteristics of each location in the User Setup dialog box (see fig. 17.1). Access the User Setup dialog box by choosing Setu**p U**ser.

The Dial area of the User Setup dialog box has three buttons for Home, Away, and Office. Beneath the buttons are the settings for each location.

To create settings for a location, follow these steps:

1. Click the button for the location you want to set.

2. Enter a dial prefix (such as 9, for an outside line) in the Dial P**r**efix box. If you previously designated dial prefixes, retrieve them from the drop-down list.

3. Type the location's telephone country code in the Count**r**y Code text box. A country code is the code used to dial a country. The country code for the United States, for example, is 1.

Fig. 17.1
Set up the dialing
characteristics
for different
locations in the
User Setup dialog
box.

4. In the **A**rea Code text box, enter the area code of the location you are
   dialing. You must enter an area code in this text box.

5. In the **I**nternational Access Code text box, enter the numbers you must
   dial to get an international line. In the United States, this number is
   011.

6. In the Long Di**s**tance Access Code text box, enter the numbers you
   must dial from your present location to get a long distance line.

7. In the **O**ff Peak Start Time box, Enter the time that off-peak hours start.
   Off-peak may refer to the time that phone rates go down, or it may
   refer to the time that people leave work and the phone lines and
   modems are more available.

8. In the Off Peak End **T**ime box, enter the time the off-peak period ends.

9. Click OK. This closes the User Setup dialog box and saves the settings
   for that location. Repeat this process for the two remaining locations,
   if necessary. For example, if you first set up preferences for the office,
   repeat the process, if necessary, for home and away.

When you change locations, choose Setu**p** **U**ser. Then click your new location in the Dial area of the User Setup dialog box. WinFax PRO displays your
currently selected location in the status bar at the bottom of the application
window.

III

Power Faxing

Using Different Locations

WinFax PRO uses the information in the Dial area of the User Setup dialog box in different areas of the program. For example, if you send a fax to an international location, WinFax PRO looks for the international access code entered in the dialog box.

Similarly, if you enter a dial prefix for a specific location, WinFax PRO automatically adds it to the recipient's phone number in the Send dialog box when you dial out.

Most notably, though, this information enables you to use different transmission methods in different locations. Set up this capability in the Send From area of either the New Recipient or Modify Recipient dialog box.

To access the New Recipient dialog box, follow these steps:

1. Make the Phonebooks window the active view either by clicking the Phnbooks button on the toolbar or choosing **F**ax P**h**onebooks.

2. In the folder list window, highlight the phonebook in which you want to add the new phone entry.

3. In the item list window, double-click the New Recipient. WinFax PRO displays the New Recipient dialog box.

4. Fill in the New Recipient dialog box. Read Chapter 6, "Using Phonebooks," for more information about creating a new phonebook record.

5. In the Send From area of the New Recipient dialog box, select the method of transmission for each location (see fig. 17.2).

Fig. 17.2
Determine the method of transmission for each location in the Send From area.

6. When you complete the New Recipient dialog box, click OK. WinFax PRO adds the new recipient to the currently selected phonebook.

To modify an existing recipient, double-click the entry in the item list window. WinFax PRO displays the Modify Recipient dialog box, which is identical to the New Recipient dialog box, except that it includes information about the recipient. Make any changes, including changes in the Send From area, and click OK. WinFax PRO saves the changes in the recipient's record.

Note that not all options are always available in the drop-down lists in the Send From area. Only the options you create in the Connections area of the Modify Recipient or New Recipient dialog box are available. Also, if you subscribe to Delrina's extra-cost Fax Broadcast service, that option also is available in the Send From area.

This ability to change the method of transmission depending on your location saves a lot of time for travelers. For example, if you move from your home office to a satellite office, you merely change your location in the User Setup dialog box.

WinFax PRO then automatically knows how to dial out of the phone system of your new location. Also, when you address a message to a specific person, WinFax PRO automatically sends the message using the correct transmission method.

Troubleshooting

When WinFax PRO dials a number, it incorrectly adds a dialing prefix.

Chances are that you haven't selected the correct location. For example, you may need a dial prefix at the office to get an outside line. If you try to dial from home using your office settings, WinFax PRO incorrectly adds the dial prefix numbers. Change your location in the User Setup dialog box, which you access by selecting Setup User.

Laptop Installation

One simple but helpful way to make life easier for travelers is available during the initial installation of WinFax PRO. As discussed in Chapter 1, "Installing WinFax PRO," one installation option is the Laptop Installation.

The Laptop Installation installs only the minimum number of files necessary to run WinFax PRO. It is particularly appropriate for laptop and notebook computers for the following reasons:

- Laptop and notebook computers often don't have as much hard drive capacity as desktop computers. The Laptop Installation method requires the minimum amount of hard disk storage possible for running WinFax PRO.

- Laptops and notebook computers often don't have as much random-access memory (RAM) as desktop computers. Some of the features of

III

Power Faxing

WinFax PRO, such as optical character recognition (OCR), require more memory than the program requires for only basic operation.

■ Laptop and notebook computers often aren't as powerful as desktop computers. Some of WinFax PRO's features, again such as OCR, require high-speed central processors to operate optimally.

To use the Laptop Installation option, simply select it during the installation process.

WinFax PRO doesn't install the following elements:

■ OCR capabilities. Read Chapter 15, "Converting Faxes to Text," for information to help you decide whether to load this capability.

■ The Covering Your Fax library of fax cover pages. This is a special library of fax cover pages, some of them amusing, that WinFax PRO includes. Even if you don't load these cover pages, you can still create your own cover pages or use quick cover pages. Read Chapter 7, "Creating and Managing Cover Pages," to learn more about cover pages.

■ The files necessary to use WinFax PRO with your organization's electronic mail system. Read Chapter 10, "Using WinFax PRO for Electronic Mail," to learn more about this capability.

The installation program also enables you to select some, but not all, of the elements described previously. Select the Custom Installation option. Read Chapter 1, "Installing WinFax PRO," for more information about the installation process.

Automatic Forwarding

Another invaluable feature for travelers is WinFax PRO's ability to automatically forward faxes. This capability is useful in several instances, such as the following:

■ You travel to a new location and expect to receive an important fax at your office. Tell WinFax PRO to automatically forward that fax—or all faxes, for that matter—directly to your new location.

■ When working at home, have WinFax PRO automatically forward faxes to you that were sent to the office.

■ When you go on vacation, have WinFax PRO automatically forward faxes to your assistant or colleagues.

Enable automatic forwarding and set it up in the Receive Setup dialog box (see fig. 17.3). Access the dialog box by choosing Setu**p R**eceive.

Fig. 17.3
The Receive Setup dialog box is where you enable automatic forwarding of faxes.

In the Receive Setup dialog box, select the Forwar**d** check box. To further refine automatic forwarding, click the S**e**tup button. WinFax PRO displays the Forward Setup dialog box (see fig. 17.4).

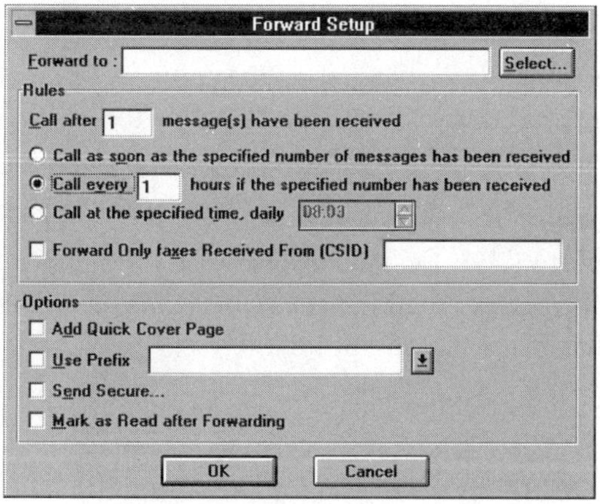

Fig. 17.4
Refine WinFax PRO's automatic forwarding capabilities in the Forward Setup dialog box.

III

Power Faxing

Use the Forward Setup dialog box to specify how often you want WinFax PRO to forward faxes, and which faxes you want it to forward.

Selecting a Forwarding Destination

Enter the fax telephone number to which you want faxes forwarded in the Forward To text box of the Forward Setup dialog box. To forward your faxes to the fax machine of a recipient in your phonebooks when you aren't sure of that person's number, select the **S**elect button. WinFax PRO displays the Select Recipient dialog box (see fig. 17.5).

Fig. 17.5

Select the location to which you forward faxes from the Select Recipient dialog box.

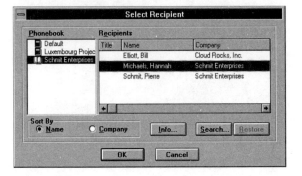

To select a recipient, follow these steps:

1. In the **P**honebook list window, double-click the phonebook containing the recipient.

2. In the R**e**cipients window, click the recipient.

3. Determine how WinFax PRO sorts the contents of the **R**ecipients window in the Sort By area. Select the **N**ame button to sort the window by name or select the **C**ompany button to sort by company.

4. For information about a specific recipient, select the recipient and click the **I**nfo button. WinFax PRO displays the Information message box, which is identical to the Modify Recipient dialog box except that you cannot change any of the information.

5. To search for a specific recipient, click **S**earch. WinFax PRO displays the Search dialog box, which is identical to an empty New Recipient dialog box. Type the information you seek in the appropriate text box. For example, type **Smith** in the **L**ast text box if you are looking for records of recipients named Smith.

6. When you complete the Search dialog box, click OK. WinFax PRO displays the results of the search in the R**e**cipients list window in the Select Recipient dialog box. To restore the full contents of the folder, click the **R**estore button.

7. After you select the recipient, click OK to return to the Forward Setup dialog box. WinFax PRO automatically places the telephone number of the recipient in the Forward to dialog box.

Setting Forwarding Rules

The Rules area of the Forward Setup dialog box determines when WinFax PRO forwards messages as well as which messages it forwards.

The first option in the Rules area works in conjunction with the other options. The Call After Message(s) Have Been Received text box tells WinFax PRO to forward messages only after it receives the number of messages you specify.

Type a number in the text box for this option. The next three options are buttons that determine when WinFax PRO forwards your messages after it receives the number of messages you specify. The three options are as follows:

- Call As Soon as the specified number of messages have been received. This option tells WinFax PRO to forward messages as soon as it receives the number of messages you specify.

- Call Every Hours if the specified number has been received. This specifies the interval, in hours, between times that WinFax PRO calls to forward new messages. However, it only calls if it receives the specified number of messages.

- Call at the Specified Time, daily tells WinFax PRO to call only at a specific time every day. Set the specific time in the box to the right of this option.

> **Note**
>
> Set specific times according to the 24-hour clock. For example, if you want WinFax PRO to forward messages at 6 p.m., specify the time as 18:00.

If you only want WinFax PRO to forward faxes from a specific recipient, select the Forward Only Faxes Received From (CSID) check box. Then enter the CSID number of the sender in the text box to the right of this option.

Setting Other Forwarding Options

WinFax PRO offers many useful additional fax forwarding capabilities. Those additional capabilities are in the Options area of the Forward Setup dialog box.

Tip

If you frequently forward your faxes to another location, make the location a telephone book entry, which makes it easy to enter the phone number in the Forward Setup dialog box.

Tip

Typically, you can find the CSID in the header of a fax you previously received from the sender. If the CSID information isn't in the header, ask the sender for the correct information.

III

Power Faxing

Select the Add Quick Cover Page check box to have WinFax PRO automatically affix a quick cover page to forwarded faxes.

To have WinFax PRO use a dialing prefix when it dials to forward the faxes, select the Use Prefix check box. Then enter the prefix in the text box to the right of this option. If you previously used the required prefix, select it from the drop-down list.

The Mark as Read after Forwarding option tells WinFax PRO to designate the fax as read in the Receive Log after it forwards the fax. The Receive Log lists unread faxes in bold and read faxes in regular type.

To add a measure of security to the forwarding process, select the Send Secure check box. When you select it, WinFax PRO displays the Send Secure dialog box (see fig. 17.6).

Fig. 17.6
The Send Secure dialog box is where you add security to the forwarding process.

Tip
To track faxes you receive while away, don't select the Mark as Read after Forwarding option. When you return, faxes you received appear in bold type in the Receive Log.

The Send Secure option requires WinFax PRO to detect a specific CSID on the fax device that is receiving the forwarded messages. If WinFax PRO does not detect that CSID, it won't forward the faxes.

In the Send Secure dialog box, enter as much of the receiving device's CSID as you know, in the Recipient's CSID text box. Click OK to return to the Forward Setup dialog box.

After you complete the Forward Setup dialog box, click OK to return to the Receive Setup dialog box. Click OK in the Receive Setup dialog box, and WinFax PRO will be set up to automatically forward faxes.

Note

Remember that after you set up automatic forwarding and leave your present location for a new location, you must leave your computer running with WinFax PRO loaded.

Troubleshooting

WinFax PRO isn't automatically forwarding faxes to me as I instructed it.

There are several possible solutions to this problem: WinFax PRO may not have received any faxes to forward, or it may not have received the number of faxes you specified. If you used the Send Secure option in the Forward Setup dialog box, you may have entered the wrong CSID of the machine that is receiving the forwarded faxes. Or perhaps you entered the wrong phone number for the recipient fax device.

Tips and Tricks for Travelers

A previous section describes the laptop installation process and automatic forwarding. Those tools are powerful aids for travelers who must keep track of their messages even while they are away.

However, there are other ways to set up WinFax PRO to help while you travel. The following sections describe these methods:

Using Your Telephone Credit Card

When you make a long distance call from a hotel room, you usually have to pay a surcharge to the hotel, in addition to the normal toll charges. If you are faxing with a notebook or laptop computer from your hotel room, use WinFax PRO's credit card capabilities to avoid these surcharges.

As described in Chapter 4, "Configuring WinFax PRO," set up WinFax PRO's credit card dialing capabilities by selecting Setu**p C**redit Card. WinFax PRO displays the Dial Credit Card Setup dialog box (see fig. 17.7), which tells WinFax PRO your credit card number and the service you use. You also can expand the dialog box to establish a specific sequence for calling out using your credit card.

Read Chapter 4, "Configuring WinFax PRO," for more information about setting up WinFax PRO for use with a credit card.

From the Send dialog box, you actually choose to use your credit card for a long distance call. In the Send dialog box, click the **O**ptions button. WinFax PRO displays the Send Options dialog box (see fig. 17.8).

Tip
Use WinFax PRO's credit card capabilities when you're visiting a client or relative and don't want to use their long distance service.

III

Power Faxing

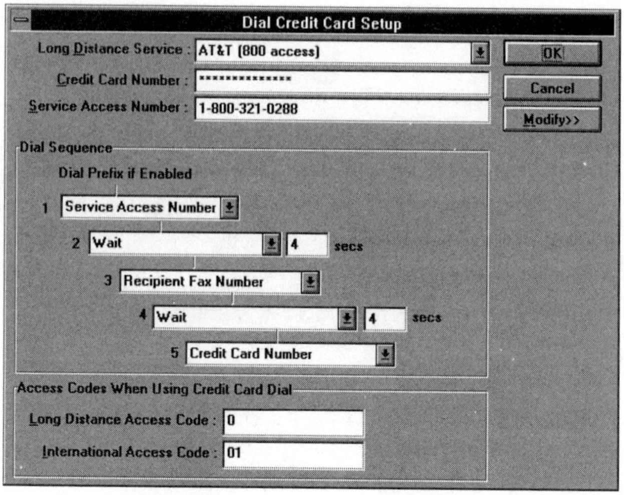

Fig. 17.7

The Dial Credit Card Setup dialog box is where you tell WinFax PRO about your telephone credit card and set a dialing sequence.

Fig. 17.8

Tell WinFax PRO to use your credit card for dialing in the Send Options dialog box.

In the Send Options dialog box, select the **C**redit Card check box. Click OK to return to the Send dialog box and proceed as you normally would.

Using the Outbox

If you are rushing to get out of the office, use WinFax PRO's Outbox to schedule faxes for a later time. This enables you to create faxes without worrying about actually sending them; WinFax PRO does that for you after you leave.

As described in Chapter 8, "Sending Faxes," to schedule faxes for later transmission, follow these steps:

1. Create your fax as you normally would.

2. Start the regular process of sending your fax. If you create your message in another application, "print" the fax using the WinFax PRO driver.

3. In the Send dialog box, select all your recipients. Access the Send dialog box by clicking the Send button in the toolbar.

4. In the **R**ecipient List window, select all recipients by selecting one recipient, holding down the Ctrl key, and selecting the other recipients.

5. Click Sch**e**dule button. WinFax PRO displays the Schedule/Modify Events dialog box (see fig. 17.9).

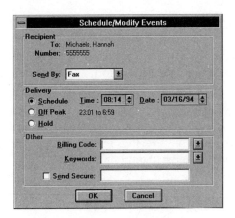

Fig. 17.9
Schedule messages for later transmission in the Schedule/Modify Events dialog box.

To schedule the transmissions for a specific time and date, select the **S**chedule button. Set a specific time and date in the **T**ime and **D**ate boxes.

To direct WinFax PRO to send the faxes at off-peak times, select the **O**ff Peak button. Define what the off-peak hours are in the User Setup dialog box, which you access by selecting Setu**p** **U**ser. Typically, off-peak hours are either when the phone rates go down or when use of your computer or modem decreases.

Finally, choose to hold faxes and schedule their transmission at a later time. Select the **H**old button in the Schedule/Modify Events dialog box.

Read Chapter 8, "Sending Faxes," for more information about sending faxes and using the Outbox.

Easing Eyestrain

The displays of laptop and notebook computers are getting better, but they still are harder on the eyes than most monitors used with desktop computers. WinFax PRO provides a couple of ways to customize WinFax PRO to make viewing easier on laptop or notebook screens.

Tip
Hold faxes that require confirmation before transmission, such as a product announcement. If the confirmation occurs while you are traveling, an assistant or colleague can schedule the fax.

III

Power Faxing

One way to reduce eyestrain is to customize WinFax PRO's toolbar. Rather than crowding the toolbar with lots of buttons, customize it so that it includes only the most-needed buttons.

To customize the toolbar, choose Setu**p T**oolbar. WinFax PRO displays the Toolbar Setup dialog box. Read Chapter 5, "Customizing WinFax PRO," for details about how to use the Toolbar Setup dialog box to customize the toolbar.

Another way to avoid eyestrain is to reduce the number of items displayed in the Send and Receive Logs. One way to do this is to use filters to display only the items you want in the Send and Receive Logs. Read Chapter 11, "Using the Send and Receive Logs," for more information about filters.

Saving Disk Space

Notebook and laptop computers often don't have as much hard disk storage space as desktop computers. A previous section of this chapter, "Minimum Installation," describes the installation option to place the minimum number of WinFax PRO files on your disk. However, WinFax PRO provides several additional methods of saving disk storage space when you are on the go:

First, move older faxes or those you infrequently reference from the Send and Receive Logs to archive folders. This automatically compresses the fax messages so they take up less disk space.

Similarly, use the Log Setup dialog box to automatically delete older messages. Access the Log Setup dialog box by selecting Setu**p P**rogram. WinFax PRO displays the Program Setup dialog box.

From the Program Setup dialog box, click the **L**og button. WinFax PRO displays the Log Setup dialog box (see fig. 17.10).

The Log Setup dialog box enables you to automatically delete messages—and their related files—from the Send and Receive Logs after the number of days you specify. For details about using the Log Setup dialog box, read Chapter 4, "Configuring WinFax PRO."

Often, when on the road, you must transfer files. For example, you may need to transfer sales reports or spreadsheets that you are working on to a colleague.

If that is the case, and you don't need to perform tasks such as logging on to a bulletin board or corporate host computer, you can avoid loading an additional data communications package. This is because, as stated in Chapter 16,

"Different Ways to Send and Receive," you can use WinFax PRO's Binary File Transfer (BFT) capabilities to transfer files.

Fig. 17.10
Delete older faxes from the Send and Receive Logs in the Log Setup dialog box.

To review, the following are the only requirements for transferring binary files using WinFax PRO:

> You use a Class 1 modem. Read Chapter 2, "How WinFax PRO Works," for details about the different classes of modems.

> You are sending (or receiving) the files from somebody using either WinFax PRO 4 or another fax software program that supports BFT.

If you meet these two requirements, you can save disk space by not installing a data communications package. Remember, you can't use WinFax PRO for tasks such as logging on to a bulletin board; you need a data communications software product for tasks such as that.

Getting Support

Getting technical support for any software product while you are traveling can be time-consuming, but you can use WinFax PRO to simplify the task.

Delrina, like most software vendors, has the right to refuse support to anybody who hasn't properly registered his or her copy of WinFax PRO. To ascertain that you properly registered WinFax PRO, a support technician may ask you for the serial number of your copy of WinFax PRO.

Tip
Make sure that you carry the right modem with you on the road. Specifically, you will need a Class 1 modem for BFT of faxes.

III

Power Faxing

Make sure that you register your copy of WinFax PRO as soon as you install it on your computer. Also, make sure you have a phonebook entry in WinFax PRO with Delrina's voice and fax technical support telephone numbers. The phone numbers are:

■ Voice technical support: (416) 441-0921

■ Fax technical support: (416) 441-0774

Even more importantly, include the serial number of your copy of WinFax PRO in the phonebook record. A good location to place the serial number is either in the Notes or **M**isc. fields in the New Recipient or Modify Recipient dialog boxes.

Fax Service Add-ons

As described in Chapter 16, "Different Ways To Send and Receive," Delrina offers an extra-cost service. Fax Broadcast provides a centralized service for broadcasting the same fax to many different recipients.

Fax Broadcast is aimed at sending out dozens or hundreds of faxes, but it also can be useful for travelers. For example, Fax Broadcast makes it easy to transmit international faxes, which can be particularly trying from hotel rooms. Also, Fax Broadcast helps avoid the hassles of busy signals and bad connections.

For more information about this extra-cost service, call Delrina Communications Services at (800) 268-6082.

Troubleshooting

I can't successfully dial out using the dialing sequence I developed in the Dial Credit Card Setup dialog box.

One possible problem is that you may have selected the wrong sequence. For example, you may have told WinFax PRO to dial the fax number before inserting a dial prefix to get an outside line. Another likely problem is that you didn't provide a pause between parts of the dialing sequence. If you did provide a pause, try making the pause longer.

From Here...

This chapter describes how travelers can make the best use of WinFax PRO. Many of these operations are basic operations that you modify slightly while you are traveling.

To review, you may want to read the following:

- Chapter 1, "Installing WinFax PRO," describes the installation procedure.

- Chapter 4, "Configuring WinFax PRO," discusses the basics of setting up WinFax PRO.

- Chapter 5, "Customizing WinFax PRO," tells you how to customize the WinFax PRO on-screen appearance.

- Chapter 8, "Sending Faxes," tells you how to send faxes from the Send dialog box.

- Chapter 11, "Using the Send and Receive Logs," tells you how to make optimal use of the Send and Receive Logs for storing your messages.

III

Power Faxing

Chapter 18

Using WinFax PRO in Other Programs

In this chapter, you learn how to do the following:

- Share phonebooks, attachments, and cover pages on the network.

- Share attachments on the network.

- Share cover pages on the network.

- Forward fax messages via e-mail.

- Connect WinFax PRO with other programs.

These days, no software program is an island. While communications programs such as WinFax PRO connect to the rest of the world, WinFax PRO connects better than most.

Connecting WinFax PRO to other programs extends its reach considerably. You also can extend the reach of WinFax PRO by sharing key parts of it on networks. This chapter tells you about using WinFax PRO with other programs and on networks.

Using WinFax PRO on Networks

Computer networks are becoming common, even in smaller organizations. In simple terms, computer networks connect desktop computers, enabling users to share files and peripherals such as printers.

III

Power Faxing

WinFax PRO 4 is primarily a stand-alone product, meaning that you load and run it on your desktop PC. However, there are several network-related uses for WinFax PRO.

One of the most common uses of networks is electronic mail, or *e-mail*. As discussed in Chapter 10, "Using WinFax PRO for Electronic Mail," WinFax PRO can replace the normal end-user e-mail interface on many systems.

In other words, WinFax PRO can send, receive, and store e-mail messages as well as faxes. This capability means that you only have to learn a single program—WinFax PRO—for both faxing and e-mail instead of learning two separate programs.

WinFax PRO also has some additional networking capabilities. The next several sections tell you about those capabilities.

About WinFax PRO for Networks

A variation of the stand-alone WinFax PRO that is the subject of this book is called WinFax PRO for Networks. This product essentially has three parts:

- The workstation software, which is virtually identical to the software that is the subject of this book. If your organization uses WinFax PRO for Networks and you are not responsible for maintaining this product, reading this book tells you virtually everything you need to know.

- Administrator's software, which enables a network administrator to control the use of WinFax PRO for Networks. For example, the administrator determines who uses WinFax PRO for Networks and what rights each user has for various functions, such as the ability to route incoming faxes to other persons on the network.

- Server software, which is the part of the WinFax PRO that an administrator installs on a special networked computer, called a server. The server software gives WinFax PRO for Networks several additional capabilities. For example, it enables:

    Those who send and receive faxes on networked fax modems to use multiple fax modems attached to multiple fax servers.

    Network administrators to set up fax servers so that network users can easily share data such as phonebooks and cover pages.

If your workgroup or department relies on faxing to conduct its business, WinFax PRO for Networks may be more appropriate than the stand-alone version that this book discusses. Specifically, consider WinFax PRO for Networks under the following circumstances:

- All the members of your workgroup or department who frequently send faxes use desktop computers connected to a computer network.

- The fax volume of your workgroup or department is high. WinFax PRO for Networks is relatively inexpensive to set up, yet handles a much greater volume of faxes than a standard fax machine. If members of your workgroup or department fax only occasionally, the stand-alone version of WinFax PRO should suffice.

- Somebody is available to set up and administer WinFax PRO for Networks. This is not a difficult or time-consuming job. However, like many software products designed specifically for networks, somebody must set the program up, give individual users the right to access the program, and perform other "administrative" tasks.

- You have the appropriate hardware to work with WinFax PRO for Networks. At the very minimum, you need a fax modem attached to the computer of one network member. However, if call volume is high, WinFax PRO for Networks works better with a dedicated fax server with at least one fax modem attached to it.

- You don't have a fax modem attached to your computer, but there is a fax modem attached to the network.

Even without WinFax PRO for Networks, however, the stand-alone version discussed in this book has some important networking capabilities. Specifically, you can share phonebooks, attachments, and cover pages with other network users. You also can forward faxes over the network.

The next several sections describe the network capabilities of WinFax PRO.

Sharing WinFax PRO Resources

WinFax PRO enables network users to share three of its key elements: phonebooks, attachments, and cover pages. Following are some examples of situations when sharing WinFax PRO resources is useful:

- Sharing phonebooks is useful in a sales department where several people are responsible for the same customers. Sharing phonebooks enables all sales personnel to send faxes to all customers.

III

Power Faxing

- Similarly, sharing phonebooks also is helpful in service and support departments where all members of the department can help any customer.

- Sharing attachments is useful in an accounting department. The department, for example, could share all relevant budget spreadsheets so that different members of the department could include the spreadsheets, when necessary, in faxes to satellite offices.

- An Accounts Receivable department could share cover pages. Specifically, one of the Cover Your Fax cover page libraries contains cover pages that tactfully, and sometimes humorously, ask customers for payment.

The next three sections specifically describe how to share phonebooks, cover pages, and attachments on the network. For the most part, there are only three rules to remember:

- You must store shared WinFax PRO resources on *shared* network drives. As the name implies, a shared network drive is a drive that many network users can access.

- When you create a new resource such as a new phonebook on a network drive, the drive you create it on must be a *read-write* drive. This means you can both read information in files stored on such drives and create new files.

- After you create new items on network drives, however, you (or, more typically, a network administrator) must make the drive *read-only*. A read-only drive is a drive that enables users to access, but not change, the files stored there.

If users can alter the data—or write to the data file, in computerese—you could irrevocably damage the information. For example, you could damage an entire phonebook if you are modifying a phonebook record when somebody else tries to use that record. Placing the phonebook in a read-only drive or directory protects the phonebook from changes.

The following guidelines discuss what you can and cannot do with information on shared, read-only drives.

- You cannot change the information and then save the information on the read-only drive. For example, you can't use the Modify Phonebook dialog box to change phonebook records and then save the modifications. If you make changes on a shared drive that you can write to, and somebody else tries to use that phonebook record as you are making the changes, you could damage the entire phonebook file.

- You can use records and change them after they become part of WinFax PRO on your desktop computer. For example, you could use a phonebook record from a phonebook stored on a shared, read-only directory to send a fax. After the record is in the Recipient List window of the Send dialog box, you can change and alter the record all you want because you copied the record from the read-only directory to your desktop computer.

- You—or the system administrator—can change a shared directory from read-only to read-write status. This enables you to add, delete, and modify information. However, to protect the files while you do this, you must prevent other users from accessing the directory. Depending on your network software, you can completely prevent access to the shared drive or directory as you are modifying records. Or you can simply tell people not to access information on that particular drive for a specific period of time as you make the modifications.

In most cases, a network administrator is responsible for maintaining the network and all information on it. The network administrator typically determines which users can access shared drives, which drives and directories are read-only, and who has access to the directories at specific times.

After the administrator sets up the shared, read-only drive for your WinFax PRO resources, he or she must temporarily grant write privileges to the network while you copy the resources to that drive. Once the information is located on the drive, the administrator changes the status to make the drive read-only. Network users can then use the shared WinFax PRO resources.

III

Power Faxing

The following three sections describe how users of the stand-alone version of WinFax PRO use shared resources.

Sharing Phonebooks

You can use a phonebook located on a shared network drive the same as a phonebook on a drive located on your desktop computer. Specifically, to add a shared phonebook to the folder list window of the Phonebooks view, follow these steps:

1. Make the Phonebooks view the active view by double-clicking the Phnbooks button on the toolbar, or by selecting **F**ax P**h**onebooks.

2. Double-click the New Phonebook/Group entry at the top of the folder list window. Alternatively, select Phone**b**ook **N**ew. WinFax PRO displays the New Phonebook/Group dialog box (see fig. 18.1).

Fig. 18.1
Add shared phonebooks to your item list window in the New Phonebook/ Group dialog box.

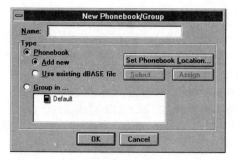

3. In the **N**ame text box, type the name of the phonebook as you want it to appear in your folder list window.

4. To add either an existing WinFax PRO phonebook located on a shared network drive or a database phonebook file in the dBASE format, select the **U**se Existing dBASE File button.

> **Note**
>
> In WinFax PRO, phonebooks are actually dBASE files, meaning that you can directly open them with the dBASE database program or any program that uses dBASE files. Thus, the name of the option is **U**se Existing dBASE file.

5. Click the **S**elect button. WinFax PRO displays the Select Phonebook/ Database File dialog box (see fig. 18.2).

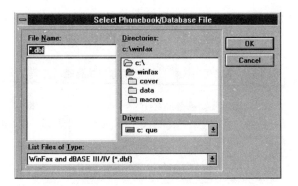

Fig. 18.2
Select a specific shared phonebook from the Select Phonebook/ Database File dialog box.

6. In the Select Phonebook/Database File dialog box, select the shared drive from the Dri**v**es drop-down list.

7. Select the shared directory from the **D**irectories list window.

8. Select the specific file name of the shared phonebook in the File **N**ame list window.

> ### Note
>
> The file name for a phonebook is not necessarily the same as the phonebook name that appears in the folder list window of the Phonebooks view. For example, the name in the folder list window might be "Eastern Region Prospects." However, because of DOS file naming rules, the file name is shorter. Also, like all dBASE files, phonebook or database files must have the DBF file name extension. As a result, the file name might be EASTREG.DBF.

9. Click OK to return to the New Phonebook/Group dialog box.

10. Click OK in the New Phonebook/Group dialog box.

At this point, one of two things happens: If WinFax PRO created the shared phonebook, this process automatically adds the phonebook to the selected folder in the folder list window.

However, if you use a dBASE file created by another program, WinFax PRO may display the Data Field Assignment dialog box. It does this if the variables in the dBASE file do not precisely match the WinFax PRO variables in the New Recipient and Modify Record dialog boxes. For example, the text box that WinFax PRO calls FirstName may have a name like FIRST in the dBASE file.

III

Power Faxing

You use the Data Field Assignment dialog box (see fig. 18.3) to link fields in the database to the appropriate fields in WinFax PRO.

Fig. 18.3

Link fields in databases created by other programs in the Data Field Assignment dialog box.

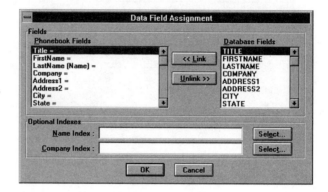

Linking fields is easy. The **P**honebook Fields list window lists all the standard WinFax PRO fields. These fields appear in the New Recipient and Modify Record dialog boxes.

The **D**atabase Fields list window contains the names of the fields in the database file you use to create a phonebook. To link the fields, follow these steps:

1. Click a field in one window.

2. Click the corresponding field in the other window. For example, highlight FirstName in the **P**honebook Fields window and FIRST in the **D**atabase Fields window.

3. Click the **L**ink button. Notice that the two field names are side by side in the **P**honebook Fields list window with an equal sign between them. To unlink the fields, click the **U**nlink Button.

4. Repeat the process until you link all the fields.

There are two additional items in the Data Field Assignment dialog box, but they require some database expertise to use. Databases use *indexes* to speed retrieval of specific information. An index is a file containing every item listed in a particular field in a database and the specific record in which the item appears.

WinFax PRO enables you to share two indexes—for the name and company variables in phonebooks. This is useful for maintaining consistency in the phonebooks used by many WinFax PRO users. Select specific indexes for names and companies at the bottom of the Data Field Assignment dialog box.

Caution

Don't use this option without assistance from your system administrator.

When you finish the Data Field Assignment dialog box, click OK to return to the New Phonebook/Group dialog box. Click OK and WinFax PRO adds the phonebook to your folder list window.

WinFax PRO informs you, in the area display window of the Phonebooks view, that the newly created phonebook is a read-only phonebook. In the Type text box in the area display window, the words "read-only" are in parentheses.

Note

Remember that you must log on to your network and gain access to the shared drive before you can use the shared phonebook. Your system administrator can grant access to the network and shared drives.

Read Chapter 6, "Using Phonebooks," for more information about using WinFax PRO phonebooks.

Troubleshooting

My system crashed while I was using a phonebook stored on the network.

Chances are that you or your network administrator forgot to designate the network directory on which the phonebook is located as read-only. As you were trying to use the phonebook, another user was either trying to use the phonebook, or tried to alter it. When this happens, you can damage the phonebook file. If the phonebook file is damaged, you may be able to repair it by making the drive it is on read-write. Then select Phonebook Optimize. In the future, make sure that the directory in which you store the phonebook is a read-only directory.

When I try to use a phonebook or other resource located on a network drive, WinFax PRO tells me it can't access it.

The problem may be simple: You may have forgotten to log onto the network. But the problem may be more complex: The network administrator may have changed drive designations (changing, for example, drive N: to drive Z:. Or the network administrator may have changed your rights to access the drive on which the WinFax PRO resource is located. Try the simple solution first—make sure that you are logged on properly. If you are properly logged on, contact your network administrator.

III

Power Faxing

Sharing Attachments

You can use attachments saved on shared drives precisely as you use attachments located on your own computer. To add an attachment located on a shared drive to an attachment folder, follow these steps:

1. Make the Attachments view the active view. Do this either by clicking the Attach button on the toolbar or by choosing **F**ax A**t**tachments.

2. Double-click the folder in which you want to add the attachment.

3. In the item list window of that folder, double-click the New Attachment item. Alternatively, select **A**ttachment **N**ew. WinFax PRO displays the New Attachment dialog box (see fig. 18.4).

Fig. 18.4
Add attachments from shared drives in the New Attachment dialog box.

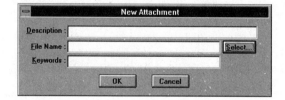

4. Add a description of the attachment in the **D**escription text box.

5. Type the drive, path, and file name of the attachment in the **F**ile Name text box. If you are not sure of the location or name of the file, click the **S**elect button. WinFax PRO displays the Select Attachment dialog box (see fig. 18.5).

Fig. 18.5
Find a specific attachment in the Select Attachment dialog box.

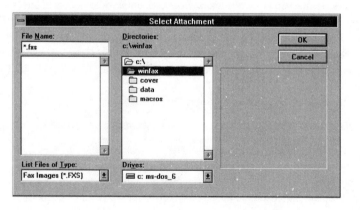

6. In the Select Attachment dialog box, select the correct drive in the Drives drop-down list and the correct directory in the **D**irectories list window. Select the type of file you want as an attachment in the List Files of **T**ype drop down list, and select the file name for the attachment in the File **N**ames list window.

7. When you finish the Select Attachment dialog box, click OK to return to the New Attachment dialog box.

8. Optionally, type one or more keywords in the **K**eyword text box.

9. Click OK. WinFax PRO adds the attachment to the currently selected attachment folder.

For more information about attachments, read Chapter 12, "Assembling Faxes from Many Sources."

Sharing Cover Pages

The process for adding cover pages stored in shared directories is similar to that for adding attachments.

1. Make the Cover Pages window the active view either by clicking the Cvr Pgs button on the toolbar or selecting **F**ax Cover P**a**ges.

2. Select the folder into which you want to place the cover page by double-clicking it in the folder list window.

3. In the item list window, double-click the New Cover Page entry. Alternatively, select Co**v**er Page **N**ew. WinFax PRO displays the New Cover Page dialog box (see fig. 18.6).

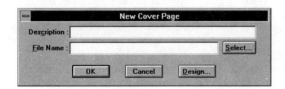

Fig. 18.6
Add cover pages from shared drives in the New Cover Page dialog box.

III

Power Faxing

4. Type a description of the cover page in the Des**c**ription text box.

5. Type the drive, directory, and file name of the cover page in the **F**ile Name text box.

If you are not sure, click **S**elect. WinFax PRO displays the Select Cover Page dialog box (see fig. 18.7).

Fig. 18.7
Select a specific cover page in the Select Cover Page dialog box.

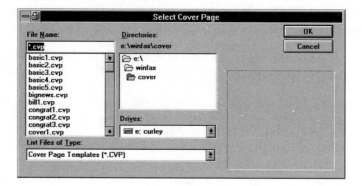

6. In the Select Cover Page dialog box, select the correct drive in the Dri**v**es drop-down list and the correct directory in the **D**irectories list window. Select the specific cover page file in the File **N**ame list window. Notice that WinFax PRO displays a thumbnail of the selected cover page.

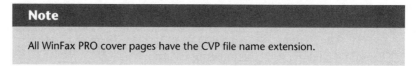

Note

All WinFax PRO cover pages have the CVP file name extension.

7. After you complete the Select Cover Page dialog box, click OK to return to the New Cover Page dialog box.

8. Click OK. WinFax PRO adds the cover page from the shared directory to the currently selected folder.

Tip
To save disk space on your desktop computer, ask the network administrator to load all cover pages on the network.

For more information about cover pages, read Chapter 7, "Creating and Managing Cover Pages."

Forwarding Faxes Over the Network

One other network trick that the stand-alone version of WinFax PRO performs is forwarding faxes received through network electronic mail. Forwarding faxes to e-mail recipients is the same as forwarding faxes to other fax recipients:

1. Make the Receive Log the active view by clicking the Rcv Log button on the toolbar.

2. Select the folder containing the fax you want to forward in the folder list window by double-clicking the folder.

3. Select the fax you want to forward in the item list window of the Receive Log.

4. Select **L**og For**w**ard. WinFax PRO displays the Forward dialog box (see fig. 18.8).

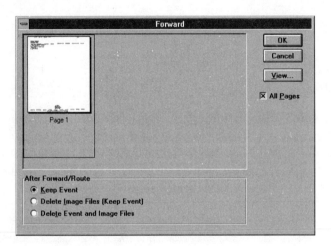

Fig. 18.8
Forward faxes via e-mail in the Forward dialog box.

5. In the Forward dialog box, select the All **P**ages check box to forward all the pages of the fax.

6. To send only specific pages, deactivate the All **P**ages check box, hold down the Ctrl key, and click the thumbnails of all the pages to forward.

7. View a specific page by selecting its thumbnail and clicking **V**iew.

8. In the After Forward/Route area of the dialog box select one of three options for handling the message after you forward it:

Keep Event keeps the fax in the Receive Log or related folder after forwarding.

Delete **I**mage Files (Keep Event) deletes the files related to the fax, but keeps the notation of the fax in the Receive Log or related folder.

Dele**t**e Event and Image Files deletes both the notation of the fax and the files related to the fax.

Tip
Use this process to eliminate the cover page that originally came with the fax and then add your own cover page from the Send dialog box.

III

Power Faxing

9. When you finish the Forward dialog box, click OK. WinFax PRO then displays the Send dialog box.

> **Note**
>
> If you select multiple faxes to forward via e-mail, WinFax PRO skips the Forward dialog box and goes directly to the Send dialog box.

10. In the Send dialog box, select the e-mail recipients you want. You also can add attachments or make any other changes you want.

11. Click **S**end. WinFax PRO forwards the fax via e-mail to the recipients you chose.

If the recipient has chosen WinFax PRO to receive his or her e-mail, the forwarded fax appears in the Receive Log as an e-mail message with an attachment. To view the forwarded fax, double-click it in the Receive Log. As with any received e-mail message, WinFax PRO displays the forwarded e-mail message in the Mail Message Contents dialog box (see fig. 18.9).

Fig. 18.9
View faxes
forwarded via
e-mail in the Mail
Message Contents
dialog box.

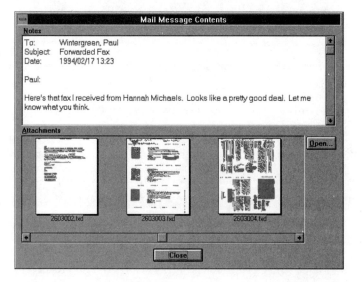

Your e-mail software may present different dialog boxes and may require different actions on your part. See your e-mail software guide for detailed information.

If you added a quick cover page to the forwarded fax, the text appears in the **N**otes window of the Mail Message Contents dialog. Thumbnail images of the fax pages and icons representing any attachments appear in the **A**ttachments area of the Mail Message Contents dialog box.

To view a fax page or open an attachment file, click **O**pen. For fax pages, WinFax PRO starts Viewer and loads the selected fax page. For attachments, WinFax PRO loads the attachment file using the appropriate application.

Troubleshooting

I want to copy an attachment to the shared drive, but I couldn't find the drive.

The problem probably is that the network administrator didn't give you permission to access the shared drive. Talk to the network administrator about gaining access to the drive.

I have access to the shared drive, but I can't seem to copy an attachment to it from my computer.

In this case, the problem probably is that the drive is read-only, which means that you cannot copy files to the drive. To copy files to the drive, the network administrator must change its status.

The fax I forwarded via e-mail never got to its destination.

You may have the wrong address for the recipient's network e-mail. In most cases, your network e-mail package informs you of this. Another possible problem is that too many people were on the network at the same time. This slows down the speed at which e-mail and other data move through the network. If you forwarded a large fax during a peak time, it may take a bit longer to get to its destination.

I forwarded an attachment via e-mail, but the recipient's WinFax PRO won't load the attachment.

Chances are that the recipient doesn't have the proper application. For example, if you forwarded a Microsoft Excel spreadsheet and the recipient doesn't have that application, WinFax PRO obviously can't load it.

Another problem could be that the recipient doesn't have the correct Windows association for the attachment. A Windows association tells WinFax PRO to load the program that created the attachment as well as the attachment itself. Read the Windows user's guide for information about associations and how to create them.

III

Power Faxing

Connecting to Other Programs

WinFax PRO provides two methods for connecting with other Windows applications. The first method is to use one of the macros that come with WinFax PRO.

Macros are like small programs created by an application that enable it to do special things. The macros included with WinFax PRO create a special WinFax item in the File menus of the applications.

This WinFax selection placed in the File menu of other applications is a great time-saver. It enables you to send a fax directly from the application without changing printer drivers as described in Chapter 8, "Sending Faxes." Instead, the macros automatically load the WinFax PRO printer driver. When you finish sending the fax, the macro automatically restores the normal printer driver.

WinFax PRO includes macros for some of the most popular Windows applications, such as WordPerfect for Windows 6.0 and Microsoft Excel 5.0. As discussed in Chapter 1, "Installing WinFax PRO," you copy the macros to your disk when you install the program. WinFax PRO copies the macros to the \WINFAX\MACROS subdirectory.

You don't run the macros from WinFax PRO, you run them from the application as you normally would run a macro in that application. Read the application's documentation to learn how to run macros.

When the macro finishes executing in the application, the WinFax item is in the application's File menu. To send a fax, simply create your document and click the WinFax option.

Another way that WinFax PRO connects with other applications is when the application vendor, not WinFax, makes the connections. Specifically, several personal information managers (PIMs) connect directly to WinFax PRO. This enables you to use the phonebooks of those PIMs to send faxes.

Check the documentation of your PIM to determine whether it can connect directly to WinFax PRO.

From Here...

This chapter told you how to extend WinFax PRO's reach by connecting either to a network or to other applications. To review, you may want to read the following chapters:

- Chapter 6, "Using Phonebooks," tells how to create phonebook entries.

- Chapter 7, "Creating and Managing Cover Pages," describes how to manage cover pages using folders.

- Chapter 8, "Sending Faxes," describes how to send faxes, including how to forward faxes.

- Chapter 10, "Using WinFax PRO for Electronic Mail," describes electronic mail and how WinFax PRO works with it.

- Chapter 12, "Assembling Faxes from Many Sources," tells you about attachments, how to add them to WinFax PRO, and how to use them in faxes.

Reference

WinFax PRO Menu Commands

This appendix lists the menu commands for WinFax PRO. The appendix is designed to provide a quick overview of the menu commands, not explain them in detail. For a detailed explanation of the menu commands, read the appropriate chapters of this book.

Note that not all menus are available at all times. In those cases, the table notes when specific menus are available.

Menu	Command	Description
Fax		
	Outbox	Opens Outbox view
	Attachments	Opens Attachments view
	Cover P**a**ges	Opens Cover Pages view
	P**h**onebooks	Opens Phonebooks view
	Copy	Copies selected item to new folder
	Move	Moves selected item to new folder
	View	Views selected item
	Print Log	Prints currently active log
	Print Eve**n**t	Prints currently selected item
	Printer **S**etup	Sets up printer

(continues)

Menu	Command	Description
Fax		
	Export	Exports phonebooks and logs
	Import	Imports phonebook databases and cover pages
	E**x**it	Exits WinFax PRO
Attachment (visible only when Attachments window is active)		
	New	Creates new attachment
	Modify	Modifies attachment information
	Remove	Removes selected attachment
	Sear**c**h	Searches for specific attachment
	Res**t**ore	Restores normal attachment item list window
	Expand Folder	Displays all subfolders
	Collapse folder	Hides all subfolders
Co**v**er Page (visible only when the Cover Pages window is active)		
	New	Creates new cover page
	Modify	Lets you modify cover page information
	Remove	Removes selected cover page
	Set **D**efault	Sets selected cover page as default
	Always Use Cover Page	Requires cover page use
	Sear**c**h	Search for specific cover page
	Res**t**ore	Restores normal cover page item list window
	View All Thumbnails	Shows thumbnails of all cover pages in folder
	OLE	Creates new cover page using OLE
	Expand Folder	Displays subfolders
	Collapse Folder	Hides subfolders

Menu	Command	Description
Log (visible only when Send and Receive Logs are visible)		
	New	Creates new archive folder
	Modify	Modifies log record information
	Remove	Removes item from log
	Forward	Forwards selected item to a new recipient (available only when Receive Log is visible)
	Resubmit/Forward	Resubmits message to original recipient (available only when Send Log is visible)
	Info	Displays information about selected item
	Save Attachments	Saves binary attachments on received e-mail and BFT transmissions
	Add to Phonebook	Adds e-mail sender's name to phonebook
	Text	Shows editable text of OCR'd messages
	Pages	Shows pages of OCR'd messages
	Sort	Sorts items in current folder
	Search	Searches for specific item
	Restore	Restores log window
	Filters	Applies and creates filters
	Collapse Folder	Hides subfolders
	Expand Folder	Displays subfolders
Outbox (visible only when Outbox is currently active view)		
	Modify	Modifies information about selected item
	Remove	Removes selected item
	Hold	Holds message for later scheduling
	Release	Releases and sends held item
	Hold All	Holds all items in folder for later scheduling
	Release All	Releases and sends all held items

(continues)

Menu	Command	Description
Outbox (visible only when Outbox is currently active view)		
	Send Now	Sends selected item
	Res**c**hedule	Reschedules selected item
	Change **D**estination	Changes recipient of selected item
	Filter	Applies filter to selected folder
Phone**b**ook (visible only when Phonebook view is active)		
	New	Adds new phonebook recipient
	Modify	Modifies selected recipient
	Remove	Removes selected recipient
	Optimize	Optimizes phonebook database
	Sort by N**a**me	Sorts phonebook by name
	Sort by Compan**y**	Sorts phonebook by company
	Search	Searches for specific recipients
	Res**t**ore	Restores normal phonebook item list window
	Collapse Folder	Hides subfolders
	Expand Folder	Displays subfolders
Send		
	Fax	Sends fax from Send dialog box
	Log	Displays Send Log
Receive		
	Manual Receive Now	Receives a fax on command
	Log	Displays Receive Log
	Automatic Receive	Enables or disables automatic reception
Setu**p**		
	Program	Sets options relating to program operation
	Fax/Modem	Sets modem options

Menu	Command	Description
Setup		
	User	Sets information about the user and his/her phone system
	Credit Card	Establishes credit card information for automatic dialing
	Receive	Sets options for receiving messages
	MS At **W**ork	Sets options for Microsoft At Work
	Mail	Sets e-mail options
	Toolbar	Customizes toolbar
S**e**rvices (visible only if you selected extra-cost advanced services during installation and registration)		
	Fax Broadcast **R**eport	Receives reports on broadcast faxes
	Fax Broadcast **S**etup	Sets up use of the Fax Broadcast service
Mail (visible only if you selected to use WinFax PRO with electronic mail during installation)		
	Login	Logs you into your electronic mail system
	Retrie**v**e Mail	Retrieves electronic mail waiting for you
	C**o**mpose	Create an electronic mail message
	Re**p**ly	Reply to sender of currently selected message
	Reply **A**ll	Reply to sender of selected message and those who received copies
	For**w**ard	Forward current electronic mail message
Window		
	Tile Horizontally	Tiles all open windows horizontally on-screen
	Tile **V**ertically	Tiles all open windows vertically on-screen
	Cascade	Displays open windows in cascade pattern
	Arrange **I**cons	Arranges all document window icons at bottom of WinFax PRO desktop

(continues)

Menu	Command	Description
Window		
	Close **A**ll	Closes all open WinFax PRO document windows
	Toolbar	Shows or hides toolbar
	St**a**tus Bar	Shows or hides status bar
	Display **I**nformation	Displays text information in display area window
	Display **T**humbnails	Displays thumbnail images in display area window
	Zoom	Zooms display when showing fax message in display area window
	Pre**v**ious Page	Shows previous fax page when showing fax message in display area window
	Ne**x**t Page	Shows next page when showing fax message in display area window
Help		
	Contents	Displays help system contents
	Search for Help On	Search for specific help topic
	Glossary	Glossary of terms relevant to WinFax PRO
	Using Help	Help about getting help
	Technical Support	How to get technical support
	A**b**out	About WinFax PRO, register and also request Fax Broadcast

Appendix B

Viewer and Cover Page Designer Menu Commands

This appendix lists the menu commands for WinFax PRO's Viewer and Cover Page Designer. Viewer is the menu where you view, annotate, and apply character recognition to faxes. Cover Page Designer is the menu where you create new fax cover pages.

This appendix is designed to provide a quick overview of the menu commands, not explain them in detail. For detailed explanations of the menu commands, read the appropriate chapters of this book.

Viewer Menu Commands

The following table lists the menu commands found in WinFax PRO's Viewer. Viewer is the part of WinFax PRO that enables you to view and annotate faxes.

Viewer has three views:

- Viewing mode, where you view the fax.

- Annotation mode, where you annotate the fax.

- Recognition mode, where you apply optical character recognition to the fax. Recognition mode has two modes: normal Recognition mode where you set up and launch OCR, and interactive Recognition mode where you edit the results of OCR.

Some options are available in one view or mode and not the others. If there is no notation with an item, it is available in all modes. However, note the following:

* means the option is available only in Viewing mode

** means the option is available only in Annotation mode

*** means the option is available only in Recognition mode

**** means the option is available only during Interactive Recognition mode

Menu	**Command**	**Description**
File		
	Open	Opens file for viewing and annotation
	Save As****	Saves recognized text to file
	Return to Fa**x******	Returns to Annotation mode
	Export	Exports file in graphics format
	Load Template***	Loads recognition zone template
	Save Template***	Saves recognition zone template
	Save* **	Saves annotated file
	Merge Annotation with Fax**	Makes annotation part of fax
	Re**v**ert**	Reverts to unannotated format
	Print	Prints fax
	P**r**inter Setup	Sets up printer
	Return to **V**iewer	Returns to Viewing mode
	E**x**it	Exits Viewer
Edit		
	Undo	Undoes previous action
	Select area*	Selects area for action
	Cu**t**	Cuts selected area and pastes to Windows clipboard

Menu	Command	Description
Edit		
	Copy	Copies selected area to clipboard
	Paste	Pastes clipboard contents into work area
	Delete* ***	Deletes selected area
	Delete object**	Deletes selected object
	Du**p**licate*	Duplicates selected area on another part of image
	Paste Bit**m**ap**	Pastes bitmap image onto fax image
	Bring to **F**ront**	Brings selected object to front of view
	Send to **B**ack**	Places selected object behind other objects
	Select All** ***	Selects all objects
	Invert*	Inverts white and black in selected area
	Cleanup*	Cleans up stray pixels from fax image
View		
	100%	Shows fax at 100% of its size
	50%	Shows fax at 50% of its size
	25%	Shows fax at 25% of its size
	Fit in Window	Shows entire fax in work area
	F**i**t Sides	Fits fax in work area horizontally
	Zoom In	Zooms in for closer view of fax
	All Pages	Shows all pages of fax
	Show **M**iniature	Shows window with miniature view of fax
	Show **G**rid**	Shows annotation grid
	Hide **T**oolbar	Hides Viewer toolbar
	Enhance View	Enhances the view of fax
	S**h**ow Graphics**	Shows either graphic image or a box substitute for image

(continues)

Menu	Command	Description
View		
	Fast Display**	Speeds display of graphic images
	In**v**ert Display*	Inverts black and white in entire fax or page
Page		
	Next Page	Moves to next page of fax
	Previous Page	Moves to previous fax page
	Go to Page	Moves to a specific page
Text**** (available only *after* interactive recognition)		
	Left Justify	Left-justifies selected text
	Center Justify	Center-justifies selected text
	Right Justify	Right-justifies selected text
	B**o**ld	Bolds selected text
	Italic	Applies italic to selected text
	Underline	Underlines selected text
	Normal	Eliminates bold, italic, or underline from selected text
	Font	Selects fonts for selected text
	S**p**elling	Spell-checks selected text
Options		
	Rotate Current Page	Rotates current page 90 or 180 degrees
	Rotate **A**ll Pages	Rotates all pages 90 or 180 degrees
	Brush Width*	Selects width of Pencil tool
	Eraser Size*	Selects size of Eraser tool
Annotate		
	Show*	Shows Annotation toolbar when in Viewing mode
	Hide**	Hides Annotation toolbar when in Annotation mode

Menu	Command	Description
Annotate		
	Sha**d**e**	Sets shading options for objects
	Border**	Sets border options for objects
	Text**	Sets text options for objects
	Font**	Sets font for text
	S**p**elling**	Spell checker for text
	Graphic**	Inserts graphic image
	S**t**amps**	Inserts stamp image
	Grid Set**u**p**	Sets grid dimensions
	Snap to Grid**	Snaps items to grid points
Recognize (available only in Viewing and Recognition modes)		
	Selected Areas***	Recognizes areas you select
	Current Page*	Starts OCR process on current page
	Select **P**ages*	Selects pages for the OCR process
	S**e**tup*	Sets up recognition process
Line" (available only in Annotation mode)		
		Selects various thicknesses for lines and arrows
Help		
	Contents	Shows contents of help system
	Search for Help On	Searches for help on specific topic
	Glossary	Glossary of WinFax-related terms
	Using Help	How to use the help system
	Technical Support	How to get support from Delrina
	A**b**out	About WinFax PRO

Reference

Cover Page Designer Menu Commands

This section lists the commands available in the Cover Page Designer, the module where you design and edit fax cover pages.

Menu	Command	Description
File		
	New	Starts new cover page
	Open	Opens existing cover page
	Save	Saves current cover page
	Save **As**	Saves current cover page with different name
	Print	Prints cover page
	P**r**inter Setup	Sest up printer
	Pre**f**erences	Sets preferences for Cover Page Designer
	E**x**it	Exits Cover Page Designer
Edit		
	Cu**t**	Cuts selected item to clipboard
	Copy	Copies selected item to clipboard
	Paste	Pastes item from clipboard
	Delete	Deletes selected item
	Paste Text **F**ile	Pastes text file into work area
	Paste **B**itmap	Pastes image into work area
View		
	100%	Shows fax at 100% of its size
	50%	Shows fax at 50% of its size
	25%	Shows fax at 25% of its size
	Fit in Window	Shows entire fax in work are
	Fit **S**ides	Fits fax in work area horizontally

Menu	Command	Description
View		
	Grid Setup	Sets up work area grid
	Snap to Grid	Aligns objects to grid points
	Sho**w** Graphics	Displays graphic images or box representing them
	Fast Display	Displays graphic images faster
Object		
	Bring to **F**ront	Brings selected object to front of view
	Send to **B**ack	Places selected object behind other objects
	Select All	Selects all objects
	Graphic	Inserts graphic image
	St**a**mps	Inserts stamp image
	Bor**d**er	Changes border of selected object
	Tabbing **O**rder	Changes fill-in order of text fields
Shade		
	White Transparent	Sets object shading as white transparent
	White **O**paque	Sets object shading as white opaque
	Black	Sets object shading as black
	Gray	Sets objects shading as gray
Text		
	White Text	Uses white text in text box
	Black Text	Uses black text in text box
	Left Justify	Left-justifies selected text
	Center Justify	Center-justifies selected text
	Right Justify	Right-justifies selected text
	Bold	Bolds selected text
	Italic	Applies italic to selected text

(continues)

Menu	Command	Description
Text		
	Underline	Underlines selected text
	Normal	Eliminates bold, italic, or underline from selected text
	Font	Selects fonts for selected text
	S**p**elling	Spell-checks selected text
Va**r**iable (Inserts the following variables into cover pages)		
	Recipient Name (First and Last Names)	Inserts full name
	Recipient **F**irst Name	Recipient's first name
	Recipient **L**ast Name	Recipient's last name
	Reci**p**ient Title	Recipient's job title
	Recipient Fax N**u**mber	Recipient's fax phone number
	Recipient **C**ompany Name	Recipient's company
	Recipient Address **1**	First part of recipient's address
	Recipient Address **2**	Second part of recipient's address
	Recipient Ci**t**y	Recipient's city
	Recipient Stat**e**	Recipient's state
	Recipient **Z**ip Code	Recipient's zip code
	Date	Date of fax transmission
	Time	Time of fax transmission
	Tot**a**l Number of Pages	Pages in fax transmission
	Sub**j**ect	Subject of fax
	Sender name	Sender's name
	Sender Compan**y**	Sender's company
	Sender Fa**x** Number	Sender's fax number
	Sender **V**oice Number	Sender's voice number

Menu	Command	Description
Variable		
	Notes field	Contents of Notes field in recipient record
	Misc field	Contents of Misc field in recipient record
	Billing Code	Billing code in recipient record
Line (available only in Annotation mode)		
		Select various thicknesses for lines and arrows
Help		
	Contents	Displays help system contents
	Search for Help On	Searches for specific help topic
	Glossary	Glossary of terms relevant to WinFax PRO
	Using Help	Help about getting help
	Technical Support	How to get technical support
	A**b**out	About WinFax PRO

Reference

Index

A

GO AHEAD. PLUG YOURSELF INTO
PRENTICE HALL COMPUTER PUBLISHING.

Introducing the PHCP Forum on CompuServe®

Yes, it's true. Now, you can have CompuServe access to the same professional, friendly folks who have made computers easier for years. On the PHCP Forum, you'll find additional information on the topics covered by every PHCP imprint—including Que, Sams Publishing, New Riders Publishing, Alpha Books, Brady Books, Hayden Books, and Adobe Press. In addition, you'll be able to receive technical support and disk updates for the software produced by Que Software and Paramount Interactive, a division of the Paramount Technology Group. It's a great way to supplement the best information in the business.

WHAT CAN YOU DO ON THE PHCP FORUM?

Play an important role in the publishing process—and make our books better while you make your work easier:

- Leave messages and ask questions about PHCP books and software—you're guaranteed a response within 24 hours
- Download helpful tips and software to help you get the most out of your computer
- Contact authors of your favorite PHCP books through electronic mail
- Present your own book ideas
- Keep up to date on all the latest books available from each of PHCP's exciting imprints

JOIN NOW AND GET A FREE COMPUSERVE STARTER KIT!

To receive your free CompuServe Introductory Membership, call toll-free, **1-800-848-8199** and ask for representative **#597**. The Starter Kit Includes:

- Personal ID number and password
- $15 credit on the system
- Subscription to CompuServe Magazine

HERE'S HOW TO PLUG INTO PHCP:

Once on the CompuServe System, type any of these phrases to access the PHCP Forum:

GO PHCP   **GO BRADY**
GO QUEBOOKS   **GO HAYDEN**
GO SAMS   **GO QUESOFT**
GO NEWRIDERS   **GO PARAMOUNTINTER**
GO ALPHA

Once you're on the CompuServe Information Service, be sure to take advantage of all of CompuServe's resources. CompuServe is home to more than 1,700 products and services—plus it has over 1.5 million members worldwide. You'll find valuable online reference materials, travel and investor services, electronic mail, weather updates, leisure-time games and hassle-free shopping (no jam-packed parking lots or crowded stores).

Seek out the hundreds of other forums that populate CompuServe. Covering diverse topics such as pet care, rock music, cooking, and political issues, you're sure to find others with the sames concerns as you—and expand your knowledge at the same time.

Teach Yourself
with QuickStarts from Que!

The ideal tutorials for beginners, Que's QuickStart Books use graphic illustrations and step-by-step instructions to get you up and running fast. Packed with examples, QuickStarts are the perfect beginner's guides to your favorite software applications.

MS-DOS 6 QuickStart

Suzanne Weixel

This is the easy-to-use graphic approach to learning MS-DOS 5. The combination of step-by-step instruction, examples, and graphics make this book ideal for all DOS beginners.

DOS 6

$21.95 USA
1-56529-096-8, 420 pp., $7^3/8$ x $9^1/8$

Windows 3.1 QuickStart

Ron Person & Karen Rose

This graphics-based text teaches Windows beginners how to use the feature-packed Windows environment. Emphasizes such software applications as Excel, Word, and PageMaker, and shows how to master Windows' mouse, menus, and screen elements.

Through Version 3.1

$21.95 USA
0-88022-730-3, 500 pp., $7^3/8$ x $9^1/8$

1-2-3 Release 2.4 QuickStart

Release 2.4

$21.95
0-88022-986-1, 500 pp., $7^3/8$ x $9^1/8$

1-2-3 Release 3.4 QuickStart

Releases 3.4

$21.95 USA
1-56529-007-0, 550 pp., $7^3/8$ x $9^1/8$

1-2-3 for Windows QuickStart

1-2-3 for Windows

$19.95 USA
0-88022-723-0, 500 pp., $7^3/8$ x $9^1/8$

Excel 4 for Windows QuickStart

Version 4 for Windows

$21.95 USA
0-88022-925-X, 400 pp., $7^3/8$ x $9^1/8$

Q&A 4 QuickStart

Versions 3 & 4

$19.95 USA
0-88022-653-6, 450 pp., $7^3/8$ x $9^1/8$

Quattro Pro 4 QuickStart

Through Version 4.0

$21.95 USA
0-88022-938-1, 450 pp., $7^3/8$ x $9^1/8$

WordPerfect 5.1 QuickStart

WordPerfect 5.1

$21.95 USA
0-88022-558-0, 427 pp., $7^3/8$ x $9^1/8$

WordPerfect 6 QuickStart

Version 6

$21.95 USA
1-56529-085-2, 400 pp., $7^3/8$ x $9^1/8$

WordPerfect 5.2 for Windows QuickStart

WordPerfect 5.2 for Windows

$21.95 USA
1-56529-174-3, 400 pp., $7^3/8$ x $9^1/8$

Word for Windows 2 QuickStart

Version 2

$21.95 USA
0-88022-920-9, 400 pp., $7^3/8$ x $9^1/8$